Lifting the Veil of

Revelation

by Michael D. Miesch Jr. PhD OP

outskirts
press

THIS BOOK IS DEDICATED TO

THE FATHER,

THE SON AND

THE HOLY SPIRIT

UNDER WHOSE GUIDANCE THIS BOOK WAS WRITTEN

My deepest appreciation is expressed to my dad and my mother, Donovan and Alma Miesch, for their constant love and encouragement, especially when I was struggling through grade school, high school and college with a severe hearing loss and speech impediment.

Indebtedness is expressed to my brother, Dr. Pete Miesch, who started school with me at the age of four, and helped me through grade school, high school and parts of college. To my Aunt Julia Miesch, I give thanks for my religious training and for insisting that I attend two weeks of Bible school every summer even through my sophomore year in college.

Last, but not least, is my deep love and appreciation to my wife, Ann, for her help in the preparation of this manuscript and for her patience for the time I spent on the manuscript.

The author is extremely grateful to Bill Ivie who introduces me to the life in the Spirit and to Ruth Kageler who guided me in the life in the Spirit after my baptism in the Spirit in 1970.

Deep appreciation to my many prayer partners: Barney Bailey, Dr. Dan Morgan, Roger Boos, Al Bastinelli, George Allman, Bill Alexander, Conrad Hopperstead and Michael D. Miesch III for their role in seeking the Lord's discernment and guidance in the preparation and writing of this manuscript.

The author wishes to express his gratitude to Conrad Hopperstead, Mrs. Katherine Morgan, Mrs. Dolores Costello, Robert Mock, and Mark David Miesch for proofreading parts of the manuscript. Great appreciation is express to Trudy Smith and Reverend Philip N. Powell O.P. for editing the manuscript. The writer is grateful to Jim Hustead for help with grammar. To my sister, Dr. Mary Sue Tiller and Michael D. Miesch III, the author wishes to acknowledge their suggestions and help in preparation of this manuscript. The author is grateful to Wayne McGowen for reading, suggestions and encouragement on the manuscript and to Reverend Peter Phan, formerly head of the Theology Department at the University of Dallas, for encouraging me to publish the manuscript. The author is indebted to Nancy Ward for advice on the manuscript.

In a dream, the Lord revealed that I was involved in a checker game as I was making the moves to get the manuscript written, read and published. The Lord said I was too deeply involved in the game to back out; however, there had been a setback, and I was going to have to make the right moves to get the book published. I asked a prayer partner to pray with me for discernment about the setback. We received words that it had to do with the phrase I had written in the dedication of the book. I dedicated the book to the Father, Son and Holy Spirit, under whose guidance this book was written. Someone felt I was either acting in faith or being presumptuous that this manuscript was written under the guidance of the Father, Son and Holy Spirit. I knew this manuscript was written under their guidance but I did not want to be accused of being presumptuous or acting in faith so I decided to remove this phrase. The Lord revealed that I had spent considerable time in prayer and fasting as I wrote this book and that this book was truly written under the guidance of the Father, Son and the Holy Spirit. The following words were spoken:

> Do not remove the phrase "under whose guidance this book was written." These words are Holy Fire, which will carry your book throughout this nation and many others, not only in your generation but in generations to come. The adversary is immensely strong, but with just these words, the enemy has no power. Give the glory to God.

There is no way I could have written this book and another book, "Seven Vital Truths for God's Children" without the numerous visions, messages and guidance that my prayer partners and I received from the Father, Son and Holy Spirit.

Declaration

This is not a book on Catholic doctrines and teachings. This is a book of private revelations received in prayer. The contents of this book are the author's own understanding of Revelation after much prayer, fasting and studying.

Table of Contents

Tables

# Preface

The purpose of this book is to stimulate man's inquiry as to who he is. Where did he come from? Where is he going? What is his purpose on earth? What is his destiny? And, what can he do about it?

In 1973, I had a dream in which my wife and I and our two oldest boys woke up and walked out onto a porch. I had knowledge that this was the midnight hour and the Lord was coming for His bride. There was a glow of light coming from the sky above. I could not see directly up as we were under a porch. There was a tremendous feeling of excitement. The scripture about the ten virgins waiting to meet the bridegroom came to me. The Lord put a strong desire in my heart to study the end times.

On December 22, 1978, I had three dreams in which different people spoke to me and said, "You are going to graduate school to prepare for evangelic work." On December 26, 1978 I had a vision of two white-haired priests, dressed in black suits wearing derby hats, each carrying a Bible, walking with a brisk pace on the road in front of my house. As they reached and turned into my driveway, they suddenly had Ph.D.'s caps and gowns on. I had knowledge that these two men were the Lord's two witnesses and that they had all wisdom, knowledge, understanding and discernment. Six years later, I asked two prayer partners to pray with me to the Lord for an understanding.

These two men were angels of the Lord coming as Doctors of the Church to bestow the gift of knowledge, and understanding upon you. The angels in priest's suits indicated that the gift of knowledge and understanding was related to spiritual matters. The Ph.D.'s garment is symbolic of the highest level of knowledge and understanding.

The Lord had been prompting me for several years to write on what I had learned in my studies on the Book of Revelation. I finally got started in May of 1980. After I had written 8 to 10 pages, the Lord showed me a vision of what I had written and said, "This will not do." The Lord not only prompted me to write but also guided me as I wrote. The Lord gave me a deeper understanding as I prayed and searched the scriptures for knowledge and truth.

This book was written in an effort to unveil the revealed knowledge of the mysteries of the Book of Revelation and to discuss and answer such questions as: What is the time-frame of the major events that occur during the Seventieth Week of Daniel? Who is the sun-clothed woman and her children? Who is the Man-child? Jesus did not call his disciples His Bride. Why?

The disciples of John the Baptist came to Jesus and said, "John and his disciples fast often. How come You and Your disciples do not fast?" Jesus replied, "How can the wedding guests or attendants fast as long as the Bridegroom is with them?"

Have you ever wondered why Jesus did not call His disciples the "Bride?" The answer to this question is revealed in the Book of Revelation. I asked that you bear with me. The Lord spoke to Daniel and said "Seventy weeks are decreed on my people. Seven weeks plus sixty-two weeks until the coming of the Messiah, which at that time, He will be cut off, i.e. crucified." There is one week left. The scripture says a prince of the people who destroys Jerusalem will in the future make a covenant with My people for one week. The Romans were the ones who destroyed Jerusalem in 68 – 70 AD. Daniel said a future prince of the Roman people will make a covenant of peace with Israel for one week (seven years). In the middle of the week the covenant will be broken with the abomination of desolation of the temple. Jesus said, "When you see the abomination of desolation spoken of by Daniel the Prophet, there shall be a great tribulation like the world has never seen. There are only 3 ½ years left in the seventieth week of Daniel when the covenant is broken. The beast has authority to wage war against God's people for 3 ½ years (Revelation 13:5).

The Book of Revelation speaks of a book of seven seals and seven trumpets. When the seventh trumpets is blown in Revelation 11:15, the scripture says it is finished, for the kingdom of this world becomes the kingdom of our Lord Jesus Christ. In Revelation 12, the woman, after giving birth to the man-child, flees into the wilderness for 3 ½ years. There cannot be an additional 3 ½ years, as the beast only has authority to wage war for 3 ½ years. This means that Revelation 12 must go back and overlap Revelation 4 to fit within the time frame of the seventieth week of Daniel.

The very moment the man-child is born and taken up to heaven, is the very moment that a door is opened in heaven in Revelation 4 and suddenly there is a multitude before the throne. This multitude is the man-child. Revelation 14 calls this multitude the first fruits unto the Lamb. This multitude follows the Lamb where ever He goes. It is the Bride that follows the Lamb wherever He goes.

When the dragon cannot get the man-child or the woman, he makes war with the remnants of the woman's seeds who keeps the commandments of God and has the testimony of Jesus Christ. This shows that there are Christians left on earth after the Lord came for His Bride. This is the same story of the ten virgins – five were ready, five were not. Revelation 8 calls those that are gathered by the angels immediately after the great tribulation "servants". They do not follow the Lamb wherever He goes. This group is so numerous that they cannot be counted.

Question? What is involved in being a part of the Man-child Rapture? What is the prize of the high calling that Paul ran a race for with all his might? Who is the bride of Christ? Who are the guests who are invited to the marriage feast of the Lamb? The bride is not invited as she naturally has a place of honor next to the groom. Who is the bride of God, the Father? What is the Great Tribulation, the Day of the Lord and the Wrath of God? What is the city of many nations and languages that is called the Whore of Babylon? The scriptures do not teach that this city is Rome or the Catholic Church. If the Whore of Babylon is a city then the sun-clothed woman must also be a city. How many raptures are there? Will the Christians go through the Great Tribulation and the Wrath of God? When will the Lord Jesus Christ and the resurrected saints return to the earth to begin the millennium? What does the Bible reveal about the millennium and life on earth during the millennium?

It is the intention of the author that these thought-provoking questions will challenge the reader to search for the deep knowledge and truths hidden in the scriptures. My prayer is that each reader will gain an understanding of the need to truly repent and make reparation for each sin he has ever committed; understand the necessity of receiving the Body and Blood of Christ as often as possible; the need to instill a desire to read and study God's Word each day; and the necessity of praying at all times especially in the spirit.

This book gives an insight into God's plan for man on his journey through life, a vision of how to run the race for the prize of the high calling, and an understanding of how man can win the highest reward with glory and honor for all eternity.

The following poem written by my wife, Ann Milburn Miesch, when she was sixteen years old, gives one a glimpse of man's pilgrimage through life on the planet earth.

As I came to be,
           the world never missed a turn.
                      Why?
Was it not a miracle,
           that I evolved
From love, hope and clay
           into a world of matter, essence and life,
To develop into an individual
           of self-choice,
To exist, live, discover, hope,
           dream, desire, mature, settle,
Only to be rushed hurriedly back
           into the realms of the unknown,
Where life is forever,
           hope is unknown, and love is Godly.

Question?

I was reluctant to ask the Lord this question. The question was – Am I doing what is necessary to be worthy to be a part of the bride of Christ?

My son, My son, no man ever lived, who could do
enough to deserve this. It is Mine to give, and I give
it to whom I please.

Book may cause controversy

While in prayer the Lord said, "This book may cause controversy; controversy is not always bad, controversy can do a lot of good."

What is written is written

I have received many visions and powerful personal messages which I had knowledge that they were to be shared and published. After finishing the writing of the manuscript and being concerned about sharing these very personal visions and messages, I asked the Lord if I should remove these very personal messages. The Lord said:

"What is written is written. Do not make any changes".

While I was praying for those reading my manuscript, the Lord said:

Walk a straight line, Mike. This line exemplifies the Holy Spirit. This Spirit is Who wrote your book. Do not yield to any spirit other than Mine. Your book shall be carried to all nations, so that they may hear. Do not modify or change it in any way. Critics, in whom you have a great deal of respect, will try to change your book. But they were not of the anointing of the Spirit, when your pen was in action. So listen to no one, except those with whom you pray for learning of my truths.

While in prayer, the Lord revealed to me that He wanted me to get the manuscript blessed. I asked the Lord, whom I should get. He said:

Mike, it makes no difference who blesses the book. The person does not carry the blessing. The person only administers the blessing. The blessing is Mine to give. The person is for you to choose. Anyone with the office of presbyter that you choose, I will honor.

I was having trouble deciding between two priests. Finally, the Lord told me to use both of them. I asked the Lord why two priests?

Two priests are used in the blessing of this book, for it is through them that I send My glory and My honor, glory and honor that many angels can use to minister the fruits of your labor. When one prays, a thousand angels are put to flight. Prayer, like sacred blessings, is the extension of man's realm into the presence of God. When one asks Me to come into his presence, I come. The petition must be made, however, for the will of man cannot be made united with the will of God unless the prayer or blessing has been committed. It is a form of respect and love for Me, which I will in no way reject. My army is fortified by prayers and communal blessings that men on earth supply Me in their devotion to Me. Love others as I have loved you, by expressing to them what I have given you and the road to joy and happiness will be simple and straight forward.

The book has doubled in size since it was originally blessed by Reverend Daniel Clayton and Reverend Don Fisher. I asked Reverend Andrew Kolzow O.P. to give the book another blessing.

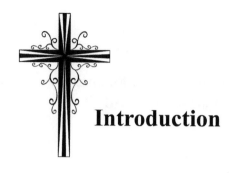

Introduction

The Millennium And Reign Of Christ

The millennium or thousand years' reign of Christ on earth was accepted and taught by the Apostles and the early Fathers of the Church. Papias, St. Justin Martyr, St. Irenaeus of Lyons, Tertullian, Hippolytus of Rome, St. Methodius of Olympus, Lactantius, all living in the first three centuries, believed and taught that Christ would return and reign in Jerusalem for one thousand years. **The Apostles and the early Fathers of the Church believed in the physical, second coming of Jesus, reigning in an earthly millennium kingdom.** Their belief was never condemned by the Church.

St. Justin Martyr, in dialogue with Trypho, wrote that he and other true Christians believe in the resurrection of the dead and a thousand year reign's with Christ in the rebuilt and enlarged city of Jerusalem, as foretold by Ezekiel, Isaiah and others prophets. Justin stated that there was a man among them named John, one of the Apostles of Christ, who wrote that the resurrected followers of Christ would dwell in Jerusalem with Christ for one thousand years. After the general resurrection and thousand year's reign, there would be an eternal resurrection of the dead and judgment of all men. (1, 2)

"The Teachings of the Catholic Church," published in 1952 with the seal of the Church, stated that it is not contrary to Catholic teaching to believe in some mighty triumph of Christ on earth, before the final consummation of all things. Then Cardinal Joseph Ratzinger, now Pope Benedict XVI, has declared that the Holy See has not made any definite pronouncement in regard to the era of peace (millennium) or an age to come before the end of human history. (2)

The millennium has never been condemned by the Church.

Although Apollinaris was condemned by Pope St. Damasus, at the Council of Rome in 381 A.D., for his belief in "the human truly rational soul in Christ", his belief in the millennium was not condemned at this council. Though many in the Church condemn the belief in the millennium and the reign of Jesus Christ on earth, this belief has not been officially condemned by the Church. (3)

No pope has spoken ex cathedra, that is, from the chair of Peter, condemning the belief in Jesus' physical reign on earth or in the millennium.

Many in the Church today believe neither in a physical reign of Christ on earth with His resurrected saints nor in the millennium (2, 3).

**The Lord's comment about His return and physical reign
on earth as King and in the millennium.**

My prayer partner and I, while praying, asked the Lord if He had any comment about people being skeptical concerning **His physical return to reign on earth as King with His resurrected saints in the millennium.** There was a vision of the Lord riding a mighty and frisky, white stallion with vapors snorting out of its nostrils. The Lord said,

"Let My Word speak for itself".

The Lord's words below and in other parts of this manuscript clearly speak of His physical return and reign on earth.

The angel told Mary in Luke 1:30-33 that she would have a Son and that He would sit on the throne of His father, David. **David's throne was a throne on earth.**

In Acts 1:6-7, 11, the **Apostles asked the Lord when He was going to set up His earthly kingdom? Jesus did not deny an earthly kingdom.** He replied that only the Father knew. Two angels told the disciples that **Jesus would return to the earth the same way He left.**

Jesus returns with His holy ones.

Zechariah 14:4-5, 9 speaks of **Jesus returning with His holy ones.** His feet will touch the Mount of Olives causing it to split into a large valley. On that day, **Jesus will be King over all the earth. This is not a Eucharistic reign.**

The Lord's throne will be in the temple.

Scripture speaks of the Lord coming through the eastern gate into the inner court of the temple. The Spirit brought Ezekiel into the inner court. The Lord said to Ezekiel, "**Son of man, this is the place of My throne and the place of the soles of My feet,** where I will dwell among the sons of Israel forever." (Ezekiel 43:1-7)

Zechariah 6:12-13 shows that the **Lord will build the temple, and His throne will be in the temple. He will sit and rule on His throne.** Thus, He will be a priest on His throne, and the counsel of peace will be between the two offices. **This will be on earth during the millennium as there will be no need of counsel for peace in heaven.**

People from other nations will help the Lord build the temple.

Scriptures in Zechariah 6:15 and Isaiah 60:10-11 show that the gentiles and foreigners will help the Lord build His temple. Gentiles were not allowed in the temple in the Old Testament.

When new Jerusalem came down out of heaven after the millennium John said he saw **no temple in it, for the Lord God, the Almighty, and the Lamb, are its temple** (Revelation 21:2, 22). **This proves that the temple mentioned in Ezekiel and Zechariah is the millennium temple as there is no structural temple after the millennium.**

The Lord will reign as King on Mount Zion in Jerusalem.

We read in the Book of Jeremiah in verses 23:5-6 and 33:15-16 that the **Lord will reign as King and will execute justice and righteousness on the earth.** Jerusalem is shown in Isaiah 2:2-3 to be the world capitol. **The Lord will reign on Mount Zion in Jerusalem.** (Isaiah 24:23) **For the law will go forth from Zion, and the Word of the Lord from Jerusalem.**

The Lord will be visible to the people on earth.

Both Isaiah 30:19-20 and Ezekiel 39:28-29 state that **the Lord will no longer hide His face, but He will be visible to the people.**

The Lord will receive an allotment of land in the millennium.

Ezekiel 48:9 teaches that the Lord will receive an allotment of land just as each of the twelve tribes of Israel **during the millennium.** In the Old Testament, the Levites lived among the different tribes and did not have an allotment of land.

In the millennium the Levites will have an allotment of land just as the other tribes.

Isaiah 65:17-25 says as the years of a tree so shall be the years of My people. If a child dies at the age of 100 years, it will be consider a curse. People will be born, living to a ripe old age and dying. This is not heaven; this is the millennium on earth as no one dies after entering heaven.

Revelation 20:4-6 speaks of the **Lord reigning on earth with His resurrected saints for a thousand years.** The male child is made up of the saints that overcame and will rule nations with a rod of iron. The saints will return with the Lord and reign with Him for a thousand years.

Saints shall rule nations with a rod of iron.

The Scriptures say that Jesus Christ is the Ruler of the kings of the earth. In Revelation 2:26-28, 5:10 and 12:5, Jesus promised the saints who overcame and prevailed to the end that He would give them authority to rule over nations. Nations are on earth. The Scriptures do not speak of nations in heaven. The saints will be kings and priests who will rule the earth with a rod of iron. I cannot imagine or visualize a loving God ruling His people in heaven with a rod of iron. Ruling with an iron rod pertains to rebellious people who are born, live, and die on earth in the millennium.

Satan and his angels are chained in prison in the millennium. When the millennium is completed, Satan and his angels will be release to test the people that were born and lived in the millennium. He will deceive and gather people for battle against the Lord and His saints. Those deceived will be as numerous as the sand of the sea. People who rebel will be destroyed by fire coming down from heaven at the end of the millennium. People will not be rebellious in heaven. (Revelation 20:7-9)

The millennium and the physical reign of Jesus on earth as King, is the fulfillment of God's covenant to His people, the Israelites.

Jesus said, "Let My Word speak for itself."

The scriptures speak very clearly of Jesus' physical reign on earth with His resurrected saints during the millennium. Can anyone argue against the clear teachings of God's Word? We need to be very, very cautious in saying God's Word does not mean what it says.

St. Augustine, at first, believed in the second coming of Jesus and the millennium. It was later that he changed his mind. It has been reported that **St. Augustine changed his opinion three times.** Many of the writers in the Church have accepted the opinions and beliefs of St. Augustine, stating that Jesus will not physically return to the earth and that there is no millennium. (2) The writings of St. Augustine, St. Jerome and others are **private opinions and are not matters of faith.** There is no scripture that support the opinions and beliefs of St. Augustine and St. Jerome and many in the Church.

"The Question Corner" by Father John Dietzen published in the East Texas Catholic newspaper on September 2nd, 2005, stated that St. Thomas Aquinas and many other theologians often disagreed with St. Augustine (4). Who is right, St. Thomas Aquinas and the other theologians or St. Augustine? **What St. Augustine wrote, concerning the second coming of Jesus, is contrary to the teaching of Scripture, which is the Word of God.**

St. Augustine, the Catechism of Catholic Church, nor the writers that follow the teachings of St. Augustine are infallible. **We need to be very cautious in calling the belief in the millennium and the physical reign of the Lord Jesus on earth, a heresy, as this is clearly contrary to the teachings of the scripture and the Apostolic Fathers of the Church. Jesus said "Let My Word speaks for itself".**

With the teachings of St Augustine, the Catholic Church has been called the new Israel. The Catholic Church **is not the new Israel** as **the Lord is still dealing with Israel.** The Lord told Moses that, if the Israelites did not keep His commandments, He would scatter them to all nations of the world, which He did. (Deuteronomy 28:64) The Lord also told Moses that He would re-gather His people from all nations of the world. This has happened in our lifetime. (Deuteronomy 30:4-5) As was foretold in Isaiah 66, Israel became a nation in one day on May 14, 1948 by the decree of the United Nations. (5) The Israelites have come back to their homeland from every nations of the world. If the Lord is no longer dealing with Israel, why did He bring His people home?

Roman 11:26 teaches that all of Israel will be saved. One of the current writers on Revelation interprets this to mean that Jesus cannot return until all of Israel has been converted or saved. This writer believes this because he does not believe in the millennium. (3) This belief is also stated in the Catechism of the Catholic Church (674) (6). In reality, the Israelites will not be converted until Jesus is reigning on earth as their King, which includes the 144,000 of the twelve tribes who will be sealed and protected during the Wrath of God as written in Revelation 8. If the Lord is no longer dealing with Israel, why will He anoint and seal the 144,000 of the twelve tribes for protection during the wrath of God? This scripture shows that God is still dealing with Israel. All of Israel will be saved when Jesus is reigning on His earthly throne in the temple in Jerusalem in the millennium.

St Augustine originally accepted the teachings of the Apostolic Fathers of the Church. The writings of St. Augustine show that he changed his opinion three different times. An opinion not back by scripture is just an opinion. Jesus said "Let My word speak for itself." Why are we allowing the opinion of a man who changed his opinion three times take precedent over Scriptures which is God's Word and the teaching of the Apostolic Fathers of the Church?

Note – numbers are for references cited at the end of the book.

Revelation Terms

NOTE: These terms are supported in the text of this book, <u>Lifting the Veil of Revelation</u>.

Revelation is the only book of the Bible that opens and closes with a promise of a special blessing to those who read, study and keep the words written within (Revelation 1:3, Revelation 22:7).

Revelation reveals God's plans concerning the coming of our Lord Jesus Christ and His kingdom on earth.

Jesus' physical reign on earth -- I asked the Lord if He had any comments about the unbelief of His physical return and reign on earth during the millennium. There was a vision of our Lord Jesus Christ riding a mighty and frisky, white stallion that was snorting with vapors coming out of its nostrils. Jesus said, "Let My Word speak for itself."

Seventieth Week of Daniel - This is the last week of the 70 weeks decreed upon the Jewish people by Daniel the Prophet. The first 69 weeks occurred before the crucifixion of our Lord. The events described in the Book of Revelation will take place during the 70th week of Daniel, which is yet to come.

The 70th week will begin the moment the prince of the Roman people (the Beast or Antichrist) makes a 7-year covenant with Israel (Daniel 9:26-27). Isaiah 28:15 calls this a covenant with death. This covenant will be broken in the middle of the week with the abomination and desolation of the temple as spoken by Daniel and Jesus (Matthew 24:15). There are three and half years left in the seventieth week of Daniel after the covenant is broken.

It is important to understand that the beast only has authority to wage war and to persecutes the Christians and Israelites for 3 ½ years. Since the sun-clothed woman flees into the wilderness for 3 ½ years in Revelation 12, chapters 12 to 22 must overlap Revelation chapters 4 to 11 to fit into the time-frame of 3 ½ years. The minutes the Lord Jesus Christ received a crown and a kingdom as recorded Revelation 4, 5 and 6, He rides forth on a white horse. The scripture says He goes forth to conquer and to conquer. This is the same moment Satan is being driven from the heavens to the earth by Michael and his angels (Revelation 12). Satan is a defeated foe. He cannot be the one riding the white horse as many people think. This is discussed in the text.

Week – 7 years. Laban spoke to Jacob and said: "Fulfill your week, 7 years and I will give you Rachael as a wife also." (Genesis 29:28) 70 weeks is 490 years.

The Lord also decreed three other 70-week periods:

1. 70 weeks of the family of Abraham,
2. 70 weeks of the Judges,
3. 70 weeks of the Kings.

It is interesting that Bishop Fulton Sheen said something significant happens every five hundred years in the history of the church.* Five hundred years is very close to 490 years. These 70-week periods are supported in the text.

    * Bishop Sheen's tape

Book of the Seven Seals is the title deed to the earth (Revelation 5:1). The Lord Jesus Christ takes this book from the hands of His

Father and receives a crown and a kingdom. The book of the Seven Seals is the book that Daniel was told to seal until the time of the end (Daniel 12:4). The events described in Revelation take place at the time of the end. The opening of the seals of this book is the process of reclaiming the earth that was lost when our first parents sinned.

Four horsemen of the Apocalypse – When Jesus opens the first seal of the title deed to the earth, He receives a crown and rides forth on a white horse to conquer and reclaim the earth (Revelation 6:1-2). In Revelation 14:14, He is seen with a crown on His head. In Revelation 19:12, He wears many crowns. The rider of the White Horse in Revelation 6:2 is Jesus Christ. One must read the text to understand.

Four horsemen of the Apocalypse – The riders of the red, black and pale horses in Revelation 6 are the angels of the Lord, which are also mentioned in Zechariah 1:7-12 and 6:1-8. The angels, the riders of the different colored horses in the Zechariah, patrol, protect and bring peace to the earth. Angels in Revelation 7:1-3 hold back the forces of darkness and destruction, until the 144,000 Jews can be sealed with the seal of the living God. The angels that ride the red, black and pale horses in Revelation 6 release or remove the forces that prevent war, famine, death and destruction on earth.

Great Tribulation begins when the 7-year covenant with Israel is broken by the Antichrist in the middle of the week with the abomination and desolation of the temple in Jerusalem, as spoken in Daniel 9:27, and by Jesus in Matthew 24:15, 21. This occurs 3 ½ years after the 7-year covenant is made. There are 3 ½ years (or 42 months or 1260 days) left in the 70th week of Daniel, when the covenant is broken.

Abomination and desolation of the temple – When the temple is rebuilt, the Jews will start offering bloody sacrifices and grain offerings in the temple as foretold by Daniel. The abomination and desolation occurs, when the Antichrist stops the sacrifices and grain offerings and sets himself up in the temple, proclaiming himself to be God. People will be forced to bow down and worship him, or be put to death.

The first 3½ years of the 70th week of Daniel are peace; the last 3½ years are the Great Tribulation and the Wrath of God.

The Great Tribulation is the first part of the last 3½ years.

The Wrath of God is the last part of the last 3½ years.

The Great Tribulation includes the sequence of events covered by the first five seals. When the sixth seal is opened, the Great Tribulation is over, as the sun is darkened and the moon turns blood-red (Revelation 6:12). Matthew 24:29 says that the Great Tribulation is over, when the sun is darkened, and the moon does not give its light. When the moon does not give its light, it turns red.

The Great Tribulation is when the Beast or the Antichrist persecutes those who do not worship him and take his mark.

The Wrath of God is when the Lord pours out His judgment on those who worship and takes the mark of the beast. God's judgment involves natural phenomena such as seas and rivers turning to blood; red-hot flaming meteors falling into the sea, into rivers or on land; men are afflicted with boils and sores; the sun and the moon not giving their light (three days of darkness); severe earthquakes, etc.

The Wrath of God begins with the opening of the seventh seal, which includes the seven trumpets (Revelation 8 –11) and seven bowls (Revelation 15 –16).

Revelation 4 through 11 covers the Great Tribulation and the Wrath of God. Revelation 12 through 22 must be superimposed on

Revelation 4 through 11. This is supported in the text.

Sun-clothed woman in Revelation 12 is our mother, heavenly Jerusalem, which is also described in Isaiah 66:7-13 and Galatians 4:21-31. The sun-clothed woman flees into the wilderness after the birth of the male child, where she is protected from the dragon for 3 ½ years. The dragon immediately makes war with the remnant of the woman's children who keep the commandments of God (Jews), and have the testimony of Jesus Christ (Christians) (Revelation 12:17). This shows that all Christians are not taken up in the pre-tribulation rapture. Many Christians will go through the Great Tribulation.

Isaiah 66:7-13 describes a similar scene. The woman, Jerusalem, our mother, gives birth to a male child before she goes into labor (pre-tribulation rapture). After she goes into labor (The Great Tribulation) she brings forth the rest of her children.

When the seventh trumpet is blown in Revelation 11, the Scripture says it is finished for the kingdom of the world has become the kingdom of our Lord Jesus Christ. In Revelation 12 the woman flees into the wilderness for 42 months or 1260 days after the birth of the manchild. There can not be an additional 42 months after Revelation 11 as the Antichrist has authority to wage war for only 42 months. This means Revelation 12 has to go back to Revelation 4 to fit within the time-frame of 42 months left in seventieth week of Daniel after the covenant is broken. The moment the woman flees into the wilderness is the beginning of the Great Tribulation.

When the man-child is born and taken up to heaven in Revelation 12, is the same moment in which a door is opened in heaven in Revelation 4, and suddenly there is a multitude of people before the throne. This multitude before the throne is the man-child which also includes the 144,000 in Revelation 14. Revelation 14:1-5 calls this multitude before the throne the first fruits unto the Lamb. The first fruits follow the Lamb wherever He goes. This is the bride. The bride is the one who follows the Lamb wherever He goes.

The man-child rapture is the midnight hour rapture, which occurs when the Lord comes for His bride. Afterwards, Revelation 14:6 speaks of angels flying through the air preaching the Gospels. Revelation 14:9 warns all not to take the mark of the beast. This shows that the man-child rapture takes place prior to the beginning of the Great Tribulation.

Bride of Christ is the pre-tribulation rapture or the midnight hour rapture, which includes the 144,000 mentioned in Revelation 14, is the first fruits into the Lamb. They are pure and holy without blemish, stain or deceit. They follow the Lamb wherever He goes. This is the bride who follows her husband wherever He goes. The bride is the prize of the high-calling for which Paul ran a race for with all of his might. Those that win this prize are numbered.

John the Baptist's disciples asked Jesus why He and His disciples did not fast. Jesus, Who identified Himself as the Bridegroom said, "How can the wedding guests or attendants fast as long as the Bridegroom is with them?" (Mark 2:18-20, Matthew 9:14-15) Jesus called His disciples His wedding guests or attendants because, at that point in time, they had not yet won the race for the prize of the high-calling for which Paul ran for with all of his might.

Paul in Philippians 3:10-14 said "I hope that I may arrive at resurrection from the dead. I am racing to grasp the prize if possible. My entire attention is on the finish line which is life on high in Christ Jesus."

Paul is not talking about the general resurrection or the Harvest Rapture that occurs immediately after the Great Tribulation (Matthew 24:29-31). Paul is hoping to make the midnight resurrection, when the Lord comes for His Bride. If Paul were hoping to make the general resurrection or the Harvest Rapture, then you and I would not have a chance.

In 2 Timothy 4:6-7, Paul speaks of finishing the race.

The title of the 45th Psalm in the New American Bible is called "Nuptial Ode for the Messianic King". Many people are at the wedding, but not everyone is the Bride. Many are invited to the marriage feast of the Lamb (Revelation 19:9), but the Bride is not invited, as she does the inviting.

The Bride will help the Lord govern the earth in the millennium – Those who make the Man-child rapture will rule nations with a rod of iron. Ruling with a rod of iron is for rebellious people that are being born, living and dying in the millennium. There will be no ruling with a rod of iron in heaven as there will be no rebellious people in heaven.

> Revelation 2:26-27: And he who overcomes, and who keeps My deeds until the end, to him I will give authority over the nations and he shall rule them with a rod of iron, . . (6)

> Revelation 5:10: And hast made us unto our God kings and priests:
> And we shall reign on the earth. (4)

> Revelation 12:5 And she gave birth to a son, a male child, who is to rule all nations with a rod of iron; and her child was caught up to God and to His throne. (6)

The Man-child or male child (Revelation 12:5) will help the Lord govern the nations and cities of the world as kings and priests. Those involved in the Harvest Rapture or the general resurrection are not involved in governing the cities and nations of the world as Scripture calls them servants.

The words of knowledge, received in prayer, revealed that the Bride of Christ will be those who:

1. have accepted His name,
2. have walked in faith,
3. are prayer warriors,
4. are diligent workers for Christ's sake, and
5. have brought many into the kingdom.

The Bride of Christ will have more rewards and honors, more knowledge and understanding of the nature of God than those who just make it within the door of the kingdom. God's judgment will determine those, who will be the Bride of Christ.

The Bride of Christ, the prize of the high calling will include people from every walk of life - from janitors, housewives, mechanics, and doctors to evangelists, priests and missionaries who are on the frontlines bringing people to the Lord. These people all have one thing in common: They are prayer warriors, who spend considerable time in prayer. These prayer warriors bind the forces of darkness and pray to the Lord of harvest to send laborers into the field to gather the harvest. Those who realize that there is a prize to be won will plunge into the race and run with all their might. The prize is for all eternity.

Whore of Babylon is the woman who rides the seven-headed dragon, the mother of all of the abominations on earth. She is described as a city of many nations and languages. The Jews have returned to Israel from all the nations of the world. Jerusalem is a city of many nations and languages. Jerusalem is the whore of Babylon. (Revelation 17:5, 15) Details are covered in the text.

Ezekiel 16 called Jerusalem a harlot, saying she has done worse than her sisters, Sodom and Samaria.

Revelation speaks of two great cities called Babylon. One is religious Babylon, which is Jerusalem. The other great city is commercial Babylon, which is the city of the Beast or the Antichrist. The merchants rejoice at the destruction of religious Babylon (Revelation 17:1-18) but weep at the destruction of commercial Babylon, which is probably Rome (Revelation 18:1-24). Religious Babylon is destroyed over a period of time; commercial Babylon is destroyed in one hour.

Two Witnesses – The two prophets are the two witnesses who will walk the streets of Jerusalem for 42 months, warning the people not to take the mark of the Beast (Revelation 11:3-13). They are believed to be Elijah and Moses. This is discussed in the text.

The two witnesses are killed in the street of that "Great City called Sodom and Egypt, where our Lord was crucified". This Great City is Jerusalem. When an earthquake destroys Jerusalem, scripture says that Babylon was remembered by the Lord (Revelation 16:19).

The Seven-headed Dragon – Satan (Revelation 12:9). The seven heads represent Satan's seven kingdoms throughout history: Egypt, Assyria, Babylon, Persia, Greece, the Roman kingdom at the time of Christ, and the Roman kingdom at the time of end.

The False Prophet – in Revelation 13, is believed to be the false or black pope (prophetic messages).

Antichrist – The Beast, the Little Horn, the prince of the Roman people, is from Greece. One must read the text to understand this. He has power to wage war with God's people for 42 months (3 ½ years) (Revelation 13:5-8).

Mark of the Beast – no one may buy or sell unless they have the mark or name or number of the Beast in their right hand or on their forehead. The number of the Beast is 616 instead of 666. Earlier manuscripts used the number 616 instead of 666.

Two divided into four gives two, which is a whole number. Two into five gives two and a half, which is not a whole number. Each Greek letter has a numerical value. It is interesting that when all the Greek letters that have the name Jesus alone or a phrase or a complete sentence are added up, the sum total of the name Jesus or phrase or sentence with the name of Jesus can be divided by 37 or 111 and get a whole number. This is true for all scriptures with the name Jesus. This phenomenon was only recently discovered. This is truly amazing since different writers wrote the scriptures in this manner, unknowingly, long ago.

The number 616 can be divided into any sentence that has to do with the mark of the Beast and get a whole number, but this cannot be done with 666. Proof of this is supported in the text.

Kingdom of Iron and Kingdom of Clay – These are two different kingdoms, which make a covenant with each other to form one kingdom, under the Beast. Scripture says that they will not adhere to each other (Daniel 2:32, 41-43).

Kingdom of Iron represents ten nations, which are under the Beast, the prince of the Roman people (Daniel 2:32, 41-43).

Kingdom of Clay represents the nation of the North and her allies mentioned in Ezekiel 38:1-23. Just as there are ten nations of iron, there are also ten nations of clay. Toward the end of the 70th week of Daniel, the Kingdom of Clay will break its covenant with the Antichrist and invade Israel. The breaking of this covenant and the invasion of Israel precipitates the Battle of Armageddon. This is explained in the text.

Temples – There are six temples mentioned in the Bible: temple in the wilderness, Solomon's temple, Zerubbabel's temple, Herod's temple, temple during the Great Tribulation, and millennium temple, described in Ezekiel. After the millennium, there is no structural temple, as the temple is the Lord God Almighty and the Lamb (Revelation 21:22).

The Great Tribulation's temple has to be built so that abomination and desolation of the temple spoken of by Daniel (Daniel 9:26-27), Jesus (Matthew 24:15, 21) and Paul (II Thessalonians 2:3-4) can take place. The Beast or the Antichrist will defile the temple. The Jews will own the land only within the temple walls. The land outside of the temple will belong to the Gentiles – the Muslims (Revelation 11:1-2). This shows that the tribulation temple will be built on Mt. Moriah, next to the Dome of the Rock. If the temple were built someplace else, the Jews would see that they owned the land outside the temple's wall as well.

The 144,000 in Revelation 14 are part of the bride of Christ, the first-fruits unto the Lamb. They are pure and holy, without blemish or deceit. They follow the Lamb wherever He goes, which is the characteristic of the Bride, who follows her husband wherever He goes. These 144,000 are in heaven, before the Great Tribulation begins.

The 144,000 in Revelation 7 are the twelve tribes of Israel. They are not sealed and protected until after the opening of the seventh seal after the Great Tribulation is over. They are on earth and are protected throughout the Wrath of God. They are part of the people over whom the Lord will be king, when He sets up His kingdom on earth during the millennium (Revelation 20:4).

Angels preach the gospel during the Great Tribulation – The commission given to the apostles to preach the gospels apparently is over, as the angels fly through the air, preaching the gospel (Revelation 14:6-13).

Harvest Rapture is described in Matthew 24:29, Revelation 7:9-17, and Revelation 14:14-16. This group is so numerous that they cannot be counted. This group serves the Lord day and night as servants in the temple. They do not follow the Lamb wherever He goes. The Harvest Rapture takes place immediately after the Great Tribulation, when the sun is darkened and the moon turned red, (Matthew 24:29-31, and Revelation 6:12-17).

Millennium is the thousand year reign of the Lord Jesus Christ on earth (Revelation 20:4).

1. Jesus' throne will be in the Temple in Jerusalem (Ezekiel 43:6, Zechariah 6:12-13).
2. The Lord is given an allotment of land, along with the twelve's tribes of Israel (Ezekiel 45:1, Ezekiel 48:9).
3. The Lord will no longer hide His face, but will be visible to the people (Isaiah 30:19-20, Ezekiel 39:28-29).
4. He will reign on Mt. Zion in Jerusalem. (Isaiah 24:23).
5. Jerusalem will be the world capitol (Isaiah 2:2-3).
6. Weapons of war will be no more (Isaiah 2:4).

Millennium Temple – The Gentiles and Jews will help the Lord build the millennium temple (Zechariah 6:15 Isaiah 60:10-11). Prior to the millennium, Gentiles were not allowed in the temple.

The saints, living and dead who were raptured, will return to the earth with our Lord, Jesus Christ, when He reigns for 1,000 years (Revelation 20:4). The saints will rule over nations with a rod of iron (Revelation 2:26-28, Revelation 12:5). The Lord Jesus Christ will marry His bride prior to His return to the earth (Revelation 19:7-10).

Earth changes during the millennium:

1. Jerusalem will be on a mountain surrounded by a plain (Zechariah 14:10, Isaiah 40:1-5, Revelation 20:7-9).
2. The desert will bloom (Isaiah 35:1-2, Isaiah 35:7, Isaiah 41:18-19, Isaiah 51:3, Isaiah 55:13).
3. Water will flow from the sanctuary of the temple in Jerusalem into the Dead Sea and into the Mediterranean Sea (Zechariah 14:8).
4. The Dead Sea will become a living sea. (Ezekiel 47:1-5,8).
5. The Dead Sea will become alive with fish. Fishermen will make a living fishing in the Dead Sea (Ezekiel 47:9-10).
6. Salt will be obtained from marshes and swamps (Ezekiel 47:11).
7. Fruit trees will bear fruits every month of the year, because of the water from the sanctuary. Fruits will be food for the people. The leaves will be medicine for the healing of the people (Ezekiel 47:12). Sin, sickness and death will occur in the millennium.
8. Wild animals will become tame (Ezekiel 34:24-25, 28)
9. The lion will eat straw like an ox (Isaiah 11:6-7, Isaiah 65:25).
10. The wolf and lamb will graze together (Isaiah 65:25).
11. A baby will play by the hole of a cobra (Isaiah 11:8-9).
12. The Lord will make a covenant with the wild birds of the air and beasts of the field to lie down in safety (Hosea 2:18-20).

13. People will build their own houses and raise their own food (Isaiah 65:21- 24).
14. The years of the people will be as trees, during the millennium, as it was before the flood. If a child dies at the age of 100, it will be considered a curse (Isaiah 65:19-20,22).

Bloody sacrifices and grain offerings during the millennium – Both Jews and Gentiles will offer bloody sacrifices and grain offerings during the millennium. If the Gentiles of other nations do not come up to Jerusalem to pay respect to the Lord, they will not receive rain for their crops (Ezekiel 43:18-27, Zechariah 14:16-21, Isaiah 56:6-7). The bloody sacrifices are to remind the people what the Lord went through in atoning for their sins.

Lord's Supper will be celebrated in the millennium. In Matthew 26:29, Mark 14:25 and Luke 22:18, the Lord said He would not partake of the fruit of the vine until He drank it new with them in His Father's kingdom.

Satan and his angels are bound in prison during the 1,000 years' reign of the Lord on earth (Revelation 20:1-3). At the end of the millennium, Satan and his angels will be loosed so the people born and living during the millennium, can be tempted and tested before the final judgment i.e. the Great White Throne judgment (20:7-10).

White Throne judgment takes place at the end of the millennium (Revelation 20:11-15).

The Beast and the False Prophet are cast into the Lake of Fire at the end of the seventieth week of Daniel prior to the millennium (Revelation 19:20). They are still alive at the end of the millennium, when the 1,000 years are up (Revelation 20:10).

Satan and his angels are cast into the Lake of Fire at the end of the millennium, and the wicked people are cast into the Lake of Fire, after the White Throne judgment (Revelation 20:11-15, Matthew 25:31-46).

God the Father will not be visible to the people on earth until after the millennium (Revelation 21:3).

God the Father will marry His bride after the millennium.

All of this is discussed in the text.

CHAPTER 1

Personal Messages Given To Me While Writing My Books

After I started receiving visions and messages from the Lord, the Lord indicated I was to use caution with whom I shared these.

> Do not distribute what is holy and of God to the dogs. It's like giving away treasures that are bestowed upon you. The Holy Spirit directs writings among people, but such writings cannot be disclaimed or criticized too harshly for it is the same nature as grieving the Holy Spirit's works. Just be very careful to whom you issue holy writings and make sure that nothing is said to destroy anything that is of the Lord.

Now, I have received knowledge that I am to share the messages I have received in regard to visions or pictures, words spoken or of knowledge received, even those that are very personal. I have a great reluctance to share many of the personal messages as I feel I am vulnerable, opening myself up to much criticism. A prayer partner said these messages would be a source of comfort to those who receive them. The Lord wants us to know that He wants a warm, individual, close personal relationship with each one of us. The Lord is bountiful in His gifts to those who are open to receive His treasures and understandings. He manifests these gifts differently in each individual. **I did not receive any of the messages directly. Each of the messages was spoken to me through**

1

one of the many prayer partners while we were in prayer. Each message was related to a vision or a picture, a word of knowledge, a word, or words that were spoken to me, or a question that I asked the Lord. I did not choose my prayer partners. The Lord said He selected my prayer partners. The Lord obviously spoke to me through prayer partners so the messages would not be contaminated with my words or thoughts. These visions and messages were received over a period of 30s years.

Vision - a young black boy standing before me wanting to know if he can pray with me. When I told him yes, he had a big happy smile. The Lord said:

> You have not chosen your prayer partners. You have allowed Me to choose for you. You are free.

I am going to share some of the things I have received in prayer: Whenever I have a vision, a picture or have received a word, I ask a prayer partner to discern if this is from the Lord. If so, does the Lord have a message? A vision or a picture is really the same. The messages my prayer partners received are quoted after the description of each vision, dream or question I asked the Lord:

What you have written

A prayer partner spoke the following words to me.

> My son, what you have written, I give to you so that you might learn more deeply who I am. I give you this knowledge so that you will grow in faith and trust so that you will know without a doubt the tremendous, loving, limitless God I am. To share this knowledge with others who do not have your spiritual light will bring difficulties. They will not understand but you must share it.

Vision of my prayer partner carrying a brown grocery bag:

A prayer partner spokes the following words to me.

> The bag contains the fruits of knowledge, wisdom, understanding, love and peace, which were present in the Garden of Eden at the time of Adam and Eve. By prayer and faith you are to continue in love for Me as I have loved you. I will reveal many things to you by means of visions to impart truth to you individually and for which you will be responsible for delivering to others in need of spiritual guidance. My words are given to you freely so you must give them freely to others in return. Be not selfish but give with concern and love for others in need. Be not alarmed by the words, which I give. They are words not comprehended easily by mortal man, if not received by the help of My Spirit. Deliver My words with courage and be always certain in your spirit that you are hearing from Me. Your Adversary is strong, stronger than you are, if you do not pray for My protection first.

Vision of a small blue flame (similar to a pilot light) in a small white stove:

> A small effort on your part is like a pilot light for a great fire of results. When you are faithful in prayer and sacrifice, great things happen.

The midnight hour rapture

In 1973, I had a dream in which my wife and I woke up at the midnight hour and walked out onto the porch with our two oldest sons who were 8 and 9 years old. There was an unusual light or glow coming down from above. I could not see directly up, as we were under the porch. I had knowledge that this was the midnight hour rapture and the Lord was coming for His bride. There was a tremendous feeling of excitement. The scripture that came to me was the story of the ten virgins waiting to meet the Bridegroom. I was puzzled why our youngest son, who was two years old, was not with us. Seven years later, I received understanding that the bride is the prize of the high calling for which Paul ran a race for with all of his might. A two-year-old child is not capable of running a race for the prize of the high calling. I do not wish to imply that I or any of my family have won the race of which Paul spoke. The Lord put a strong desire in my heart to study and learn about Book of Revelation and the end times.

Dreams - You are going to graduate school to prepare for evangelistic work.

On December 22, 1978, I had several dreams, in which three different people spoke to me and said, "You are going to graduate school." In the first dream, two of my associates at work spoke to me and said, "Graduate school requires studying." In the second dream, an elderly Christian lady said, "Mike, you are going to school." In the third dream, another Christian lady friend said, "I told you a long time ago you are going to school to prepare for evangelistic work."

I did not actually go to school; however, I spent considerable amount of time reading, studying, praying, and seeking the Lord for understanding and guidance in the writing of this manuscript. I shared this dream with the third lady, who was a very friendly person. It is interesting that she was very cool to me afterwards. I don't blame her. Who would believe that the Lord would be telling a deaf person with a severe speech impediment to go to graduate school to prepare for evangelistic work?

4

Vision – Two priests with Ph.D.'s caps and gowns walking into my yard.

On December 26, 1978 I had a vision of two white-haired men, dressed in black priest's suits wearing derby hats, each carrying a Bible, walking with a brisk pace on the road in front of my house. When they turned and walked into my driveway, they suddenly had Ph.D.'s caps and gowns on. I had knowledge that these two men were the Lord's two witnesses and that they had all wisdom, knowledge, understanding and discernment. Six years later, I asked two people to pray with me for understanding.

> These two men were angels of the Lord coming as Doctors of the Church to bestow the gift of knowledge, and understanding upon you. The angels in priest's suits indicated that the gift of knowledge and understanding related to spiritual matters. The Ph.D.'s garment is symbolic of the highest level of knowledge and understanding.

The second prayer partner received and spoke the following words to me.

> I love you Mike so I will instruct you with wisdom, instruction and love. Continue steadfastly with the work that the Lord has given you the opportunity to present. Pray with these two men for forgiveness of sins of the people. The prayers and fasting with which you have honored Me, are about to unfold with their reward.

Strong thoughts kept coming to me to write on the Book of Revelation.

The Lord had been prompting me, for several years, to write on the Book of Revelation. I finally began in May of 1980. After I had

5

written 8 to 10 pages, the Lord showed me a vision of what I had written and said, "This will not do." The Lord not only prompted me to write, but also guided me as, I wrote.

The Lord did not allow me to have a spiritual director. He kept me isolated from theologians. One priest told me I was out of my field. The Lord allowed me to share my work with only a few people. He spoke to me through dreams and visions, and guided me through several prayer partners throughout the writing of this manuscript.

The Lord provided me with a prayer partner.

While attending a retreat, I asked someone, whom I had met and spoken to only a few times, to pray with me for a discomfort in my neck. While praying, he started speaking the following message to me. I had not said anything to him about my book.

> Give the first part of the morning to Me. Give the other part of the time to your family. Rest in Me, I have much to teach you. I want you to enjoy the fruits of your labor, as you bring the knowledge of My glory to the people of this planet. At this moment, I have already begun to put into motion the people who will publish and distribute your book to all the people of this planet, so that they may know of My glory.

A week later, the word "Releemer" was spoken and spelled to me as I was coming out of my sleep at 5 A.M. As I prayed for understanding, I had a vision of myself standing on a sidewalk. The Lord, dressed in a white robe, was on the sidewalk. He was bending over, picking up loose bricks and building a brick wall on both sides of the walkway. As the Lord moved forward to pick up more bricks, I would back up. The brick walls were approximately two feet wide and three feet high. The brick walls and walkway led to what looked like a two storey tall building with two large columns about 75 yards away. This building was the Jewish temple. After praying for three days receiving no understanding, I called the friend, who spoke the above prophecy. As we began to pray, he spoke the following words to me.

> Son of man, you will be a witness, as the Apostles of old were witnesses to My Son, Jesus. I have given you wisdom, knowledge, understanding and discernment about the restoration of My people. I will allow you to see this restoration of My people, because I love you. Each brick is symbolic of a person being restored to My bulwark that I am building, for the protection of My Church. This is the Lord God Yahweh Who speaks. I am your Father Who has redeemed you by the blood of My Son, Jesus, Who has brought you to an awareness of My nature through the Person of the Spirit. I am pleased with your prayer time. Be patient, as you continue your work, for through it, many people will come to know the glory of My name. Be conscious of My Word. Research My name, for in it you will find the meaning of life.

"Releemer" is a spiritual term, which refers to a type of communication men receive from Christ. Christ presents His view, objective, direction and guidance, with the help of the Holy Spirit, to many people who believe in His name. This means of communication bridges the gap between God and man in the exchange of ideas.

While in prayer, a prayer partner received the following words.

> My son, walk with Me. Bring Me your burdens, for I am the way, the truth and the life. I am calling you

7

to come to know Me as the Apostles of old. I would have you to know the nature of My being and the character of My nature. Rest in Me, My son, for it is within Me that I will reveal the mysteries of life to you. You ask to know the meaning and the purpose of life. At this moment, My Spirit wants to reveal Himself to you. Come to Me in order that I may reveal those things you need to know about Me to complete the work that I am doing through you. Be strong; be committed; be humble; be My servant. Allow Me to mold your character to that of one of My chosen. The Apostles of old allowed themselves to be surrounded in My love. Do the same, for I want you to be one of My own. At this moment, all that is of concern to you is in My control. I love you. Be patient; for My work is not yet complete. Your book is in the hands of those whom I would have to come to know My nature. Pray for them daily. Pray for their souls daily in order that My words will fall on fertile soil. For many are called, but few are chosen. The Lord God Yahweh speaks.

Do not have fear.

Fear not, for I have all things under My command. You are the first of many brothers. You are to have no fear, for I am your Father, and all things are under My authority. There is no situation that I would allow, which would disturb the peace that I would have for you. For in the name of My Son, Jesus, all good things will abound to you. Rest in His name (Jesus) and in the light of My name, Yahweh. You are precious to Me, My son, because of your work and love for Me. You need to have no fear, for all things will turn to My good. Continue with your writings, your study and your prayer. Make them one, just as I am one with the Son and the Spirit. Unite yourself to Me in prayer and fasting. Your faith is the faith of Abraham. Your blessings will be the same. Remember that My Son Jesus, died and rose and ascended to Me. You too will die, and rise and ascend to Me. Be patient with all those people who seem to be annoyances for Jesus has died for them as well. I love them as I love you. Your work (book) will one day be complete. I love you. Continue on unfalteringly with your prayer, studies and writings. I will make your face as that of Moses. I love you.

Nature of God

After I had finished my manuscript on the Book of Revelation, I had knowledge that I was supposed to write another chapter on the nature of God. I was puzzled, as this did not seem to fit in with the Book of Revelation. I asked a prayer partner to pray with me. The following words were spoken to me.

My son, when you begin to write about My nature, I would have you to pray in the Holy Spirit. Begin at the beginning with what I have given you so far in regard to My nature. I say to begin at the beginning of the Holy Word. It is in the first few chapters of My Word that you will come to an understanding of My triune nature. Seek out what it is about My Holy Spirit that is revealed in the early writings of the Book of Genesis, for it is in the beginning, I was. It is in the writings of the prophets that the presence of My Son is first revealed. Carry this particular part

9

of your work on through the New Testament. Flow with the wind of the Holy Spirit. Allow the flow and movement to be the movement of the Holy Spirit. Allow Him to come upon you to engulf you, to refresh you and to use you, to bring about what My love is. I would have the movement of your writings be that of a symphony by starting slowly, moving toward a crescendo, all the time allowing the beauty of My nature to be revealed. Move slowly, but exactly, for this is an important part of My overall work that you are presenting in your writing. I love you for your diligence. I have many blessings in store for you. For he who reads My Word and believes, shall have everlasting life.

Vision of a moon-like trumpet

While in prayer early in the morning of January 19, 1984, somehow in a vision I was walking on the grounds of the U.S. Capitol with some of the national monuments in the background. As I walked on the sidewalk through the park, I saw a soft white moon-like light in the sky, in the form of a long trumpet. The sky was purple.

The Lord had previously revealed to me that purple was a call for repentance. In the Old Testament, the trumpet was an instrument used to give certain signals or calls to the people. Because the moon-like trumpet was in a purple sky, in the presence of the U.S. Capitol, I felt the Lord wanted to sound a trumpet call to the people of this nation to repent for their sins and for the sins of their leaders and their nation. The Lord is asking the people to repent and to turn from their sins and their wicked ways, and to pray for a spiritual revival, so that this nation may be restored as one nation under God. As I continued to seek the Lord about the meaning of this vision, the following words were spoken to me:

The pen is mightier than the sword and
My sword is the sharpest pen known to mankind.
Take up My pen, which is My Word and
write about the need for national repentance.
Do this now in order that
you will be ready to publish it, at the appropriate time.
All that is important for you to know at this time is that
I would have you to write about the need for repentance in
your nation.
Trust in Me, for the message of repentance in your land must
come forth.

Allow the Lord to help.

Be still, My son. Allow Me to assist you in your work. You will have the final discernment on the book. Others will proofread, some will try to change. Not all have purity at heart. This is why I chose you for this work. My Word will stand regardless of any effort to change it. Yours is the final decision as to what will come to print. Be patient with those whom I have given to help in assembling your material. Pray for them in order that their discernment will be the same as Mine. Have confidence that your work will be completed as I desire. For my desire is for us to be one.

The Lord calls the book, His book.

My son, be at peace about My book, for I have it in the hands of those I would have to receive great blessings from it. Even though the progress seems minute to you, the blessing has been great for those who have handled it, for a day is as a thousand years and a thousand years are as a day. Do not despair, My son, for many great healings must first take place, in order for your work to be finished. Continue to persevere for My name's sake. Dedicate all your actions, in regard to this book, to Me. All things are in My control. Be patient, persevere and have hope that this work will be complete.

The Lord's book is near completion.

I have given you the means by which I can give My people the solutions to their problems. My book is near completion. Keep in mind My attitude about prayer. Vigilance, persistence and self-denial are the necessary ingredients for successful and victorious encounters against the Adversary. My scripture is the embodiment of all truth. Write as I have instructed you in the past with an open mind, a contrite heart and diligence for the truth. My Word will speak for itself. Concern yourself with only the truth. Trust Me, for I am with you always.

I asked the Lord if I was to write about faith and praying in tongues.

My words at this moment are on their way to you. My thoughts in regard to prayer of faith, you already know. Be direct, descriptive and scriptural. Brevity is important. Directness of trust is imperative. Begin with the description about the Spirit. Begin with a description of the power of praying in the Spirit. All else flows, as the river of life flows in the eternal city in paradise. Ask the saints to pray for you, because the resistance of the Adversary is strong. Call on your patron saint to stand with you and ask for divine guidance. I am pleased with your cooperation and collaboration with My Holy Spirit. Pray as you write, and My thoughts will come forth for you.

Do not be deceived into thinking that this information came from yourself.

You are a storehouse of information. You have had My truths deposited within you because they are part of the nature of My Spirit that has dwelled within you since baptism. These truths are not yours, they are Mine. Be sensitive to the prompting of the Spirit as to who is to receive them. For those who receive them will receive My blessings. The origin of these truths is always Me, your Father. Never be deceived into believing that they came from yourself or another. Test them always, before dispensing them. This way, there will be no error as to the source, from which they came. I would have you, at this time, to bring My truths to a larger number of people. Use these means that I have given you to take advantage of the opportunities that present themselves. For it is important that My Word go forth, for the time of the end draws near.

The Lord speaks on faith.

My son, your faith is as strong as Abraham, Isaac and Jacob. It is, because of your faith that you are able to understand the mysteries of My nature. It is because of your faith in Me, Yahweh your God, that you are able to ask for and receive the desires of your heart. This faith of yours is a gift from Me, Yahweh your God. Cherish and protect it, for it is your children's children's legacy. The enemy tries to weaken your faith by deception and untruths about the mysteries of My plan of salvation and redemption. Remain committed, faithful and strong in your search of scriptural truths, which are contained in the book that I have commissioned you to transcribe. The importance of My truths must be the foremost endeavor of this work (book). In time, you will come to know the totality of My glory. For now be patient, and accept it in the same faith of your forefathers - Abraham, Isaac, Jacobs and Moses. I will draw to you, those people that are needed as helpers for you to finish this work. Be patient, work with diligence, and know that I am in control of this project. I love you. Continue with your prayers, as you have in the past. Your reward will be great, when this book is complete. It is Yahweh Who speaks.

The Lord is pleased. (These words were spoken on two separate occasions.)

I am pleased with your commitment to search for the deep knowledge hidden in the scripture.

I am pleased with your witness and testimony, your faithfulness and fidelity to My Word. I am pleased that you yield yourself to the prompting of My Spirit. I love you very much. I have many great gifts for you. Do not look for these gifts to come from the world, for these are not the rewards I have for you. Look for these gifts to arrive through the vehicle of My written Word. I will be giving you a deeper knowledge, wisdom and understanding of My nature. Be open to receive, for I want you to know and experience the totalness of My love for you.

14

Writing of the manuscript is completed.

My son, your faithfulness in your endeavor to write My revealed knowledge of the Book of Revelation in a clear 20th Century manner is to be commended. The work is now to be entrusted to those in whom you have confidence. Listen to their criticisms, advice and discernment. The part you play, in bringing this manuscript forth, is now complete. I will be in charge of the discernment process, just as I was in charge of the writing. The positive feedback will strengthen your faith. The apparent negative feedback will purify your work effort. Do not allow anyone to hinder or stop this manuscript from being published. The words that you have written for Me are words for this hour. I do want them to come forth at this time. These are My words. I will let no man keep them from being read by others. Be conscious of the enemy, so that he will not distract from the truth that is contained in this manuscript. Pray for those, who will be reading this manuscript in order that they may be guided by the Holy Spirit, just as you were guided by the Holy Spirit in writing it. Your part is complete. It is now time for others to play their part, for it is the Lord God Yahweh Who speaks.

Rest for now.

Rest and be peaceful at this time. In the creation of the universe, there was a day left to rest. You have labored generously with the project that I have given you. You are in the seventh day, the beginning of a new week. Rest for now. The work that I am doing within you is one of developing a peaceful and harmonious spirit. Do your everyday chores of the world. At the same time, allow yourself the opportunity to rest in Me. Your load is light, at this time, in order that you may be more attentive to Me and My will for you. Be cautious of the spirit of hastiness, for I am a God of order, patience, power and might. Your role in the war with the enemy of darkness, death and destruction is one of greatness. I choose, at this time, for you to relax and be peaceful, so that you will be able to discern the part that I would have for you to play. Come quietly before Me each day. Seek ye My face, in order to know My will for you, at this time.

I had a vision of two blue eyes looking at me. Blue is symbolic of holiness, but for some reason, I knew these eyes were evil.

Do not be deceived by those who would appear in the eyes of men to be holy. For not all holiness is of God. The Pharisees appeared to be holy, however, they were as dead inside as Pharaoh of Ancient Egypt. Be cautious in trusting yourself to those who appear to be holy. Trust the Spirit of God that seems to be present in them. Not all of the men that came to Me were of God, My Father. There were those, who wanted to use me (Judas Iscariot) for themselves and for the benefit of others. Know this My son, I have given you all wisdom and knowledge to discern the intentions of those, who would come in the appearance as holy men. I am in charge. Trust in Me, for this is the Lord God Yahweh, Who speaks.

Dream – I was at the top of a large round cube, approximately 18 feet off the ground. I knew it was time to get down.

I have placed you in a position at the top of the bulwark, in order that you may see the work that is being done in the restoration of My Church, of which you are a part. I am allowing you to see both sides of the wall. I would like for you at this time to allow Me to help you down, in order that you can become part of the restoration, by helping the laborers, who are already at work. For now, I have a new work for you, which I will reveal to you in My time. Be at peace, and know that I am with you and that My Holy Spirit is guiding you. Trust in Me to show you your new place and work.

Dream and prophesy:

I had knowledge that a priest had read my manuscript. This priest walked into a room with about twenty people and said, "Who has Mike's book?" Someone stood up with the book. The priest walked over and took the book, saying something about Revelation. Another person stood up and said, "Revelation makes me not want to be a Catholic. Revelations turns me away from the Catholic Church." The priest said, "This book (Lifting the Veil of Revelation) will bring them to me."

> My son, be not alarmed of those, who would be turned away from the Catholic Church because of the Book of Revelation. This book was written by My evangelist, John. It is My desire that this book (Lifting the Veil of Revelation) be read by all men. My Holy Spirit has been its discerner, and many people will be drawn to Me through it. Trust Me, knowing that My Father has approved this.

17

Tell the people about the Lord.

> I have raised you up, in order for you to do My work of telling people, who I am, what I am like, where I am, why I am, because at this time the work of My Church and My Magisterium and My written Words are under attack by the world, self, and Satan himself. The gift of written communication skills comes to you for the purpose of bringing My divine character and nature to others, who do not know of Me. It is also an alternative to those things of the world and the devil that will deceive people from knowing Me as the Lord God Almighty. I am with you at all times. The questions that you have about Me will always be answered, for I have you in the world to be a disseminator of information about Me and My kingdom. This is the Lord God Yahweh Who speaks. (Our desire is to know, love and serve Him and to be happy with Him forever on earth and in heaven.)

While I was praying for those reading my manuscript, the Lord said:

> Walk a straight line, Mike. This line exemplifies the Holy Spirit. This Spirit is Who wrote your book. Do not yield to any spirit other than Mine. Your book shall be carried to all nations, so that they may hear. Do not modify or change it in any way. Critics, in whom you have a great deal of respect, will try to change your book. But they were not of the anointing of the Spirit, when your pen was in action. So listen to no one, except those with whom you pray for learning of my truths.

Dream - The Lord revealed that I was involved in a checker game as I was making the moves that involved getting the manuscript written, read and published. The Lord said I was too deeply involved in the game to back out; however, there had been a setback, and I was going to have to make the right moves to get the book published. We prayed and asked the Lord about the setback. The Lord revealed that it had to do with the phrase I had written in the dedication of the book. I dedicated the book to the Father, the Son and the Holy Spirit, under whose guidance this book was written. Someone felt I was being presumptuous that this manuscript was written under the guidance of the Father, the Son and the Holy Spirit. I knew the manuscript was written under their guidance but since I did not want to be accused of being presumptuous, I decided to remove that part. My prayer partner said the Lord had revealed to him that I had spent considerable amount of time in prayer, as I wrote this book and that this book was truly written under the guidance of the Father, the Son and the Holy Spirit. The Lord said:

> Do not remove the phrase "under whose guidance this book was written." These words are Holy Fire, which will carry your book throughout this nation and many others, not only in your generation but in generations to come. The adversary is immensely strong, but with just these words the enemy has no power. Give the glory to God.

A picture of a friend who said, "The Lord is well pleased with the book."

I spoke back immediately and said, "Thank you, Jesus."

The Lord said people will come into His Body 1011 ways. Then there was a vision in which I was serving as a Eucharistic minister, holding a golden chalice filled with a powdered form

of the Body of Christ. Using a silver spoon, I was spoon-feeding the Body of Christ to the people as they came to the altar. As we began to pray, the Lord spoke.

> My message is for all people, which includes both male and female of all races and creeds. My message comes to them for the washing of their soul and body to regenerate new life. Once new life is formed, it is unsoiled, pure as white linen, with the days of old unable to stain the white garments that bathe and clothe their new life. Sin is no longer a deadly sting to claim its victim. Thousands upon thousands of people will accept My name in the near future. They will come into My kingdom like you and Mike. Bring My message to them with vigor and steadfast prayer. Have faith in Me so that I may come to them through you and Mike. My message will be heard by millions of people through a book that will be under the authorship of Michael D. Miesch Jr. Stand by Mike when he publishes this book, and believe that it will come forth to My sheep in this generation and generations to come. This book will be a tool to serve as a guideline for millions of people, who will come to Me to accept My glory.

Vision - I was talking with a priest outside a new church building. The priest, wearing a black cassock with a white surplice, walked into the church through a door near the altar. I followed the priest and stood behind him on the altar to his right, facing the people. The church was round and beautifully constructed with a high dome. The seats were filled with people. There was a long procession of priests getting ready to march into the church. Though I was very comfortable standing on the altar behind the priest, the priest was very nervous and uncomfortable with me standing behind him. He kept turning around looking at me, but he did not say anything.

When the Lord walked the streets of His hometown, many people of that so-familiar site refused to have faith in Jesus as a healer of divine origin. God's very own Son was able to do nothing miraculous amongst the people because of their own unbelief. Jesus delivered a message to His people, but the message was not received. Faith is the ultimate receptacle that must be a part of the people before the power of the Almighty Holy Spirit can be made manifest to bring forth a healing. The process is two fold: the people must provide the faith and God will provide the power. The priest within Christ's Church is representative of many of the high priests that were in command of religious order in Jesus' day. If the priest's own faith is as little as the faith of the people of Nazareth, there is little hope of him receiving the power of the almighty Holy Spirit. Many priests all over the world are with little faith in Jesus Christ. Whatever comments or remarks they may make, about Mike's book, must not be taken to heart, if their words are not guided by the Spirit. They must have receptacles of faith to be responsive to what the Holy Spirit saith. The book will make many of the priests nervous, because it strikes fear into them regarding their own convictions. However, it will bless them in the final moments of their ministries, when they realize the truth of the message is that of the Holy Spirit.

Vision - a priest sitting behind a desk with his feet propped upon the desk reading my manuscript. Then, there was a picture of a man to my right looking at me.

> The Lord is going to send some people to talk to you about the manuscripts. One of the people will speak with half-truths. The Lord wants you to listen to what they have to say, but to come before Him, before making any changes or decisions.

Vision – a building was being constructed.

This building was solidly reinforced with different width boards (6,8,10 and 12 inch boards) nailed at an angle, not only on the sides but also on the roof. This building was strongly reinforced to be able to weather a fierce storm.

> The Lord said this building was His Church. He said my son (Michael III) and I were carpenters that were helping to rebuild, restore and renew His Church just as St. Francis of Assisi did. The Church is going to have to be reinforced this strong to weather the storm that is coming. The Church is the body. The body is the people. The people are going to have to be strong in their faith to weather the storm that is coming.

While praying for my book, I had a vision of a long and narrow yellow and green ribbon-like flag, flying from a pole.

Yellow symbolizes the presence or the light of the Lord. Green symbolizes new life.

> The door of life shall be opened by your book, to reveal the glory of the Lord upon His people. Thus they will be raised to the height, to which I have called them.

Praying for my book

While praying for my book, I had a vision of a farmer wearing a black, wide brim, flat top hat, white shirt and beige pants like those worn in 1800's. The farmer had his hands on a plow that was being pulled by an ox, breaking the ground for planting. The sun was shining on the farmer's face, but not on anything else.

As the farmer tills the ground for planting seeds, so am I preparing America and the world for a harvest, unparalleled to this time.

While praying for my book, I had knowledge that there was something within me, blocking the publication of this book.

I refer to the book as my book. The Lord said this is not my book but His book, that He only used me as an instrument to write the book. I must turn loose of the book and give it to Him, so that he can do with it what He wants.

Vision of a white-hot dove that looks like metal, when it is super heated: This dove, which resembled the emblem of the Holy Spirit, was descending downward head first.

I have given you My words and have set them in your heart. It is on fire from My Holy Spirit. I shall interpret what it means to each person, as My Spirit speaks to their hearts. You have done all that I have asked of you. You shall have your just reward. Do not turn to change anything. You have given it to Me. Do not try to take it back. Blessing and curse comes from the tongue. So it is with My words. It will divide and join. Many will come to sit at your feet. Be prepared in all areas of your life. I am taking you on a new path, a path of different colors. They shall be joined to Me through you. Turn back to what I have taught you. Be ready to use it. Much joy is coming. Rejoice, for I am near and hear your voice day and night. You have taken a place in My heart. I rejoice in your personal praise and the open love that you show Me. I love you, My son. Know that I love you.

Vision – I had shown a priest something I had written. Later, the archbishop dropped in. As the archbishop was leaving, the priest walked up to him and asked if he had time to look at this paper. To my surprise, he glanced at it, and then he sat down to read it. I had written something about the Holy Spirit. The archbishop looked something up in the Catholic dictionary and said, "That is right" and continued to read. Then he read something about a giraffe. Again, he looked it up in the Catholic dictionary and said, "That is right".

> The Archbishop is symbolic of the higher authorities of the Church. The giraffe meant that this work, at first glance, appears to be too simple and uncomplicated to be valid by the typical, wise learned theologians of the Church. This work appears to be ridiculous. The Archbishop was saying that this was a valid work of the Holy Spirit.

Dream – I had knowledge that I was to be on TV. I asked a friend if he thought my book was from the Lord? He said, "No decision has been made, but they would know tonight." I had knowledge that I was to be interviewed by a lady with premature white hair who had the gift of discernment. Then my friend asked me a question, "What if it is not from the Lord?" I responded by saying, "If it is not of the Lord, I will get rid of the book."

The "night of decision" mentioned in the dream, does not indicate "tonight", rather "a time" of prayer and discernment about your book, which will be seriously considered. The lady, with white hair, is a spirit of truth who will be interviewing not only you, but those, who will be discerning your book. The question, "What if the book is not of God?" is made to you by God, not your friend. Your answer is the right answer. The "television" you will be on is the deep scrutiny you will be under because of your book.

Dream – Someone said to me, "I understand the Lord has been speaking to you about Abraham Lincoln". I said, "Yes!" Then another person said, "I understand the Lord has been speaking to you about Abraham Lincoln." I said, "Yes!"

> The Proclamation of Emancipation was for all slaves in bondage against their will, and they were set free by the direction of Abraham Lincoln. Such will be the emancipation of all believers and unbelievers alike as they will be guided by the light of God through this book.

Dream – I had written a manuscript or something in which the code to what I had written had been lost. I do not know to whom I was talking, but I told him to interpret it the way it read.

> The Lord has the code. Those reviewing the manuscript are to interpret the document "just the way it reads". This is meant only for reviewers.

Someone with whom I have prayed with on a few occasions, who asked to read the manuscript, said this hit him right between the eyes, as he really had intentions of editing the manuscript.

Vision of a white bearded man, standing close to me, looking sideways to the ground: My prayer partner received the following words.

> This man was Moses. He was standing beside you explaining what is going to happen to the earth. He said you had written of it and will understand. I asked, "Why Mike?" Moses responded, "He will be part of what was, what is, and what is to come!"

Vision of several pieces of white paper blowing with the wind in a pasture or meadow: Each sheet of paper was like a blinding light.

Something you have written has been rejected by those who should read it. This writing will be found to be of God and will reflect God's will.

Praying before the Blessed Sacrament after Mass:

> I want you to show My people My mercy throughout your book that I gave you. When there is a tragedy or calamity, show My mercy to My people, My children. Show how I love them. I will give you the words to write. My words will be understood by children as well. They will be simple and they will be Mine. I want My children to know why I am doing this for them. I do not want them to have fear. I would have them to be joyous and happy that I would do this for them. My words will be full of peace and love.

Words received

What you have written will endure the test of time.

Vision of an abstract picture - I was in a classroom talking to a teacher. The teacher's face and upper portions of the chest and arms suddenly became as an abstract picture. I saw several different views

26

of the picture. One view had a purple outline of the face. Then the power of God came upon me and the abstract picture became a living person in front of me looking at me.

> The Lord revealed that the full understanding and meaning of an abstract picture is only known to the artist. This is the same with the Book of Revelation. The Book of Revelation is like an abstract picture in which only the Lord knows the full meaning of all the symbols and things written therein. These meanings become clear to those to whom the Lord chooses to reveal them. I could see several different views in an abstract form, but when the power of God came upon me, I could see this person who was a teacher very clearly. I asked my prayer partner to pray with me for understanding as to who this person was. My prayer partner laughed after praying. The Lord revealed that this person was one of several angels that are around me at all times ministering to me.

Dream – a book of perilous verses

I was holding a book that I had seen in a previous dream. I placed the book on a table saying that my book was finished (not referring to the book on the table). There were two young men close by. They were trying to get a glance at the cover of the book that was placed on the table. When a priest picked up the book, I asked him, if it was his book. He said, "Yes". Later, after I woke up and was praying my regular prayers, I had a vision of the priest in the dream. He asked me, "What is your favorite verse?" I replied, "To know, love and serve the Lord, thy God, with thy whole heart, whole mind, and whole soul", which is the first commandment. I had forgotten about the dream, which I remembered after the vision. My prayer partner received the following message:

This book is a writing of perilous verses. (My prayer partner did not know what perilous meant. Perilous means dangerous or hazardous.) This priest will write a book against your book. He will use your book against you. He will slander your name, misinterpret the scriptures and will almost certainly come to the point of abusing the Holy Scriptures. Scriptures are the sword. Remember the first commandment, have it in your mind and heart at all times for your protection, and the enemy will not penetrate your spiritual realm. Your flesh will be very weak and battered, but your spirit will be unharmed. Do not mind those that believe in what that priest says. They shall also falter in their walk in the Lord. Just remember the words you spoke after the priest asked you what your favorite verse was. People who blindly abuse the Holy Scripture will be smitten by the sword. My people suffer for the lack of knowledge.

The Lord speaks

My son, do not concern yourself about anyone who would take issue with your work. Your work is unlike any other work undertaken on the Book of Revelation. The book in the dream is not yours because it belongs to someone else. The person to whom it belongs has his own opinion, which is different than yours. Others have already written and will write on the subject matter that is the same as yours. Yet, their work will not be the same as yours. You need not worry or concern yourself about someone taking issue with your work or discrediting your work or slandering your name, because you have been obedient to My will, which is to know, love and serve Me with your whole heart, soul and mind. The priest represents the mainline Christian denominations and not a specific priest.

The Lord says:

Be cautious and move with diligence. Gather your materials and make preparation to contact prospective publishers. In time, I will make known to you the responsible agent for the publication, printing and distribution of your work. Gather facts about those, who you believe will be prospective candidates for publication. Move with confidence, knowing that you have a work of God to be brought forth. Anyone who leads you into believing that he is doing you a favor in publishing the work should be eliminated. Those that present themselves as a serving-agent of God's work on this earth are to be considered. Any others, who endeavor to dazzle you with their operation, need not be considered. Only consider the best who are exemplified as Christ-like character. Don't rush, for all things will come to pass in My time. Patience, diligence, discernment, observation and scrutiny are the watch-words for now.

The book

The book will print. It will reprint. It will sell many, but only to those who choose to know.

The sun-clothed woman and the Blessed Mother

I made the statement that the Sun-clothed woman is not the Blessed Mother; yet, there are prophecies, supposedly from the

Blessed Mother, saying that she is the Sun-clothed Woman. While I was praying asking the Lord for an understanding, I had a picture of a head of an alligator with its mouth wide open with many teeth. A few days later, while praying, I had a vision of the Blessed Mother. I asked three of my prayer partners to come together and pray with me for an understanding. I asked the Lord if I was to change the statement about the Blessed Mother not being the Sun-clothed Woman. We received the following message and words of knowledge:

> We, who are of many tribes, come together to worship and adore My Father and the Holy Spirit. My message is the same, yet, I speak in a way that those who are searching will understand. I have twelve tribes, not all understand in the same way. I speak loudly and intellectually to one, and I give dreams to another. Just as at the Tower of Babel, My people have been confounded. Yet, I am speaking and they are each hearing Me differently. Does this mean what I have spoken or made known to you is wrong? "Nay!" I say, "Nay!" What you have been given is for those of the tribe I have directed you to. Because they challenge, charge, argue, assail, laugh, distort, curse or lie about my revelation to you is no consequence to you. I give this to you that those, who will see or hear it, will be touched, blessed and a part of my whole message which has been imparted to them. My other messengers are speaking the same message and it is disseminated to them in a way that they will understand. Stand firm, speak boldly, do not concern yourself with the message I have given others to speak. They are reaching those that I am sending to them and reaching others that they themselves are reaching out to. My messengers will

cross paths and will sometimes be misunderstood. Do not separate yourself from them. Know that I will use those who are willing and even some that are not. Go to those that I have sent you to and be at peace for I am Peace and Love.

Head of an alligator with its mouth wide open with many teeth

The Lord said, "Do you believe what you have written wholeheartedly with all that is within you?" I replied, "Yes!" Then He replied, "The alligator with its mouth wide open will be the people trying to tear at you and bring you down. " I am a God of covenant. I dwell within My covenant. Apart from it, there are grave consequences. Stay within its protection and there will be blessings and fruits. Apart from it, there is death.

Another prayer partner received the following words of knowledge:

The Lord is the author of your work. You do not need to apologize for what He has given you to understand and how He has instructed you to write. He has a covenant with you in the writing of this book. It is His task to open the understanding of each one, who has access to it.

Vision of the Blessed Mother

Be comforted my son. You do not need to be concerned about tomorrow, for it will take care of itself. Be of good cheer for my Son loves you.

Vision in which three different colored solutions were being injected into the tree. The color of the three solutions was red, blue and yellow.

> This tree is the "Tree of Life". Red is the blood of man, which is the manifestation of the Spirit of Life. Blue is the Living Water, which is the Spirit of Life. Yellow is the Light of His Word, which never changes. These colors symbolized the chemistry of our existence. Trust My Word. Let the light shine, as in My Word to show that the blood of man, the once fallen race, shall be saved for all eternity. This is what My Son has done for mankind, to set man free. Thereby, I say unto you, do the same for others, just as He has done for you. Let no man persuade you against the truth, which is My Word, which shall never change. The goodness of your heart is all that will remain from your present physical existence. Stand steadfast in My Word, which will keep your heart in My good will. These three things are the Spirit of existence. The fourth thing is knowledge of the disorder of nature which could not harmonize with the goodness of the tree of knowledge. Because of redeemed man, God had to cut out that portion of the tree, which was the nature of sin through Jesus Christ, Who was the atonement for that portion of the tree, which was man's disobedience to God's Word.

Dream – I had knowledge that I had asked Jesus for permission to ascend upward to be enlightened so I could finish the Book of Revelation. I spoke to Jesus, Who was standing at my right and said, "Thank you Jesus."

Study My heart. Study My soul. Let My mind be in yours. Know Me. Study how I forgive. Study how My revenge will prevail over Satan. Know My love. Know My will. Many have forgotten that have tasted My love and My presence. They have forgotten about My wrath that is to come. All they want is to feel good. They have gone back to pagan ways. They have chosen to be lied to - to feel O.K. I want you to be ready to tell them and so shall those, who will follow you. I love you My son. You are Mine!

Dream - I came upon a man in the street, carrying a package, wrapped in a roll of newspapers. This roll was tightly bound with string. This man and I were in a struggle over this package. I managed to pull out a small package rolled very tightly in newspaper, the size of a hot dog bun. I spoke to the man and said, "I have it." I had knowledge that package contained meat. This man dressed in a brim hat and a coat that covered his hips said to me, "Eat it". I refused to eat it, as I did not know what it was. As I began to unroll the tightly wrapped newspaper off the package, I got a glimpse of a white blinding light, then it looked like white gold. I asked a prayer partner to pray with me for discernment. Is this from the Lord?

Prophecy-

My son, you have fought and struggled to know and understand My Word and Me. I am happy to tell you of the great blessing that has been made ready for you. In the box was My hidden Word. You have brought it to the light. Your work has been tested by fire for the truth. It has produced pure white gold. It is ready to be shared with the world. My Words are that of brilliant gold. My Words are in you and through you about to speak to My people. Your heart

33

is so full that many will reject you as they did Moses. Many will open their hearts to your words of Me. Speak slowly and gently. Let your words be kind and building. Many will be spring lambs. Very few will be able to consume the greatness I have taught you. Let My Words flow from My heart to your heart. Let your lips bring joy, acceptance, and forgiveness. Some you now know will scatter. Know this now and do not be shaken when it happens. I will be with you. Take care of your physical person. Much will be demanded of you.

I asked my prayer partner to pray with me about my book.

Be prepared for disappointment. Have faith that My Word will not come back void. For My Word is like a mighty hammer, driven into the spirit and flesh. Be humble of heart and obedient unto My authority and you shall be blessed. Submit to My perfect will. Send it (the book) to the publishers that have been mentioned. If not those, I will close or open the doors. Trust in Me, for I will choose the one that will publish the book. Be prepared to be tested.

I gave a copy of my book to a friend to read. At that time, she received understanding that she was to speak a word from the Lord to me at another time. Later she received this message.

The Lord says that it is time to publish the books!
Don't get hung up on ecclesiastical looks.
The opinions and statements of man are
only snares and traps to hinder, what I've told you to do before hand.
Go forth and cast down your nets.
The fish are waiting and you will have pockets to let.

34

It is time for the nation to hear
what I've spoken privately in your ear.
It is time for My people to read about the spiritual truths
that you have paid the price to receive.
Now listen! Don't hold back
for I have gone before you and slain the devilish pack.

My son, you have stayed before Me,
loving Me, delighting yourself in My presence
for surely I will give you the desires of your heart.
You have cried out to Me to open the door.
Now I have unlocked (previously closed opportunities).
Much more, than you have asked, is in store.

Your life is a testimony to be shared
for those beloved saints that have physically been impaired.
For know that you are one chosen to overcome
Even now you have victory and are proof that
battles have been fought and won by the Son.

Your anointed praise and intercession
is a sweet smelling fragrance to Me.
Because of your dying to self, so many have been set free.
Many walk in health and deliverance today,
because I've called you to pray.

The days ahead will be busy and time-consuming.
Be aware there are still snares.
Again, doors will swing wide open that have been closed
to speak to the family's unhearing ears.
For you this will be a good spiritual year.

Press on My son, move forward,
for it is time for others to know those

35

revelations and knowledge to you I did show.
Don't wait! Don't hesitate!

The lull, the pause is over.
Now I'm releasing you to move forward.
I will fill you with My anointing, My love and My power
To enlighten mankind this last hour.
Selah

A few years ago, I asked the Lord if I was to make any changes in my book. The Lord said:

No, do not make any changes, you will in time. What you have written will go out on power lines through-out this nation and the world.

While in prayer, the Lord said:

This book may cause controversy; controversy is not always bad, controversy can do a lot of good.

Dream – Someone spoke to me very excitedly about me teaching Revelation. In a second dream this person said there was a division in the ocean. In a third dream, he said there was a great division in the ocean.

Michael, the time is now. Go and prepare your notes. Set into place - markers. Arrange your cards. Prepare your highlights. Make your notes clear. Arrange each step so that My weak will understand. Choose no one to serve you. I will send My own to be by your side. They in turn will go out into the hinterlands. As time passes many will separate themselves through My churches. Many have been misled and wander to know the truth. When the false comes more will separate themselves looking for peace. Go, prepare, write, rewrite. Do not be discouraged. You will be taken away when no more can be done. I have made a place for you and yours.

As I was waking up I heard these words:

"My son, you have been given a trumpet to raise the dead from the dead."

While praying very early in the morning, I had five or six visions of a blinding light.

The Lord said, "I am coming soon. It is time to get your books published.

My beloved holy one of Mine. Prepare to travel. Not as you have done before, for I call you away. I have much for you to do. You must be prepared to travel light. Be prepared to go when My angel beckons. All is cared for. You have much to do for Me. Do not be afraid. Learn now to give up what you do not need for those things you will need. I am your arm chair and comforter. I will bring you to My place for you to rest and work. My eyes are looking into your eyes to see My will.

Embraced by the Lord Jesus Christ

I was sitting in a chair at home with my eyes closed saying my prayers. Someone grabbed both of my upper arms giving me a gentle shake. When I opened my eyes, there was no one in the room. I had assumed this was an angel as I have been touched many times by angels to get my attention. I asked my prayer partner to pray with me for an understanding.

Jesus said, "It is Me! It is Me! It is Me! It is good that you are here. I will comfort you here."

A month later

I had laid a book down to close and rest my eyes. Suddenly my hands were on the upper arms of a person. I started squeezing and feeling the muscles with my hands. I knew immediately this was Jesus. I started telling him how much I love Him over and over. I pulled His head over my shoulder to hug Him. I did not dare open my eyes as I knew He would disappear the minute I opened my eyes. This lasted for less than a minute.

I received understanding that Jesus was extremely pleased that I wrote and am publishing the two books that He asked me to write. He expressed His appreciation by allowing me to physically touch and embrace Him.

The Lord said, "You have My strength. I have you in the palm of My hands. I will never leave you nor forsake you.

CHAPTER 2

God's Blessing On Those Who Study Revelation

We were created by God to love and serve him with our whole heart and soul. We are on a pilgrimage on earth for a very short period of time which will determine our fate in the next life which is for all eternity. Many of us work or study real hard to get an education, to be doctors, lawyers, successful business men and women to prosper, to achieve fame and honor in this life with no concern for the next life. We came into the world naked. When we leave this world we cannot take anything with us except the goodness of our hearts. One hundred years ago we were not here. A hundred years from now we will not be here.

The mysteries of God, His nature and His plans for man are written in the pages of the Bible. Life on earth is as a grain of sand on the seashore or a drop of water in the ocean, in contrast to time in eternity. The manner in which we develop a relationship with God, spending time in prayer, studying His Word, and being sensitive to knowing and doing His will, will determine our fate for all eternity. There are many rewards and honors in the kingdom. Some will have crowns or many crowns. Some will be kings and priests. The Lord said those that prevail to the end, He will give them authority to rule nations with a rod of iron. Some will be rulers over five cities, some over ten cities, and some over one city. Some will receive many honors and rewards and will shine brightly as stars for all eternity.

Some will be the bride of the Lamb and will follow Him wherever He goes. Some will be servants. Some will just make it within the door of the kingdom.

Once we cross the line from time to eternity, our fate is sealed for all eternity. There will be no advancement, as there is in the business world today. There is nothing more serious or important in this life than our relationship with God, and an understanding of God's plan of the things to come. This understanding affects our ability to know and to do God's will, and to run the race for the prize of the high-calling that Paul sought to run and win with all of his might.

The books of Daniel and Revelation contain the keys to understanding God's plan in regard to the Jews, the gentiles, the seventieth week of Daniel and the return of the Lord to the earth. There are more differences and opinions concerning the books of Daniel and Revelation than any other books of the Bible. Since the subject is deep and difficult to understand, most people are discouraged from even discussing it.

Lord promises a special blessing to those who read and study the Book of Revelation.

Most people think Revelation is a book full of mysterious symbols which God did not intend for us to understand. This is not true. God promises a special blessing to those who will read, study and attempt to understand the Book of Revelation.

> Revelation 1:3: Blessed is the one who reads the words of this prophecy, and blessed are those who hear it and take to heart what is written in it, because the time is near (7).

What must one do to get this blessing?

1. Blessed is he who reads the words of this prophecy.
2. Blessed is he who hears the words of this prophecy.
3. Blessed is he who takes to heart what is written in it, because the time is near.

Simply stated, you must read, hear and meditate on the things written in Revelation to receive this blessing. God began and finished the book of Revelation with a promise of a blessing. God is encouraging us to read, study and attempt to understand the things written in the Book of Revelation. The Lord will lift the veil and give understanding to those who will seriously pray, study and attempt to understand the signs, symbols and the things written in this book. The Lord does not want us to be ignorant of the mysteries and secrets hidden in the Book of Revelation. He wants us to have an understanding of the teachings and meaning of this book.

A thorough understanding of the Book of Revelation, the seventieth week of Daniel and its time frame, will give us some understanding of God's plan of the things to come, and will inspire us to run the race each day, for the prize that Paul sought to win with all of his might. Our reward is for all eternity.

When someone discourages you from studying Revelation, he is discouraging you from receiving the special blessing God promises to those who read and study it.

Keeping the words of this prophecy

> Revelation 22:7: Behold I am coming soon! Blessed is he who keeps the words of the prophecy in this book (7).

The Book of Revelation is the only book in the Bible that the

Lord opens with a promise of a special blessing in the first chapter and closes with a promise of a special blessing in the last chapter. The Lord has made it very clear that He wants everyone to know, study and understand the things written in the Book of Revelation, so we can prepare for the times that are coming. Those who read, study and understand Revelation will realize that there is a race to run, a prize to win, and the reward is for all eternity. You have to read, study and have some understanding of Revelation to keep the words of this prophecy.

Do not seal the words of this prophecy.

> Revelation 22:10: . . . Do not seal up the words of the prophecy of this book because the time is near (7).

In the 12th Chapter of Daniel, the Lord told Daniel the revelations he had received were to be sealed for they were not to be revealed until the time of the end.

> Daniel 12:1–4: At that time Michael, the great prince who protects your people, will arise. There will be a time of distress such as has not happened from the beginning of nations until then. But at that time your people – everyone whose name is found written in the book – will be delivered. Multitudes who sleep in the dust of the earth will awake: some to everlasting life, others to shame and everlasting contempt. Those who are wise will shine like the brightness of the heavens, and those who lead many to righteousness, like stars for ever and ever. But you, Daniel, close up and seal the words of the scroll until the time of the end. Many will go here and there to increase knowledge. (7)

Now, the Lord is saying, "Do not seal the words written in the book of Revelation." The book of Revelation was written to be read, studied and understood. The Lord wants us to pray, study and search for the deep mysteries written and hidden in the book of Revelation. Understanding the great mysteries of Revelation will enable and encourage one to live, desire and strive for the greatest, highest reward and honor for all eternity. (8)

What is prophecy?

> Revelation 1:3: Blessed is the one who reads the words of this prophecy, . . . (7).

Prophecy indicates something that is going to happen in the future. The book of Revelation was given to John on the Island of Patmos, which is off the coast of Turkey, approximately 95 A.D. At this time, most of the apostles were dead, and John was an old man.

The Book of Revelation was the revelation of Jesus Christ that God gave to show and teach His people the things that must soon take place.

> Apocalypse 4:1: . . . , Come up hither, and I will show thee the things that must come to pass hereafter (9).

Revelation was written at the close of the first century when Christ revealed the things that must soon take place. Those who try to find Revelation as a fulfillment of pre- or early Christian history will be deceived, for there is no way these events could have already happened if the scripture tells us they are yet to take place.

Revelation is a book of signs and symbols.

Why did God speak in mysterious signs and symbols? Why didn't He speak to us with words that we can understand? Jesus often taught by using parables. Puzzled and mystified, the apostles asked the Lord why He spoke in parables, Jesus replied,

> Matthew 13:11-13: . . . The knowledge of the secrets of the kingdom of heaven has been given to you, but not to them. Whoever has will be given more, and he will have an abundance. Whoever does not have, even what he has will be taken from him. This is why I speak to them in parables: Though seeing, they do not see; though hearing, they do not hear or understand. (7)

The mysterious signs and symbols in Daniel and Revelation are similar to the parables. These are the mysteries of God that are revealed to the humble, reverent, faithful believers... the babes, but are hidden from the wise and learned. Those who faithfully study and attempt to understand the Book of Revelation will receive an abundance of knowledge of the secrets of the kingdom of heaven. The Lord will make revelation very easy to understand. (8)

How can the mysterious signs and symbols in the Book of Daniel or Revelation be understood?

Revelation must be interpreted literally, except where signs and symbols are used. Signs and symbols can be identified or understood in the same text where they are mentioned or in other books of the Bible. A thorough knowledge of the Bible is required to accurately interpret and fully understand the meaning of the mysterious signs and symbols. (8) The Book of Revelation cannot be understood without a thorough understanding of the other books of the Bible.

The Lord wants us to study the scriptures with an open mind and contrite heart, to correctly divide the word of truth.

> II Timothy 2:15: Study to show thyself approved unto God, a workman that needeth not to be ashamed, rightly dividing the word of truth (10).

All interpretations must be tested on scriptural evidence.

The Book of Revelation is not only deeply rooted in and interwoven with the Old Testament, but also with the gospels and the epistles of the New Testament. The Books of Daniel and Revelation show the Lord's plan to bring the kingdom of this world to an end, to defeat Satan, and to set up His own kingdom.

What must we do to understand the Book of Revelation?

We must remember the following:

1. It is a prophetic book, i.e. it concerns things that will come to pass in the future. Since the Book of Revelation was written around 95 A.D., it concerns the things that will happen after 95 A.D.

2. The Book of Revelation must be studied in chronological order. It cannot be taken out of context. For example, in the book of the seven seals, the first seal is opened before the second seal. The second seal is opened before the third seal. If one tries to show that the events in the seventh seal happen before the events in the first seal, then the scriptures are taken out of context and out of chronological order.

3. An understanding of the time-frame will help put the chronological series into perspective. The seventieth week of Daniel, which covers seven years, begins the moment when the Beast (Antichrist) makes a covenant with Israel for seven years. The covenant is broken by the Beast in the middle of seven years, which means that there are 42 months, or three and half years left in the seventieth week of Daniel. The Great Tribulation begins with the breaking of the covenant (Matthew 24:15-21, Daniel 9:27). This is significant

in the fact that the Beast has power and authority for 42 months to wage war against the Christians and Jews. The two witnesses walk the streets of Jerusalem for 42 months and the sun-clothed woman flees into the wilderness for 1260 days, which is 42 months. The first 42 months of the seven years is peace. The first part of the last 42 months is the Great Tribulation. The last part of the last 42 months is the Wrath of God.

> Revelation 13:5-7: The beast was given a mouth to utter proud words and blasphemies and to exercise his authority for forty-two months. He opened his mouth to blaspheme God, and to slander his name and his dwelling place and those who live in heaven. He was given power to make war against the saints and to conquer them. (7)

4. When the seventh trumpet is blown in Revelation 11, the scripture says the kingdom of this world has become the kingdom of our Lord Jesus Christ. Yet, Revelation 12 speaks of the woman fleeing into the wilderness for another 42 months or three and one-half years. There cannot be another three and one-half years for a total of seven years as the beast only has power to wage war for three and half years. This shows that Revelation 12 has to go back overlap Revelation 4 to fit within the time-frame of three and one-half years that are left in the seventieth week of Daniel after the covenant is broken. The very moment the man-child is born and taken up to heaven in Revelation 12 is the very same moment that a door is open in heaven in Revelation 4 and there is a

multitude before the throne. Revelation 14 called this
multitude the first fruit unto the Lamb.

5. There are two main chronological series of events in
   the Book of Revelation.

   a. First series - Chapter 1 through 11 covers the
      Lord's messages to the seven churches and the
      opening of the book of the seven seals. The sev-
      enth seal consists of seven trumpets. When the
      seventh trumpet is blown, the kingdom of this
      world is finished, for the scriptures say it be-
      comes the kingdom of our Lord Jesus Christ.

   b. Second series - Chapter 12 through 22 starts over
      again, filling in the details, which were not cov-
      ered in the first series (8). The seventh trumpet
      consists of seven bowls or vials judgments which
      are called the seven last plagues. Though the sev-
      enth trumpet is blown in Revelation 11 the seven
      last plagues do not begin until Revelation 15.

As long as the events are placed and studied in chronological order, Revelation will be easier to understand. Since the kingdom of this world becomes the kingdom of our Lord Jesus Christ
in Revelation 11:15, the events mentioned in Revelation 12 to 22
have to be superimposed over the events mentioned in Revelation 4
through 11. Evidence for this is discussed in Chapter 16.

Revelation must be approached in a prayerful attitude, with an
open mind, for serious, detailed study. The Lord knew that many
would be discouraged from reading and studying Revelation. This
is why the Lord promised a special blessing to encourage us to read
and study it. Revelation is the only book in the Bible that open and
closes with a promise of a special blessing to those who read and
study it. (11)

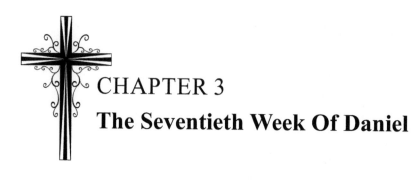

CHAPTER 3
The Seventieth Week Of Daniel

When people speak of seven years of the Great Tribulation or three and one-half years of the Great Tribulation, and three and one-half years of the Wrath of God, they are confused.

Where do the seven years or three and one-half years originate?

The seven years are not mentioned in Revelation. We have to turn to Daniel for an understanding of the seven years, or three and one-half years.

> Daniel 9:24-27: Seventy weeks have been decreed for your people and your holy city, to finish the transgression, to make an end of sin, to make atonement for iniquity, to bring in everlasting righteousness, to seal up vision and prophecy and to anoint the most holy place (or Holy One). So you are to know and discern that from the issuing of a decree to restore and rebuild Jerusalem until Messiah the Prince there will be seven weeks and sixty-two weeks; . . . after sixty-two weeks the Messiah will be cut off . . . the people of the prince who is to come will destroy the city and sanctuary. . . . And he (the prince) will make a firm covenant with many for one week, but in the middle of the week, he will put a stop to sacrifice and grain offering; and on the wings of abominations will come one who makes desolate, even until a complete

destruction, one that is decreed, is poured out on the one who makes desolate. (12)

Before we can answer the question where the seven years or three and one-half years originate, we must analyze Daniel 9:24-27. The Lord decreed seventy weeks upon the Jewish people. There were seven weeks and sixty-two weeks until the coming of the Messiah plus one week yet to come. The one week yet to come is the seventieth week of Daniel.

How long is a week?

Daniel 9:25 speaks of seven weeks and sixty-two weeks from the issuing of the decree at the end of the Babylonian captivity until the crucifixion of the Messiah. If a week is spoken of as seven days, then it would be a little more than a year, from the end of the Babylonian captivity to the crucifixion of the Messiah - - - far too short a time to consider a week as seven days.

In Genesis 29:27, Laban was speaking to Jacob about giving him Rachel to be his wife. The scripture says, "Fulfill her week and we will give thee this also for the service, which thou shalt serve with me yet seven other years" (10). Here a week is spoken of as seven years.

It is from the seventieth week of Daniel that people refer to the seven years of the Great Tribulation or the Wrath of God. However, the Great Tribulation and the Wrath of God cover only part of the seventieth week of Daniel. We will discuss this and the three and one-half years later.

When did the seventy weeks begin?

Daniel 9:25 speaks of the seventy weeks beginning when Cyrus, the King of Persia, issued a decree to restore and rebuild Jerusalem. This decree occurred at the end of the seventy years of Babylonian captivity.

Ezra also shows Cyrus issuing a command to rebuild the temple in Jerusalem during his first year in office.

> Ezra 1:1-2: Now in the first year of Cyrus king of Persia, in order to fulfill the word of the Lord by the mouth of Jeremiah, the Lord stirred up the spirit of Cyrus king of Persia, so that he sent a proclamation throughout all his kingdom, and also put it in writing, saying, "Thus says Cyrus king of Persia, 'The Lord, the God of heaven, has given me all the kingdoms of the earth, and He has appointed me to build Him a house in Jerusalem, which is in Judah.'" (12)

What is the significance of seven weeks and sixty-two weeks?

Seven weeks is forty-nine years. Gordon Lindsay said seven weeks was the length of time from the going forth of the command by Cyrus to rebuild the temple until the temple was completed. Lindsay said this was supported by the fact that both "Ploetz's Dictionary of Dates" and "Putman's Dictionary of Events" show that there were forty-nine years from the first year of Cyrus to the thirty-second year of Darius Hyspastes (Nehemiah 13:6) when the temple was completed. (13)

The seven weeks plus sixty-two weeks was the length of time from the command by Cyrus to rebuild the temple to the crucifixion of our Lord Jesus Christ, the Messiah. These sixty-nine weeks were a total of 483 years (13).

What is the seventieth week of Daniel?

> Daniel 9:26-27: . . . the people of the prince who is to come will destroy the city and the sanctuary. . . . And he (the prince) will make a firm covenant with many for one week, but in the middle of the week,

he will put a stop to sacrifice and grain offering; and on the wing of abomination will come one who makes desolate, even until a complete destruction, one that is decreed, is poured out on the one who makes desolate. (12)

The seventieth week of Daniel begins when the prince of the people, who destroyed Jerusalem, makes a covenant with Israel for one week (seven years). The seventieth week comes after the sixty-ninth week. The sixty-ninth week ended with the crucifixion of the Messiah (Daniel 9:26 . . . the Messiah will be cut off . . .). The seventieth week will have to come after the crucifixion. The people, who destroyed Jerusalem, after the crucifixion, were the Romans in 68 to 70 AD (13). Jesus foretold this destruction in Luke.

Luke 21:20, 24: But when you see Jerusalem surrounded by armies, then recognize that her desolation is at hand. . . . and they will fall by the edge of the sword, and will be led captive into all the nations; and Jerusalem will be trampled underfoot by the Gentiles until the times of the Gentiles be fulfilled. (12)

Jesus indicated that the destruction of Jerusalem would happen in the future after the sixty-ninth week.

What does the scripture, "The people of the prince who is to come will destroy the city and the sanctuary . . . and he will make a firm covenant . . ." mean? When does the seventieth week of Daniel begin?

The people who destroyed Jerusalem were the Romans. "The prince, who is to come" indicates that the prince will come at a future date, making a covenant with Israel for one week (seven years).

When the covenant is made, that will be the beginning of the seventieth week of Daniel. Isaiah 28:15 called this covenant "a covenant with death." (13)

What is the abomination in the temple?

Daniel 9:27 says the prince will break the covenant in the middle of the week, stopping sacrifice and grain offering, bringing on an abomination in the temple. Paul in his letter to Thessalonians said the temple would be defiled.

> II Thessalonians 2:3-4: Let no one in any way deceive you, for it (the day of the Lord) will not come unless apostasy comes first, and the man of lawlessness is revealed, the son of destruction, who opposes and exalts himself above every so-called god or object of worship, so that he takes his seat in the temple of God, displaying himself as being God. (12)

Jesus spoke of the abomination in the temple.

> Matthew 24:15,21: Therefore when you see the abomination of desolation which was spoken of through Daniel the prophet, standing in the holy place (temple), . . . for then there will be a Great Tribulation, such as has not occurred since the beginning of the world until now, nor ever shall. (12)

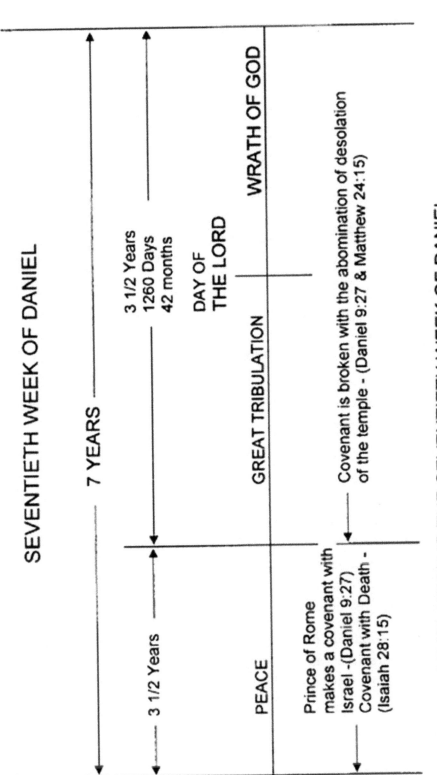

SEVENTIETH WEEK OF DANIEL

7 YEARS

3 1/2 Years

3 1/2 Years
1260 Days
42 months

PEACE

GREAT TRIBULATION

DAY OF
THE LORD

WRATH OF GOD

Prince of Rome
makes a covenant with
Israel -(Daniel 9:27)
Covenant with Death -
(Isaiah 28:15)

Covenant is broken with the abomination of desolation
of the temple - (Daniel 9:27 & Matthew 24:15)

TABLE 1 - REVELATION IS THE SEVENTIETH WEEK OF DANIEL

The abomination of desolation, spoken of by Daniel, Paul and our Lord Jesus Christ takes places when the prince, who makes the covenant with Israel, breaks the covenant by setting himself up in the temple as God.

When is the covenant broken?

Daniel 9:27 speaks of the covenant being broken in the middle of the week, i.e. after three and one-half years of peace. When the covenant is broken, there are exactly three and one-half years left in the seventieth week of Daniel. The scripture speaks of 1260 days; 42 months; and time, times and half a time as referring to three and one-half years. This is very significant, considering that there are only three and one-half years left after the covenant is broken.

When does the Great Tribulation begin?

Jesus said, the Great Tribulation will begin immediately after the abomination of desolation spoken of by Daniel the prophet (Matthew 24:15, 21).

1. The seventieth week of Daniel begins the moment the prince of the Roman people makes a covenant with Israel for one week (seven years).
2. We will know from the moment the covenant is made that the abomination will take place in three and one-half years.
3. The Great Tribulation begins with the abomination of desolation of the temple (Matthew 24:15-21).

Did the abomination of desolation take place when Antiochus Epiphanes desecrated the temple of God in 168 BC by sacrificing a sow on the altar?

Daniel 11:35 speaks of these events happening at the time of the end (13).

In Daniel 11:36, the desecrator will exalt and magnify himself above every God (12). Paul, in II Thessalonians 2:2-4 said, this was yet to come.

Daniel 11:45 and 12:1 show that the desecrator is destroyed at the close of the Great Tribulation (12). This is confirmed in Revelation 19:20 when the Beast is thrown into the Lake of Fire and the Lord Jesus Christ returns to the earth.

Jesus, in Matthew 24:15 said, "When you see the abomination of desolation spoken by Daniel, the prophet," thus indicating it was yet to come.

No covenant with Israel was known to have been made by Antiochus Epiphanes (13).

Did the seventieth week of Daniel take place at the time of Christ or afterward?

1. Daniel 9:26 spoke of the Messiah being cut off (crucified) at the end of sixty-nine weeks.
2. There was no seven-year covenant made. Jesus made a covenant at the Last Supper, which has been in effect for almost 2000 years.
3. Certainly Jesus was not the one to desecrate the temple (13).
4. No known desecration of the temple as described by Daniel took place at the time of Christ.
5. No known covenant was made in 68 to 70 AD. If a covenant had been made, it would have been scripturally recorded.
6. In Matthew, Jesus places the time of the Great Tribulation at the end of the age, just prior to His return.

> Matthew 24:29-31: But immediately after the tribu-
> lation of those days, the sun will be darkened, and
> the moon will not give its light, and the stars will
> fall from the sky, and the powers of the heavens will
> be shaken, and then the sign of the Son of Man will
> appear in the sky, and then all the tribes of the earth
> will mourn, and they will see the Son of Man coming
> on the clouds of the sky with power and great glory.
> And He will send forth His angels with a great trum-
> pet and they will gather together His elect from the
> four winds, from one end of the sky to the other. (12)

This scripture shows that the seventieth week of Daniel takes place just prior to the return of the Lord.

Can there be an interruption or break between the sixty-ninth and the seventieth week of Daniel?

Let us consider I Kings.

> I Kings 6:1: In the four hundred and eightieth year af-
> ter the Israelites had come out of Egypt, in the fourth
> year of Solomon's reign over Israel, . . . he began to
> build the temple of the Lord (7).

The actual time from Exodus to the building of the temple is:

In the wilderness	40 years	Joshua 5:6
Joshua and the elders	20 years *	Number 14:29
Period of the Judges	450 years	Acts 13:18-21
Reign of King Saul	40 years	Acts 13:21
Reign of King David	40 years	II Samuel 5:4
4th year of King Solomon	4 years	I Kings 6:1
Total	594 years	

The years added up seem to contradict the 480 years in I Kings 6:1. Many theologians consider this an error in the scripture. Mr. E. W. Bullinger gives an explanation for this in his book "Number in the Scripture." There were seven oppressions during the times of the Judges. The oppressions were the times when the Israelites were out of favor with God and were under the reigns of the gentiles.

The seven oppressions are:

1. Mesopotamia	8 years	Judges 3:8
2. Moabite	18 years	Judges 3:12-14
3. Canaanite	20 years	Judges 4:2-3
4. Midianite	7 years	Judges 6:1
5. Usurpation of Abimelech	3 years	Judges 9:22
6. Philistine and Ammonite	18 years	Judges 10:7-8
7. Philistine	40 years	Judges 13:1
Total oppression	114 years	

Actual time from Egypt to building of the temple	594 years
Total oppression	114 years
The Lord's determined time	480 years

* Gordon Lindsay explained the twenty years in detail in his book (14).

It can be seen that the Lord's timetable stops when the children of Israel were out of order and were under the reign of a foreign king or people (12, 15). Gordon Lindsay discusses this thoroughly in his book, "The Prophecies of Daniel Series" in Volume III. Lindsay explains that a person may work forty hours a week. This does not mean a man works forty hours without interruption. This means that a man works a total of forty hours in a week's time. The actual time in a week is 168 hours. The determined work time was forty hours. (13)

This is the same principal in I Kings 6:1. The 480 years was the determined time, while the 594 years was the actual time. This shows there is no problem with an interruption between the sixty-ninth and seventieth weeks of Daniel. (12, 15) The seventy weeks of Daniel is the time determined upon the Jewish people. The sixty-ninth week ended with the crucifixion of the Messiah (Daniel 9:26). The seventieth week comes just prior to the return of the Lord to the earth (Matthew 24:29, Acts 1:11 and Zechariah 14:4).

There has been 2,000 years since the crucifixion of our Lord Jesus Christ. The seventieth week of Daniel has not been fulfilled, as the Lord Jesus Christ will return to the earth to set up His own kingdom when the seventieth week of Daniel is over. The large gap between the sixty-ninth week and the seventieth week of Daniel shows that there is a difference between the Lord's determined time and the actual time involved. The Lord's determined time stops with the crucifixion of the Messiah and will begin again the moment the prince of the Roman people makes a seven-year covenant with Israel. The seventy weeks is Lord's determined time on the Jewish's people.

What does Daniel 12:11 mean? What do the three time periods in Daniel 12 mean?

> Daniel 12:11: From the time that the daily sacrifice is
> abolished and the abomination that causes desolation
> is set up, there will be 1,290 days (7).

This scripture alone, without the understanding of the whole chapter of Daniel 12, gives the impression that there are 1290 days between the abolishing of the daily sacrifice and the abomination of the temple. If there are 1290 days between the abolishing of the daily sacrifice and the abomination of the temple, then there is no way the Great Tribulation and the Wrath of God can fit within the time frame of the seventieth week of Daniel. What are the facts?

Daniel 12 speaks of three time-periods: 1260 days, 1290 days, and 1335 days. To understand the meaning of these time-periods, we need to review Daniel 12.

An angel appeared to Daniel and told him about the coming of a time of distress that is unprecedented in the history of the world. The time is referred to as the time of Jacob's trouble.

> Jeremiah 30:7: How awful that day will be! None will be like it. It will be a time of trouble for Jacob, but he will be saved out of it. (7)

Also at this time, which is the time of the end, there will be a resurrection of many people, including Daniel, who are sleeping in the dust of the earth. Daniel, being curious, asked the angel when and how long it would be before these astonishing things would be fulfilled? The questions Daniel asked are the keys to understanding Daniel 12:11 and the three time-periods.

In response to Daniel's question, the angel replied that it would be a time, times and half-a-time before all of these events are fulfilled. A time, times, and half-a-time is 1260 days. This is the time that is left in the seventieth week of Daniel when the covenant is broken in the middle of the week. This is the actual time of the reign of the Antichrist.

> Revelation 13:5, 7: The beast was given a mouth to utter proud words and blasphemies and to exercise his authority for forty-two months. . . . He was given power to make war against the saints and to conquer them. And he was given authority over every tribe, people, language and nation. (7)

Daniel 9:27 speaks of the covenant being broken in the middle of the week, with the abolishing of the sacrifice and the abomination

59

of the temple. Matthew 24:15, 21 show that the Great Tribulation and the Wrath of God does not begin until after the abomination of the temple.

Daniel 12:11 has to be looked at and understood from the questions Daniel asked and the answers that the angel gave. The 1260 days (42 months) began with the breaking of the covenant in the middle of the week and ended at the end of the seventieth week of Daniel. The two time-periods of 1290 days and 1335 days also began with the breaking of the covenant and ended thirty days and seventy-five days after the reign of the Antichrist.

The angel told Daniel that these events would be fulfilled after the end of 1260 days, 1290 days, and 1335 days. The reign of the Antichrist and seventieth week of Daniel both ended at the same time.

"If" the sacrifice is stopped in the middle of the week, and the abomination of the temple takes place 1290 days later, then the Great Tribulation and the Wrath of God would have to begin after the seventieth week of Daniel has ended. This cannot be, for this would put the Great Tribulation and the Wrath of God beyond the seventieth week of Daniel, beyond the time-frame God designated for this to take place. Daniel 9:24 shows that everything is to be finished within the seventy weeks that have been decreed upon Daniel's people.

> Daniel 9:24: Seventy weeks have been decreed for your people and your holy city, to finish the transgression, to make an end of sin, to make atonement for iniquity, to bring in everlasting righteousness, to seal up the vision and prophecy, and to anoint the most holy place. (12)

Everything must be finished within the time-frame of the seventieth week of Daniel. Therefore, there cannot be 1290 days between the end of the sacrifice in the middle of the week and the abomination of the temple, for this would put the Great Tribulation and the Wrath of God beyond the time-frame of the seventieth week of Daniel.

Secondly, it is the Antichrist who abolishes the sacrifice and causes the abomination of the temple. How can the Antichrist be responsible for abolishing the sacrifice and still be in power forty-three months later to cause the abomination of the temple, when he is in power for only forty-two months? If the abomination of the temple took place forty-three months after stopping the sacrifice in the middle of the week, then the Antichrist would have to be in power another forty-two months as the Great Tribulation does not begin until after the abomination of the temple (Matthew 24:15, 21). This would put the time of Jacob's trouble, the time of the greatest distress in the history of the world, outside the time frame of the seventieth week of Daniel. This cannot be.

The 1260 days (42 months) reign of the Antichrist over the saints and the holy people of God begin with the breaking of the covenant in the middle of the week. The breaking of the covenant begins with the abolishing of the sacrifice and the abomination of the temple. The reign of the Antichrist ends when the Lord Jesus Christ returns to the earth with His saints to capture the Beast (the Antichrist) and the false prophet and throws them alive into the Lake of Fire.

> Revelation 19:11,14,19-20: And I saw heaven opened; and behold, a white horse, and He who sat upon it is called Faithful and True; and in righteous-ness He judges and wages war. . . . And the armies which are in heaven, . . . were following Him on white horses. . . . And I saw the beast and the kings

61

of the earth and their armies, assembled to make war against Him who sat upon the horse, and against His army. And the beast was seized, and with him the false prophet who performed the signs in his presence, by which he deceived those who had received the mark of the beast and those who worshiped his image; these two were thrown alive into the lake of fire which burns with brimstone. (12)

The thirty day's and seventy-five day's time-periods are not fulfilled until after the Lord Jesus Christ returns to the earth to begin the millennium. It is my belief that the reign of the Antichrist and the seventieth week of Daniel both end at the same time with the return of the Lord Jesus Christ. If the thirty days and seventy-five days, after the reign of the Antichrist, are part of the seventieth week of Daniel, then the covenant would have to be broken two and one-half months before the middle of the week so that the Antichrist can reign for forty-two months. Yet the scripture says the covenant is broken in the middle of the week (seven years) which is 42 months.

Daniel 12:11 does not mean that there are 1290 days between the abolishing of the daily sacrifice and the abomination of the temple. Daniel speaks of 1290 days as the end of a time-period that started with the abolishing of the sacrifice and the abomination of the temple. The end of the two time-periods of 1290 days and 1335 days occurs after the end of the seventieth week of Daniel and after the Lord returns to the earth to begin the millennium.

Daniel 12:12: Blessed is the one who waits for and reaches the end of the 1335 days (7).

Gordon Lindsay said the thirty days and seventy-five days after the reign of the Antichrist is the time necessary for deliverance to be consummated (16). St. Vincent Ferrer believed that the 45 days after the 1290 days is time given by God for the conversion of those that had been seduced by the Antichrist. However, he does not believe they will be converted (17).

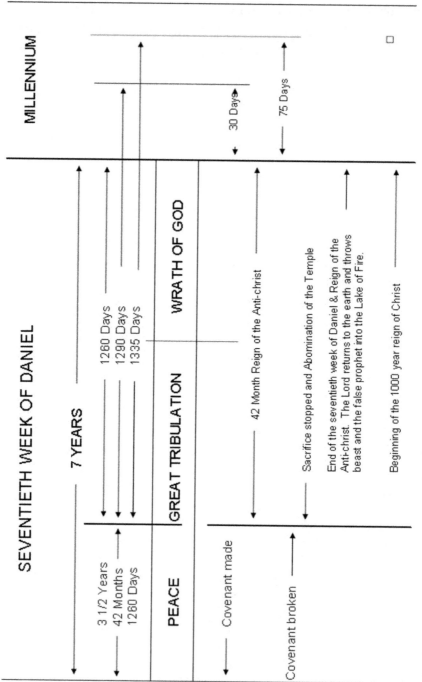

TABLE 2 - SHOWS ALL THE EVENTS OCCURRING WITHIN THE TIME-FRAME OF THE
SEVENTIETH WEEK OF DANIEL

CHAPTER 4
The Temple

Will the temple be rebuilt?

Daniel, Jesus and Paul all referred to the temple. Daniel spoke of stopping sacrifice and grain offering, as well as the desecration of the temple. Jesus and Paul spoke of the desecration of the temple.

Daniel 9:27 says the prince will break the covenant in the middle of the week stopping sacrifice and grain offering, bringing on an abomination in the temple. Jesus, in Matthew 24:15, speaks of the abomination of desolation of the holy place (the temple). Paul, in II Thessalonians 2:2-4, refers to the son of destruction, who opposes and exalts himself above every so-called god or object of worship, so that he takes his seat in the temple of God, displaying himself as being God.

Since Jesus said the desecration takes place just prior to His return (Matthew 24:29-31) and the present temple was destroyed in 68 and 70 AD, then it is obvious that another temple must be built. Otherwise, how will the son of destruction bring about the abomination of the holy place proclaiming himself to be God?

Desmond Birch reported that the following Fathers, Doctors and Saints of the Church: St. Hippoltus, St. John Damascene, St. Irenaeus, St. Ephrem, St. Ambrose, and St. Anselm expressed the belief that the tribulation temple must be rebuilt in Jerusalem so that the abomination of desolation spoken of by Daniel, Jesus, and

Paul can take place. (3)

The Scriptures speak of six different temples:

1. Tent of the Tabernacle - This was a nomadic type tabernacle that the Lord dwelt in when the children of Israel were wandering in the wilderness. According to Cruden's Concordance, the tabernacle was twenty cubits wide and sixty cubits long. (18) A cubit is considered to be one-half of a yard. This means that the tabernacle was ten yards wide and thirty yards long. The walls of the tabernacle were made of curtains. The walls that surrounded the inner court and the tabernacle were fifty cubits wide and a hundred cubits long. This shows that the walls that surrounded the inner courtyard and the tabernacle were twenty-five yards wide and fifty yards long. The area outside the walls was the outer courtyard.

2. Solomon's Temple - This was the first permanent temple built. It was built on the threshing floor of the Jebusite, where David built an altar.
According to I King 6:2, this temple was sixty cubits long and twenty cubits wide and twenty-five cubits high. This shows that Solomon's Temple was the same width and length as the tent of the tabernacle. Solomon's Temple was destroyed by Nebuchadnezzar at the time of the Babylonian captivity.

3. Zerubbabel's Temple - This temple was built by Zerubbabel after the Jews returned to Jerusalem from Babylonian captivity (Nehemiah 7:7 and Zechariah 4:9). This temple stood until the building of Herod's Temple (19).

4. Herod's Temple - Herod built this temple to gain favor with the Jews. The construction of this

temple was started in 19 BC just before the birth of Jesus (19).

5. Tribulation Temple - This temple has to be built so the prophecies spoken by Daniel, Jesus, and Paul can be fulfilled. The Tribulation Temple is mentioned in Revelation 11:1-2.

6. Millennium Temple - The Millennium Temple will be built by the Lord with the help of the Gentiles from many nations during the millennium (Ezekiel 40-48). The Millennium Temple will be discussed in Chapter 29, 32 and 33.

Which direction did the temple face?

Ezekiel shows that the temple faced toward the east.

Ezekiel 8:16: . . . And behold, at the entrance to the temple of the Lord, between the porch and the altar, were about twenty-five men with their backs to the temple of the Lord, and their faces toward the east; and they were prostrating themselves eastward toward the sun. (12)

This shows that the temple axis was east and west.

Does the Mosque of Omar have to be destroyed for the temple to be rebuilt?

Many people believe that the Mosque of Omar has to be destroyed before the temple can be rebuilt. The Mosque of Omar, a sacred Moslem shrine, is a dome structure over a round rock where Abraham supposedly attempted to offer Issac as a sacrifice to the Lord. This rock is 6 feet high, 45 feet long and 36 feet wide. (20) Since the temple was 90 feet long and 30 feet wide, there is no reason to believe that the temple would have been built on a small uneven rock that is only half the size of the temple and protrudes six feet above the ground. This rock is not large or level enough to hold the temple and it is too large to fit within the temple or the inner courtyard.

Archaeological evidence shows that the original temple was built north of the Mosque of Omar (Dome of Rock).

Asher S. Kaufman reported in "Biblical Archaeology Review" that archaeological findings indicate that the Holy of Holies is believed to be under the Dome of the Tablets, which is 330 feet northwest of the Dome of the Rock. The original site of the temples of Solomon and Herod is believed to be located on most of the northern part of the pavement platform that surrounds the Dome of the Rock. The outer courtyard wall of the temple, at its closest point to the Dome of the Rock, would be approximately 85 feet.

The structure of the Dome of the Rock does not have to be destroyed for the temple to be rebuilt. If the temple is rebuilt on its original site, most of the pavement platform that extends north of the Dome of the Rock will have to be removed. There is no reason why the temple could not be rebuilt next to the pavement, except for the fact the Jews may want the temple to be rebuilt on its original sites. The maps in "Biblical Archaeology Review" show that there is plenty of room to rebuild the temple without touching or affecting the Mosque of Omar. (21)

Israeli Architect Tuvia Sagiv proposed a southern site below the Dome of the Rock as the original site of the temple.

The Temple Mount is an area of 45 acres. Israeli Architect Tuvia Sagiv placed the site of the original temple south of the Dome of the Rock on a spot occupied by El Kas Fountain which is halfway between the Dome of the Rock and Al-Aqsa Mosque. Mr. Sagiv based his theory on the need of flowing water the priests need for ritual baths and for cleansing the area where animal sacrifices were offered. Rabbinical law requires flowing water, not water stored in a cistern. The temple would have to be below the source of flowing water as water cannot flow up a hill. (22)

Will the Jews own the land in the outer courtyard of the Tribulation Temple?

> Revelation 11:1-2: I was given a reed like a measuring rod and was told, "Go and measure the temple of God and the altar, and count the worshipers there. But exclude the outer court; do not measure it, because it has been given to the Gentiles. They will trample the holy city for 42 months. (7)

The scriptures teach that the Jews will only own the temple and the inner courtyard. The outer courtyard will belong to the gentiles. This proves that the temple will be built on Mount Mariah. If the temple were built on a different site away from Mount Mariah, the Jews would certainly see that they own the land in the outer courtyard. This shows that the Mosque of Omar, which is in the outer courtyard, belongs to the Gentiles. The land on Mount Mariah in the temple area belongs to the Moslems.

Could the new synagogue, which is being built about a mile from Mount Mariah, be the new temple?

No, because the Jews will be making sacrifices and grain offerings according to the Old Testament (Daniel 9:27). The Jews do not offer sacrifices in a synagogue (23).

The Ark of the Covenant

The Ark of the Covenant was last seen before the Babylonian captivity. According to the second Book of Maccabees, at the time of the Babylonian captivity, Jeremiah, the prophet, under the guidance of the Lord hid the Ark of the Covenant. He took the Ark of the Covenant, the tent and the incense, and hid them in a cave on Mount Nebo, which is in Jordan next to the Dead Sea. Jeremiah reprimanded those that tried to follow and mark the place where the Ark, the tent and the incense were hidden, saying that they were not to be found until the Lord regathers His people again.

> 2 Maccabees 2:1-8: You will find in the records, not only that Jeremiah the prophet ordered the deportees to take some of the aforementioned fire with them, but also that the prophet, in giving them the law, admonished them not to forget the commandments of the Lord or be led astray in their thoughts, when seeing the gold and silver idols and their ornaments. With other similar words he urged them not to let the law depart from their hearts. The same document also tells how the prophet, following a divine revelation, ordered that the tent and the ark should accompany him and how he went off to the mountain which Moses climbed to see God's inheritance. When Jeremiah arrived there, he found a room in a cave in which he put the tent, the ark, and the altar of incense; then he blocked up the entrance. Some of those who followed him came up intending to mark the path, but they could not find it. When Jeremiah heard of this, he reproved them: "The place is to remain unknown until God gathers his people together again and shows them mercy. Then the Lord will disclose these things, and the glory of the Lord will be seen in the cloud, just as it appeared in the time of Moses and when Solomon prayed that the Place might be gloriously sanctified. (24)

Though some of the Israelites came back from the Babylonian

captivity and the temple was rebuilt, the Ark of the Covenant was never found nor mentioned in the scriptures. Jeremiah was apparently referring to the time of the second regathering of the people when Israel would become a nation and Jerusalem its capitol. Israel became a nation in 1948 for the first time since the Babylonian captivity. Israel was under the Roman Empire at the time of Christ.

At the appropriate time, the Lord will arrange for the Ark of the Covenant, the tent and the incense to be found on Mount Nebo. When this happens, the glory of the Lord will appear in a cloud over the Ark, as it did in the days of Moses and Solomon. The finding of the Ark will definitely be an incentive to rebuild the temple, if at that time it has not already been rebuilt. Notice that the tent was also hidden with the Ark. If the temple is not built when the Ark is found, the Ark will be placed in the tent.

Desmond Birch reported that many prophecies foretell that the Ark of the Covenant will be found by Elijah the prophet (3).

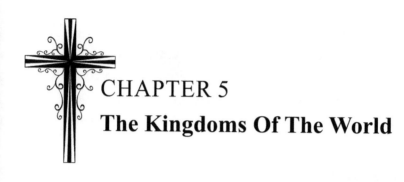

CHAPTER 5

The Kingdoms Of The World

What is God's plan concerning the coming kingdoms of the world?

Nebuchadnezzar, the King of Babylon, had a disturbing dream, which he could not remember. The Lord revealed the dream and the interpretation of it to Daniel. Daniel said to Nebuchadnezzar, "Before you went to sleep, you were wondering what was going to happen in the days to come. While you were asleep, the Lord revealed to you the things that were to come to pass."

In the dream, Nebuchadnezzar saw a very large and bright statue, whose appearance was terrifying. The head of the statue was pure gold, its chest and arms were silver, its belly and thighs were bronze, the legs were iron, and its feet were part iron and clay. While he was looking at the statue, a stone was cut from the mountain without hands. This stone struck the feet of iron and clay breaking them in pieces. The iron, clay, bronze, silver and gold all crumbled, and became as chaff, which the wind blew away. The stone, which struck the statue, became a great mountain and filled the whole earth. This was the dream Nebuchadnezzar had.

Daniel gave the interpretation of the dream. The head of gold was Nebuchadnezzar's kingdom. The silver, bronze, iron, and iron and clay represented the four world kingdoms that followed Nebuchadnezzar's.

Gold	Kingdom of Babylon
Silver	Medo-Persian Kingdom
Bronze	Greek Kingdom of Alexander the Great
Iron	Roman Kingdom at the time of Christ
Iron and Clay	Roman Kingdom at the time of the end
Stone	Kingdom of our Lord Jesus Christ

The feet and toes, Nebuchadnezzar saw, were partly clay and partly iron, meaning that it will be a divided kingdom. The scriptures say that the toes represent the kings of the kingdom. Daniel 2:44 says that in the days of those kings the God of heaven will set up a kingdom, which will never be destroyed. The stone, which was cut without hands, became a great mountain and filled the whole earth. The stone is the kingdom of our Lord Jesus Christ.

The Lord revealed to Nebuchadnezzar His plan concerning the five world kingdoms, the last being our Lord's kingdom. The Lord's kingdom will be set up in the days of the ten kings at the time of His coming.

What is interesting is that the Lord revealed to Daniel the coming of the kingdoms of the worlds long before it happen. Three of the kingdoms silver, bronze and the iron have not come to pass. The kingdom of Iron (Rome) was foretold 500 years before hand. The death of the Lord Jesus Christ was foretold 483 years prior to His coming and death. Only a living God could have foretold all of this 500 years in advance. There are two more kingdoms yet to come: Kingdom of iron and clay which is the Roman kingdom and the kingdom of stone which is the kingdom of our Lord Jesus Christ.

What is the difference between the kingdoms of two legs of iron, and the feet and ten toes of clay and iron?

The Roman Kingdom is divided into two eras: The first

part, two legs of iron, represents the kingdom at the time of Christ. The second part with feet and ten toes, a mixture of clay and iron, will be the kingdom just prior to the Lord's return to the earth.

Do the scriptures teach that there are two different Roman Kingdoms?

Daniel 9:26-27 says that the people, who destroy Jerusalem, will have a prince who will come later and make a covenant with the Jewish people for one week (seven years). The Romans destroyed Jerusalem and the temple in 68 to 70 AD. (13) The Jews were taken into captivity and scattered to all nations of the world. The Jewish people have not been in a position to make a covenant until this century. This covenant has not yet been made. Daniel 9:26-27 shows that there are two different Roman kingdoms, separated by a great period of time, as only part of the prophecy in Daniel 9:26-27 has been fulfilled.

Revelation 17:8, 10-11 shows that the angelic prince of the Roman Kingdom at the time of Christ will not be the angelic prince of the Roman Kingdom at the time of the end. The two angelic princes also prove that there are two Roman Kingdoms. The angelic princes are princes of darkness.

What does scripture say about clay and iron in the feet?

> Daniel 2:41-43: . . . the feet and toes, partly of potter's clay and partly of iron, it will be a divided kingdom . . . so some of the kingdom will be strong and part of it will be brittle. And in that you saw the iron mixed with common clay, they will combine with one another in the seed of men; but they will not adhere to one another, even as iron does not combine with pottery. (12)

Iron and clay will make a covenant with one another to form one kingdom. The iron will be strong, while the clay will be weak. After a period of time, the clay and iron will separate, causing the kingdom to be divided.

What is the iron in the kingdom of iron and clay?

Iron is the Roman Kingdom that probably covers the territory of the Old Roman Empire. This kingdom will not be known until a covenant is made with Israel for seven years.

What is the clay in the kingdom of iron and clay?

After spending time in prayer seeking the Lord for an understanding of the kingdom of iron and clay, a voice spoke to me in a dream, said:

> Clay is another substance like iron, gold, silver, bronze and stone. Clay is another kingdom that will combine with the kingdom of iron to form one kingdom.

> The only kingdom in the same geographical area that could combine with iron is probably Russia and her allies.

Is there any scriptural evidence that Russia and her allies may be the kingdom of clay?

Ezekiel 38 and 39 speak of the Nations of the North invading Israel at the time of the end, when Israel is living in peace and security in unwalled villages.

The invasion of the northern army is mentioned in Joel 2:20. An understanding that the event in Joel 2:1-2, 10-11 occurs before Joel 2:20 shows that the invasion will take place after the day of the Lord, which is the beginning of the Wrath of God. The Wrath of God is the last phase of the seventieth week of Daniel. The day of the Lord will be discussed later.

In the Old Testament, Assyria and Babylon were called the Nations of the North. In reality, these nations were really to the northeast and east of Israel. These nations are not in power today. Russia, one of the most powerful nations in the world, is directly north of Israel. It is interesting that Rosh, the Bible name of the northern nation, is similar to the name Russia. (16)

The scriptures in Daniel 2 tell us that the ten toes represent the kings in the kingdom of iron and clay. The mixture of iron and clay in the ten toes seems to indicate there will be ten nations in the kingdom of clay and ten nations in the kingdom of iron.

Russia and her allies before the break-up had ten nations, which would correspond to the ten nations of iron in the Roman Kingdom (25).

Kingdom of Clay:

1. Russia	4. Poland	7. Hungary	10. Lithuania
2. East Germany	5. Bulgaria	8. Estonia	
3. Czechoslovakia	6. Romania	9. Latvia	

We will not know the exact nations until the time comes. Nevertheless, Russia, one of the most powerful nations on earth today, will likely play a role with the Antichrist and in the invasion of Israel. For these reasons, it is believed that Russia and her allies will be the kingdom of clay that combined with the kingdom of iron to form one kingdom. The nations mention in Ezekiel 38 will most likely be the kingdom of clay. This will be discussed in Chapter 27.

If the ten nations of the Roman Kingdom combine with Russia and her allies, it is easy to see why the Beast or the Antichrist Kingdom would be the most powerful and the most feared kingdom in the world. As the scripture in Revelation 13:4 says, "Who is like the beast, and who is able to wage war with him?"

Daniel 2:41-43 points out that the kingdom of iron and clay will be a divided kingdom. "They will combine together in the seed of men, but will not adhere to one another even as iron and clay does not mix together." (12)

The fact that the iron and clay come together in a covenant relationship, and then break the covenant, shows that clay is a strong kingdom, even though iron is the stronger of the two. What other kingdom could be almost as strong as the ten nations Roman Empire, if it is not Russia and her allies?

An example of this type of a covenant was a covenant between Germany and Russia at the beginning of World War II. This pact lasted approximately 666 days before Germany turned on Russia. If Russia and Germany had remained united, they would probably have won World War II. (13)

The Roman prince is spoken of in Daniel 9:27 as making a covenant with many. The prince apparently makes a covenant with Russia and her allies to form one kingdom, just as he makes a seven-year covenant with Israel. However, Israel is not a part of the Beast Kingdom in the same sense as Russia and her allies. Israel's covenant is for peace and protection.

While the Roman Kingdom (iron) is combined with Russia and her allies (clay), they will be the most powerful and feared kingdom in the world.

When will the battle of Armageddon begin?

Toward the end of the seven years of the seventieth week of Daniel, Russia and her allies, being the kingdom of clay, will break relationships with the kingdom of iron and will invade Israel. The prince of the Roman Kingdom will be furious, and he will attack Russia and her allies in Israel. This will be the moment for which all the other nations of the world have been waiting. While the Kingdoms of Iron and Clay are united, they are the most feared kingdom of the world. Once they break relationship and start fighting each other, other nations will sense an opportunity to defeat the Beast. This will be the beginning of the battle of Armageddon.

Is the Invasion of Israel by the Nations of the North and the battle of Armageddon the same event?

Many biblical scholars believe that the Nations of the North are Russia and her allies and that the invasion of Israel by the northern armies is a separate battle from the battle of Armageddon. They believe Russia will invade Israel prior to the seventieth week of Daniel before the Great Tribulation. However, other biblical scholars believe that the invasion of Israel by Russia and her allies and the battle of Armageddon is the same event. (26, 27)

What comparative scriptural evidences do we have that the invasion by the Nations of the North described in Ezekiel 38 and 39 is the beginning of the battle of Armageddon?

The battle of Armageddon begins, when the seventh angel in Revelation 16:16-17 pours out his bowl into the air. The events described in Revelation 16:18-21 are similar to the events mentioned in Ezekiel 38 and 39.

The great earthquake

Revelation 16:18: . . . there was a great earthquake, such as there had not been since man came to be upon earth, so great an earthquake was it, and so mighty. (12)	Ezekiel 38:19: And in My zeal and in My blazing wrath I declare that on that day there will surely be a great earthquake in the land of Israel. (12)

Mountains and cities will be leveled

Revelation 16:19-20: The great city split into three parts and the cities of nations collapsed. . . . Every Island fled away and the mountains could not be found. (7)	Ezekiel 38:20: The fish of the sea, the birds of the air, the beasts of the field, every creature that moves along the ground, and all the people on the face of the earth will tremble at my presence. The mountains will be overturned, the cliffs will crumble and every wall will fall to the ground. (7)

Revelation speaks of Jerusalem and the cities of nations being destroyed. The earthquake in Revelation affects the cities of many nations. The earthquake described in Ezekiel appears to be worldwide, since all the fish of the sea, and all the people of the earth trembled. Since the mountains are leveled in both Revelation and Ezekiel, this earthquake has to be the most severe earthquake the world has ever seen. I am not aware of any mountain ever being leveled or severely affected by an earthquake.

Ezekiel speaks of the people trembling at the presence of the Lord. The scriptures do not speak of the Lord being visible until the rapture and when He returns to the earth at the battle of Armageddon.

Huge Hailstones

Revelation 16:21: From the sky huge hailstones of about a hundred pounds each fell upon men. And they cursed God on account of the plague of hail, because the plague was so terrible. (7)	Ezekiel 38:22: I will execute judgment upon him with plague and bloodshed; I will pour down torrents of rain, hailstones and burning sulfur on him and on his troops and on the many nations with him. (7)

Hailstones are mentioned in both Revelation and Ezekiel. Hailstones of one hundred pounds will be very severe and destructive.

Call to the fowl of the air to the great supper of our God

Revelation 19:17: And I saw an angel standing in the sun, who cried in a loud voice to all the birds flying in midair, "Come, gather together for the great supper of God, so that you may eat the flesh of kings, generals, and mightymen, of horses and their riders, and the flesh of all people, free and slave, small and great. (7)

Ezekiel 39:4: On the mountains of Israel you will fall, you and all your troops and the nations with you. I will give you as food to all kinds of carrion birds and to the wild animals. (7)

The feast for the fowl of the air is similar in both Revelation and Ezekiel.

The rest of the people are killed by the sword of the Lord

Revelation 19:21: The rest of them were killed with the sword that came out of the mouth of the rider on the horse and all the birds gorged themselves on their flesh. (7)

Ezekiel 39:5-6, 17-21: You will fall in open field, for I have spoken, declares the Sovereign Lord. I will send fire on Magog and on those who live in safety in the coastlands, and they will know that I am the Lord. . . . Call out to every kind of bird and all the wild animals: Assemble and come together from all around to the sacrifice I am preparing for you, the great sacrifice on the mountains of Israel. There you will eat flesh and drink blood. You will eat the flesh of mighty men and drink the blood of the princes of the earth . . . At the sacrifice I am preparing for you, you will eat fat till you are glutted and drink blood till you are drunk. At my table you will eat your fill of horses and riders, mighty men and soldiers of every kind . . . and all the nations will see the punishment I inflict and the hand I lay upon them. (7)

In Revelation, the sword that comes out of the mouth of the Lord kills the sinful people who were not killed at the battle of Armageddon. Likewise, in Ezekiel, the Lord sends fire on those who live in safety in the coastlands, . . . and all the nations will see the punishment He will inflict upon them. In both Ezekiel and Revelation the fowl of the air and the beasts of the field will feast on the mighty men and princes of the earth. The princes of the earth indicate leaders from all over the world. The judgment in Ezekiel is worldwide, as it involves more than the Nations of the North. It is as severe as the judgment in Revelation, as the Lord said that all nations will see His hand and the punishment He will inflict upon them.

The Lord will reign over His people

In Ezekiel, the Lord has re-gathered His people. He will be their God and they will be His people. He will no longer hide His face from them.

Ezekiel 39:28-29: Then they will know that I am the Lord their God, for though I sent them into exile

81

among the nations, I will gather them to their own land, not leaving any behind. I will no longer hide my face from them, for I will pour out my Spirit on the house of Israel, declares the Sovereign Lord. (7)

When the Lord says He will no longer hide His face, this means He has returned to the earth to sit on the throne of His father, David, the kingdom of stone as seen in Daniel 2:44. The millennium has begun. This will take place after the battle of Armageddon.

There is an identical parallel of events in both the invasion of Israel by the Nations of the North and the battle of Armageddon. In Ezekiel, during the invasion by the Nations of the North, the Lord pours out His wrath not only in Israel but on the nations of the world and those who live in safety on the coastlands. Since the events described in Ezekiel 38 and 39 are similar to the events which occur at the battle of Armageddon, and the destruction and the catastrophe is so great and widespread in both occasions, it is difficult to believe that these are two separate events.

The comparative study above was made after receiving a newsletter from a prominent nationally known minister stating that the invasion of Israel by the Nations of the North was a separate event from the battle of Armageddon. After making a comparative study, I said, "Lord, I see the comparison, but how can I show that these two events are the same event?" After praying on this for two days, I got up at 5:30 one morning to spend time in prayer. While I was pacing the floor, praising the Lord, a very strong thought came to me. The thought was so strong that I knew it was not my thought. The thought was, "If the invasion of Israel by the Nations of the North is a separate event from the battle of Armageddon, and the mountains of Israel are leveled when the Nations of the North invade Israel, where are the mountains to be leveled at the battle of Armageddon?"

The mountains of Israel can be level only one time. Since the mountains of Israel can be leveled only once, the invasion of the Nations of the North in Ezekiel and the battle of Armageddon in Revelation have to be one and the same event.

The reasons that the invasion of the Nations of the North and the battle of Armageddon are the same event:

1. Identical events occur at both the invasion of the Nations of the North and the battle of Armageddon.
2. The mountains of Israel can only be leveled one time; therefore, this can not be two separate events.
3. The earthquake in Revelation 16:18 and in Ezekiel is equally the most severe and destructive earthquake the world has ever seen.
4. The judgment in Ezekiel involves more than Israel and the Nations of the North. This judgment is worldwide in scope as the Lord inflicts His wrath upon all nations and princes of the earth.
5. In Ezekiel 39:28-29, the Lord says He will no longer hide His face. This means He will be visible to the people living on earth from that point on (Isaiah 30:19-20, and Chapter 28 of this book). This does not happen until the Lord returns to the earth at the end of Armageddon to begin the Millennium. Therefore the events in Ezekiel could not occur before the battle of Armageddon.

All of this proves that the invasion of the Nations of the North and the battle of Armageddon is same event.

The kingdom of iron (the Beast Kingdom) and the kingdom of clay (the northern kingdom) make a covenant to form one kingdom. Toward the end of the seventieth week of Daniel, the kingdom of clay breaks the covenant with the kingdom of iron and invades Israel. The Beast is furious and goes to fight the kingdom of clay in Israel. This precipitates the battle of Armageddon. As the scriptures in Daniel 2:41-43 say, ". . . they will combine with one another in the seed of men, but will not adhere to one another even as iron does not combine with pottery."

Using a symbol of a man made of gold, silver, bronze, iron and clay, the Lord showed Daniel and Nebuchadnezzar His plans concerning the Gentile kingdoms and His coming kingdom on earth.

Are there any other teachings in the scriptures in regard to these kingdoms?

The seventh chapter of Daniel gives further understanding on the worldly kingdoms and the kingdom of our Lord Jesus Christ. Daniel had a dream and visions in which he saw the four winds of heaven stirring up the great sea and four beasts come up from the sea, different from one another (Daniel 7:2-3)

What are the four beasts that come up from the sea?

The four beasts are four-world kingdoms that are coming upon the earth. The beasts are said to come out of the sea. What is the sea? The sea might be the Mediterranean Sea where these kingdoms are located. However, there is probably a deeper meaning. The water or sea in Revelation 17:15 refers to a multitude of people of different nations and tongues. This means the beasts came up from among the people. (26)

The Beast in Revelation 13:1 is spoken of as coming out of the sea (people). Revelation 13:18 calls the Beast a man.

The four winds that strove upon the sea

The four winds that strove upon the sea probably refer to the four princes of darkness, such as the prince of Persia and the prince of Greece, which are mentioned in Daniel 10:13, 20.

Paul, in Ephesians 6:12, tells us that "our struggle is not against flesh and blood, but against the rulers, against the authorities, against the powers, against the world forces of this darkness, against the spiritual wickedness in the heavenly places." (12)

The four winds represent each of the princes of darkness that are princes over each of the world kingdoms.

In Revelation 7:1, the four angels of the Lord are told to hold back the four winds, until the servants of God are sealed. The four winds are the princes of darkness.

The four beasts

First beast – the lion - the Kingdom of Babylon

The first beast in Daniel 7 was as a lion with the wings of an eagle. The wings were plucked and the lion was lifted from the ground and made to stand on two feet like a man. A human mind was given to it.

The lion, with wings of an eagle, refers to the kingdom of Babylon. The plucked wings refer to Nebuchadnezzar losing his mind (insanity). Being lifted from the ground and given a human mind refers to Nebuchadnezzar being restored to sanity (Daniel 4).

"Bible Reading for the Home Circle" in 1914 reported that the lion, the first of the four great beasts, like the golden head in Nebuchadnezzar's dream, represented the kingdom of Babylon. Just as the lion symbolizes the king of the beasts, gold is considered the most precious of metals. The eagle's wings represented the rapidness with which Babylon extended its kingdom under Nebuchadnezzar. (28)

Second beast - the bear - the Kingdom of Medo-Persia

The second beast, which resembles a bear, refers to the Medo-Persia Kingdom.

Third beast - the leopard - the Kingdom of Greece

The third beast was a leopard with four bird-like wings and also four heads. This beast refers to the Kingdom of Alexander the Great of Greece.

"Bible Reading for the Home Circle" says that, if the wings of the eagle on the lion meant the swift movement of the Kingdom of Babylon, then the four wings of the leopard symbolized the swiftness of Alexander the Great in conquering and defeating other nations. The four heads on the leopard meant that Alexander's kingdom would be divided four ways after his death. The Kingdom of Alexander the Great was actually divided among his four generals.

Fourth beast - an unidentified terrifying beast - the Roman Kingdom

The fourth beast was dreadful, terrifying and extremely strong. It had large iron teeth and claws of bronze. This Beast devoured, crushed and trampled down the remainder with its feet. The beast had ten horns. While Daniel was looking at the ten horns, a little horn came up pulling the first three horns out by their roots. The little horn had eyes like a man and a mouth uttering great boasts.

Daniel was greatly disturbed over the fourth beast. The angel that appeared to Daniel explained the meaning of the fourth beast. The fourth beast is the fourth kingdom on earth, which will devour the whole earth and tread it down and crush it.

The little horn gives further understanding of the kingdom of the ten kings symbolized by the feet and ten toes of clay and iron. The ten horns, as the ten toes, refer to the ten kings. The little horn will conquer or subdue three of the kings (countries) and the other seven (countries) will quickly submit to the Beast. This is shown by the fact that the little horn, when it sprung up, quickly uprooted three of the big horns. The little horn is the prince or the Beast that is to come. The iron teeth of the terrifying beast correspond to the iron in the legs and feet of the man in Nebuchadnezzar's dream. The bronze claws, which represent Greece, is significant and will be discussed later.

The Beast, the little horn, will wage war with the saints and overpower them. He will speak out against the Most High, and will wear down the saints of the Highest One. They, the Christians and the Jews, "will be given into his hands for time, times and half of time," which is three and one-half years (Daniel 7:25). The Beast will make a covenant with Israel for one week (seven years). He, the Beast, will break the covenant in the middle of the week. After the breaking of the covenant, the Beast will have power for three and half years to persecute the Jews and Christians. God is permitting Satan to have his hour through the Beast before he is defeated. Russia, being the clay part of the feet and ten toes of the beast, likewise defeated three nations - Estonia, Latvia and Lithuania at the beginning of World War II before taking over seven other nations. This is similar to what the Beast will do in the kingdom of iron. (29)

Daniel (Daniel 7:9) kept watching the vision of the Beast until thrones were set up, and the Ancient of Days took His seat. Thousands upon thousands were attending Him, and myriads upon myriads were standing before Him. The court sat and the books were opened. (This is the judgment scene in heaven described in Revelation 4 and 5 before God pour out His judgment on earth).

Daniel continued to watch the Little Horn that was speaking boastful words until the Beast was slain, and cast into the Lake of Fire. This is also described in Revelation 19:20.

Daniel kept looking at the vision until he saw one like the Son of Man, coming with a cloud of heaven, Who came up to the Ancient of Days, the Father, and was presented before Him. He was given dominion, glory and a kingdom that all the peoples, nations and men of every language might serve Him. His dominion is an everlasting dominion, which will not pass away. His kingdom is one, which will not be destroyed. The Son of Man's kingdom is the kingdom of stone.

The man of gold, silver, bronze, iron and clay in Daniel 2, and the four beasts in Daniel 7, which symbolized the four world kingdoms were doubled to Daniel just as Pharaoh's dream of the cows and the ears of corn were doubled to Pharaoh. Genesis 41:32 said the doubling of Pharaoh's dream meant that this event was foreordained of God, and that God would bring it to pass.

Are there any other seventy weeks periods in the Old Testament or in the history of the Church?

Mr. E. W. Bullinger in his "Number in Scripture" (15) showed that there are four periods of seventy weeks of years (490 years):

1. The family of Abraham
2. The period of the Judges
3. The time of the Kings
4. The seventy weeks of Daniel

The period of the judges was not quite seventy weeks, as the Israelites demanded a king before God was ready to give them a king.

Gordon Lindsay did a beautiful job using graphs, dates and determined times in discussing the four seventy week periods (14). It is interesting that Bishop Fulton J. Sheen reported that something drastic happens approximately every five hundred years in the history of the Church. Four hundred and ninety years is almost five hundred years (30).

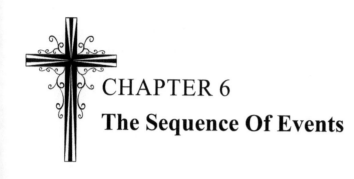

CHAPTER 6
The Sequence Of Events

We have shown:

1. The book of Revelation is the seventieth week of Daniel.
2. The seventieth week of Daniel is the time God is dealing with the Jewish people.
3. The seventieth week of Daniel begins the moment the prince of the Roman nations makes a seven year covenant with Israel.
4. The covenant is broken with the abomination of desolation of the holy place, the temple, in the middle of the week.
5. The Great Tribulation begins with the breaking of the covenant.
6. There are three and one-half years left in the seventieth week of Daniel, when the covenant is broken.

The following table shows the breakdown of the seventieth week of Daniel into peace, the Great Tribulation, the Day of the Lord and the Wrath of God. The key to understanding the seventieth week of Daniel is to know when the different events occur.

The Great Tribulation, the Day of the Lord, the Wrath of God, and the events that occur during the seventieth week of Daniel will be discussed later.

The Second Coming of Christ

There are those that scoff at the idea of the Second Coming of Christ. Peter spoke of these scoffers:

> II Peter 3:3-4: First of all, you must understand in the last days scoffers will come, scoffing and following their own evil desires. They will say, "Where is this 'coming' he promised? Ever since our fathers died, everything goes on as it has since the beginning of creation." (7)

Many people believe that the Second Coming of Christ is spiritual instead of a physical return. The scriptures teach differently.

> Acts 1:9-11: . . . as they were looking on, he was lifted up, and a cloud took him out of their sight. And while they were gazing into heaven as he went, behold, two men stood by them in white robes and said, "Men of Galilee, why do you stand looking into heaven? This Jesus, who was taken up from you into heaven, will come in the same way as you saw him go into heaven." (31)

> Zechariah 14:3,4,9: Then the Lord will go forth . . . And in that day His feet will stand on the Mount of Olives, which is in front of Jerusalem on the east; . . . And the Lord will be king over all the earth; . . . (12).

These scriptures show that the Lord Jesus Christ will return to the earth and to the same mountain in the same way He left. At this time Jesus will reign as king over all the earth.

If there were a literal first coming of the Lord as the scriptures teach, there will be a literal second coming of the Lord, as there are many more scriptures pertaining to the second coming than to the first coming. If

> Luke 1:31: And behold, you will conceive in your womb and bear a son, and you shall name Him Jesus.

was literally fulfilled, then

> Luke 1:32,33: He will be great and will be called the Son of the Most High; and the Lord God will give Him the throne of His father David; and He will reign over the house of Jacob forever; and His kingdom will have no end. (12)

will have to be literally fulfilled also. (32)

The throne of David was an earthly throne, not a spiritual throne.

COVENANT WITH ISRAEL FOR SEVEN YEARS

P E A C E

3 1/2

BREAKING OF THE COVENANT - MANCHILD RAPTURE

ABOMINATION OF THE TEMPLE

BOOK OF THE SEVEN Seals

   1st Seal - White Horse

   2nd Seal - Red Horse

   3rd Seal - Black Horse

   4th Seal - Pale Horse

   5th Seal - People under the Altar

T R I B U L A T I O N

G R E A T

3 1/2

6th Seal - Sun is Darken, Moon is Blood-red

HARVEST RAPTURE

DAY OF

THE LORD

7TH Seal - SEVEN TRUMPETS

   1st Trumpet

   2nd Trumpet

   3rd Trumpet

   4th Trumpet

   5th Trumpet - 1st Woe

   6th Trumpet - 2nd Woe

   7th - Trumpet - 3rd Woe - Seven Bowls

     1st Bowl

     2nd Bowl

     3rd Bowl

     4th Bowl

     5th - Bowl

     6th - Bowl

     7th Bowl

W R A T H   O F   G O D

7 Y E A R S

S E V E N T I E T H   W E E K   O F   D A N I E L

TABLE 3 - A PICTURE OF THE SEVENTIETH WEEK OF DANIEL SHOWING THE PART OF THE WEEK IN WHICH EACH SEAL, TRUMPET AND BOWL FALL UNDER

CHAPTER 7

Son Of Man - His Messages To The Overcomers

John, the beloved apostle of Jesus, while on the Island of Patmos, heard a loud voice like a trumpet,

> Revelation 1:11-20: . . . which said, "Write on a scroll what you see and send it to the seven churches." . . . And when I turned I saw seven golden lampstands, and among the lampstands was someone "like a son of man, dressed in a robe reaching down to his feet and with a golden sash around his chest. His head and hair were white like wool, as white as snow, and his eyes were like blazing fire. His feet were like bronze glowing in a furnace, and his voice was like the sound of rushing waters. In his right hand, he held seven stars, and out of his mouth came a sharp double-edged sword. His face was like the sun shining in all its brilliance. When I saw him, I fell at his feet as though dead. Then He placed his right hand on me and said: "Do not be afraid. I am the First and the Last. I am the Living One; I was dead, and behold, I am alive forever and ever! And I hold the keys of death and Hades." Write, therefore, what you have seen, what is now and what will take place later. The mystery of the seven stars that you saw in my right

hand and of the seven golden lampstands is this: The seven stars are the angels of the seven churches, and the seven lampstands are the seven churches. (7)

Descriptions of the Son of Man

1. "His head and hair were white as snow." This is the description of the Ancient of Days in Daniel 7:9.
2. "His eyes were like blazing fire." Here is all-penetrating intelligence, burning with power to read secrets, to warm and to search all hearts at a single glance. These eyes will comfort the good and terrify the wicked (11).
3. "His feet were like bronze glowing in a furnace." Bronze feet, glowing white in a furnace, present an image of pureness and holiness. With these feet the Lord shall walk among the churches, and tread down all abominations and defeat the Antichrist and Satan. His feet, glowing in a furnace, speak of judgment. (11)
4. "His voice was like the sound of rushing water." This is the voice of power, majesty and authority (10, 33).
5. "Out of his mouth came a sharp two-edged sword." The two-edged sword is the Word of God.
6. "His face was like the sun." When Jesus was transfigured with Moses and Elijah, His face was like the sun (Matthew 17:2). In Malachi 3:20 or 4:2, He is called the "Sun of righteousness".

Letters to the seven churches

Jesus told John to write on a scroll a letter to each of the seven churches what is now, and what will take place later. Revelation 2 and 3 are the letters to the seven churches. Christ, in writing to the seven churches, has words of encouragement to those that overcome the obstacles that are before them.

Christ's promises to the overcomers:

1. Church in Ephesus	Revelation 2:7: . . . To him who overcomes, I will give the right to eat from the tree of life, which is in paradise of God (7).
2. Church in Smyrna	Revelation 2:11: . . . He who overcomes will not be hurt at all by the second death (7).
3. Church in Pergamum	Revelation 2:17: . . . To him who overcomes, I will give some of the hidden manna. I will also give him a white stone with a new name written on it, known only to him who receives it. (7)
4. Church in Thyatira	Revelation 2:26-28: To him who overcomes and does my will to the end, I will give authority over the nations. He will rule them with an iron scepter; he will dash them to pieces like pottery. - just as I have received authority from my Father. I will also give the morning star. (7)
5. Church in Sardis	Revelation 3:5: He who overcomes will be dressed in white. I will never erase his name from the book of life, but will acknowledge his name before my Father and his angels. (7)

6. Church in Philadelphia	Revelation 3:12: Him who overcomes, I will make a pillar in the temple of my God. Never again will he leave it. I will write on him the name of God and the name of the city of my God, the new Jerusalem, which is coming down out of heaven from my God; and I will also write on him my new name. (7)
7. Church in Laodicea	Revelation 3:21: To him who overcomes, I will give the right to sit with me on my throne, just as I overcame and sat down with my Father on his throne. (7)

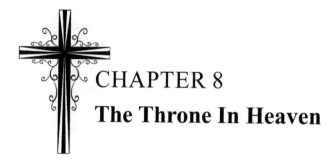

CHAPTER 8

The Throne In Heaven

A door opens in heaven

> Revelation 4:1-4: After this I looked, and there before me was a door standing open in heaven. And the voice I had first heard speaking to me like a trumpet said, "Come up here, and I will show you what must take place after this." At once I was in the Spirit, and there before me was a throne in heaven with some one sitting on it. And the one who sat there had the appearance of jasper and carnelian. A rainbow, resembling an emerald, encircled the throne. Surrounding the throne were twenty-four other thrones, and seated on them were twenty-four elders. They were dressed in white and had crowns of gold on their heads. (7)

After the Lord had finished speaking to John about the seven churches, John saw a door open in heaven. A voice spoke, "Come up here, and I will show you what must take place after this." John said, immediately, he was in the Spirit before the throne in heaven.

When do the events described in Revelation 4 through 22 take place?

In 95 AD, the Lord told John in Revelation 4:1 that these events to be discussed were yet to come. Everything mentioned in Revelation 4 through 22 was yet to come. If we try to place these events prior to 95 AD, we will be deceived.

What is the throne that is being set in heaven?

As soon as the door was opened, John saw a throne being set. The man-child rapture (discussed in Chapter 18) would have to occur before all the elders could sit on the thrones. Therefore, John saw the thrones being set after the door was opened.

The throne being set in heaven is similar to the one described in Daniel, where a throne was set in heaven in the days of the ten kings, prior to the Lord's return to the earth.

> Daniel 7:9-10: As I looked, thrones were set in place, and the Ancient of Days took his seat. His clothing was white as snow; the hair of his head was white like wool. His throne was flaming with fire, and its wheels were all ablaze. A river of fire was flowing, coming out from before him. Thousands upon thousands attended him; ten thousand times ten thousand stood before him. The court was seated, and the books were opened. (7)

The description of Ancient of Days in Daniel 7:9-10 is similar to the description of the Son of Man in Revelation 1. The Ancient of Days is a term used to describe either the Father or the Son. In Daniel, the Ancient of Days appears to be the Father, as Daniel 7:13-14 speaks of the Son of Man coming before the Ancient of Days to receive His kingdom.

> Daniel 7:13-14: In my vision at night I looked, and there before me was one like a son of man, coming with the cloud of heaven. He approached the Ancient of Days and was led unto his presence. He was given authority, glory and sovereign power; all peoples, nations and men of every language worshiped him. . . . (7)

Revelation gives further description of the throne described in Daniel.

> Revelation 4:5-6: From the throne came flashes of lightning, rumbling and peals of thunders. . . . Also before the throne there was what looked like a sea of glass, clear as crystal. . . . (7).

The throne set in heaven is obviously a judgment scene, since:

1. Daniel 7:10 speaks of the books being opened.
2. Daniel 7: 9-10 speaks of the throne being ablaze with flames and a river of fire flowing out before the Lord.
3. The flashes of lightning, thunder and fire were also the scene when the Lord poured out judgment on Egypt in the days of Moses (34).
4. Daniel 7:21-22 speaks of the Little Horn (the Beast) waging war against the saints and defeating them. Then the Ancient of Days came and pronounced judgment in favor of the saints of the Most High and the time came when they possessed the kingdom.

The scripture in Revelation 4:1 speaks of a door opening in heaven. **What is the significance of this door?**

In Daniel 7:13-14 the scripture speaks of the Son of Man coming before the Father to receive sovereign power, honor, glory and authority, and that the people of every nation and language will worship Him. These people are part of the multitude standing before the throne in Daniel 7:10.

Revelation 4:4 speaks of the 24 elders, seated on the thrones, with golden crowns on their heads. The elders are redeemed saints. Throughout the Old and New Testaments, elders are referred to as men not angels. In Revelation 3:21, the Lord promises those who overcome will sit down with Him on His throne. It is men, not angels, who will sit on the throne.

Revelation 4:6 describes a sea of glass, clear as crystal, before the throne. Revelation 17:15 speaks of the sea or water as a multitude of people of every nation and language.

It is obvious that the elders and the sea of glass are the redeemed saints standing before the throne (first fruits of the Old Testament saints and the first fruits of the New Testament saints) (34).

If these elders and saints are standing before the throne, before the Son of Man received His kingdom and before the books are opened, when did the elders and the saints come before the throne?

The only time these saints could have come before the throne was when the door was opened in heaven in Revelation 4:1. This company of believers is obviously the Man-child rapture described in Revelation 12 and 14. All the multitudes around the throne are not redeemed saints for some are angels as mentioned in Revelation 5:11.

Jesus said, "I am the door" (John 10:9). When the door was opened, the Man-child rapture took place. Paul tells us in I Thessalonians 4:13-17 that the dead in Christ will rise first, and then those that are alive will be caught up to meet the Lord in the air. For these people to be gathered around the throne, a rapture would have had to occur. This shows that this scene in heaven takes place at the time of the end.

Was there a first-fruit resurrection of the Old Testament saints at the resurrection of Jesus?

> Matthew 27:50-53: And when Jesus had cried out again in a loud voice, he gave up his spirit. At that moment the curtain of the temple was torn in two from top to bottom. The earth shook and the rocks split. The

tombs broke open and the bodies of many holy people who had died were raised to life. They came out of the tombs, and after Jesus' resurrection they went into the holy city and appeared to many people. (7)

This is obviously a resurrection of many of the Old Testament saints. It doesn't seem right that these dead saints would have to die a second death after being raised from the dead. I believe that this is the resurrection of the first fruits of the Old Testament saints that went to heaven to be with the Lord.

I believe that the Old Testament saints are part of the group that were standing before the throne with the first fruits of the New Testament saints, when Christ is shown receiving His kingdom before the opening of the seven seals.

> John Leary received this message on April 12, 2009, Easter Sunday. Jesus said: "My people, My death on the cross opened the gates to heaven because I paid the ransom for all the sins of mankind, both in the past and the future. The souls, who were pure enough to enter heaven, were released from the place of the dead. Easter was a glorious time for all souls. (Matt. 27:52, 53) 'And the graves were opened: and many bodies of the saints that had slept arose, and coming out of the tombs after His Resurrection, came into the holy city, and appeared to many.' This event gave hope to those still living and further hope to those living today that you also could be resurrected one day. Give praise and thanks to Me for all of My gifts to My faithful. Repent and follow My laws, and you will have your reward in heaven." Sunday, April 12, 2009: (Easter Sunday) (35)

What do the twenty-four elders and the twenty-four thrones represent?

The twenty-four elders and twenty-four thrones probably represent both the Old and the New Testament saints. Twelve of the elders could represent the twelve tribes of Israel and the other twelve elders could represent the twelve apostles.

What is the significance of the rainbow around the throne?

The rainbow is a reminder of the covenant God made with man (Noah) not to destroy the earth by flood again (11). Though this is a judgment scene in heaven, it is not a judgment to destroy the earth but to reclaim the earth for the saints of God.

The seven lamps – the seven Spirits of God

Revelation 4:5: Before the throne, seven lamps were blazing. These are the seven Spirits of God (7).

Isaiah 11:2-3 speaks of the spirits of God (7, 36):

1. Spirit of the Lord will rest on him
2. Spirit of wisdom
3. Spirit of understanding
4. Spirit of counsel
5. Spirit of power
6. Spirit of knowledge
7. Spirit of the fear of the Lord

Four living creatures

Revelation 4:6-8: . . . In the center, around the throne, were four living creatures, and they were covered with eyes in front and back. The first living creature was like a lion, the second was like an ox, the third had a face like a man, the fourth was like a flying eagle. Each of the four living creatures had six wings and was covered with eyes all around, even under his wings. Day and night they never stopped saying, "Holy, holy, holy is the Lord God Almighty, who was, and is, and is to come." (7)

What are the four living creatures?

The four living creatures in Revelation are similar to the four living creatures described in Ezekiel.

> Ezekiel 1:10: Their faces looked like this: Each of the four had the face of a man, on the right side each had the face of a lion, and on the left the face of an ox; each also had the face of an eagle (7).

The four faces of the four living creatures represent the four faces of the Lord.

1. Face of a man - the Lord emptied Himself of His divinity of God and became man.
2. Face of a lion - Jesus is known as the Lion of the tribe of Judah.
3. Face of an ox - an ox is a servant. Jesus came as a servant.
4. Face of an eagle - the eagle soars in the heavenly places. The Lord also soars in the heavenly places. (37)

Book of the Seven Seals

> Revelation 5:1-7: And I saw in the right hand of Him who sat on the throne a book written inside and on the back, sealed up with seven seals. And I saw a strong angel proclaiming with a loud voice, "Who is worthy to open the book and to break its seals? And no one in heaven, or on the earth, or under the earth, was able to open the book, or look into it.

> And I began to weep greatly, because no one was
> found worthy to open the book, or to look into it;
> and one of the elders said to me, "Stop weeping;
> behold, the Lion that is from the tribe of Judah, the
> Root of David, has overcome so as to open the book
> and its seven seals. And I saw between the throne
> and the elders a Lamb standing as if slain, having
> seven horns and seven eyes, which are the seven
> Spirits of God, sent out into all the earth. And He
> came, and He took it out of the right hand of Him
> who sat on the throne. (12)

An angel proclaimed with a loud voice, "Who is worthy to open the book with seven seals?" When no one was found worthy, John, who was witnessing this scene, started weeping. Then one of the elders spoke to John and said, "Do not weep for the Lion of the tribe of Judah, the Root of David, has overcome." He is worthy to open the book of the seven seals.

What is the Book of the Seven Seals?

Daniel was told to seal up the book for it was not to be opened and revealed until the time of the end. The only sealed book mentioned in the New Testament is the Book of the Seven Seals in the Book of Revelation. Revelation is the seventieth week of Daniel, which occurs at the time of the end just prior to the Lord's return to the earth.

> Daniel 12:9-13: And he said, "Go your way, Daniel,
> for these words are concealed and sealed up un-
> til the end time. Many will be purged, purified and
> refined; but the wicked will act wickedly, and none
> of the wicked will understand, but those who have
> insight will understand. And from the time that the
> regular sacrifice is abolished, and the abomination

of desolation is set up, there will be 1,290 days. How blessed is he who keeps waiting and attains to the 1335 day! But as for you, go your way to the end; then you will enter into rest and rise again for your allotted portion at the end of the age. (12)

William DeBurgh believes that the book of the seven seals is the book that was revealed to Daniel. Mr. DeBurgh called the book of the seven seals "The Book of Christ's Inheritance", i.e. the book contains an account of the redemption of Christ's inheritance and purchased possession. The book of the seven seals is the title deed to the earth. Daniel was told to seal up the book because Jesus had not yet paid the price to reclaim the earth. (38)

When God created the earth, He gave dominion of the earth to Adam and Eve. When Adam and Eve sinned, the dominion was passed to Satan. This was shown by the fact that Satan told Jesus that if He would bow down and worship him, he would give Him the kingdom of this world. Jesus did not challenge Satan's right to give Him the kingdom of this world.

Why did John weep bitterly, when no one in heaven, on earth or under the earth could be found, who was worthy to open the Book of Seven Seals?

> Revelation 5:4: I wept and wept because no one was found who was worthy to open the scroll or look inside (7).

This book was so important that John, viewing the scene unfolding in heaven, began to weep and weep because no one was found who was worthy to open the book. Why was this book so important that John wept openly and bitterly? The book is obviously the title deed to the earth. An elder told John not to weep that the Lamb of

God, who was slain for our sins has prevailed, and He was worthy to open the book of the seven seals.

Mr. Burgh explained that in the Old Testament if a man lost or sold his property, disinheriting his children, any kinsman could buy the land back at any time by paying the purchase price; then the land could be restored to its rightful owners. This process was called redemption. The man, who bought the land back, was known as the redeemer. The land would pass back into the hand of the heirs, and they would move onto the land to posses it. This was called redemption of the purchase possession.

When a kinsman redeemed the property, a deed was written up and sealed. The sealed deed was given to the original owners or heirs. The heirs, after breaking the seal, used the open deed as their authority to take possession of the land (Jeremiah 36: 6-15). (38)

Jesus defeated Satan 2,000 years ago with his death on the cross. Nevertheless, Satan and his angels are still the prince and the powers of the air and the rulers of darkness (Ephesians 6:12). The opening of the book and each of the seven seals are the final steps in reclaiming the earth as an inheritance for the kinsmen, the brothers and sisters of Jesus Christ.

> Matthew 12:50: For whoever does the will of my Father in heaven is my brother and sister and mother (7).

> Romans 8:16-17: The Spirit Himself bears witness with our spirit that we are children of God, and if children, heirs also, heirs of God and fellow-heirs with Christ, if indeed we suffer with Him in order that we may also be glorified with Him. (12)

The saints, the children of God, the brothers and sisters of the Redeemer, our Lord Jesus Christ, the descendants of Adam and Eve are the rightful heirs of the earth. The Lord Jesus Christ, our kinsman and Redeemer, paid the price by His sacrifice and death on the cross. The openings of each of the seven seals are steps in opening the sealed deed to reclaim the earth.

What do the seven horns and seven eyes on the Lamb that is standing as slain, symbolize?

The Lamb standing as slain is the Lord Jesus Christ. Stuart says the horn denotes power throughout the scripture. The ten horns are symbolic of the ten kings or kingdoms. The Lamb with seven horns and seven eyes symbolizes supreme power and omniscience. (39)

Golden bowls – the prayers of the saints

Revelation 5:8: . . . Each one had a harp and they were holding golden bowls full of incense, which are the prayers of the saints (7).

God created us and everything that is in heaven and on earth. There isn't anything that God needs. God has given us a free will. We can obey and serve Him, or we can do our own thing. The one thing that really pleases God is for us to spend time with Him in prayer, praising Him, thanking Him and adoring Him.

Just as we record the message of a good speaker, God collects the praises and prayers of the saints, putting them into golden bowls to be displayed before the angels and saints. The praises and the prayers of the saints really please God. Since our prayers are substances, which are collected in bowls to be displayed before the angels and saints for all eternity, we need to make a sincere effort to spend time each day to praise and worship the Lord not only for Who He is but for what He has done for us. We do not want our bowl to be empty for all eternity. Notice that the prayers are substances, which give off incense or odor that is pleasing to God.

CHAPTER 9

The Opening Of The Book
Of The Seven Seals

The Beginning Of The
Great Tribulation

In the scene before the throne, John saw the Son of Man take a book with seven seals, His inheritance, the deed to the earth, from the hands of His Father, the Ancient of Days, and receive a kingdom. With the opening of the book of the seven seals, the Lord begins the process of reclaiming the earth that was lost through the sins of Adam and Eve.

Though the opening of the book of the seven seals coincides with the beginning of the Great Tribulation, the Great Tribulation does not begin with the opening of the book of the seven seals. Jesus said, "The Great Tribulation begins with the abomination of desolation of the temple, which was spoken of by Daniel, the prophet. (Daniel 9:27, Matthew 24:15, 21)

The first five seals cover the period of the Great Tribulation.

Riders of the four horses

As the Lamb of God opens the first four seals of the book of the seven seals, four riders come forth, each on a different colored horse. The four riders and the four horses each ride out from the presence of the four living creatures and those standing before the throne.

Who are the four horsemen that ride the different colored horses?

The different colored horses are mentioned in Zechariah 1 and 6 (38).

> Zechariah 1:8-11: I saw at night, and behold, a man was riding on a red horse, and he was standing among the myrtle trees which were in the ravine, with red, sorrel, and white horses behind him. Then I said, "My lord, what are these?" And the angel who was speaking with me said to me, "I will show you what these are." And the man who was standing among the myrtle trees answered and said, "These are those whom the Lord has sent to patrol the earth." So they answered the angel of the Lord who was standing among the myrtle trees, and said, "We have patrolled the earth, and behold, all the earth is peaceful and quiet. (12)

> Zechariah 6:2-8: With the first chariot were red horses, the second chariot black horses, with the third chariot white horses and with the fourth chariot strong dappled horses. Then I spoke and said to the angel who was speaking with me, "What are these my lord?" And the angel answered and said to me, "These are the four spirits of heaven, going forth after standing before the Lord of all the earth, with one of which the black horses are going forth to the north country; and the white ones go forth after them, while the dappled ones go forth to the south country. When the strong ones went out, they were eager to go patrol the earth. And He said, "Go, patrol the earth." So they patrolled the earth. Then He cried out to me and spoke to me saying, "See, those who are going to

the land of the north have appeased My wrath in the land of the north." (12)

The Amplified translation says, "Have quieted my spirit (of wrath) and caused it to rest in the north country."

It can be seen from Zechariah that the riders of the different colored horses are angels of the Lord that patrol the earth. In Zechariah 6:8, the angel of the Lord, while patrolling the north country, brings peace by appeasing the Wrath of God.

If the angels of the Lord that patrol the earth can bring peace by holding back the forces of God's wrath, then the angels can bring forth God's wrath by removing the restraining forces. This can be seen in Revelation 7, wherein the four angels hold back the four winds, the forces of destruction, until the 144,000 of the twelve tribes of Israel can be sealed with the seal of the Living God. The four winds mentioned in Daniel 7 were called the four princes of darkness, as discussed in Chapter 5.

If one questions whether angels can pour out judgment upon the earth, what about the angels that blow the seven trumpets and pour out the seven vials on earth during the Wrath of God? The angels that pour out the vials are redeemed saints as shown in Revelation 17:1 and 19:9-10.

Although the angels of the Lord are involved in some of the drama that unfolds with the opening of the seven seals, they, in reality, remove themselves as the restraining forces during the Great Tribulation, giving the Beast and Satan complete freedom to make war, and to persecute and kill people.

The Great Tribulation is when the Beast persecutes and kills the people, who will not bow down worship him or his image and take his mark. The Wrath of God is when the Lord pours out

His wrath on the Beast and on the people that take the mark of the Beast.

Opening of the first seal – the rider of the white horse

> Revelation 6:1-2: And I saw when the Lamb broke one of the seven seals, and I heard one of the four living creatures saying as with a voice of thunder, "Come". And I looked, and behold, a white horse, and he who sat on it had a bow; and a crown was given to him; and he went out conquering, and to conquer. (12)

Who is the rider of the white horse?

It is seen in Zechariah, that the riders of the horses are the angels of the Lord who patrol the earth. In an effort to determine who the rider of the white horse is, we need to remember:

1. A judgment throne is set in heaven.
2. Jesus, the Son of Man, has just taken the book of the seven seals out of the hands of His Father, the Ancient of Days, and received a kingdom.
3. The book of the seven seals is the title deed to the earth. Jesus is reclaiming the inheritance that was lost by Adam and Eve by opening the seals of the deed to the earth.
4. We know the Lord is the rider of the white horse in Revelation 19:11.
5. When Jesus opened the first seal, one of the four living creatures said, "Come." Before John and the throne was a rider on a white horse. A crown was given unto him. He rode out from the throne going forth, conquering and to conquer.

Some people believe the rider of the white horse is Satan. Jesus Christ has just opened the first seal of the title deed to the earth. It is hard to believe that in this solemn moment, Satan would appear as an Angel of Light on a white horse before the throne to receive a crown and then ride forth, conquering and to conquer. The question is, "Why would Satan receive a crown before the throne, before the Lord and His angels and saints?"

In the most solemn moment of all eternity, when the Lord Jesus Christ takes the book of the seven seals, the title deed of His inheritance, from the hands of His Father and receives a kingdom with power, glory and honor with the opening of the first seal, the beginning of the process of reclaiming the earth, the rider of the white horse can be none other than the Lord Jesus Christ.

The Son of Man received a kingdom from His Father, the Ancient of Days, in Daniel 7, which is the same scene as seen Revelation 4 and 5. If the Son of Man received a kingdom, He should also receive a crown at the same time. In Revelation 6:1-2, the rider of the white horse does receive a crown. When Jesus is seen in Revelation 14:14, he has a crown on His head. At the beginning of the judgment scene, when the Son of Man takes the book from the hands of His Father, he does not have a crown on His head. If the Lord has a crown on His head in Revelation 14:14, when did He receive this crown, if it were not at the appearance of the rider on the white horse at the opening of the first seal?

With the opening of the first seal of the deed to the earth, a rider emerges on a white horse going forth conquering and to conquer. The Lord Jesus Christ is the only one that goes forth conquering and to conquer. Revelation 12, which is the beginning of the second chronological series and is parallel with the opening of the first seal, shows Michael and his angels driving Satan and his angels from the heavens onto the earth. Satan does not receive a crown to ride through the heavens going forth to conquer, but is driven from the heavens at the time the rider of the white horse receives a crown. Satan is a defeated foe that has less than three and one-half years at this moment to do his work.

Some say that the Lord cannot open the seals and at the same time participate in the drama that is unfolding. If the Lord cannot participate in the riding of the white horse with the opening of the first seal, He cannot participate in the drama in any of the other seals that He opens. There is no question that the Lord appears in the scene with the opening of the sixth seal as written in Revelation 6:16 and 14:14.

In Revelation 10:8-10, John, an apostle, who is watching the opening of the seals and the drama that unfolds, is asked to participate with the eating of the open book that had been sealed with the seven seals. This shows that the Lord can open the first seal and still ride the white horse. (34)

Is the bow a weapon of the Lord?

Some say the weapon of the Lord is the sword that comes out of His mouth and that the rider of the white horse carries a bow, which is not a weapon of the Lord. The following scriptures show that a bow is a weapon of the Lord.

> Psalm 7:11-13: God is a righteous judge, a God who expresses his wrath every day. If he does not relent, he will sharpen his sword; he will bend and string his bow. He has prepared his deadly weapons; he makes ready his flaming arrows. (7)

> Isaiah 41:2: Who has aroused one from the east whom He calls in righteousness to His feet? He delivers up

nations before him, and subdues kings. He makes them like dust with His sword, as the wind-driven chaff with His bow. (12)

It can be seen from Psalm 7:11-13 and Isaiah 41:2 that the bow is a weapon of the Lord (34).

There should be no question that the rider of the white horse is the Lord Jesus Christ, Who received a crown at the moment He received a kingdom from His Father at the beginning of the judgment scene. He rides forth to conquer and reclaim the earth.

Opening of the second seal – the rider of the red horse

Revelation 6:3-4: And when He broke the second seal, I heard the second living creature saying, "Come." And another, a red horse, went out; and to him who sat on it, it was granted to take peace from the earth, and that men should slay one another; and a great sword was given to him. (12)

As discussed earlier, the angels of the Lord hold in check the forces of destruction in Revelation 7:1-8 until the 144,000 of the twelve tribes of Israel can be sealed with the seal of the Living God.

I truly believe the angels of the Lord hold in check the forces of darkness through the intercessory prayers of the saints on earth (Daniel 10:1-21). With the rapture of the first fruits, the man-child, the church is greatly weakened. The intercessory prayers that restrain the forces of darkness are gone.

The rider of the red horse goes forth to remove the restraining forces, which allow peace to be taken away from the earth, so that men may slay one another. A sword was given to the rider of the red horse to bring forth war. Since the rider of the white horse is the

Lord, then the riders of the red, black and pale horses must be the angels of the Lord as is shown in Zechariah 1:8-11 and 6:1-8. (34)

Opening of the third seal – the rider of the black horse

> Revelation 6:5-6: And when He broke the third seal, I heard the third living creature saying, "Come". And I looked, and behold, a black horse; and he who sat on it had a pair of scales in his hand. And I heard as it were a voice in the center of the four living creatures saying, "A quart of wheat for a denarius, and three quarts of barley for a denarius; and do not harm the oil and the wine." (12)

As we saw with the opening of the second seal, the rider went forth to take peace from the earth and to slay one another. When war is going on, it is difficult to raise food such as wheat and barley. When there is not enough wheat and barley to go around, they are weighed on a scale. In a time of plenty, wheat and barley are not weighed.

This scripture says do not harm the oil and wine. Oil is produced from olives and wine comes from grapes. Olive trees and grapes will continue to produce without much attention, while barley and wheat require care and attention as the fields need to be cultivated, seeds planted and the crop harvested. (40)

We should also remember that the two witnesses mentioned in Revelation 11 come on the scene prior to the abomination of desolation of the temple to warn the people not to take the mark of the Beast. These two witnesses, who are given forty-two months to walk the streets of Jerusalem, have power to shut up the sky in order that rain may not fall during the days of their prophesying. If rain does not fall during the days of their prophesying, there would certainly be famine in the land.

On August 19,1996, John Leary received the following message: Listen to Me, My people. I wish to stress this message to you tonight and follow Me. There is coming a great famine over all the earth. This will be one of the many coming chastisements to purify the earth. I have told you of such famines before as with Joseph and the Pharaoh's dream. Those who do not heed My words, will suffer the ravages of starvation. At this time tell everyone and your government to make preparation for this trial. Put aside food and water for yourselves. It would be better that all people prepare as such, so looting and stealing of food will not be rampant. I will be repeating this theme of, "a ration of food will be given at the proper time." This ration will be needed twice. First, before the tribulation, and then during the tribulation when I will provide My Manna for you in hiding. I am watching over you by giving you these warnings. These food shortages will later fall into the hands of the Antichrist, who will demand allegiance and his mark to buy and sell this food in short supply. It is at this time you must flee into hiding with My angel. He will show each of you your way, and provide you with the heavenly bread. Listen and heed My words, for your chastisements will be increasing. (41)

A denarius was shown in Matthew 20:2 to be the ordinary wage for a full day labor. A quart of wheat or three quarts of barley is very little food for a day's wage. How can a man feed and clothe his family, pay his rent and buy the other necessities of life with one denarius? It would be difficult to feed and provide for a family with one quart of wheat for a day's wage. A quart of wheat is not even a loaf of bread. (11)

The fourth seal – the rider of the pale horse

> Revelation 6:7-8: And when He broke the fourth seal, I heard the voice of the fourth living creature saying, "Come." And I looked, and behold, an ashen horse; and he who sat on it had the name of "Death"; and Hades was following with him. And authority was given to them over a fourth of the earth, to kill with sword and with famine and with pestilence and by the wild beasts of the earth. (12)

The rider of the pale horse obviously removes the restraining forces, giving the Beast, known as the prince of the Roman people, the Little Horn or the Antichrist, power over a fourth of the earth, to kill with the sword, famine, pestilence, and the beasts of the earth. Notice that the Beast only has control over a fourth of the earth. The area controlled by the Beast certainly includes most of Europe, Russia, the Middle East and parts of Africa. The Beast does not have control of Edom, Moab and Ammon (Daniel 11:41). This is the wilderness area to which the Israelites were told to flee. The Beast does not have control of the whole world. If he did, how would the different nations of the world make war with the Beast at the battle of Armageddon?

The power of the Beast will be felt by all nations of the world. This can be seen by the fact that if the Beast controls the oil in the Middle East, and he has control of the buying and selling of goods, his presence and power will definitely be felt by all the nations of the world.

The Beast received power to kill with the sword. Revelation 13:7 says, "Authority was given unto him to wage war with the saints and overcome them."

Famine can be caused by war, lack of rain and control of food. The two witnesses have power to shut up the sky so it does not rain during the three and a half years of their prophecies, just as it was in the days of Elijah (Revelation 11:6). Rampages of insects, insect-borne diseases, plant diseases, and contagious human diseases, due to war and unsanitary conditions, could cause pestilence.

"To kill with . . . the wild beasts of the earth." Although lions and wild beasts could be used to kill the saints, in a manner similar to the days of the early church in Rome, this is highly unlikely the meaning of this verse. The Lord, in Matthew speaks of this time as a time of tribulation and persecution like the world has never seen.

> Matthew 24:21 for then there will be a great tribulation, such as has not occurred since the beginning of the world until now, nor ever shall (12).

All we have to do is look back to Hitler's Germany, where his lieutenants (the beasts) killed six millions Jews plus millions of other people such as the Gypsies and Polish people in concentration camps (41). World War II resulted in the death of millions of soldiers and people caught in the war. The Lord in Matthew said the Great Tribulation would be the greatest persecution the world has ever seen. The only way for the Great Tribulation to be worse than what Hitler did, would be for a greater number of people to be killed. The gross crimes committed by Hitler and his lieutenants against humanity in concentration camps were unbelievable.

Slaughter will be great

> Matthew 24:22: And unless those days had been cut
> short, no life would have been saved; but for the sake
> of the elect those days shall be cut short (12).

During the reign of the Beast, the slaughter will be so great that almost no one will survive. This persecution will obviously be against the Jews, the Christians and those, who will not worship the Beast or take his mark. The Lord said, "for the sake of the elect those days will be shortened."

The beasts of the earth are obviously the lieutenants of the Beast, the prince of the Roman people.

Opening of the fifth seal – the people under the altar

> Revelation 6:9-11: And when He broke the fifth
> seal, I saw underneath the altar the souls of those
> who had been slain because of the word of God,
> and because of the testimony which they had main-
> tained; and they cried out with a loud voice, saying,
> "How long, O Lord, holy and true, wilt Thou refrain
> from judging and avenging our blood on those who
> dwell on the earth?" And there was given to each
> of them a white robe; and they were told that they
> should rest for a little while longer, until the num-
> ber of their fellow servants and their brethren who
> were to be killed even as they had been, should be
> completed also. (12)

Who are the people under the altar?

The people under the altar are those that had been killed by the Beast during the Great Tribulation. These people cried out to the Lord from under the altar asking, "When wilt thou judge and avenge our blood on those dwelling on earth?" The Lord tells them that they must be patient and wait until the rest of their fellow brethren, who are to be killed, have been killed as they had. A period of time is allotted to the Beast to do his dirty work.

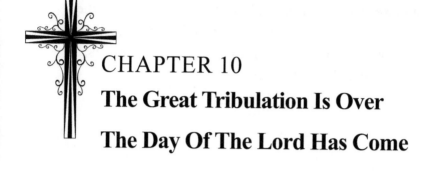

CHAPTER 10

The Great Tribulation Is Over

The Day Of The Lord Has Come

The sixth seal – sun is darkened - moon turned blood-red

> Revelation 6:12-17: I watched as he opened the sixth
> seal. There was a great earthquake. The sun turned
> black like sackcloth made of goat hair, the whole moon
> turned blood red, and the stars in the sky fell to earth, as
> late figs drop from a fig tree when shaken by a strong
> wind. The sky receded like a scroll, rolling up, and ev-
> ery mountain and island was removed from its place.
> Then the kings of the earth, the princes, the generals,
> the rich, the mighty, and every slave and every free man
> hid in caves and among the rocks of the mountains.
> They called to the mountains and the rocks, "Fall on us
> and hide us from the face of him who sits on the throne
> and from the wrath of the Lamb! For the great day of
> their wrath has come, and who can stand?" (7)

In Matthew 24:29, Jesus refers to the sun being darkened and the
moon not giving its light immediately after the tribulation. When the
sun is darkened, the moon will turn red.

**Are there any scriptures that speak of the sun being darkened
and moon turning red, before the great day of the Lord?**

There are several scriptures that refer to the sun being

darkened and the moon turning blood-red, before the great day of the Lord comes.

> Joel 2:30-31: I will show wonders in the heavens and on the earth, blood and fire and billows of smoke. The sun will be turned to darkness and the moon to blood before the coming of the great and dreadful day of the Lord. (7)

Peter quotes Joel, the prophet, in Acts:

> Acts 2:20: The sun shall be turned into darkness, and the moon into blood, before that great and notable day of the Lord comes (10).

> Zephaniah 1:14-18 speaks of the great day of the Lord as a day of wrath.

Signs and wonders immediately after the Great Tribulation but before the great day of the Lord

Jesus, in Matthew 24:29-31, 38, 39, speaks of certain signs and wonders happening immediately after the Great Tribulation. Revelation 6:12-17 shows that the events described in Matthew take place during the opening of the sixth seal.

The events that happen immediately after the tribulation are:

Sun is darkened and moon becomes blood red

Matthew 24:29: But immediately after the tribulation of those days the sun will be darkened, the moon will not give its light, . . . (12)

Revelation 6:12: I watched as he opened the sixth seal. There was a great earthquake. The sun turned black like sack-cloth made of goat hair, the whole moon turned blood red, (7)

The stars fall from the sky

Matthew 24:29: . . . the stars will fall from the sky, and the powers of the heavens will be shaken, . . . (12).

Revelation 6:13: . . . and the stars in the sky fell to the earth, as late figs drop from a fig tree when shaken by a strong wind. (7)

People will see the sign of the Son of Man

Matthew 24:30:. . . and then the sign of the Son of Man will appear in the sky, . . . (12).

Revelation 6:14: The sky receded like a scroll, rolling up, and every mountain and island was removed from its place. (7).

People will see the Son of Man and fear will strike them

Matthew 24:30: . . . then all the tribes of the earth will mourn, and earth, they will see the Son of Man coming on the clouds of the sky with power and great glory. (12)

Revelation 6:15-16: Then the kings of the the princes, the generals, the rich, the mighty, and every slave and every free man hid in caves and among the of rocks the mountains. They called to the mountains and rocks, "Fall on us and hide us from the face of him who sits on the throne and from the wrath of the Lamb." (7)

Gathering his elect

Matthew 24:31: And He will send forth His angels with a great trumpet and they will gather together His elect from the four winds, from one end of the sky to the other. (12)

Revelation 7:9,14: After this I looked and there before me was a great multitude that no one could count, from every nation, tribe, people and language, standing before the throne and in front of the Lamb. They were wearing white robes and were holding palm branches in their hands. . . . These are they who have come out of the great tribulation; they have washed their robes and made them white in the blood of the Lamb. (7)

The Day of the Lord – the Wrath of God

Matthew 24:38-39: For as in those days which were before the flood they were eating and drinking, they were marrying and giving in marriage, until the day that Noah entered the ark, and they did not understand until the flood came and took them all away, so shall the coming of the Son of Man be. (12)

Revelation 6:16-17: They called to the mountains and rocks, "Fall on us and hide us from the face of him who sits on the throne and from the wrath of the Lamb! For the great day of their wrath has come, and who can stand? (7)

The comparison of events in Matthew 24:29-31 with Revelation 6:12-17 and 7:9, 14 shows that the Great Tribulation is over with the opening of the sixth seal (40).

There are several scripture passages in Revelation that speak of the sun, moon and the stars, but not in the same manner, as revealed in Matthew 24:29 and Revelation 6:12-13.

During the fourth trumpet, in Revelation 8:12, the sun, moon and stars are partially darkened for one-third of a day and night. The other events such the coming of the Son of Man, and gathering of the elects, etc., are not mentioned in Revelation 8:12.

The sun is darkened by the smoke of the pit during the fifth trumpet, but the moon, stars and other events are not mentioned. The fourth and fifth trumpets occur during the Wrath of God. The Great Tribulation is over before the Wrath of God begins. The only place where the events mentioned in Matthew 24:29-31, 38, 39 are found, is during the opening of the sixth seal. All the events in Matthew 24:29-31, 38, 39 take place immediately after the Great Tribulation, but before the day of the Lord mentioned in Revelation 6:16-17.

The Great Tribulation is the period of persecution by the Antichrist or the Beast against the Christians, Jews and those who will not take the mark of the Beast. The day of the Lord or the Wrath of God is the period after the Great Tribulation, when the Lord pours out His wrath on the inhabitants of the earth, especially on the Beast and those that received his mark.

What causes the sun to darken and the moon to turn blood-red?

Gordon Lindsay reported that when large forest fires broke out in Oregon, where he lived as a boy, that smoke would cause the sun to darken and the moon would turn blood red. The light of the sun seems to diffuse into space, causing the sun to darken or disappear. The moon, having no light of its own, reflects the light of the sun, becoming red. (40)

During the eruption of the volcano, Mt. St. Helen, in the state of Washington in May 1980, a heavy cloud of ash covered the whole state, causing the sun to darken or disappear, while the moon turned blood red. (Radio and TV)

How this phenomenon will occur after the Great Tribulation, no one knows, especially on a worldwide scale. Revelation 9:2, during the fifth trumpet, speaks of the sun being darkened by smoke arising from the furnace in the bottomless pit. Though the fifth trumpet is a separate event, which happens after the sixth seal, it does show that the sun is darkened by smoke arising from the earth.

Revelation 6:12 speaks of a great earthquake. Acts 2:19 says, "I will show wonder in heaven above and signs on earth below, blood and fire, and billows of smoke." That is a lot of smoke. Whether the earthquake caused the earth to open up, and smoke to pour out as in Mt. St. Helen, no one knows. Nevertheless, when that day comes, the Lord will cause this manifestation to occur. This phenomenon will probably last at least several days.

The 144,000 Jews

> Revelation 7:1-4: After this I saw four angels standing at the four corners of the earth, holding back the four winds of the earth to prevent any wind from blowing on the land or on the sea or on any tree. Then I saw another angel coming up from the east, having the seal of the living God. He called out in a loud voice to the four angels who had been given power to harm the land and the sea. "Do not harm the land or the sea or the trees until we put a seal on the foreheads of the servants of our God." Then I heard the number of those who were sealed: 144,000 from all the tribes of Israel. (7)

What are the four winds that the four angels of the Lord hold back?

The four winds are not ordinary winds, as an ordinary wind does not hurt the land, sea or trees. These four winds are probably the winds mentioned in Daniel 7, which were shown to be the princes of darkness that give power to the four beasts' kingdoms on earth. These four winds are the spiritual forces of darkness that will harm the land, the sea and the trees. The four angels of the Lord hold these forces of darkness in check until 144,000 of the twelve tribes of Israel can be sealed.

Who are the 144,000 from the twelve tribes of Israel?

Many people believe that the Church is raptured before the Great Tribulation, and that these 144,000 Jews will be evangelists who will preach the gospel during the Great Tribulation. These people also believe that the rapture that takes place immediately after the Great Tribulation will be those converted by the 144,000 Jews during the Great Tribulation. (32)

What are the facts? (See Table 3 of the seventieth week of Daniel in Chapter 6). We must remember:

1. The Great Tribulation is over with the opening of the sixth seal.
2. The Harvest Rapture takes place immediately after the Great Tribulation (Matthew 24:31, Revelation 7:9-17, 14:15-16).
3. When the sixth seal is opened, the scriptures speak of the day of the Lord, and the great day of His wrath. However, the day of the Lord or the great day of His wrath does not begin until the opening of the seventh seal in Revelation 8.
4. The 144,000 Israelites are not sealed until after the opening of the seventh seal. At this time, the Great Tribulation is over. The Harvest Rapture has already taken place.
5. It is inconceivable to believe that these 144,000 Jews who were not sealed until after the Great Tribulation is over, would be preaching the Gospel during the Great Tribulation.

6. If these Jews were preaching the Gospel during the Great Tribulation, why were they not raptured, when the Great Tribulation was over with many of the other Christians?

7. The scripture in Revelation 9:4 shows that these 144,000 Israelites go through the Wrath of God, but nothing can hurt them. The scriptures do not speak of a rapture after the Harvest Rapture with the exception of the two witnesses who are called up to heaven three and a half days after they had been killed.

8. These 144,000 Israelites are on earth when the Lord returns with His saints to rule the nations of the world. These 144,000 Jews are obviously God-fearing Israelites living by the laws of the Old Testament. They have not at the time of their sealing, accepted Jesus Christ as their Lord and Savior. These Jews are part of the remnants the Lord will be king over, when He begins His kingdom during the millennium.

If these 144,000 Israelites had accepted Jesus Christ as their Lord and Savior and were preaching the gospel during the Great Tribulation, they would no longer be Jews but Christians. If they were Christians, they would have gone up in the Harvest Rapture immediately after the Great Tribulation.

Notice that Revelation 7:9 shows people from all tribes standing before the throne along with people from all nations of the world. This shows that a large number of Jewish people accepted Jesus Christ as their Lord and Savior, and went up in the Harvest Rapture. These 144,000 Israelites, however, were not part of the Harvest Rapture.

CHAPTER 11
The Harvest Rapture

The Rapture

The rapture takes place when Jesus send His angels with the sound of the trumpet to gather His elects as spoken in Matthew 24:29-31, I Thessalonians 4:13-17 and in I Corinthians 15:51-52. There is a rapture of the first fruits in Revelation 4 when the door in heaven is open and suddenly there is a multitude before the throne. The Harvest rapture occurs immediately after the Great Tribulation as spoken in Matthew 24:29-31. This will be discussed later.

People of all nations, tribes and languages standing before the throne. These are they who went through the Great Tribulation.

> Revelation 7:9-11,13,14 After this I looked and there before me was a great multitude that no one could count, from every nation, tribe, people and language, standing before the throne and in front of the Lamb. They were wearing white robes and were holding palm branches in their hands. And they cried out in a loud voice: "Salvation belongs to our God, who sits on the throne, and to the Lamb." All the angels were standing around the throne and around the elders and the four living creatures. They fell down on their faces before the throne and worshiped God, . . . Then one of the elders asked me (John), "These in white robes - who are they,

and where did they come from?"

John did not know from where these people in white robes came. The elder told John,

> . . . These are they who came out of the great tribulation; they have washed their robes and made them white in the blood of the Lamb. (7)

It can be seen that a large number of Christians will go through the Great Tribulation as shown in the scripture above. These Christians were not evangelized by the 144,000 Israelites as many believed, because these Israelites are not Christians. The 144,000 Israelites were not sealed until after the Harvest Rapture, after many of the Christians had been taken out of the earth to heaven.

All Christians are not taken up

Before I heard of John Leary and his messages, I asked my prayer partner to ask the Lord if there would be Christians going through the Wrath of God? The following words were spoken to us.

> I tell you My son that you have asked a most important question. This I will tell you. There are those who would serve out their time in purgation before entering heaven with Me. There are those that have acknowledged Me as Lord but do not have the ability to live out what is necessary for them to be ready to enter. Of these I will say no more.

This message indicates that all Christians will not go up, when the Harvest Rapture takes place.

John Leary received understanding that those, who had not made reparation for their sins, will not enter the kingdom of heaven, when the rapture occurs. Since June 1993, John Leary has been receiving messages from the Lord daily on preparing His people for the Great Tribulation and the Era of Peace during the millennium. The Harvest Rapture takes place after the opening of the sixth seal. Yet, the Lord continues to give instructions to His people on events, which take place during the Wrath of God, which is after the Harvest Rapture. It is obvious that the people to whom He is talking are Christians. In the following prophecy Jesus tells His people that He will protect them, when He sends a comet to the earth during the trumpets judgment, which is after the Harvest Rapture and during the Wrath of God.

> I am showing you again My chastisement not to frighten you but to tell you it is close for the comet to come. - - - I have shown you the path of fire and the resulting fumes which choke some as the sun's light will cease for a time. Be in a spot protected from the air so you do not have to breathe these fumes. Much of the oxygen will be consumed and breathing will be difficult, but once this trial has passed, you will be resplendent in my glory, for no one can imagine how beautiful life will be for My faithful. On the other hand, those not loyal will meet a bitter fate. 9/17/94 (43)

All Christians will not go up in the Harvest Rapture, which takes place immediately after the Great Tribulation. Jesus said, He will take some that are still alive up into space, while He renews the earth. Others, their angels will lead to a place of safety.

> Many have asked questions about what it will be like at the end of the tribulation. As a Christian you know it is a time of judgment, but it is also a time of sharing in My victory. When I purify the earth, I will draw many into safety from the evil ones. At that time I will

let your angels assist you into moving to a safe place. For some who are still alive, I will draw you up into space out of the clutches of the evil ones until I renew the earth. Then when the chosen time is at hand, I will call My worthy faithful back down to enjoy the era of true peace I have promised. 9/5/95 (44)

It is stated here that only some will be taken up into space. (Note - Mr. Leary calls the whole last 3 1/2 years of the seventieth week of Daniel the tribulation. He does not differentiate between the Great Tribulation and the Wrath of God.)

Jesus emphasizes reparation for sin before entering heaven.

John Leary had a vision of people suffering in flames and they had a cloth over their nose and mouth because of the stench. Jesus said,

These are the souls who were not purified enough on earth. They suffer like those in hell except that they have been promised heaven one day. You can make sufferings on earth to help alleviate this torture later. Also, you can pray with the saints to diminish the souls' stay in Purgatory. Many souls cry out for help to their relatives on earth but those on earth do not think of them. - - - 11/2/93 (45)

Some of the other numerous prophecies received by Mr. Leary are:

I tell you many souls have come to this place you call purgatory. Let Me assure you, it does exist and indeed it is a part of My justice. It is a place where souls who had died and had not yet reached a state of spiritual perfection worthy of heaven. It is rare that souls avoid this without some major suffering or great spiritual awakening. . . . 11/2/94 (45)

My people, many ask why there is a need for purification. You know that I am all merciful, yet I must abide by My Father's justice as well. When sin becomes so hideous, it calls for My purification. In order to free someone of their sins, they must seek My forgiveness, and there must be some payment for that sin. My death on the cross has enabled you to reach heaven, but still there must be some recompense for My justice to be satisfied. This is why some must suffer the fire of purgatory to rid all guilt and justify their actions. This also occurs for nations as well as individuals. Your sins of abortion in your country are so vile in My eyes, that you will face great chastisement by fire to cleanse this evil from your land. Pray My people, and turn from your evil ways if you expect to be received in My arms. 2/4/96 (44)

The burning fire for the spirit soul you will see, if you experience them, are much more painful than that of the body. You would rather spend a short time in pain on earth than an unknown length of time in purgatory. 5/7/96 (44)

You should make an effort in prayer and fasting to make reparation for the punishment due for your sins. Your sins are forgiven, but My justice still demands some payment either in suffering on earth or in purgatory in the afterlife. Give up to Me all of your sufferings on earth to lessen your pain in the afterlife. Bring yourself by this work, closer to Me in heaven. 6/27/96 (44)

Give all of your pain up to Me as a prayer that I will

store in heaven as payment for the reparation of your sins. 7/6/96 (41)

John Leary had a vision of souls suffering in a dark dingy place calling out for help. Jesus said:

> My son, you are seeing in this vision how many are still suffering for their sins. I have made this real for you, so you can witness to everyone that truly this place you call purgatory, does exist. It is truly a place of reparation for the temporal punishment due to your sins. Those, who do not have their suffering on earth for their sins, will have to be purified in this place of torment. In the upper levels of purgatory as you see, the worst suffering is to be without My presence. There is open to you an option to suffer for your sins on earth. Some of those, who suffer much before death, have gained heaven in this way. Pray for these poor souls regularly to alleviate their suffering. Especially, remember to pray for your own relatives and friends. 11/2/96 (46)

> My people, I come to add My blessing over the people for their intentions. You are to know that those souls in heaven and purgatory are all a part of My One Body of faithful. Those souls, who are condemned to hell, are no longer accepted members, since they have rejected My call. As you make a remembrance of these souls, never forget them and pray for them continually through the years. Many are suffering in purgatory longer since their relatives have forgotten them. Pray also for those souls who have no one to pray for them. I want to remind all of you to be ever

watchful over your own souls, so you maybe ready for your own death. . . . 11/3/96 (46)

Those on earth who have not been purged or purified of their sins will not go up in the Harvest Rapture.

What is the duty of the Christians in the Harvest Rapture?

Revelation 7:15: Therefore, they are before the throne of God and serve him day and night in his temple; . . . (7).

The Christians in the Harvest Rapture are called tribulation saints. They are not the first fruits unto God, as those on Mount Zion mentioned in Revelation 14. They are not the highest order of the redeemed. They do not rule as kings or priests. They do not follow the Lamb wherever He goes. They are servants. They serve the Lord day and night in the temple. (40)

What are the teachings of the Lord concerning the Jews, Jerusalem, the time of his Second Coming and the end of the age?

Luke 21: 5-6 (Matthew 24:1-3): Some of his disciples were remarking about how the temple was adorned with beautiful stones and with gifts dedicated to God. But Jesus said, "As for what you see here, the time will come when not one stone will be left on another; every one of them will be thrown down." (7)

Jesus was referring to the temple being destroyed.

Matthew 24:3: As Jesus was sitting on the Mount of Olives, the disciples came to him privately. "Tell us," they said, "when will this happen, and what will be the sign of your coming and of the end of the age?" (7)

Jesus said,

> Luke 21:20-24: When you see Jerusalem surround-
> ed by armies, you will know its desolation is near.
> Then let those who are in Judea flee to the moun-
> tains, let those in the city get out, and let those in
> the country not enter the city. For this is the time
> of punishment in fulfillment of all that has been
> written. How dreadful it will be in those days for
> pregnant woman and nursing mothers! There will
> be great distress in the land and wrath against this
> people. They will fall by the sword and will be tak-
> en as prisoners to all the nations. (7)

The Lord gave warning to the Jews that when they see
Jerusalem surrounded by armies, they were to flee out of the city
to the mountains and unto the wilderness. History tells us that
in 68 to 70 AD, the unbelieving rebellious Jews took fortress
within the city, defying the Roman army. The believing Christian
Jews fled to the mountains and wilderness. After a long siege, the
Roman army finally broke through, and put most of the inhabitants to the sword. The rest of the Jews were led into captivity as
slaves to all nations of the world. (13)

Gordon Lindsay wrote that the Roman soldiers tore down every
stone in the temple to collect the gold that had melted into the rock
after a fire had broken out in the temple. (47)

Jerusalem trodden down by the gentiles

Luke 21:24 speaks of Jerusalem being trodden down by the
Gentiles until the times of the gentiles is fulfilled. In 1967 Jerusalem
was taken over by the Jews. Jerusalem is no longer in the hands of
the Gentiles. The times of the Gentiles have been fulfilled. Jesus

said, "When Jerusalem is in the hands of the Jews, it would be one of the signs that His Second Coming was near."

In respect to His Second Coming, Jesus answered: "Watch that no one deceives you."

1. "Many will come in My name, claiming 'I am Christ', and will deceive many" (Matthew 24:5) (7). There are many Christians and non-Christians in different denominations and cults, coming in Christ's name claiming that Jesus is Lord, but are misleading and deceiving people with wrong doctrines and teachings.

2. "You will hear of wars and rumors of wars. Nation will rise against nation and kingdom against kingdom" (Matthew 24:6-7) (7). In this country alone, our nation has been involved in World War I and II, the Korean War, the Vietnam War, Dessert Storm, Haiti, Kosovo, Afghanistan and Iraq. There have been hundreds of skirmishes across the globe.

3. "There will be famines and earthquakes in various places" (Matthew 24:7) (7). Jesus said these things must happen but the end is not yet. . . . These things are the beginning of birth pains."

4. "Many will be persecuted and put to death" (Matthew 24:9) (7). There have been a large numbers of martyrs behind the Iron and Bamboo Curtains, in Africa, India and the Middle East especially by the hands of Muslims.

5. "Wickedness shall increase." Love grows cold. (Matthew 24:12) (7). Marriages and homes are breaking up. Divorces are increasing. Greed is everywhere. Abortion, murder, lying, stealing and the

sins of Sodom and Gomorrah are prevalent. God, the Ten Commandments, and prayers are being kicked out of our schools and government.

6. The Gospel is to be preached to the whole world before the end comes (Matthew 24:14).

After all these things, the end of the age shall come. This is not the end of the world, but the end of the age. The Lord will return with His saints to set up His kingdom. This will be discussed later (47).

The abomination spoken by Daniel, the prophet

Matthew 24:15-22: Therefore when you see the abomination of desolation which was spoken of through Daniel the prophet, standing in the holy place (let the reader understand), then let those, who are in Judea flee to the mountains; let him who is on the housetop not go down to get the things out that are in his house; and let him who is in the field not turn back to get his cloak. But woe to those who are with child and to those who nurse babes in those days! But pray that your flight may not be in the winter, or on a Sabbath; for then there will be a great tribulation, such as has not occurred since the beginning of the world until now, nor ever shall. And unless those days had been cut short, no life would have been saved; but for the sake of the elect those days shall be cut short. (12)

Matthew 24:15 speaks of the abomination of desolation of the temple, which was foretold by Daniel which we know is the beginning of the Great Tribulation.

When the abomination takes place, what does the Lord warn the people?

1. "Let them that are in Judea flee to the mountains." Judea is very mountainous, where traveling will be difficult. The Beast is not likely to go into this area looking for the Jews or Christians.

2. "Let those that are on housetops or in the fields not go into the house to get their belongings." Why? When the abomination takes place, people will have a very short time to escape before the roads are blocked, and all means of escape are cut off. Those that try to get their belongings will be caught. They will be forced to worship the Beast, or his image, or be killed.

3. The women, who are pregnant or those with children, will have difficulty traveling or trying to escape.

4. "Pray that your flight be not in the winter." If the abomination takes place in the winter, those that escape will suffer greatly due to the lack of food, warm clothing and shelter.

5. "Pray that your flight be not on a Sabbath." The Orthodox Jews have returned to the old customs of not walking more than a Sabbath mile on the Sabbath day. It would be very easy for the Beast, who has spent the week working in Rome to decide to have some fun on the weekend. If the Beast flew to Jerusalem on Friday night or Saturday, which is the Jewish's Sabbath to set up the abomination of desolation of the temple spoken by Daniel the prophet, the God-fearing Jews would be caught like sitting ducks not wanting to break the law of Sabbath by walking more than one mile on the Sabbath's Day. These are the reasons the Lord said to pray that the

abomination does not take place in the winter or on the Sabbath.

When did Jesus speaks of the rapture taking place?

> Matthew 24:29-31: But immediately after the tribulation of those days the sun will be darkened and the moon will not give its light, and the stars will fall from the sky, and the powers of the heavens will be shaken, and then the sign of the Son of Man will appear in the sky, and then all the tribes of the earth will mourn, and they will see the Son of Man coming on the clouds of the sky with power and great glory. And He will send forth His angels with a great trumpet and they will gather together His elect from the four winds, from one end of the sky to the other. (12)

Jesus, in His whole Olivet discourse, only speaks of the rapture taking place immediately after the tribulation of those days after the sun has darkened and the moon turned blood-red. This has been shown to take place after the opening of the sixth seal.

Did Christ or any other writers of the Gospels or Epistles teach that the rapture would take place before the Great Tribulation?

Let us look at some of the scriptures and see if they give any indication that refers to a different rapture than the one the Lord revealed in Matthew 24:29-31.

> I Thessalonians 4:13-17: But we do not want you to be uninformed, brethren, about those who are asleep, that you may not grieve, as do the rest who have no hope. For if we believe that Jesus died and rose again, even so God will bring with Him those who have fallen asleep in Jesus. For this we say to you by the

> word of the Lord, that we who are alive and remain until the coming of the Lord, shall not precede those who have fallen asleep. For the Lord himself will descend from heaven with a shout, with the voice of the archangel and with the trumpet of God; and the dead in Christ shall rise first. Then we who alive and remain shall be caught up together with them in the clouds to meet the Lord in the air, and thus we shall always be with the Lord. (12)

There is nothing in this scripture to indicate that it is a different rapture from that mentioned in Matthew 24:29-31.

> II Thessalonians 2:1-4: Concerning the coming of our Lord Jesus Christ and our being gathered to him, we ask you, brothers, not to become easily unsettled or alarmed by some prophecy, report or letter supposed to have come from us, saying that the day of the Lord has already come. Don't let anyone deceive you in any way, for that day will not come until the rebellion occurs and the man of lawlessness is revealed, the man doomed to destruction. He opposes and exalts himself over everything that is called God or is worshiped, and even sets himself up in God's temple, proclaiming himself to be God. (7)

This scripture in II Thessalonians supports the teaching of Jesus in Matthew 24:29-31. Paul said not to be deceived concerning the coming of our Lord Jesus Christ, because the man of sin, who sets himself up in God's temple as God, has to be revealed before Jesus comes.

The Great Tribulation begins, when the man of lawlessness sets himself up in the holy place, the temple. Paul said this would happen before the coming of our Lord Jesus Christ. There is no teaching of the pre-tribulation rapture here.

> II Thessalonians 2:6-8: And you know what restrains him now, so that in his time he may be revealed. For the mystery of lawlessness is already at work; only he who now restrains will do so until he is taken out of the way. And then the lawless one will be revealed whom the Lord will slay with the breath of His mouth and to an end by the appearance of His coming. (12)

As will be shown later, the Bride of Christ is the pre-tribulation rapture which occurs at the mid-night hour. The beast, the lawless one, is restrained by the prayers of the Bride, the prayer warriors. When the Bride is taken up, there are no prayers to restrain the beast.

We will all be transformed in a twinkling of an eye.

> I Corinthians 15:51-52: . . . We will not all sleep, but we will all be changed in a flash, in the twinkling of an eye, at the last trumpet. For the trumpet will sound, the dead will be raised imperishable, and we will be changed. (7)

This event will happen, when the rapture occurs in Matthew 24:29-31. There is no teaching in the Gospels or Epistles that shows a definite pre-tribulation rapture.

God has not destined us for his wrath.

> I Thessalonians 5:2, 9: For you yourselves know full well that the day of the Lord will come just like a thief in the night. . . . For God has not destined us for wrath, but for obtaining salvation through our Lord Jesus Christ. (12)

We need to remember that the Great Tribulation and the Wrath of God are two different events. The Great Tribulation is the persecution of the saints of God (Jews and Christians) by the Antichrist. The Great Tribulation is over with the opening of the sixth seal. The Wrath of God begins with the opening of the seventh seal, after the Great Tribulation and the rapture. The Wrath of God is God's judgment against the Antichrist, those who have taken his mark, and the wicked people on earth.

As I Thessalonians 5:9 says, "God has not destined us for wrath." This is true; some of the Christians will be raptured immediately after the Great Tribulation, as shown in Matthew 24:29-31 and Revelation 7:9-17. Others, the Lord will send His angels to protect and lead them to a place of safety.

John Leary had a vision of a huge angel the size of a ten-story building with a large white cross up above the angel. Jesus said:

> My people, you are witnessing in this vision the glory of My coming protection during the tribulation. You will see My angels visible in power before you at these places of refuge. The power of My grace and My Presence will lead you to these safe havens. You will receive My Heavenly Manna from My angels. My angels will protect you from any evil spirits at that time. There will be such a glorious display of My grace and power at these permanent signs of My cross, that the faithful will flock to these places. You will see by these manifestations that I will not leave you orphans. My saving power will be among you in a miraculous way, that Satan will have no power over it. I have told you that fear is useless. Trust in My protection and I will see to all of your physical

and spiritual needs. 8/25/96 (41)

Mr. Leary uses the term tribulation to include both the Great Tribulation and the Wrath of God.

Neither Christ nor the scriptures promise that the Christians would not be persecuted or that they would not go through the period of the Great Tribulation or the Wrath of God.

> Matthew 24:6-9: You will hear of wars and rumors of wars, . . . Nation will rise against nation, and kingdom against kingdom. There will be famines and earthquakes in various places. All these are the beginning of birth pains. Then you will be handed over to be persecuted and put to death, and you will be hated by all nations because of me. (7)

The Lord revealed that we would be persecuted and many would be put to death.

Israel – the fig tree

The Lord told the disciples in the parable of the fig tree that, when the fig tree sprouts its leaves, knows that summer is near. The fig tree is Israel. When Israel becomes a nation, know that the kingdom of God is near (Luke 21:29-31).

This generation that sees Israel become a nation, will not pass away until all these things have been fulfilled.

> Luke 21:32-33: I tell you the truth, this generation will certainly not pass away until all these things have happened. Heaven and earth will pass away, but my words will never pass away (7).

This generation of people, who sees Israel become a nation, will not pass away until all things are fulfilled. Israel became a nation in 1948 (16).

Pray that you may be able to escape all that is about to happen.

> Luke 21:34-36: Be careful, or your hearts will be weighed down with dissipation, drunkenness and anxieties of life, and that day will close on you unexpectedly like a trap. For it will come upon all those who live on the face of the whole earth. Be always on the watch, and pray that you may be able to escape all that is about to happen, and that you may be able to stand before the Son of Man. (7)

Jesus did not say that if you accepted Him as your Lord and Savior or if you are a Christian, you would escape. Jesus said to pray that we may be considered worthy to escape the things, which are about to come to pass.

There is a pretribulation rapture; however, there are no scriptures in the Gospels or Epistles that prove it. There are some scriptures like the one just quoted "pray that you may be considered worthy to escape the things that are to come to pass", but these scriptures do not prove the pretribulation rapture. The only way to prove the pretribulation rapture is in Revelation, with an understanding of where the events occur during the seventieth week of Daniel. We will discuss the pretribulation rapture in studying Revelation 12 and 14.

CHAPTER 12
The Wrath Of God

Seventh seal – the seven trumpets

> Revelation 8:1: When he opened the seventh seal, there was silence in heaven for about half an hour (7).

Why was there silence in heaven for half of an hour?

The scripture does not say; however, this is not difficult to understand. The Great Tribulation is over. The Harvest Rapture has taken place. The day of the Lord has come. The Wrath of God is about to begin. With the opening of the seventh seal, the Lord begins the purification of the earth, removing the wicked and renewing the earth, as it was in the Garden of Eden.

Gordon Lindsay said this is a solemn moment that compares with the seriousness of the flood in the days of Noah. The angels and saints were silent for thirty minutes, knowing that the wicked people on earth were going to be tormented, destroyed and purged from the face of the earth. (40)

The angels with the seven trumpets

> Revelation 8:2: And I saw the seven angels who stand before God, and to them were given seven trumpets (7).

The angels, as they blow the trumpets, bring the judgments of God upon the earth and in heaven. The intensity of the judgments increases with each trumpet. The first four trumpets affect the grass, trees, sea and rivers on earth, and the sun, moon, and stars in heaven. The last three trumpets deal with man. They are called the "three woes" because of the seriousness of the judgment. (40)

The first four trumpets affect one-third of the grass, trees, sea, rivers on earth, and one-third of the sun, moon and stars in the heaven. The seventh trumpet in Revelation 15 is the seven bowls or vial judgments which affect all the grass, trees, sea, rivers and sun, moon, and stars.

The prayers of the saints

> Revelation 8:3-5: Another angel, who had a golden censer, came and stood at the altar. He was given much incense to offer, with the prayers of all the saints, on the golden altar before the throne. The smoke of the incense, together with the prayers of the saints, went up before God from the angel's hand. Then the angel took the censer, filled it with fire from the altar and hurled it on the earth; and there came peals of thunder, rumblings, flashes of lightning and an earthquake. (7)

After the angel offered the incense with the prayers of the saints, he took the censer and filled it with fire from the altar, and hurled it to the earth.

What happened after the angel hurled the censer with fire to the earth?

The scriptures speak of thunder, lightning and earthquakes, which are the judgments of God. The prayers of the saints apparently play an important role in the Wrath of God, in the defeat of Satan, the Beast and the wicked people, and in bringing forth the kingdom of our Lord Jesus Christ on earth.

J.A. Seiss speaks of the fire as a great consumer associated with wrath, torture and destruction of the wicked, taking vengeance upon those who know not God, nor obey the gospel of our Lord Jesus Christ (48).

First trumpet – hail, fire and blood

> Revelation 8:7: The first angel sounded his trumpet, and there came hail and fire mixed with blood, and it was hurled down upon the earth. A third of the earth was burned up, a third of the trees were burned up, and all the green grass was burned up. (7)

The first trumpet judgment is similar to the judgment God poured out on Egypt, during the days of Moses (48).

> Exodus 9:22-25: Now the Lord said to Moses, "Stretch out your hand toward the sky that hail may fall on all the land of Egypt, on man and on beast and on every plant of the field, throughout the land of Egypt." And Moses stretched out his staff toward the sky, and the Lord sent thunder and hail, and fire ran down to the earth. And the Lord rained hail on the land of Egypt. So there was hail, and fire flashing continually in the midst of the hail, very severe, such as had not been in all the land of Egypt since it became a nation. And the hail struck all that was in the field through all the land of Egypt, both man and beast; the hail also struck every plant of the field and shattered every tree of the field. (12)

The first trumpet judgment and the judgment in Egypt are very similar. The only difference is that the judgment in the day of Moses affected only Egypt, while the first trumpet judgment affects one-third of the earth.

Hail and fire mingled with blood

The scripture speaks of hail and fire mixed with blood, falling on the earth. Fire could either be lightning or red-hot fragments from a meteorite.

What is the possible explanation of blood falling out of the sky?

Blood-red rain and blood-red snow has been reported falling on small areas of the earth on a number of occasions. Seiss reported that on August 17, 1819, that Captain Ross saw the mountains at Baffin's Bay covered for eight miles with blood-red snow several feet deep. It was also found on Mt. St. Bernard in 1878. It was recorded in the Roman Senate by Cicero that on one occasion the sky rained blood. (48)

Meteorites are one possible explanation. As a red-hot meteorite travels into the earth's atmosphere, it burns up, leaving dust-like debris of ferric oxide. Ferric oxide, a red water-insoluble pigment, gives a bloody-red appearance in water or snow.

Immanuel Velikovsky reported that blood raining from the sky has been observed in small limited areas in recent times, and that this phenomena was due to red dust coming from volcanic eruptions, or the falling of meteorite dust from cosmic spaces. (49)

Second trumpet – a red hot meteorite the size of a mountain

> Revelation 8:8: The second angel sounded his trumpet, and something like a huge mountain, all ablaze, was thrown into the sea. A third of the sea turned into blood, a third of the living creatures in the sea died, and a third of the ships were destroyed. (7)

The apostle John saw something like a mountain on fire, falling into the sea. This is not an earthly mountain. This is probably a red-hot meteor falling into the sea from outer space. A meteor, as large as a mountain, is a very large meteor.

What would happen if a flaming meteor, as large as a mountain, hit the earth or sea?

A meteor, which fell in Russia, is the only recent indication of what might happen, if a large meteor should hit the earth. Leonid A. Kulik, a mineralogist with Lomonossoff Institute, Russian Academy of Sciences in Moscow, reported that a meteor weighing at least several thousand tons, but not as much as several ten thousand tons, fell in central Siberia on June 30, 1908. At 7:00 A.M., a long blue and white flaming meteor was seen to hit the earth, causing a fireball explosion, sending a column of fire, black smoke and dust high into the atmosphere. The fire scorched and burned trees up to 12.5 miles from the center of the impact. Trees were leveled for 20 to 25 miles in a radial direction from the impact.

Powerful airwaves were recorded on barographs in Western Europe and North America. These airwaves traveled around the world and were registered for the second time at Potsdam, Germany.

A number of nomadic villages were destroyed. A man, whose uncle lived in this area, had over 1500 reindeer that were killed. A man, standing on his porch fifty miles away, was knocked unconscious. These airwaves knocked fences down, 250 miles away. At 375 miles away, an engineer of the Trans-Siberian Railway had to stop his train to keep from being derailed. Horses, 473 miles away, were knocked off their feet. (50, 51)

Trees, being leveled to the ground, are not hard to visualize after the eruption of Mt. St. Helen. The National Geographic described the force behind the eruption of Mt. St. Helen on May 18, 1980 as five hundred Hiroshimas, which leveled trees as far as seventeen miles away. (52)

If a small meteor, as the one in Siberia or the eruption of Mt. St. Helen, can pack such a wallop, then it is understandable how a large meteor the size of a mountain could easily destroy one-third of the fish and ships in the sea. A large meteor, falling into the sea, would produce shock waves and tidal waves, destroying all life in its path just as the eruption of Mt. St. Helen destroyed all trees, birds and animals in its path.

One-third of the sea turned to blood and the fish died

This is similar to a judgment in Egypt.

> Exodus 7:20-21: So Moses and Aaron did even as the Lord had commanded. And he lifted up the staff and struck the water that was in the Nile, in the sight of Pharaoh and in sight of his servants, and all the water that was in the Nile was turned to blood. And the fish that were in the Nile died, and the Nile became foul, so that the Egyptian could not drink water from the Nile. And the blood was through all the land of Egypt. (12)

Exodus shows that the water turning to blood is one of the judgments of God on Egypt. Like in the second trumpet, the fish in the river of Egypt died.

John Leary had a vision of red lava flowing in a crevice or water turning blood-red, and then, he received the following message from Jesus.

> . . . Your age has had many signs to indicate that you are in the end times. The vision is showing you of

severe earthquakes and large crevices as my Second
Coming is near. The red flow represents one of the
plagues you will receive as an angel will turn the
river into blood similar to the plagues of Egypt. . . .
12/31/96 (46)

Ferric oxide, a red hematoid pigment and debris left by a burning meteorite, will kill fish. Whether the phenomena of the sea turning to blood is caused by ferric oxide from a meteorite or stirring
of chemicals in the earth, or by an angel actually turning water into
blood, we do not know.

John Leary has seen a number of visions of a comet striking the
earth. On September 24, 1993, he had a vision of a comet striking
the Atlantic Ocean causing big waves and clouds of dust. He received the following message:

A comet will strike the Atlantic Ocean and it will send
out huge tidal waves. The burning trail will send up
huge clouds of smoke, which will cloud the sun for
three days. Prepare and have your life in order. (45)

On August 8, 1994, John had a vision of a comet headed for the
earth. A number of rockets were sent up to destroy it, but angels de-
flected them. God's justice was about to purify the earth.

Jesus said: ". . . I will purify the earth of all evil, since
it is an abomination in My sight. You are indeed seeing My instrument of destruction, as well as how fu-
tile man's attempt will be. Know I am God and ruler
of the Universe." (43)

Another vision of a comet hitting the ocean and Jesus said:

You are seeing the vehicle of my judgment of the

earth. You will experience a cataclysmic event which will shorten the reign of the Anti-Christ and his persecution of My faithful. Even though the earth will shudder and great events will be terrifying to the inhabitants of earth, know that My ending of evil is near with this event. You will almost welcome this intervention when you see how terribly evil things will get on earth. Those against Me will perform all kinds of perversions and the demons will torment them. I and your guardian angels will show you how to hide and avoid these evil people. You must pray constantly to withstand this time. Do not lose hope, I will be watching over you. It will be unnerving with these events but with your trust in Me you will live to see My splendor even on earth in a short time away. Again pray and be faithful to My will. 5/17/94 (45)

Third trumpet – a second red-hot meteorite hits the earth

Revelation 8:10-11: The third angel sounded his trumpet, and a great star, blazing like a torch, fell from the sky on a third of the rivers and on the springs of water - the name of the star is Wormwood. A third of the waters turned bitter, and many people died from the waters that had become bitter. (7)

A great star, blazing like a torch, falling from the sky, is also a description of a falling star or meteorite. The star or meteor is called Wormwood after a bitter herb because the water is made bitter.

Gordon Lindsay, in his Revelation Series, stated that if a poisonous meteor fell in a mountainous area in Europe where many rivers originate, it could easily poison the water supply of hundreds

154

of millions of people. This would be an overwhelming catastrophe. (40)

There are a number of elements that will cause water to be bitter or poisonous. Iron or nickel plus carbon dioxide form iron carbonyl or nickel carbonyl, which is poisonous. Iron and nickel are found in some meteorites.

If a meteor or a comet hits some nuclear power plants near streams of running water, the radioactive material could easily poison the water supply of hundreds of millions of people. John Leary received the following prophetic words:

> I have shown you nuclear plant problems before. Take note of wormwood of the Apocalypse at Chernobyl. You have seen the destruction of this radioactivity in contaminating this area. Unless care is taken, you may see more problems in this area. 4/10/96 (44)

On September 2, 1995, Mr. Leary had a vision of a flaming comet. Jesus said:

> My people, you are having a preview of the instrument of My purification of the earth. There will rain fire from on high at the proper time. This will consume and confound evil at that time. This will be a dreadful sight, especially for those who refuse Me. It will be a time when all will fall on their knees to ask God's mercy and forgiveness. For my faithful, I will take you up and protect you. For those evil ones, they will wish for death, but they will only find torture of flames. I have promised you I would cleanse the earth and it will be so in My own time. So pray much for your day of vindication My faithful children, for

your sweet reward of heaven on earth lies shortly beyond this coming tribulation. (44)

Fourth trumpet – a third of the sun, moon and stars are darkened

Revelation 8:12: The fourth angel sounded his trumpet, and a third of the sun was struck, a third of the
moon, and a third of the stars, so that a third of them
turned dark. A third of the day was without light, and
also a third of the night. (7)

This phenomena affects the light of the sun, moon and stars so
they don't shine for one-third of the day and one-third of the night.
Whether this is an eclipse of the sun and moon, somehow affecting
the stars or a period of darkness, due to some other obstruction, no
one knows.

There was a period of darkness for three days and nights during
the plagues in Egypt.

Exodus 10:21-22: Then the Lord said to Moses,
"Stretch out your hand toward the sky so that darkness will spread over Egypt - darkness that can be
felt." So Moses stretched out his hand toward the
sky, and total darkness covered all Egypt for three
days. No one could see anyone else or leave his place
for three days. (7)

There was a period of darkness from the sixth hour to the
ninth hour, when Jesus was being crucified on the cross (Matthew
27:45). (40)

What are the three woes?

Revelation 8:13: As I watched, I heard an eagle that
was flying in midair call out in a loud voice: "Woe!

Woe! Woe to the inhabitants of the earth, because of the trumpet blasts about to be sounded by the other three angels." (7)

The three woes are the three last trumpets, i.e., fifth, sixth and seventh trumpets, as shown in Revelation 8:13, 9:12 and 11:4. They are called the three woes, because these judgments are more severe than the first four trumpets.

CHAPTER 13
First Woe

Fifth trumpet – a star falls from heaven with a key to the bottomless pit.

> Revelation 9:1-2: And the fifth angel sounded, and I saw a star from heaven which had fallen to the earth; and the key of the bottomless pit was given to him. And he opened the bottomless pit; and smoke went up out of the pit, like smoke of a great furnace; and the sun and the air were darkened by the smoke of the pit. (12)

What is the star from heaven, which had fallen to the earth?

Stars are often spoken of as fixed objects in a constellation or as falling or shooting stars or meteorites. Stars are also often referred to as angels.

This star is referred to as an intelligent being since a key to the bottomless pit was given to him. This star appears to be Satan. Jesus, in Luke 10:18 said "I saw Satan fall like lightning from heaven." Isaiah speaks of Satan as a morning star, cast down to the earth.

> Isaiah 14:12-15: How you have fallen from heaven, O morning star, son of dawn! You have been cast down to the earth, . . . You said in your heart, "I will ascend to heaven; I will raise my throne above the stars of God; I will sit enthroned on the mount of assembly,

on the utmost heights of the sacred mountain. I will
ascend above the tops of the clouds; I will make myself like the Most High." But you are brought down
to the grave, to the depths of the pit. (7)

Revelation 12:4, 9 speaks of Satan as the great dragon and one-
third of the stars of heaven (fallen angels) being thrown to the earth.
The bottomless pit is a place where fallen angels are locked up for a
period of time or until judgment.

II Peter 2:4: . . . God did not spare angels when they
sinned, but cast them into hell and committed them
to pits of darkness, reserved for judgment; (12)

In Luke, a legion of demons was talking to Jesus, begging Him
not to command them to go to the bottomless pit.

Luke 8:31: And they begged him (Jesus) not to command them to depart into the abyss (the bottomless
pit) (31).

As shown in Revelation 9:14, some angels were bound in the
area of the great river Euphrates. These fallen angels apparently
were bound or locked up at some time in the past. As shown in
Daniel 10, there was a battle between Michael the Archangel and
his angels against the prince of Persia. They fought for 21 days. The
fallen angels that were defeated may have been taken captive and
thrown into the pit, or bound in some place as the river Euphrates.
Daniel 10:20 indicated that when the prince of Persia is defeated, the
prince of Greece will come and take his place. (53)

Plague of locusts

Revelation 9:3-11: And out of the smoke came forth
locusts upon the earth; and power was given them, as

the scorpions of the earth have power. And they were told that they should not hurt the grass of the earth, nor any green things, nor any tree, but only the men who do not have the seal of God on their foreheads. And they were not permitted to kill anyone, but to torment for five months; and their torment was like the torment of a scorpion when it stings a man. And in those days men will seek death and will not find it; and they will long to die and death flees from them. And the appearance of locusts was like horses prepared for battle; and on their heads as it were, crowns like gold, and their faces were like the faces of men. And they had hair like the hair of women, and their teeth were the teeth of lions. And they had breastplates like breastplates of iron; and the sound of their wings was like the sound of chariots, of many horses rushing to battle. And they have tails like scorpions, and stings; and in their tails is power to hurt men for five months. They have a king over them, the angel of the abyss; his name in Hebrew is Abaddon, and in Greek he has the name Apollyon. (12)

Huge Flying Scorpions

On January 2, 1996, John Leary had a vision of thousands of huge flying scorpions, each one about the size of three men. Jesus said:

> My people, you are witnessing in this vision one of the many plagues I will send to punish those who have rejected Me. These scorpions are the instruments of My punishment, by which they will sting the people many times, but they will not die just now. They will feel fiery darts that will sicken these condemned souls. Those who reject Me in the tribulation,

160

and give themselves over to the evil one, will suffer much. They will wish they were dead, but death will elude them until they have witnessed all of My chastisements. My faithful, your small sufferings will pale to those that these poor souls will suffer. These evil souls will have been warned in their life review of this choice for Me vs. Satan. For those who still choose Satan after being supernaturally warned, they deserve all manner of punishment they will receive for rejecting My love. (44)

What are the locusts that came out of the smoke from the pit?

The locusts that come out of the smoke from the furnace of the pit are not ordinary locusts, but are obviously spirit beings that rebelled against God and were locked up in the pit. Good angels and spirit beings like the four living creatures with four faces standing before the throne are not locked up. (53)

The characteristic of these demon spirits is that they have:

1. bodies like horses.
2. faces like men
3. hair like women
4. teeth like the lion.
5. breastplates like iron.
6. a crown of gold on their head.
7. wings that sound like many horse-drawn chariots going to battle.
8. tails like scorpions with a sting to torment men for five months. (Note - I have been stung by a scorpion. The sting of a scorpion burns like fire and is very painful.)

Spirit beings such as the Lord, the angels, Satan, fallen angels and demons are not visible to the human eye. John wrote down the things he saw in the spirit.

The Lord's army of horses and chariots

In II Kings 6:8-17, the king of Syria was warring against Israel. The king of Israel always knew what the king of Syria was doing. The king of Syria learned that Elisha was passing information about Syria to the king of Israel, and as a consequence, could never slip up on Israel. The king of Syria sent a great army with horses and chariots by night and surrounded Elisha. Early the next morning, the servant of Elisha saw an army of horses and chariots surrounding the city. He asked, "What shall we do?" Elisha said, "Fear not, for those with us are more than those against us." Then Elisha prayed that the Lord would open the servant's eyes that he might see. The Lord opened the young man's eyes, and he saw mountains full of horses and chariots of fire around Elisha.

The Lord's army of horses and chariots were on the mountains ready to defend Elisha but they were not visible to the natural eye. It was only when Elisha prayed that his servant could see the spiritual world.

There is a question as to whether or not the locust creatures out of the pit were visible to the natural eye. The scripture speaks of these creatures tormenting men for five months. Demon spirits are able to harass, torment and inflict sickness, diseases and plagues without being seen.

In Job 2:7, Satan went out from the presence of the Lord and afflicted Job with painful sores from the top of his head to the soles of his feet. We read in I Corinthians 5:5 that Paul handed a sinful man over to Satan for the destruction of the flesh so that his spirit might

162

be saved in the day of the Lord.

Jesus healed those that were blind, deaf, lame and sick by casting out demons (Matthew 4:23-24, 8:14-17, 8:28-34, 15:22-28, 17:14-18).

As with Job and the man Paul handed over to Satan, the blind, deaf, lame and sick were not able to see Satan or the demons that afflicted and tormented them. People may not necessarily see the locusts with tails of scorpions, which will torment them.

The heavenly army

The heavenly army did not fight a physical battle with the king of Syria, whose army just suddenly became blind and helpless. Elisha rounded them up on ropes, and led them single file to the king of Israel.

The locusts from the pit

The locusts out of the pit are not like ordinary locusts or grasshoppers, as they do not have the features or descriptions of locusts. These locusts were given orders not to hurt the grass, plants, or trees, but to torment those people who did not have the seal of the living God on their forehead for five months. An ordinary locust (grasshopper) feeds on grass and plants. These creatures from the pit had a king over them, while ordinary locusts do not have a king. The spirit beings from the pit were called locusts because of their large numbers as would be seen in a swarm of locusts (grasshoppers).

The book of Joel speaks of an army of locusts with the teeth of a lion, the fangs of a lioness, the appearance of horses and the sound of many chariots inflicting all kinds of plagues upon the land. This is similar to the events described in the fifth trumpet in Revelation 9. These creatures from the pit that are tormenting men without the seal of the living God, and causing all kinds of plagues, will most likely not be visible to the human eye. These creatures will be Satan's army, just as the mountains full of horses and chariots that surrounded Elisha, were the heavenly army that blinded the Syrian army. This is part of the spiritual warfare of which Paul wrote in Ephesians 6:12.

Sun and air darkened

> Revelation 9:1-2 speaks of the sun and air being darkened by the smoke that rises from the bottomless pit.

On October 29, 1993, John Leary received the following message from the Lord:

> ". . . When the demons will come, there will be so many as to blot out the sun if they had material bodies. You forget they still have angelic powers and could deceive even the elect. This is why I call on you all to a constant life of prayer so you will have the spiritual strength to overcome these future temptations. Stay close to Me and you will save your soul. (45)

If the demons are not visible, what is the possible explanation of the sun and air being darkened?

We need to remember that Satan is the prince and power of the air and darkness (Ephesians 6:12). In the book of Job, Satan manifested himself in a storm and took the lives of Job's children (Job 1:18-19). When the apostles woke Jesus from a deep sleep, there was a storm raging over the Sea of Galilee. Jesus rebuked the storm as if it were a demon spirit (Mark 4:36-39, Luke 8:23-24).

Satan and his angels can manifest themselves in the elements of the earth and the air to darken the air and the sun.

Comet's debris and smoke from volcanic eruptions is another possible explanation.

On July 23, 1996, John Leary had a vision of a large volcano spewing out black smoke, which covered the sun. Jesus said,

> My son, you are seeing a massive volcanic eruption in this vision where dark smoke was evolving. It is true that you will continue to see volcanic eruptions increase, but this one will occur as the comet strikes the earth. There will be a tremendous distortion of the earth's crust which will give rise to many such volcanoes. It will be a combination of these eruptions and the comet's own debris that will give rise to three days of darkness. Other repercussions will be a changing of the magnetic poles from their present position, and also a brief change in the earth's orbit away from the sun. The gravity of the sun will correct this change in orbit, but for a while the earth will be colder. It is during these three days of darkness that a cave or underground dwelling will afford you the best protection from the cold and the sulfur in the air depleting the oxygen for a short duration. Pray, My people, and listen to My instructions, and I will direct you where to go and how I will feed you with My Heavenly Bread. (41)

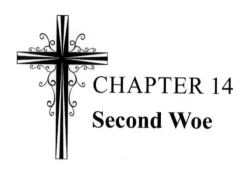

CHAPTER 14
Second Woe

Sixth trumpet – four angels slay one-third of mankind.

Revelation 9:12-19: The first woe is past; behold, two woes are still coming after these things. And the sixth angel sounded, and I heard a voice from the four horns of the golden altar which is before God, one saying to the sixth angel who had the trumpet, "Release the four angels who are bound at the great river Euphrates." And the four angels, who had been prepared for the hour and day and month and year, were released, so that they might kill a third of mankind. And the number of the armies of the horsemen was two hundred million; I heard the number of them. And this is how I saw in the vision the horses and those who sat on them: the riders had breastplates the color of fire and hyacinth and of brimstone; and the heads of the horses are like the heads of lions; and out of their mouths proceed fire, smoke and brimstone. A third of mankind was killed by these three plagues, by the fire and the smoke and the brimstone, which proceeded out of their mouths. For the power of the horses is in their mouths and in their tails; for their tails are like serpents and have heads; and with them they do harm. (12)

What is the significance of the golden altar with four horns?

The golden altar with four horns before the throne of God is similar to the altar that was in the temple in the wilderness and in Jerusalem. The altar with horns is mentioned in Exodus 37:26 and Amos 3:14.

In the Old Testament, the altar was one of mercy. Now the altar is calling for judgment. At this time, wickedness of the earth is so great, that the altar, which ordinarily gives mercy, is crying for vengeance. The cry of the four horns of the altar comes from the immediate presence of God, indicating the intensity of the demand for vengeance (retribution). (47, 53)

Who are the four angels bound at the Euphrates River?

The four angels bound at the Euphrates River are bad angels, as good angels are not bound (48).

Peter and Jude speak of angels being confined to hell.

> II Peter 2:4: For if God did not spare angels when they sinned, but cast them into hell and committed them to pits of darkness, reserved for judgment; . . . (12).

> Jude 6: And angels who did not keep their own domain, but abandoned their proper abode, He has kept in eternal bonds under darkness for the judgment of the great day (12).

The Greek word for hell is not Hades but Tartarus, which is a prison for angels. Whether the prison for the angels at the river Euphrates is the same as Tartarus we do not know (53).

What does the scripture mean that the angels were prepared for the hour, day, month and year to slay one-third of mankind?

The Lord knows everything that has happened, or is going to happen from the beginning to the end. The Lord had the evil angels prepared or ready to slay one-third of mankind at the appropriate moment and time that only He knows.

Who are the 200,000,000 horsemen?

These creatures and their riders are probably the spirit beings that were called locusts, which were released from the pit during the fifth trumpet. They were commanded not to kill, but to torment men who are without the seal of the living God for five months. With the release of the four angels at the river Euphrates during the sixth trumpet, the time has come to slay one-third of mankind with all kinds of plagues.

The riders of these 200,000,000 horses are obviously fallen angels, as there is no earthly army with this many soldiers and horses. The horses are similar to the creatures previously described, with the heads of lions and tails of serpents. Mankind is killed by fire, smoke and brimstone, the elements of hell, which proceed from horses' mouths. These creatures will go throughout the world, killing with all kinds of plagues, just as the angels of death killed people and animals during the Passover in Egypt (Exodus 11 and 12), and also when David committed the sin of taking a census of the people in Israel (II Samuel 24:1-25).

When the sixth trumpet sounded, the four angels, the princes of Satan apparently assumed leadership over the locust-like creatures that came up out of the pit during the fifth trumpet, to kill one-third of mankind. During the first woe, they were not allowed to kill. Now they have permission to kill men.

Will the woes cause men to repent?

> Revelation 9:20-21: And the rest of mankind, who were not killed by these plagues, did not repent of the works of their hands, so as not to worship demons, and

idols of gold and of silver and of brass and of stone and of wood, which can neither see nor hear nor walk; and they did not repent of their murders nor of their sorceries nor of their immorality nor of their thefts. (12)

Man has hardened his heart against God and will not repent. There is no indication that the 144,000 Jews are evangelizing anyone to the Lord.

The mighty angel

Revelation 10:1-3: And I saw another strong angel coming down out of heaven, clothed with a cloud; and the rainbow was upon his head, and his face was like the sun, and his feet like pillars of fire; and he had in his hand a little book which was open. And he placed his right foot on the sea and his left on the land; and he cried out with a loud voice, as when a lion roars; . . . (12)

Who is the strong angel?

Gordon Lindsay, F. J. Dake and J. A. Seiss all believe that the strong and mighty angel is Christ (53, 35, 48). The reasons are:

1. The angel was clothed in a cloud. Jesus is spoken of as coming on a cloud (Matthew 24:30).
2. The angel had the rainbow upon his head. The rainbow was a sign of the covenant God made with man to never destroy the earth by water again. The rainbow was around the heavenly throne in Revelation 4.
3. The angel's face was like the sun. The Son of Man's face was like the sun in Revelation 1:16. In Matthew 17:2, Christ's face shone like the sun when He was transfigured.

4. The angel's feet were spoken of as a pillar of fire. Revelation 1:15 speaks of the Son of Man's feet like burnished bronze, which glows in a furnace.

5. The angel cried out with a loud voice as when a lion roars. The Lion of the tribe of Judah is one of the characteristics of Jesus.

6. The angel, in Revelation 11:3, speaks of the two witnesses as "my two

Witnesses." No angel other than Christ could speak of the two witnesses as "My two witnesses".

7. In the Old Testament, the Son of God is described as Jehovah - Angel (48).

8. Jesus has appeared, in the book of Revelation, as a Lamb, a Lion and an armed warrior with a bow. There is nothing to prevent His appearance as an angel, since men are also seen as angels. The angels that poured the bowl or vial of judgments during the seventh trumpet are redeemed men.

We will discuss this in Chapter 24.

The open book

> Revelation 10:2: . . . and he had in his hand a little book which was open. And he placed his right foot on the sea and his left on the land. (12)

What is the open book the angel had in His hand?

As we have shown above, the angel is Christ. The book is called an open book, indicating that it was once a closed, sealed book (48). In Revelation 5, Christ received a book sealed with seven seals. William DeBurgh believed the sealed book is the book that God told Daniel to seal until the time of the end. When Christ had opened the seventh seal, the book became an open book. DeBurgh called this book the "title deed to the earth". (38) This was discussed in Chapter 8. The opening of the book of seven seals was steps in the process of defeating Satan and reclaiming and taking possession of the earth.

The angel, who was Christ, had His right foot on the sea and His left foot on the land. This act, which was the symbolic way the children of Israel took possession of the land in the Old Testament time, is befitting of Christ, but not for a created angel. (48)

> Deuteronomy 11:24: Every place on which the sole of your foot shall tread shall be yours; . . . (12).

Now Christ, as He stands on the land and the sea, is about to take possession of the earth. Who can resist the Lord, whose legs are as pillars of fire, standing on the land and sea? (53).

Book, sweet as honey, yet bitter

> Revelation 10:8-10: And the voice which I heard from heaven, I heard again speaking with me, and saying, "Go take the book which is open in the hand of the angel who stands on the sea and on the land." And I went to the angel, telling him to give me the little book. And he said to me, "take it, and eat it; and it will make your stomach bitter, but in your mouth it will be sweet as honey." And I took the little book out of the angel's hand and ate it, and it was in my mouth sweet as honey; and when I had eaten it, my stomach was made bitter. (12)

Why was the book sweet as honey in John's mouth, but bitter in his stomach?

The little book, being the title deed to the earth, was given back to man. John, being a representative of God's elect, ate the book to take full possession of the earth. The book, the title deed to the earth, was as sweet as honey in his mouth because it was joyful, wonderful and exciting for man to have possession and control of the earth again. The book became bitter in John's stomach because of the wrath of God that was to be poured out to take the final possession of the earth. (53)

Ezekiel was told to eat a scroll

> Ezekiel 2:8-10, 3:1-4, 7: Now you, son of man, listen to what I am speaking to you; do not be rebellious like that rebellious house. Open your mouth and eat what I am giving you." Then I looked, behold, a hand was extended to me; and lo a scroll was in it. When He spread it out before me, it was written on the front and back; and written on it were lamentation, mourning and woe. Then He said to me, "Son of man, eat what you find; eat this scroll, and go, speak to the house of Israel." So I opened my mouth, and He fed me this scroll. And He said to me, "Son of man, feed your stomach, and fill your body with this scroll which I am giving you." Then I ate it, and it was sweet as honey in my mouth. Then He said to me, "Son of man, go to the house of Israel and speak with My words to them. . . . yet the house of Israel will not be willing to listen to you, . . . (12)

Ezekiel is speaking to the house of Israel, a rebellious people prior to Babylonian captivity. The scroll speaks of mourning, lamentation and wailing, which will take place with the destruction of Jerusalem, and for those living in exile. The scroll contains the judgment of God. This is similar to the open scroll or book of the seven seals that spoke of the Great Tribulation and Wrath of God.

Similar to the scroll in Revelation, the scroll in Ezekiel, the Word of God, was sweet as honey in the mouth. Though the word, bitter in the stomach, was not spoken of in Ezekiel, it does speak of judgment and difficult times for the people in Babylon captivity, which is bitter.

CHAPTER 15
My Two Witnesses

The two witnesses will prophesy for 1260 days.

> Revelation 11:3-4: And I will grant authority to my
> two witnesses, and they will prophesy for twelve
> hundred and sixty days, clothed in sackcloth. These
> are the two olive trees and two lampstands that stand
> before the Lord of the earth. (12)

Who are the two witnesses?

This scripture says the two witnesses are the two olive trees and
two lampstands who stand before the Lord of the earth. The two olive trees and two lampstands are first mentioned in Zechariah. In
Zechariah 4:14, the two olive trees and the two lampstands are called
the anointed ones, who are standing by the Lord of the whole earth.

Is Elijah, the Prophet, One of the Two Witnesses?

> Malachi 4:5-6: Behold, I am going to send you Elijah
> the prophet before the coming of the great and ter-
> rible day of the Lord. And he will restore the hearts
> of the fathers to their children, and the hearts of the
> children to their fathers, lest I come and smite the
> land with a curse. (12)

This scripture shows that Elijah will return to the earth before
that great and terrible day of the Lord.

Is John the Baptist Elijah?

The angel talking to Zacharias, the father of John the Baptist about John said:

> Luke 1:17: And it is he who will go as a forerunner before Him in the spirit and power of Elijah, to turn the hearts of the fathers back to the children, and the disobedient to the attitude of the righteous; so as to make ready a people prepared for the Lord. (12)

This scripture did not say John the Baptist was Elijah, but that he went forth in the spirit and power of Elijah.

The disciples ask Jesus about the coming of Elijah. Jesus said:

> Matthew 17:11-13: . . . Elias indeed is to come and will restore all things. But I say to you Elias has come already, and they did not know him, . . . Then the disciples understood that he had spoken to them of John the Baptist (9).

(Elias is another spelling for Elijah.)

John the Baptist was asked if he were Elijah?

> John 1:21, 23: And they asked him, "What then? Are you Elijah?" And he said, I am not." Are you the Prophet?" And he answered, "No." . . . He said, "I am a voice of one crying in the wilderness, 'Make straight the way of the Lord,' as Isaiah the prophet said." (12)

John the Baptist said he was not Elijah. John should know if he were Elijah. As John the Baptist was the forerunner at the first coming of Christ, Elijah will be the forerunner at the second coming of Christ, just before the great and terrible day of the Lord (54).

St. Augustine said, "It is a familiar theme in the conversation and heart of the faithful, that in the last days before the judgment, the Jews shall believe in the true Christ, that is our Christ, by means of this great and admirable prophet Elias* who shall expound the law to them." (55)

Jerome wrote, "Elias himself, who will truly come in the body at the second coming of Christ, has now come in the spirit through the medium of John the Baptist" (56).

The scriptures teach that Elijah never died, that he was taken up to heaven alive, and that he will return to the earth before the great and terrible day of the Lord.

If Elijah, an Old Testament prophet, is one of the two witnesses, then the other witness will obviously be an Old Testament prophet. This is because the time of the gentiles is over. God is dealing with the Jews during the seventieth week of Daniel.

Who is the second witness?

Many theologians believe that Enoch will be the second witness.

> Hebrews 11:5: By faith Enoch was taken up so that he should not see death; and he was not found because God took him up; for he obtained the witness that before his being taken up he was pleasing to God (12).

The scriptures teach that Enoch should not see death. The scriptures do not say Elijah should not see death (54). Since the scriptures say that Enoch should not see death, Enoch cannot be the second witness, as the two witnesses are killed on the streets of Jerusalem.

If Enoch is not the second witness, what Old Testament prophet could be the second witness?

The Jerome Biblical Commentary reported that the Jewish

176

tradition holds that the two witnesses will be Moses and Elijah, and that they will return to the earth to preach repentance before the great and terrible day of the Lord (56). The day of the Lord occurs during the seventieth week of Daniel, immediately after the Great Tribulation and the Harvest Rapture, before the Lord's second coming to the earth.

The big question is, if Moses died and was buried, how could he be the second witness?

Even though Moses died and was buried (Moses was buried by the Lord, not by the Israelites - Deuteronomy 34:5-6) as the Bible teaches, it could be that Moses was raised again in his physical body as some of the Old Testament people instead of in a glorified body. Examples:

1. Elijah raised the widow's son from the dead.
2. Jesus raised Lazarus from the dead.

If Moses were raised from the dead, there was no way he could be resurrected in a glorified body because Jesus had not yet been raised from the dead. If Moses were actually resurrected in a glorified body, how could Jesus be the first fruit of them that slept? (I Corinthians 15:20) (54)

Dispute over the corpse of Moses

The scriptures teach in Jude 9 that there was a dispute over the body of Moses.

> Jude 9: Not even the Archangel Michael, when he was engaged in argument with the devil about the corpse of Moses, dared to denounce him in the language of abuse; all he said was "Let the Lord correct you" (57).

"A New Catholic Commentary on Holy Scripture" by Fuller, Johnston and Kearns, in reply to Satan arguing with Michael the Archangel over the body of Moses in Jude 9 made reference to Origen's belief in the assumption of Moses after his death.

Origen (185 - 255 AD) an early Christian writer and commentator in Clement Alexandria expressed the belief in his *"Adumbrationes in Epistulam Jude, De Principilis_3,2,1"* that Moses in his physical body was raised from the dead and taken up to heaven after his death. (58)

The footnote in the *New Jerusalem Bible* says, "Almost certainly a reference to the apocryphal assumption of Moses." It is interesting that the commentators of the New Jerusalem Bible find that this passage refers to Moses' body being taken up to heaven and then say that the scripture doesn't mean what it says.

When interpreting scripture, there is danger in saying the scripture doesn't mean what it says, or doesn't say what it means, unless there are other scriptures to show that there has to be another interpretation.

The question is, if Moses' body were to be left in the grave, why would there be an argument between Michael the Archangel and the devil about a corpse that would rot to dust? The only reason for the devil to argue would be that Moses was actually raised physically from the dead.

If Elijah and Enoch were taken up to heaven in a physical body before Jesus was raised from the dead, is there any reason why Moses could not have been taken up in a physical body? It is interesting that Moses, though he was 120 years old, when he died, his eyes were not weak nor was his strength gone (Deuteronomy 34:5-7). (54)

The transfiguration

> Matthew 17:1-3: And six days later Jesus took with Him Peter and James and John his brother, and brought them up to a high mountain by themselves. And He was transfigured before them; and His face shone like the sun, and His garment became white as light. And behold, Moses and Elijah appeared to them, talking with Him. (12)

Notice that Moses and Elijah appeared at the transfiguration and were seen talking to Jesus.

What kind of body did Moses have at the Mount of Transfiguration?

1. Moses and Elijah were both seen talking to Jesus.
2. Jesus had a physical body.
3. Elijah had a physical body as he was taken up alive to heaven.
4. The transfiguration took place before Jesus was crucified and was raised from the dead. Scripture says that Jesus was the first of them that slept to be raised from the dead (I Corinthians 15:20). There was no way Moses could have a glorified body at the Mount of Transfiguration.

Since Elijah has a physical body, and Jesus had not yet been crucified and raised from the dead, Moses had to have had a resurrected physical body.

The two witnesses have the power of Moses and Elijah.

> Revelation 11:5-6: And if any one desires to harm them, fire proceeds out of their mouth and devours

their enemies; and if any one would desire to harm them, in this manner he must be killed. These have the power to shut up the sky, in order that rain may not fall during the days of their prophesying; and they have power over the waters to turn them into blood, and smite the earth with every plague, as often as they desire. (12)

The two witnesses will have the power to do the things that both Elijah and Moses did, when they were on earth:

1. Fire proceeds out of their mouth and devours their enemies. Elijah had the power to call fire (lightning) down from heaven to destroy his enemies (I Kings 18:38, II Kings 1:10-12).

2. The two witnesses have the power to shut up the sky so that rain may not fall during the days of their prophesy. Elijah had this power.

   James 5:17: Elijah . . . He prayed earnestly that it would not rain, and it did not rain on the land for three and a half years. Again he prayed, and the heaven gave rain and the earth produced its crops (7).

3. The three and a half years mention in this scripture is the time the two witnesses are on earth during the seventieth week of Daniel. This is the time given to the Antichrist to wage war against the Christians and the Jews. This is the time left in the seventieth week of Daniel, when the covenant is broken with the abomination and desolation of the temple.

4. They have the power to turn water into blood. Moses had the power to turn water into blood (Exodus 7:19-20).

5. The two witnesses have power to smite the earth with every plague as often as they desire. Moses had the power to call down plagues.

The two witnesses have power to do the identical things that Moses and Elijah did, while they were on earth. Since the scriptures teach that:

1. Elijah, an Old Testament prophet, will return to the earth before the great and terrible day of the Lord, then the second witness would probably be an Old Testament prophet, as God is dealing with Israel.
2. Both Moses and Elijah were present at Jesus' transfiguration.
3. Both Moses and Elijah were talking to Jesus.
4. Jesus and Elijah had physical bodies; Moses would have had to have a physical body.
5. The two witnesses have the power to do what Moses and Elijah did on earth.
6. Jude 9 implies that Moses' body was taken from the grave.

These teachings indicate that Moses could possibly be the second witness. Though the scriptures seem to support the fact that Moses is the second witness, there is no way we can be dogmatic about this.

When do the two witnesses appear?

Revelation 11:3: And I will give power to my two witnesses, and they will prophesy for 1,260 days, . . . (7).

Twelve hundred and sixty days is the same as three and one-half years. This is the time that is left in the seventieth week of Daniel after the Beast breaks the covenant with Israel in the middle of the week. Since the two witnesses are killed during the sixth trumpet (the time of the second woe), before the seventh trumpet (the time of the third woe), prior to the end of the seventieth week of Daniel, they will have to appear on the scene before the abomination and desolation of the temple takes place.

Table 4 shows that the two witnesses appearing on the scene before the Great Tribulation begin to warn the people to repent and not to take the mark of the Beast.

Two witnesses are killed

> Revelation 11:7-8: And when they have finished their testimony, the beast that comes out of the abyss will make war with them, and overcome them and kill them. And their dead bodies will lie in the street of the great city which mystically is called Sodom and Egypt, where also their Lord was crucified. (12)

The Beast, who is discussed in Revelation 13, is allowed to overcome the two witnesses and kill them. Their bodies will lie on the street of the great city Jerusalem, where their Lord was also crucified. All nations will look at their dead bodies.

> Revelation 11:9: And those from the people and tribes and tongues and nations will look at their dead bodies for three days and a half, and will not permit their dead bodies to be laid in a tomb (12).

How will all nations of the world be able to view the dead bodies?

Before this century, everyone thought this would have been impossible. With television and satellites, all nations of the world will be able to view the corpses of the two witnesses. This was foretold long before we knew how this could be possible.

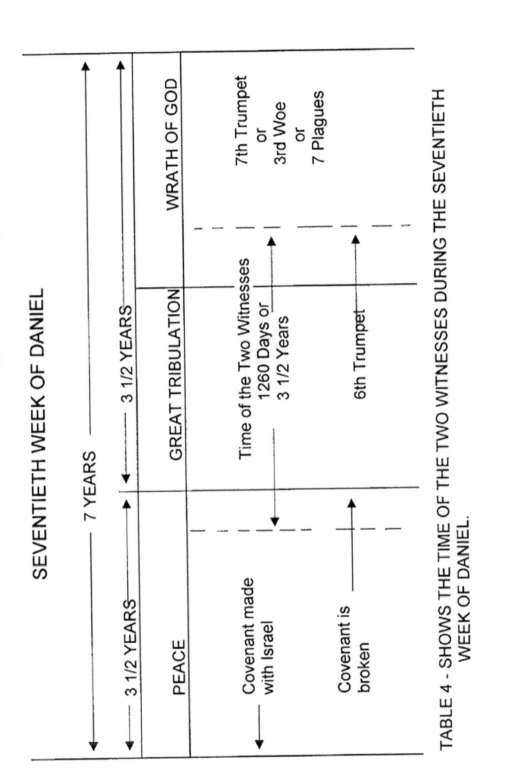

TABLE 4 - SHOWS THE TIME OF THE TWO WITNESSES DURING THE SEVENTIETH WEEK OF DANIEL.

People will rejoice because the two witnesses are dead.

> Revelation 11:10: And those who dwell on the earth
> will rejoice over them and make merry; and they will
> send gifts to one another, because these two prophets
> tormented those who dwell on the earth (12).

The two witnesses, coming on the scene before the Great Tribulation, have been preaching and tormenting those that dwell on earth for forty-two months with plagues, famines, drought, turning water into blood, etc. Just as Moses called the plagues on Egypt, the two witnesses are somehow involved in calling down the trumpet judgments with the exception of the seventh trumpet. The two witnesses are killed during the sixth trumpet. The people will hate the two witnesses as they associated them with the plagues, drought, famines, pestilence and torment. During the time of their prophecies, no one was able to hurt or harm them. Anyone who attempted to harm them was killed.

Now the people of the world are rejoicing because the two witnesses who tormented them for three and a half years are dead. People are celebrating the death of the two witnesses with big parties and sending gifts to one another.

People of all nations of the world will want to view the bodies of the two witnesses that tormented them, not permitting them to be buried. The Beast is a hero, because he has killed the two witnesses that tormented them for so long. (54)

The two witnesses are resurrected

> Revelation 11:11-13: And after three days and a half
> the breath of life from God came into them, and they
> stood on their feet; and great fear fell upon those who
> were beholding them. And they heard a loud voice from

heaven saying to them, "Come up here." And they went up into heaven in the cloud, and their enemies beheld them. And in that hour there was a great earthquake, and a tenth of the city fell; and seven thousand people were killed in the earthquake, and the rest were terrified and gave glory to the God of heaven. (12)

The two witnesses, after being killed by the Beast and laying in the street of Jerusalem for three and a half days, will come back to life, and will be taken up to heaven. Fear will come upon the people. An earthquake will destroy one-tenth of the city and kill 7,000 people. The Beast is now exposed. He is no longer a hero. The people are now giving the glory to God. (54)

How do we know the two witnesses are killed during the sixth trumpet?

After discussing the two witnesses, Revelation 11:14 says, "The second woe is past, the third woe is coming quickly" (12). The two witnesses are killed during the second woe, which is the sixth trumpet.

About 13 years after I wrote this chapter on the two witnesses, I had a vision as I glanced upward into the heavens; I saw two small specks of silver light. While my prayer partner and I were praying for an understanding, the following words came to us.

These are my two sons of righteousness, Elijah and Moses. Their light will become brighter and brighter as the days go on.

I had a vision of a white bearded man standing next to me looking sideway toward the ground. It is interesting that my prayer partner received understanding that this man was Moses.

This man is Moses. He was standing beside you explaining what is going to happen to the earth. Moses said I had written of it and will understand. Prayer partner asked, "Why Mike?" Moses responded, "He will be part of what was, what is and what is to come!"

Seventh trumpet - third woe – the seven plagues – the Kingdom of this World becomes the Kingdom of our Lord Jesus Christ.

Revelation 11:15: And the seventh angel sounded; and there arose loud voices in heaven, saying, "The kingdom of the world becomes the kingdom of our Lord, and of His Christ; and He will reign forever and ever" (12).

What is the third woe, which is the seventh trumpet?

You will notice that there is no discussion in Revelation 11 on the seventh trumpet or the third woe. The seventh trumpet or the third woe is not discussed until Revelation 15, where scripture says the Wrath of God is finished with the seven plagues.

CHAPTER 16
Second Chronological Series

What evidence do we have that Revelation 12 goes back to Revelation 4, which is the beginning of the Great Tribulation, and that Revelation 12 through 22 has to be superimposed over Revelation 4 through 11?

1. The Beast or Antichrist makes a covenant with Israel for one week (7 years). He breaks the covenant in the middle of the week which means there are three and one half years or 42 months left in the seventieth week of Daniel after the covenant is broken.

2. Revelation 13:5-7, speaks of the Beast being given the power for 42 months to wage war with the saints and to overcome them.

3. Revelation 4 through 11 covers the last three and half years of the seventieth week of Daniel. The scripture says with the sounding of the seventh trumpet in Revelation 11:15 it is finished for the kingdom of this world has becomes the kingdom of our Lord Jesus Christ.

4. In Revelation 12, the sun-clothed woman flees into the wilderness for 1260 days or 42 months after the birth of the man-child. There cannot be an additional 42 months after Revelation 11:15 as the Beast only has power to wage war against God's people for 42 months. This means Revelation 12 to 22 has to overlap Revelation 4 through 11 to fit within the

time-frame of the seventieth week of Daniel.

5. The Great Tribulation is over in Revelation 6 with the darkening of the sun and the moon turning blood-red as spoken in Matthew 24:29-31. The tribulation saints are standing before the throne before the Lamb in Revelation 7. If the Beast does not come into power until Revelation 13, then who killed the saints in the Great Tribulation?

6. An angel in Revelation 14:9 flies through the air warning people not to take the mark of the Beast. Why is the warning given in Revelation 14 to not take the mark of the Beast when the Great Tribulation is over in Revelation 6:12 with the opening of the sixth seal?

7. How can the Beast kill the two witnesses during the sixth trumpet in Revelation 11, if he does not come into power until Revelation 13?

All of these questions and statements show that the Beast or the Antichrist cannot come into power after the Great Tribulation and trumpet judgments are over in Revelation 11. After the sounding of the seventh trumpet, the scripture says everything is finished, for the kingdom of this world has becomes the kingdom of our Lord and His Son, Jesus. This proves that Revelation 12 through 22 is a new chronological series that has to be superimposed over Revelation 4 through 11 to fit within the time-frame of the seventieth week of Daniel as shown in Table 5. Revelation 12 through 22 covers the Great Tribulation, the Wrath of God and the millennium filling in details not covered in the first chronological series. (29)

Table 5 shows that the Sun-clothed woman gives birth to the Man-child just prior to the beginning of the Great Tribulation, and flees into the wilderness for three and one-half years, which is the time of the Great Tribulation and the Wrath of God.

THE SEVENTIETH WEEK OF DANIEL				MILLENNIUM	ETERNITY
MID-NIGHT HOUR MAN-CHILD RAPTURE →	THE GREAT TRIBULATION	DAY OF THE LORD →		WHITE THRONE JUDGEMENT →	
		HARVEST RAPTURE	WRATH OF GOD		NEW HEAVEN NEW EARTH
Covenant made - beginning of the 70th week of Daniel	Covenant broken in middle of week	6th Seal Sun is darkened Moon turned blood-red 144,000 Jews Rev. 6:12-17 and 7:9-17	7th Seal Seven trumpets Last 3 trumpets are 3 Woes. 3rd Woe not discussed in Rev. 11 or Rev. 8-11	Christ reigns as visible King and High Priest on earth. Satan is chained for 1,000 years	God the Father will be visible and will live on earth among the people
	Five Seals of book opened Rev. 4:1-6:11				
	144,000 First Fruits before the throne Rev. 12:17 - 14:13	Son of Man on cloud and every eye shall see Him Rev. 12:13	7th trumpet - 3rd Woe - 7 Bowls of Plagues Rev. 14:17 - 16:21 Also Rev. 17-19	Rev. 20	Rev. 21-22
		Rev. 12:1-16 Woman flees into wilderness for 3 1/2 years			
		← 3 1/2 Years →	Rev. 12:1-16 Woman flees into wilderness for 3 1/2 years		
← 3 1/2 Years →					
← 7 Years →				← 1,000 Years →	← Eternity
REV. 1 to 11	REV. 12 to 22				

TABLE 5 - SHOWS THE FIRST CHRONOLOGICAL SERIES OVERLAPPING THE SECOND CHRONOLOGICAL SERIES.

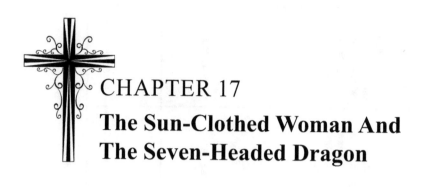

CHAPTER 17

The Sun-Clothed Woman And
The Seven-Headed Dragon

Revelation 12:1-4: A great and wondrous sign appeared in heaven: a woman clothed with the sun, with the moon under her feet and a crown of twelve stars on her head. She was pregnant and cried out in pain as she was about to give birth. Then another sign appeared in heaven: an enormous red dragon with seven heads and ten horns and seven crowns on his heads. His tail swept a third of the stars out of the sky and flung them to the earth. The dragon stood in front of the woman who was about to give birth, so that he might devour her child the moment it was born. (7)

What is the seven-headed dragon with ten horns and seven crowns that appeared as a sign in heaven?

Revelation 12:9: And the great dragon was thrown down, the serpent of old who is called the devil and Satan, who deceives the whole world; . . . (12).

This scripture shows that the dragon is Satan. The dragon is called a sign, which is a symbol representing Satan.

What is the meaning of the seven heads and ten horns?

Revelation 17:7, 9, 10: . . . I will tell you the mystery of the woman and of the beast with seven heads and

ten horns that carries her. . . . The seven heads are
seven mountains on which the woman seated; they
are also seven kings, five of whom have fallen, one
is, the other has not yet come; . . . (31)

The seven heads represent the seven mountains. A mountain is
called a kingdom. Since the dragon is Satan and Satan has been
the prince of this world since Adam and Eve sinned, then the seven
heads with crowns represent Satan's worldly kingdoms throughout
history, and the future. The seven world kingdoms are as follows:

1. Egypt
2. Assyria
3. Babylon
4. Medo-Persia
5. Greece
6. Roman Empire at the first coming of Christ
7. Roman Empire (Iron and Clay) prior to the Lord's
   Second Coming.

What are the ten horns?

Revelation 17:12: And the ten horns that you saw are
ten kings who have not yet received royal power, but
they are to receive authority as kings for one hour,
together with the beast (31).

The ten horns on the dragon are the same as the ten toes in Daniel
2 and ten horns on the Beast mentioned in Daniel 7. They are the ten
kings that represent the ten nations, which make up the Roman or
the Beast Kingdom at the time of the end.

Who is the sun-clothed woman?

This is an important question. We need to know who the sun-
clothed woman is to fully understand Revelation. We have shown

that the seven-headed dragon was a sign in the heavens representing Satan's worldly kingdoms. Satan has been the king of this world since Adam and Eve sinned. Since the dragon is symbolic of Satan's kingdom which he received when Adam and Eve sinned, then the sun-clothed woman obviously must have been in existence over an equal period of time.

The sun-clothed woman is the woman the Lord spoke of in Genesis, when he cursed Satan in the Garden of Eden and said to the serpent:

> Genesis 3:15: And I will put enmity between you and the woman and between your seed and her seed; he shall bruise you on the head, and you shall bruise him on the heel (12).

Another translation says:

> I will make you enemies of each other: you and the woman, your offspring and her offspring. It will crush your head and you will strike its heel (57).

Genesis 3:15 shows that not only are the woman and the serpent (Satan) enemies, but their offsprings are enemies (32).

Who are the offspring of the woman?

> Revelation 12:5: And she gave birth to a son, a male child, who is to rule all the nations with a rod of iron; and her child was caught up to God and to His throne (12).

> Revelation 12:17: . . . the dragon was furious (enraged) at the woman, he went away to wage war on the remainder of her descendants, who obey God's commandments and who have the testimony of

192

Jesus Christ . . . (59)

The scriptures show that the offspring of the woman are the saints who obey the commandments of God (Jews) and those that keep the testimony of Jesus Christ (Christians).

The sun-clothed woman and the dragon have been enemies since the Lord cursed the serpent in the garden. This shows that the sun-clothed woman is the symbolic mother of the Jews and the Christians. When we talk about the Jews that keep the commandments of God, we mean the spiritual Jews not the carnal Jews. Jesus differentiated between these two groups in John 8:37-44, when he said Abraham's children were those that did the deeds of Abraham, while the Jews that sought to kill him were of their father, the devil. (32)

Paul described a Jew in the book of Romans:

> Romans 2:28-29: For he is not a Jew who is one out-wardly; neither is circumcision that which is outward in the flesh. But he is a Jew who is one inwardly; and circumcision is that which is of the heart, by the Spirit, not by the letter; and his praise is not from men, but from God. (12)

Sun, moon and twelve stars

> Revelation 12:1: A great and wondrous sign appeared in heaven: A woman clothed with the sun, with the moon under her feet and a crown of twelve stars on her head (7).

We have shown that the sun-clothed woman is the symbolic mother of God's people, both the Jews and the Christians.

What are the meanings of the sun, the moon and twelve stars?

The sun is the true light. Jesus is the light. Jesus is called the sun of righteousness in Malachi 3:20 or 4:2. The woman is clothed with the sun of righteousness, which is Jesus Christ.

The moon is symbolic of the church as the moon has no light of its own but is a reflection of the light of the sun. The church, like the moon, has no light of its own but is a reflection of the light of the Lord. When we are in union with God and do His work, His light will shine on us and through us to others.

The twelve stars bring to mind the dream Joseph had in which the sun, the moon and eleven stars bowed down to him (Genesis 37:9). The eleven stars in Joseph's dream were his eleven brothers. The twelve stars could mean the twelve sons of Jacob, the leaders of the twelve tribes of Israel. The twelve stars could also refer to the twelve apostles, since the sun-clothed woman is the symbolic mother of God's people both the Jews and the Christians.

One-third of the stars of heaven

Revelation 12:4 speaks of the tail of the dragon (Satan) pulling one-third of the stars of heaven to the earth.

What are the stars the dragon pulls down from heaven?

We have shown that stars are often referred to as angels. Even Christ is called the bright morning star in Revelation 22:16. In Isaiah 14:12, Satan is called a star that has fallen from heaven to the earth. The dragon is called Satan. One-third of the stars of heaven that the dragon pulls down to the earth are probably Satan's angels that rebelled against God. Satan apparently convinced one-third of the angels to rebel against God. These angels are called fallen angels.

Man-child or male child

Revelation 12:2, 4, 5: . . . and she was with child; and she cried out, being in labor and in pain to give birth. . . . And the dragon stood before the woman who was about to give birth, so that when she gave birth he might devour her child. And she gave birth to a son, a male child, who is to rule all the nations with a rod of iron; and her child was caught up to God and to His throne. (12)

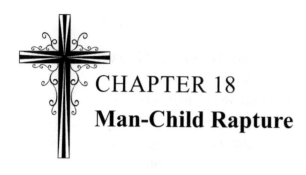

CHAPTER 18
Man-Child Rapture

Man-child or male child

> Revelation 12:2, 4-6: . . . and she was with child; and
> she cried out, being in labor and in pain to give birth.
> . . . And the dragon stood before the woman who was
> about to give birth, so that when she gave birth he
> might devour her child. And she gave birth to a son, a
> male child, who is to rule all the nations with a rod of
> iron; and her child was caught up to God and to His
> throne. And the woman fled into the wildness where
> she had a place prepared by God, so that there she
> might be nourished for one thousand two hundred
> and sixty days. (12)

When the seventh trumpet is blown in Revelation 11, the
Scripture says it is finished for the kingdom of the world has become
the kingdom of our Lord Jesus Christ. In Revelation 12 the woman
flees into the wilderness for 42 months or 1260 days after the birth
of the Man-child. There can not be an additional 42 months after
Revelation 11 as the Antichrist only has authority to wage war for
42 months. This means Revelation 12 has to go back to Revelation
4 to fit within the time-frame of 42 months left in seventieth week
of Daniel after the covenant is broken.

The very moment the Man-child is born in Revelation 12 and is
taken up to heaven is the same moment in which a door is opened in

heaven in Revelation 4, and suddenly there is a multitude of people before the throne. This multitude before the throne is the Man-child which also includes the 144,000 in Revelation 14. Revelation 14:1-5 calls this multitude before the throne the first fruits unto the Lamb. The first fruits follow the Lamb wherever He goes. This is the bride. The bride is the one who follows the Lamb wherever He goes. The bride of Christ is the prize of the high-calling for which Paul ran a race for with all of his might. Those that win this prize are numbered.

The Man-child is born and taken up to heaven before the Great Tribulation begins. The Man-child rapture is the midnight hour rapture, which occurs when the Lord comes for His bride. Afterwards, Revelation 14:6 speaks of angels flying through the air preaching the Gospels. Revelation 14:9 warns all not to take the mark of the beast. This shows that the Man-child rapture takes place prior to the beginning of the Great Tribulation, prior to the woman feeing into the wilderness for three and one-half years. Great Tribulation begins the moment the woman flees into the wilderness.

Sun-clothed woman in Revelation 12 is our mother, heavenly Jerusalem, which is also described in Isaiah 66:7-13 and Galatians 4:21-31. The sun-clothed woman flees into the wilderness after the birth of the male child, where she is protected from the dragon for three and one-half years. The dragon immediately makes war with the remnant of the woman's children on earth who keep the commandments of God (Jews), and have the testimony of Jesus Christ (Christians) (Revelation 12:17). This shows that all Christians are not taken up in the pre-tribulation rapture. Many Christians will go through the Great Tribulation.

Isaiah 66:7-13 describes a similar scene. The woman, Jerusalem, our mother, gives birth to a male child before she goes into labor (pre-tribulation rapture). After she goes into labor (The Great

Tribulation) she brings forth the rest of her children.

> Isaiah 66:7-8: Before Zion travailed she gave birth;
> before her pain came upon her she was delivered of
> a Man-child. Who has heard such a thing? Who has
> seen such things? Shall a land be born in one day?
> Or shall a nation be brought forth in a moment?
> For as soon as Zion was in labor she brought forth
> her children. (59)

Before Zion travailed means before the Great Tribulation begins. The Man-child is born before the Great Tribulation begins. This is shown in Revelation 12:6, 9, when the woman flees into the wilderness for 1260 days or three and one-half years immediately after the birth of the Man-child. The Man-child is taken up to heaven. This is the first-fruit rapture. The Man-child was born before labor began (before the Great Tribulation).

For as soon as Zion was in labor (Great Tribulation), she brought forth her children. These children are the remnant of her seed, which keep the commandment of God (Jews), and have the testimony of Jesus Christ (Christians).

Israel became a nation one day.

> Isaiah 66:8: . . . Shall a land be born in one day? Or
> shall a nation be brought forth in a moment? . . . (59)

This scripture has a double message. It not only speaks of Jerusalem as our mother and the birth of the Man-child and the coming persecution or tribulation. It also foretold that Israel would become a nation in one day. Shall a land be born in one day? Or shall a nation be brought forth in a moment? Israel became a nation in one day on May 14, 1948 by the decree of the United Nations.

Galatians calls the sun clothed woman Jerusalem, our mother.

> Galatians 4:22, 25-26: For it is written that Abraham had two sons, one by bondwoman and one by the freewoman. . . . Now Hagar is Mount Sinai in Arabia, and corresponds to the present Jerusalem, for she is in slavery with her children. But the Jerusalem above is free, she is our mother. (12)

The Man-child is to rule nations with a rod of iron.

As soon as the Man-child is born, he is taken up to heaven. This Man-child is to rule all nations with a rod of iron. The Lord promises the saints who overcome that He will give them authority over nations, and they shall rule with a rod of iron.

> Revelation 2:26-27: And he who overcomes, and he who keeps My deed until the end, to him I will give authority over the nations; and he shall rule them with a rod of iron, as the vessels of the potter are broken to pieces, as I also have received authority from My Father. (12)

"The reign of the Lord anointed"

The title of Psalm 2 in the New American Standard Bible is called "The Reign of the Lord's Anointed."

> Psalm 2:8-9: Ask of me, and I will make the nations your inheritance, the ends of the earth your possession. You will rule them with an iron scepter; you will dash them to pieces like pottery (7).

When does the Man-child rule nations with a rod of iron?

The saints will return to the earth with the Lord Jesus Christ, and reign with Him during the thousand years period called the millennium. There will be many people born, living, and dying in the millennium. Some of the people will rebel against the Lord and His saints. Only rebellious people are ruled with a rod of iron. The Lord is not going to rule the saints in heaven with a rod of iron.

> Revelation 20:4-5: And I saw thrones, and they sat upon them, and judgment was given to them. And I saw the souls of those who had been beheaded because of the testimony of Jesus and because of the word of God, and those who had not worshiped the beast or his image, and had not received the mark upon their forehead and upon their hand; and they came to life and reigned with Christ for a thousand years. The rest of the dead did not come to life until the thousand years were completed. (12)

Scriptures teach that those that have part in the first resurrection will reign with Christ for a thousand years on earth before the wicked dead are raised to life. Zechariah speaks of the Lord returning to the earth with His saints and He will be King over all the earth.

> Zechariah 14:4-5, 9: And in that day His feet will stand on the Mount of Olives, which is in front of Jerusalem on the east; and the Mount of Olives will be split in its middle from east to west by a very large valley, so that half of the mountain will move toward the north and the other half toward the south. . . . Then the Lord, my God, will come and all of the holy ones with Him! . . . And the Lord will be king over all the earth; . . . (12)

Many people think the Man-child is Christ. What are the facts?

The sun-clothed woman is not the Blessed Mother of Jesus as she is only a sign or symbol, not a literal person. (I have just come across some prophecies, supposedly from the Blessed Mother, where she said she is the sun-clothed woman. This will be discussed at the end of this chapter.)

We must remember:

1. The scriptures in Revelation 4 through 22 are prophecies of event that are going to happen in the future. The book of Revelation was written approximately one hundred years after the birth of Christ.
2. Isaiah calls the sun clothed woman, our mother, Jerusalem.
3. The moment the Man-child is born in Revelation 12 and is taken to heaven, is the same moment a door is open in heaven in Revelation 4 and there is a multitude before the throne. The Man-child is the multitude before the throne. Revelation 14 calls this multitude the first fruit unto the Lamb. This multitude follows the Lamb wherever He goes. The bride is the one who follows the Lamb.
4. The Man-child will be born during the seventieth week of Daniel, which is just before the Lord returns to the earth.
5. The Man-child will be taken up to heaven as soon as he is born. Jesus lived thirty-three years on earth before He was taken up to heaven.
6. Revelation 12:5 says that the Man-child is to rule all nations with a rod of iron. Revelation 2:26-27 says that those who prevail to the end shall rule nations with a rod of iron. The Lord promises the saints who overcome that they would rule nations with a rod of iron.
7. After the Man-child is taken up to heaven, the woman flees into the wilderness to get away from the

dragon, Satan. Satan, afterward, makes war with the remnant of her seed who keep the commandment of God and have the testimony of Jesus Christ. Gordon Lindsay said the term "remnant of her seed" shows that a large number of her seed have already been removed, not just one person as it would be if the Man-child was only referring to Christ. (31)

8. If the sun-clothed woman was the Blessed Mother, why would she be fleeing from the dragon? The dragon would be one fleeing from the Blessed Mother.

These facts show that the Man-child is not Christ but the saints that are taken up to heaven prior to the beginning of the Great Tribulation and the Wrath of God.

The Man-child Rapture: Are all Christians or saints taken up in the Man-child Rapture?

The sun-clothed woman gives birth to a man-child who is taken up to heaven before the tribulation begins (Table 5 in Chapter 16). The Man-child is not the only child, since the dragon makes war with the remnant of her seed.

> Revelation 12:17: And the dragon was enraged with the woman, and went off to make war with the rest of her offspring, who keep the commandments of God and hold to the testimony of Jesus (12).

It can be seen from the scriptures that only the Man-child is taken up to heaven. Since the dragon was unable to devour the Man-child and the woman, he makes war with the rest of the woman's children who keep the testimony of Jesus Christ.

Since the dragon makes war with the rest of the woman's children immediately after the woman flees into the wilderness for

1260 days or three and one-half years, this shows that the persecution of the Christians begins at the very beginning of the Great Tribulation. This indicates that all Christians are not taken up in the pre-tribulation rapture.

Is the Man-child Rapture a special rapture?

Yes! The Man-child rapture is the first-fruit rapture, which includes the 144,000 standing before the throne in heaven in Revelation 14.

> Revelation 14:3-4: And they sang a new song before the throne . . . and no one could learn the song except the one hundred and forty-four thousand who had been purchased (redeemed) from the earth. . . . These are the ones who follow the Lamb wherever He goes. These have been purchased from among men as the first fruits to God and to the Lamb. (12)

Later, we will show that the 144,000 in Revelation 14 are a different group from the 144,000 in Revelation 7.

Did Paul speak of a special resurrection?

> Philippians 3:10-14: I wish to know Christ and the power flowing from his resurrection; . . . Thus do I hope that I may arrive at resurrection from the dead. It is not that I have reached it yet, or have already finished my course; but I am racing to grasp the prize if possible, since I have been grasped by Christ (Jesus). Brother, I do not think of myself as having reached the finish line. I give no thought to what lies behind but push on to what is ahead. My entire attention is on the finish line as I run toward the prize to which God calls me - life on high in Christ Jesus. (60)

Paul is running a race for a special prize, the resurrection.

Paul emphasizes in six verses that he hopes to attain the resurrection of the dead.

1. It is not that I have already reached it yet (the resurrection of the dead),
2. or have already finished my course.
3. I am racing to grasp the prize (resurrection of the dead) if possible.
4. I do not think of myself as having reached the finish line (resurrection of the dead), for,
5. my entire attention is on the finish line (resurrection of the dead).
6. I run toward the prize (resurrection of the dead) to which God calls me.

Paul is not talking about salvation. Paul knew he had salvation through the grace of Jesus Christ. The scripture in Acts 2:21 say, "It shall come to pass, that whosoever shall call on the name of the Lord shall be saved." (10) If Paul was talking about salvation, who could be saved? Paul was not talking about the general resurrection (the Harvest Rapture), he was talking about the Man-child resurrection that he was running a race of which he wanted to be a part. (61)

What was the prize of the resurrection?

> Philippians 3:14: My entire attention is on the finish line as I run toward the prize to which God call me - life on high in Christ Jesus (60).

> The very top prize is Jesus, i.e., being the bride of Christ.

The 144,000

Revelation 14:4: . . . These are the ones who follow the Lamb wherever He goes. These have been purchased from among men as first fruits to God and to the Lamb (12).

The 144,000 are called the first fruits of those that have been purchased or redeemed from the earth. Those who follow the Lamb wherever He goes, is the characteristic of the bride. The bride follows her husband wherever He goes. The 144,000 are definitely part of the bride. We will discuss this later. (61)

Are there any other teachings pertaining to the Man-child or first-fruit rapture?

The mid-night hour

Matthew 25:1-13: Then the kingdom of heaven will be comparable to ten virgins, who took their lamps, and went out to meet the bridegroom. And five of them were foolish, and five were prudent (wise). For when the foolish took their lamps, they took no oil with them, but the prudent took oil in flasks along with their lamps. Now while the bridegroom was delaying, they all got drowsy and began to sleep. But at midnight there was a shout, "Behold, the bridegroom! Come out to meet him." Then all those virgins arose, and trimmed their lamps, and the foolish said to the prudent, "Give us some of your oil, for our lamps are going out." But the prudent answered, saying, "No, there will not be enough for us and you too: go instead to the dealers and buy some for yourself." And while they were going away to make the purchase, the bridegroom came, and those who were ready went in with him to the wedding feast; and the door was shut. And later the other virgins also came, saying, "Lord, lord, open up for us." But he answered and said, "Truly I say to you, I do not know you." Be on the alert then, for you do not know the day nor the hour." (12)

The allegory of the ten virgins is really a story of the Lord coming for His bride. The ten virgins represent the Body of Christ. Five of the virgins were foolish for they had oil only in their lamps whereas the wise virgins took extra vessels of oil.

Who are the virgins?

The virgins represent the Body of Christ. Paul in II Corinthians 11:2 says, "For I am jealous for you with a godly jealousy; for I betrothed you to one husband, that to Christ I might present you as a pure virgin." (12) The 144,000 in Revelation 14:4 are called virgins, being the first fruits among men redeemed from the earth. These virgins follow the Lamb wherever He goes. This is the characteristic of a bride. A bride follows her husband wherever he goes.

What is the oil?

The oil is symbolic of the Holy Spirit. The oil is the fuel that makes our light shine. The Holy Spirit is the comforter that that makes us strong Christians. The foolish virgins were told to go buy their oil. In reality, the oil, which is symbolic of the Holy Spirit, cannot be brought. However, there is a price to pay for being filled with the Spirit, i.e. having your vessel replenished and filled with oil. (46) This involves:

1. Spending time in prayer each day developing a relationship with our Lord Jesus Christ.
2. Studying and abiding in His Word so that you may know the truth and the truth will set you free. Psalm

119:105 says, "Thy word is a lamp unto my feet and a light unto my path." Studying God's Word will light your path to meet the Bridegroom.

3. Fellowship with other Christians to encourage one another and to keep each other uplifted.

Hebrews 10:24-25 . . . and let us consider how to stimulate one another to love and good deeds, not forsaking our own assembling together, as is the habit of some, but encouraging one another; and all the more, as you see the day drawing near. (12)

What is the difference between the wise and the foolish virgins?

The foolish virgins were part of the Body of Christ. Virgin means one that is undefiled, pure, holy, and without sin. The foolish virgin had lamps that were lighted. The burning light is symbolic of the light of Christ shining in and through us.

When we spend time in prayer, our vessels are replenished and filled with oil, and our light continues to shine. Other people can see this light of Christ in us. When we neglect to spend time in prayer, we dry up. We don't feel in union with God. People cannot see the light of Christ in us.

When the foolish virgins had replenished their oil and lighted their lamp, they returned and knocked on the door. The Bridegroom replied, "I do not know you." He did not say, I never knew you, as He did to those who said, "Lord, Lord, did we not prophesy in your name, and in your name cast out demons and in your name perform many miracles?" (Matthew 7:22-23). In other words, the Lord did not recognize the five foolish virgins as part of the wedding party. This doesn't mean they were not saved. This is shown by the fact that the foolish virgins had replenished their lamps with oil (Holy

Spirit) and lighted their lamp. The main difference between the foolish virgins and the wise virgins was that the wise virgins spent more time in prayer and had extra vessels of oil. The wise virgins were prepared and went up in the Man-child rapture, while the foolish virgins went up in the Harvest Rapture after the Great Tribulation. (47)

Is there a warning given in the story of the ten virgins?

Yes, the warning is: Be alert, watch and pray for you do not know the day or hour the Bridegroom comes (Matthew 25:13). This allegory implies that only some of the virgins will be the bride of Christ.

Bride of Christ

We are all part of the Body of Christ, but we are not all the bride of Christ. The bride of Christ is the prize of the high calling that Paul was running a race in an effort to win.

Gordon Lindsay used the beautiful story of Adam and Eve to illustrate this point. Eve, the bride of Adam, was taken from a rib in Adam's body. Eve was taken from a part of the body of Adam, but the whole body of Adam was not used to make Eve.

The bride of Christ will come from His body, as Eve came from the body of Adam. The whole body of Christ will not be the bride, as the whole body of Adam was not used to make his bride, Eve (62).

Who will make up the Man-child company?

Gordon Lindsay believed the Man-child will consist of people from all walks of life, from preachers, who are fighting the battle on the front lines to janitors pushing a broom. However, those who make up the Man-child company will have one thing in common; they will be "prayer warriors." They will have a disciplined prayer life. They will spend time in prayer. (62)

Intercessory prayer

Intercessory prayer is one of the highest callings a Christian can have. The Lord is almighty and all-powerful. He created everything that is in existence. He can do all things. However, He has certain guidelines that He follows. The Lord gave dominion over the earth to Adam and Eve. When Adam and Eve sinned, the dominion was passed on to Satan. Since the dominion of the earth belongs to Satan, the Lord will not do anything unless man asks Him. For example, the Lord looked all over Israel for one man, who would pray and intercede for Israel, so that the Israelites would not have to go into Babylonian captivity.

> Ezekiel 22:30-31: "And I searched for a man among them who should build up the wall and stand in the gap before Me for the land, that I should not destroy it; but I found no one. Thus I have poured out my indignation on them; I have consumed them with the fire of My wrath; their ways I have brought upon their heads," declared the Lord God. (12)

The Lord did not want to destroy Israel, but He could not find one man, who would stand in the gap to pray and intercede.

The harvest is great but the laborers are few.

> Matthew 9:37-38: Then he said to his disciples, "The harvest indeed is great, but the laborers are few. Pray therefore the Lord of the harvest to send forth laborers into his harvest" (9).

The Lord is saying that there are many, many people in the world who need to hear the gospel, but He will not supply all the laborers unless someone prays and intercedes. One can easily see the value and necessity of intercessory prayer.

Vision of Jesus kneeling by a large rock:

> God the Father said, "When My Son, Jesus, walked
> the face of the earth, He prayed without ceasing."

Jesus was a man of prayer and fasting.

Jesus is both God and man, yet He spent a major portion of His ministry in prayer. After Jesus was baptized by John the Baptist, he went into the wilderness of Judea, where He fasted and prayed for forty days (Luke 3:21).

> Luke 6:12: . . . He went off to the mountain to pray,
> and He spent the whole night in prayer to God (12).

Mark tells of Jesus getting up long before daybreak to go out alone to pray.

> Mark 1:35: Very early in the morning, while it was
> still dark, Jesus got up, left the house and went off to
> a solitary place, where he prayed (7).

Paul explains in Ephesians why we are to pray without ceasing:

> Ephesians 6:10-12, 18: Finally, be strong in the
> Lord, and in the strength of His might. Put on the
> full armor of God, that you may be able to stand firm
> against the schemes of the devil. For our struggle is
> not against flesh and blood, but against the rulers,
> against the powers, against the world forces of this
> darkness, against the spiritual forces of wickedness
> in the heavenly places. . . . With all prayer and peti-
> tion pray at all times in the Spirit, and with this view,
> be on the alert with all perseverance and petition for
> all the saints. (12)

It is through prayer and fasting that we come against the forces of darkness that hinder the Lord's work on earth. It is easy to see from these scriptures that intercessory prayer is one of the highest callings a Christian can have. Though you may go about your work, never witnessing to anyone, your constant intercessory prayers are enabling the Lord to send laborers into the harvest.

Daniel 12:3 says that those who lead many to the Lord will shine brightly like stars forever and ever. You will shine as brightly as stars for the harvest the laborer gathers through your intercessory prayers. Matthew 13:43 speaks of the righteous shinning as the sun in the kingdom of their Father.

Angels need our prayers

A friend of mine said that during her prayer time, she saw a picture of angels sitting on a curb by the road, looking depressed with their heads and arms on their knees. Then she saw a picture of herself praying. As she prayed, substances started coming out of her mouth and went into the hands of one of the angels. This angel started passing these substances, which were ammunition, to other angels. The angels all came to life and went to fight the daily battle against the forces of darkness. The woman said the Lord was showing her that when we do not pray, the angels don't have any ammunition to fight Satan and his angels. As a consequence, our prayers are not answered and the Lord's work is not done. It is easy to see why the sun-clothed woman was greatly weakened after the rapture of the Man-child. There was no one to pray and hinder the forces of darkness.

It is through the prayers of the saints that spiritual battles are fought and won. It was through the prayers and fasting of Daniel that Archangel Michael and his angels fought successfully for twenty-one days against the Prince of Persia (Daniel 10:13).

I took a trip to the Holy Land on a Gordon Lindsay's tour in 1973. I was impressed to learn that Gordon Lindsay went to bed at 9:00 p.m. so that he could get up at 4:00 a.m. and pray for two hours before beginning his day. Gordon Lindsay was a man of prayer. The fruits of his works show it.

At what hour does the Man-child Rapture take place?

In 1973, I had a dream. At that time, my youngest son was two years old. My other two boys were nine and ten years old. In the dream, my wife and I and the two older boys woke up and walked out onto a porch. It was midnight. There was a glowing light coming from the sky. I could not see directly up as we were on the porch under the roof, but I had knowledge that this was the midnight hour, and the Lord was coming for His bride. Though I did not see the rapture take place, it was a tremendous feeling of excitement, beyond description.

At that time, I did not have the understanding of Daniel, Revelation and the rapture as I do now. After the dream the story of the ten virgins came to me. I was puzzled why our youngest son was not with us on the porch. Now, seven years later, while I am writing this, I have the understanding why our youngest son was not with us on the porch. The Man-child rapture is the prize of the high calling for which Paul was running a race. This is a prize to be won. A two-year-old that has not reached the age of accountability is not in a position to run a race. I do not wish to imply that my family was part of the Man-child rapture in the dream. I will only say as Paul said, "I am running in the race for the prize of the high calling."

Obviously, it is always important to be cautious in regards to discernment of dreams. However, I feel the Lord was showing me that there will be two raptures:

1. The Man-child rapture, which occurs at the midnight hour, when the Lord comes for His bride. This rapture will not be visible to the world, as it occurs at the midnight hour, when the world is asleep.

2. The Harvest Rapture occurs during the day when every eye shall see Him. This is the rapture Christ described in Matthew 24:29-31.

I also believe the Lord was revealing to me that the Man-child rapture is the prize of the high calling, i.e. a prize to be won.

Paul was one of the apostles and one of the greatest men of God who ever lived. He was responsible for over half of the books in the New Testament. Yet, he said, "I hope to attain the prize of the high calling, the resurrection of the dead." This is a big statement. If Paul was not sure of being a part of the first resurrection (Man-child), who can be?

Jesus called His disciples His wedding guests or attendants

The Lord told me to review the scriptures that pertain to the bride of Christ, and an understanding that I previously overlooked would come forth. The understanding is this. Jesus identified Himself as the Bridegroom, but He said His disciples were His wedding guests or attendants. Why? Why didn't He call them His bride? The reason is that at that point and time, they had not yet won the race that Paul spoke of. This does not mean that they won't be a part of the bride. The bride is a prize to be won.

> Matthew 9:14-15: Then the disciples of John approached him and said, "Why do we and the Pharisees fast but your disciples do not fast? Jesus answered them, "Can the wedding guests mourn as long as the bridegroom is with them? The days will come when

the bridegroom is taken away from them, and then they will fast. (24A)

Mark 2:18-20: The disciples of John and of the Pharisees were accustomed to fast. People came to Jesus and objected,

"Why do the disciples of John and the disciples of the Pharisees fast, but your disciples do not fast?" Jesus answered them, "Can the wedding guests fast while the bridegroom is with them? As long as they have the bridegroom with them they cannot fast. But the days will come when the bridegroom is taken from them, and then they will fast on that day. . . ." (24, 63)

In another translation, Jesus called His disciples His attendants.

Mark 2:18-20: And John's disciples and the Pharisees were fasting; and they came and said to Him, "Why do John's disciples and the disciples of the Pharisees fast, but Your disciples do not fast?" And Jesus said to them, "While the bridegroom is with them, the attendants of the bridegroom do not fast, . . . But the days will come when the bridegroom is taken away from them, and then they will fast in that day." (12)

Luke 5:33-35: And they said to him, "The disciples of John fast often and offer prayers; and the disciples of the Pharisees do the same; but yours eat and drink." Jesus answered them, "Can you make the wedding guests fast while the bridegroom is with them? But the days will come, and when the bridegroom is taken away from them, then they will fast in those days." (24A)

The last days

In the gospel of Luke, the Lord talks about the last days and the day that will come suddenly upon all that dwell on earth.

> Luke 21:35-36: . . . For come it will upon all who dwell on the face of all the earth. Watch, then praying at all times, that you may be accounted worthy to escape all these things that are to be, and to stand before the Son of Man. (9)

Jesus didn't promise the Church (His Body) that it wouldn't go through the Great Tribulation. He said to pray that you may be considered worthy to escape all of these things that are going to take place in the last days. Pray that you may be a part of the Man-child rapture.

The sun-clothes woman and the Blessed Mother

I made the statement that the sun-clothed woman is not the Blessed Mother, yet there are messages supposedly from the Blessed Mother saying she is the sun-clothed woman. While I was praying asking the Lord for an understanding, I had a picture of a head of an alligator with its mouth wide open with many teeth. A few days later, while praying I had a picture of the Blessed Mother standing before me. I asked three of my prayer partners to come together and pray with me for an understanding. I asked the Lord if I was to change the statement about the Blessed Mother not being the sun-clothed woman. We received the following messages and words of knowledge:

> We, who are of many tribes, come together to worship and adore My Father and the Holy Spirit. My message is the same, yet I speak in a way that those who are searching will understand. I have twelve tribes, not all understand in the same way. I speak loudly and intellectually to one, and I give dreams

to another. Just as at the Tower of Babel, my people have been confounded. Yet, I am speaking and they are each hearing Me differently. Does this mean that what I have spoken or made known to you is wrong? Nay! I say, nay! What you have been given is for those of the tribe I have directed you to. Because they challenge, charge, argue, assail, laugh, distort, curse or lie about My revelation to you is of no consequence to you. I give this to you that those who will see or hear it will be touched, blessed and a part of My whole message which has been imparted to them. My other messengers are speaking the same message and it is disseminated to them in a way that they will understand. Stand firm, speak boldly, do not concern yourself with the message I have given others to speak. They are reaching those that I am sending to them and reaching others that they themselves are reaching out to. My messengers will cross paths and will sometimes be misunderstood. Do not separate yourself from them. Know that I will use those, who are willing and even some that are not. Go to those that I have sent to you and be at peace for I am peace and love.

Head of an alligator with its mouth wide open with many teeth

The Lord said, "Do you believe what you have written wholeheartedly with all that is within you?" I replied, "Yes!" Then He replied, "The alligator with its mouth wide open will be the people trying to tear at you and bring you down. " I am a God of covenant. I dwell within My covenant. Apart from it, there are grave consequences. Stay within its protection, and there will be blessings and fruits. Apart from it, there is death.

Another prayer partner received the following words:

> The Lord is the author of your work. You do not need to apologize for what He has given you to understand, and how He has instructed you to write. He has a covenant with you in the writing of this book. It is His task to open the understanding of each one, who has access to it.

A vision of the Blessed Mother standing before me.

> Be comforted my son. You do not need to be concerned about tomorrow for it will take care of itself. Be of good cheer for my Son loves you.

Jesus, while dying on the cross, gave us His mother.

> John 19:26-27: Near the cross of Jesus there stood his mother. . . . Seeing his mother there with the disciple whom he loved, Jesus said to his mother, "Woman, there is your son." In turn he said to the disciple, "There is your mother." (60)

The Blessed Mother has reportedly identified herself as the Sun-clothed Woman. She is truly our mother. Nevertheless, the Man-child is not Jesus. The Man-child is the mid-night hour rapture, the first-fruit unto the Lamb, who have been redeemed from the earth. The Man-child follows the Lamb wherever He goes. This is the bride who follows her husband wherever He goes.

The bride of Christ is also discussed in Chapter 22, 27, 37 and 38.

CHAPTER 19
War In Heaven

Satan and his angels are driven from heaven.

> Revelation 12:7-12: And there was war in heaven, Michael and his angels waging war, with the dragon. And the dragon and his angels waged war, and they were not strong enough, and there was no longer a place found for them in heaven. And the great dragon was thrown down . . . to the earth, and his angels were thrown down with him. And I heard a loud voice in heaven, saying, "Now the salvation, the power, and the kingdom of our God and the authority of His Christ have come, for the accuser of our brethren has been thrown down, who accuses them before our God day and night. And they overcame him because of the blood of the Lamb and because of the word of their testimony, and they did not love their life even to death. For this reason, rejoice, O heavens and you who dwell in them. Woe to the earth and the sea: because the devil has come down to you, having great wrath, knowing that he has only a short time. (12)

What do we mean, "Satan was cast out of heaven?" Wasn't Satan cast out of heaven, when he sinned and rebelled against God?

Yes, Satan was kicked out of heaven when he sinned against God. In Luke 10:18 Jesus said, "I saw Satan fall like lightning from heaven." Apparently, there are several realms or spheres in heaven. Paul spoke of the third heaven (II Corinthians 12:2). Paul also spoke of Satan being the prince and the power of the air, and the ruler of the forces of evil in the heavenly realms (Ephesians 6:12). Daniel 10:13 shows that there was war in heaven when Michael and his angels fought against the prince of Persia.

The event, described in Revelation 12, is the final casting of Satan out of heaven onto the earth. This is probably the reason why Satan, the dragon, tried to destroy the Man-child as soon as he was born (32).

> Daniel 12:1: At that time, Michael, the great prince who protects your people, will arise. There will be a time of distress such as has not happened from the beginning of nations until then. . . . (7).

The scriptures refer to the time of the end, the Great Tribulation, which Jesus spoke of in Matthew 24:21. The Great Tribulation begins, when Satan is kicked out of heaven. Satan, knowing that he has a short time, has great wrath.

Satan, the accuser

> Revelation 12:10: . . . for the accuser of our brethren, he who keeps bringing before our God charges against them day and night, has been cast out! (59).

The following statement by Arthur Bloomfield gives an in-depth analysis of Satan, our accuser.

> This war with Satan is not just one of brute force. Such a war would be easy for Michael. There is something else involved, much more mysterious. There is the aspect of a court trial in which Satan shows cause why he should retain the bodies of the

Saints, a dispute similar to that which took place when Michael contended about the body of Moses. Satan takes up each case separately and prefers charges. He will fight over every single body. The accused answer. Again, it is a court scene. They give testimony to offset Satan's accusations. We must have the right answers. Accusation cannot be answered by accusation or excuse, or by comparing ourselves with others less virtuous or by parading our good works. All the good works of a lifetime will be totally insufficient to counter Satan's accusation. He is a master prosecutor. We will need a lawyer, a good one. If any man sin, we have an advocate (lawyer) with the Father, Jesus Christ the righteous. There is only one testimony that will win this case. That testimony is written in

Revelation 12:11: And they overcame him by the blood of the Lamb, and by the word of their testimony (10),(37).

Satan will try to hold each person that ever lived responsible for every sin he or she has committed, whether through omission or commission. Moses was one of the greatest prophets of God that ever lived; yet Satan was arguing with Michael the Archangel over the body of Moses. Satan was probably saying that Moses belonged to him because of his unrepented sins (Jude 9).

Satan has no authority over sins that have been confessed, but he does have authority over sins that have not been confessed and repented. This is why it is very important to repent for each and every sin you can remember. Ask the Lord to bring to mind the sins you do not remember so that you can repent.

Serious sins must be dealt with

Perhaps one of the most serious sins many of us have to deal with is angry and resentment. Resentment begins when a person has been insulted or had his feelings deeply hurt, creating deep bitterness to the point that he cannot forgive another person for what has happened. The scriptures say we must forgive, or we cannot receive forgiveness.

> Matthew 6:15: Your heavenly Father will forgive you if you forgive those who sin against you; but if you refuse to forgive them, He will not forgive you (64).

Another translation says,

> But if you do not forgive others their trespasses, their reckless and willful sins, leaving them, letting them go and giving up resentment - neither will your Father forgive you your trespasses (sins) (59).

This scripture teaches that it is essential to forgive others, so that we can receive forgiveness from God and enter into his kingdom.

There is no such thing as once saved, always saved.

Many people believe that once saved, you are always saved. Some of these people live in serious sin with the belief that they cannot lose their salvation regardless of what they do. This is not true. There are a number of scriptures that prove this.

Sin is an act of disobedience toward God. Serious sin will cut us off from God. This is shown by the following parable that my friend and I received while we were praying, seeking the Lord for discernment on this.

> A man was walking along the side of a straight cyclone fence that divides a highway down the middle. The fence and the highway go further than one can

see. The Lord is guarding a gate which is located a good way down the road. All of a sudden, the man jumps the fence with a great deal of effort and finds himself on the other side of the fence. The man sees where he is and it looks like he is on the other side and resumes his walk. Yet, he knows that he is not on the right side of the fence.

As we prayed for an interpretation, the following understanding came. The parable is this:

A man walks down the road of life. The cyclone fence is symbolic of one's free will. We can always see what is going on in the world. We are free to choose between good and evil which is an analogy to one walking down the road and continually being able to see what is happening on the other side of the fence. If a man finds the other side of the fence tempting and looks in that direction instead of keeping his eyes on the Lord at the gate, which appears to be so far away, he will sometimes jump the fence and find himself a part of a whole new world. This person sees the pleasures of the world while the Lord looks at him in pity for going astray. The Lord sends his helpers in abundance to steer this man back to the other side of the fence. To do this, however, the Holy Spirit must convince the man's free spirit to come to the Lord again at the gate with repentance. If the man be caught on the worldly side of the fence without first coming to the Lord at the gate in this life, he will find himself on the worldly side of the fence forevermore, living a part of the darkness that separate Hades from heaven.

God does not listen to sinners, who do not do His will.

> John 9:31: We know God does not listen to sinners, but if any one is a worshiper of God and does his will, God listens to him (31).

If God did not spare the natural branches, He will not spare you either.

> Romans 11:17-21: If some of the branches have been broken off, and you, though a wild olive shoot, have been grafted in among the others and now share in the nourishing sap from the olive root, do not boast over those branches. If you do, consider this: You do not support the root, but the root supports you. You will say then, "Branches were broken off so I could be grafted in. Granted. But they were broken off because of unbelief, and you stand by faith. Do not be arrogant, but be afraid. For if God did not spare the natural branches, he will not spare you either. (7)

Paul in Philippians 2:12, said to work out your salvation with fear and trembling.

A person whose name is written in the Book of Life is a saved person. Yet, the Lord said He will blot a sinner's name out of the Book of Life

> Exodus 32:31-33: Then Moses returned to the Lord, and said, "Alas, this people has committed a great sin, and they have made a god of gold for themselves. But now if Thou wilt, forgive their sin - and if not, please blot me out from Thy book which Thou hast written!" And the Lord said to Moses, "Whoever has sinned against Me, I will blot him out of My book." (12)

Matthew 10:22, 24:13 and Mark 13:13 say, "But the one, who endures to the end, it is he who shall be saved.

Jesus was telling John on the Island of Patmos to write letters to the seven churches of Asia Minor that were in existence at the turn of the first century. Jesus, in speaking to the church at Sardis, said:

> Revelation 3:5: He that overcometh, the same shall be clothed in white raiment; and I will not blot his name out of the book of life, but I will confess his name before my Father and before his angels (10).

A person, whose name is written in the book of life, is a saved person. Nevertheless, Jesus said if a person overcomes and prevails to the end, his name would not be blotted out of the book of life. Exodus 32:31-32 and Revelation 3:5 both show that a person's name can be blotted out of the book of life. Scripture in Revelation 20:15 says, if anyone's name was not found in the book of life, he will be thrown into the Lake of Fire. These scriptures clearly teach that there is no such thing as once saved always saved.

It is difficult to receive forgiveness if you turn your back on the Lord.

> Hebrews 6:4-6: There is no use trying to bring you back to the Lord again if you have once understood the Good News and tasted for yourself the good things of heaven and shared in the Holy Spirit, and know how good the Word of God is, and felt the mighty powers of the world to come, and then have turned against God. You cannot bring yourself to repent again if you have nailed the Son of God to the Cross again by rejecting Him, holding Him up to mocking and to public shame. (64)

Hebrews speaks of a person, who was obviously a Christian, who had a close walk with the Lord then rejected the Lord, turning his back on Him. This scripture is so strong that I turned to the Lord in prayer to see if He wanted me to quote this verse. The Lord said, "Yes". Then He spoke the following words to me:

> My Word comes to you not to hold you in condemnation already. But, that you may have knowledge of the truth of the Word of God so that you may repent and receive God's mercy through Jesus Christ.

God will deal with a person in an effort to bring him to repentance.

In the Christians community of Corinthians, there was a man, who was having sexual relations with his father's wife. Paul was very upset about this, and handed this man over to Satan for the destruction of the flesh, so that his spirit may be saved in the day of the Lord. If this man was not a Christian, Paul would not have handed him over to Satan for correction (1 Corinthians 5:12-13). Paul indicated that this man had lost his salvation, and if he did not repent and turn from his sin, he would not be saved. Repentance is a requirement to enter the kingdom of heaven. The scripture does not say that the man was handed over to Satan for the destruction of the flesh so that his spirit would be saved, but that his spirit may be saved. It is essential to repent and turn away from sin to be saved.

> I Corinthians 5:1, 5: It is actually reported that there is immorality among you, and immorality of such a kind as does not exist even among the Gentiles, that someone has his father's wife. . . . I have decided to deliver such a one to Satan for the destruction of his flesh, that his spirit may be saved in the day of the Lord Jesus. (12)

Two scriptures often quoted to prove once saved, always saved.

> John 10:27-29: My sheep hear My voice, and I know them, and they follow Me, and I give eternal life to them, and they shall never perish: and no one shall snatch them out of My hand. My Father, who has given them to Me, is greater than all: and no one is able to snatch them out of the Father's hand. (12)

> Romans 8:38-39: For I am convinced that neither death, nor life, nor angels, nor principalities, nor things present, nor things to come, nor powers, nor height, nor depth, nor any created thing, shall be able to separate us from the love of God, which is in Christ Jesus our Lord. (12)

What the scriptures say is true. No one nor any of these things can take you out of the Lord's hand and cause you to lose your salvation. However, a person, who willfully sins with an unrepentant heart, can take himself out of the Lord's hand and lose his salvation. No one nor anything can cause a person to lose his salvation except a sinner, who is unwilling to repent and turn away from his sins.

Revelation 12:10 says Satan accuses the saints before the Lord day and night. If a saint cannot lose his salvation, why does Satan waste his time accusing the saints?

Confessing our sins

A Church of Christ's friend of mine once said, "Mike, you Catholics are lucky." I asked him to explain. He said, "When you go to confession, you confess your sins to God in front of a priest. Afterward, you are free and light as a bird without any guilt or condemnation. Protestants confess their sins directly to God, then hold on to them and end up going to a psychiatrist." There is certainly some truth in this.

Jesus intended for us to confess our sins before a witness. Jesus instructed his disciples to forgive or retain people's sins.

> John 20:23: . . . whose sins you shall forgive, they are forgiven them; and whose sins you shall retain, they are retained (9).

On September 20, 1984, Steve Bell of the NBC Washington News reported on Good Morning America that a study just completed has proven that if you confide your faults to a friend or go to confession that it was beneficial to your health. This study just confirmed what the scriptures have always taught, that confessing your sins to another person will set you free, bringing health to your soul and body.

> James 5:16: Therefore, confess your sins to one another, and pray for one another, so that you may be healed. . . . (12).

I do not wish to imply that you cannot confess your sins directly to God. However, there is something about confessing your sins before a witness that sets a person free. This is also what happens when a person goes to a psychiatrist or confesses their sins to a priest.

The scriptures say that Satan continuously accuses the saints before God, day and night. If there is a court trial, where Satan shows cause why the saints belong to him, then a witness that a sin has been confessed, will make it more difficult for Satan to hold that sin against a person. Forgiveness of sins must be accepted on faith; otherwise, a person will hold onto his sins bringing guilt on himself. Confessing your sins in the presence of a witness will help set a person free.

Wisdom must be used in choosing a person to confess your sins to and to pray with you, such as a priest, a pastor or someone you trust and have confidence in. Do not confess your sins to a person who will not keep your confidence or who might use or hold your sins against you.

Jesus gave his disciples the power to forgive or retain a person's sin. A Catholic should confess his or her sins to a priest which is a sacramental confession.

> John 20:21-23: "As the Father has sent me, so I send you." Then he breathed on them and said: "Receive the Holy Spirit. If you forgive men's sins, they are forgiven them; if you hold them bound, they are held bound." (23, 60)

As mentioned earlier, Satan has no authority over sins that have been confessed, but he does have authority over sins that have not been confessed. For this reason, it is important that we confess each unrepented sin as the Lord brings them to our attention. The Lord will not reveal all of our faults or sins all at once for it would be more than we can bear. We would give up feeling condemned and hopeless.

Not wanting to bring condemnation on anyone because they cannot remember all of their unrepented sins and not wanting to de-emphasize the seriousness of confessing each of our sins, I asked a friend to pray with me seeking the Lord for some insight and understanding. While in prayer the following words came to us:

> When a person accepts the Lord Jesus Christ as his personal Savior and Redeemer, his spirit is renewed. The Lord brings to this individual a conscious awareness of his past sins and leads him into repentance.

228

The change within his heart is constantly being molded from the time of his Christian birth until his time for eternity.

These are profound words. The Lord deals with our faults, our sins, and us from the moment we are born again until He calls us home for eternity. This is an ongoing process. The scriptures say the Lord disciplines those whom He loves.

Hebrews 12:4-7,10-11,14: In your struggle against sin, you have not resisted to the point of shedding your blood. And you have forgotten that word of encouragement that addresses you as sons: "My son, do not make light of the Lord's discipline, and do not lose heart when he rebukes you, because the Lord disciplines those he loves, and he punishes everyone he accepts as a son." Endure hardship as a discipline; God is treating you as sons. For what son is not disciplined by his father? . . . Our fathers disciplined us for a little while as they thought best; but God disciplines us for our good, that we may share in his holiness. No discipline seems pleasant at the time, but painful. Later on, however, it produces a harvest of righteousness and peace for those who have been trained by it. . . . Make every effort to live in peace with all men and to be holy; without holiness no one will see the Lord. (7)

Though there is no way we can reach perfection in this life, the Lord wants us to strive for perfection.

Matthew 5:48: You, therefore, must be perfect, as your heavenly Father is perfect (that is, grow into complete maturity of godliness in mind and character, having reached the proper height of virtue and integrity). (59)

Woman flees into wilderness.

Revelation 12:6: And the woman fled into the wilderness where she had a place prepared by God, so that there she might be nourished for one thousand two hundred and sixty days (12).

Why does the woman flee into the wilderness?

We have shown that the woman is the symbolic mother of the Jews and the Christians. The Jews and the Christians are to flee from Israel and the nations controlled by the Beast when the abomination of the temple takes place.

Jesus gives a warning.

Matthew 24:15-18,21: Therefore when you see the abomination of desolation which was spoken of through Daniel the prophet, standing in the holy place (let the reader understand), then let those who are in Judea flee to the mountains; let him who is on housetop not go down to get the things out that are in his house; and let him who is in the field not turn back to get his cloak . . . for then there will be a great tribulation, such as has not occurred since the beginning of the world until now, nor ever shall. (12)

When the abomination takes place, Jesus is telling the Jews and the Christians to waste no time in getting out of the cities into the wilderness, for if they delay, their escape will be blocked. The wilderness of Judea is a rocky mountainous terrain with no roads into this area. God has a place in the wilderness to protect and nourish His people who heed His command quickly for the remainder of the three and half years.

The great eagle

> Revelation 12:14: And the two wings of the great eagle were given to the woman, in order that she might fly into the wilderness to her place, where she was nourished for a time, and times and half a time, from the presence of the serpent. (12)

Who is the great eagle?

In scripture, an animal is often used to refer to a kingdom.

The Lion	-	Kingdom of Babylon
The Bear	-	Medio-Persian Kingdom
The Leopard	-	Kingdom of Greece
The Beast	-	The Roman kingdom

The serpent with seven heads symbolizes the seven world kingdoms. The one nation that is known for the symbol of an eagle is America. The eagle is spoken of as a great eagle. America is not only a great nation; it is one of the most powerful nations in the world today. Gordon Lindsay said the great eagle could possible be America. (40)

What do we mean by the woman flying on the wings of an eagle?

All of God's people are not in Judea or Israel. Some are in the countries controlled by the Beast. These people must also flee when the abomination takes place. The wilderness of Judea would not hold all the people that need to escape.

America has always been a home for refugees. When the Beast starts killing the Christians and Jews, America will most likely play a role in trying to help these people escape. The Jews and

Christians could fly out of Israel, and the Roman Empire nations on planes from America or other planes to America. Gordon Lindsay said America was an unknown wilderness at the time the book of Revelation was written. (47)

It is interesting that when the Jews from Yemen were being airlifted to Israel in American bombers between 1948 and 1951, they quoted the scripture from Isaiah.

> Isaiah 40:31: They shall mount up with wings as eagles (10). (65)

The flood

> Revelation 12:15: And the serpent poured water like a river out of his mouth after the woman, so that he might cause her to be swept away with the flood (12).

What is the river and the flood?

In Jeremiah 46, the Egyptian army was spoken of as rising like the river Nile to cover the land and destroy the inhabitants. Jeremiah also spoke of the nations of the north over-flowing like a flood (47).

> Jeremiah 47:2-3: . . . Behold, waters are going to rise from the north and become an overflowing torrent, and overflow the land and all its fullness, the city and those who live in it; and the men will cry out, and every inhabitant of the land will wail. Because of the noise of the galloping hoofs of his stallions, the tumult of his chariots and the rumbling of his wheels, . . (12)

The water or sea is shown in Revelation 17:15 to represent people, multitudes, tongues, and nations.

Ezekiel 38:15-16 speaks of the nations of the north coming with a great and mighty army to cover the land of Israel like a cloud. This is the kingdom of clay, which will invade Israel after breaking the covenant with the kingdom of iron. This invasion will precipitate the battle of Armageddon.

The scriptures in Jeremiah show that the water that overflows and floods the land is the invading army of the north coming into Israel. However, the invasion of the nations of the north does not take place until the seventh bowl at the end of the seventieth week of Daniel.

The serpent pours water out of his mouth after the woman at the beginning of the Great Tribulation. The woman escapes for three and one-half years. This is the length of time left in the seventieth week of Daniel after the covenant is broken with the defiling of the temple.

The Lord in Matthew 25:15-17, 21 tells the people to flee to the mountains and wilderness of Judea as soon as the Beast defiles the temple. The people who flee immediately are the ones that are symbolic with the woman fleeing into the wilderness.

The water coming out of the mouth of the serpent like a river is symbolic of the Beast and his lieutenants going after these people. When the people flee into the mountains and wilderness of Judea, they will escape. The terrain is so mountainous that the Beast and his lieutenants will not pursue the people. This is the meaning of the scripture that the earth helped the woman by opening its mouth and drank up the river. (62)

> Revelation 12:16: And the earth helped the woman, and the earth opened its mouth and drank up the river which the dragon poured out of his mouth (12).

If the sun-clothed woman was the Blessed Mother, I cannot imagine the Blessed Mother having to flee to get away from Satan, the dragon. It is my belief that Satan would flee from the presence of the Blessed Mother.

The Beast makes war with the rest of the woman's offspring.

> Revelation 12:17: And the dragon was enraged with the woman, and went off to make war with the rest of her offspring, who keep the commandments of God and hold to the testimony of Jesus (12).

The Beast makes war with those who delayed to get their belongings and thus, were trapped because all avenues of escape were cut off. Those who heed the word of the Lord and leave immediately will escape with their lives. Those, who delay, will pay for it with their lives. We will discuss the Beast in the next chapter.

Louise Tomkiel received a message from Jesus, which speaks of the last 3 ½ years, the remnant, and Michael and his angels.

> I stand ready at the helm of My ship which soon will set sail. We will pass through the great pillars leaving the turbulent seas behind and navigate our way into safe harbor of the Three Hearts; the Hearts of your Jesus, your mother Mary and daddy Joseph. Here you will find safe refuge from the battle that rages about you. Here alone will you find true peace. Covered with the mantle of Divine love you will find rest for your weary soul. My ship will sail safely through the darkest of night, unseen and unheard. It will withstand many storms as it is propelled by the breath of the Holy Spirit. It has provisions for 3 ½ years for all my precious remnant – men, women, children and various animals. The light will come from the Light of Christ and the Spirit's breath will provide the pure air needed for the entire journey.

I invite you, precious few, to be ready to board at My command. Fear not for it will be smooth sailing even in the roughest of seas. Michael and his legions of Angels are now on standby. All is ready and the darkest hour is approaching very quickly. Watch and pray for Our Father is about to signal His angels and the trumpets will blast alerting His faithful ones that departure time is upon you. (66)

CHAPTER 20
The Beast

The Beast came out of the sea

> Revelation 13:1: And I saw a beast coming out of the sea. He had ten horns and seven heads, with ten crowns on his horns and on each head a blasphemous name (7).

The seven heads are the seven world kingdoms, which was discussed in Chapter 17. Though the sea may mean the Mediterranean Sea around which the seven world kingdoms were and are situated, it more likely symbolizes a multitude of people of different nations and tongues as described in Revelation 17:15. The Beast, the Antichrist, is a man that rises up from among the people.

Why did the ten horns have crowns in Revelation 13 and no crown in Revelation 12?

In Revelation 12, the ten horns have no crowns, indicating that the ten kings had not yet come into power. In Revelation 13, the ten horns had crowns showing that the ten kings have come into power with the Beast (26).

The body of a leopard

> Revelation 13:2: And the beast which I saw was like a leopard, and his feet were like those of a bear, and his mouth like a mouth of a lion. And the dragon gave him his power and his throne and great authority (12.)

The Beast is a composite of a leopard, a bear and a lion, which were the symbols of Greece, Persia and Babylon. The Beast, who is a man, gets his throne, power and authority from Satan. He posses the strong features of each of the Beast Kingdoms i.e. the greatness of Babylon, the fierceness of the Persian bear, and the military genius and swiftness of Alexander the Great.

Babylon is represented as a lion, the king of the animal kingdom. The mouth of a lion indicates a roaring lion. Satan is called a roaring lion going about seeking whom he may devour (I Peter 5:8). The main body of the Beast was that of a leopard which supports the scriptures in Daniel 8 and Revelation 17:8, 10 that the Beast will come out of Greece. We will discuss this later.

The seventh head is fatally wounded.

> Revelation 13:3-4: And I saw one of his heads as if it had been slain, and his fatal wound was healed. And the whole world was amazed and followed after the beast; and they worshiped the dragon, because he gave his authority to the beast and they worshiped the beast, saying, "Who is like the beast, and who is able to wage war with him?" (12)

When the man (the Beast), who is the head of the seventh kingdom of the dragon is fatally wounded, a prince of Satan from the bottomless pit ascends, and enters into the man, the son of perdition to become the eighth head, which is in the body of the seventh.

> Revelation 17:8: The beast that thou sawest was, and is not; and shall ascend out of the bottomless pit, and go into perdition. . . . (10).

> Revelation 17:11: And the beast that was, and is not, even he is the eighth and is of the seven, goeth into perdition (10);

237

The scriptures teach that man can harbor evil spirits. At the Last Supper, when Judas was about to betray the Son of Man, Jesus said Satan entered into Judas, who was called the son of perdition (Luke 22:3, John 17:12).

In Ezekiel 28:12-19, the king of Tyre and Satan are described as the same individual, yet the king of Tyre was an earthly king. In the Garden of Eden, Satan manifested himself in a serpent (Genesis 3).

If Satan can manifest himself in Judas, the King of Tyre and a serpent, there should be no problem with a prince of Satan from the bottomless pit manifesting himself in the body of the fatally wounded man, the Antichrist, to become the eighth head. The eighth head is in the body of the seventh head that was fatally wounded. The prince from the bottomless pit enters into the fatally wounded Beast, and heals his body and starts making all the decisions. There will be a drastic personality change in the Beast after he is fatally wounded. (67)

Seiss says "Satan is a spirit and cannot operate in the affairs of our world except through the minds, passion and activities of men. He needs to embody himself in earthly organisms in order to accomplish his murderous will." (48)

The Beast – the son of perdition

> II Thessalonians 2:3-4: Let no one deceive you in any way, for the day of the Lord will not come unless the apostasy comes first, and the man of sin is revealed, the son of perdition, who opposes and is exalted above all that is called God, or that is worshipped, so that he sits in the temple of God and gives himself out as if he were God. (9)

The fatal wound

The wound that the Beast received is not a superficial wound, as the world would not be amazed at someone recovering from a superficial wound. The Beast is fatally wounded and lives. This would be similar to John F. Kennedy recovering and living after he was mortally wounded. People would have worshiped John Kennedy, if he had lived.

The fatal wounding and healing of the Beast will be Satan's mimicry of the death and resurrection of Christ. The world will worship and follow after the Beast because of this unusual phenomenon of being restored to life from a fatal wound. The people will worship Satan, who gives his power and authority to the Beast. They will say who is like the Beast? Who can wage war against the Beast? (67)

St. Hildegard (1098-1179) wrote that the Antichrist will appear to be crucified and then rise from the dead. Christians will be astounded and have grievous doubts about their faith, while the followers of the Antichrist will be confirmed in their false faith. The Antichrist will be murdered; his blood spilled, die, and then rise from his death sleep. With bewilderment, the world will learn that he is not dead. (68)

Is the Little Horn in Daniel 7 and 8 and the "the Prince that shall come" in Daniel 9:26-27 and the "Willful King" in Daniel 11:36-45 all one and the same individual?

The Little Horn or Beast in Daniel 7 is shown to be the prince of Rome. The Little Horn or Beast in Daniel 8 is shown to come out of Greece. Gordon Lindsay called the beast in Daniel 7 and the beast in Daniel 8 one of the most puzzling and difficult questions for Biblical scholars. Most Biblical scholars understand or accept the Beast in Daniel 7, 9:26-27 and 11:36-45 as the prince of the Roman Kingdom. They do not understand the super powerful king or Beast from Greece in Daniel 8, which will comes into power at the time of the end. This king in Daniel 8 will wages war with the saints and destroys many. It will be shown that the Little Horn in Daniel 7 and 8, and the prince that shall come in Daniel 9:26-27 and the willful king in Daniel 11:36-45 are all one and the same.

What scriptural evidences do we have to indicate that the Beast, the Prince of the Roman Kingdom, will come out of Greece?

Revelation 17:9-10 shows that the seven heads of the dragon represent the seven kings or the seven world kingdoms. These seven kingdoms are:

1. Egypt
2. Assyria
3. Babylon   -   gold
4. Medo-Persia   -   silver
5. Greece   -   bronze
6. Roman Kingdom -   iron - at the first coming of Christ
7. Roman Kingdom -   iron and clay at the time of the end.

The scriptures say that five of the kings have fallen, one is and one is to come. Egypt, Assyria, Babylon, Medo-Persia and Greece have fallen. The prince of Rome (the angelic prince) was in power at the time John was writing Revelation, yet one more prince was to come.

Revelation 17 speaks of a prince of Satan ascending out of a bottomless pit to enter into the son of perdition.

> Revelation 17:8: The beast that thou sawest was, and is not; and shall ascend out of the bottomless pit and go into perdition: . . . (10).

> Revelation 17:11: And the beast that was, is not, even he is the eighth and is of the seven and goeth into perdition (10).

The prince that ascends out of the bottomless pit was, is not and will come again.

Who is the angelic prince that was, is not, and shall ascend out of the bottomless pit to rule again?

At the time John was writing Revelation, the angelic prince "that is" was the prince of Rome, so the prince of Rome cannot be the prince that is to come. The prince "that was" would have to have come from one of the previous five kingdoms. The scriptures do not say anything about a prince coming out of Egypt, Assyria or Medo-Persia. The scriptures talk about Babylon, but the woman that rides the beast is described as the whore of Babylon. (67)

Daniel 7:19-25 speaks of a terrifying beast that rises at the time of the end to wage war and overcome the saints of the Most High and devour the whole earth. This beast has iron teeth and bronze claws. Iron represents the Roman kingdom and while bronze represents the Kingdom of Greece.

The bronze claws on the terrifying beast in Daniel 7, and the body of a leopard in Revelation 13, indicate that the angelic prince of Greece, is the prince that was, is not, and who shall ascend out of the bottomless pit to rule the seventh kingdom of Rome at the time of the end.

The king of Greece

The scriptures teach that a king will arise out of Greece at the time of the end. The ram and goat, in Daniel 8:3-8, 20-22, are identified as Medio-Persia and Greece. Daniel 8:9-15, 23-26 shows that the little horn that comes into power at the time of the end will come out of Greece.

The Angel Gabriel spoke to Daniel in Daniel 8:19 and said, "Behold, I am going to let you know what will occur at the final period of indignation, for it pertains to the appointed time of the end." The Living Bible translation says,"I am here to tell you what is going to happen in the last days of the coming time of terror - for what you have seen pertain to that final event in history." The final period of indignation takes place during the seventieth week of Daniel at the time of the end, just prior to the return of the Lord to the earth.

> Daniel 8:23 And in the latter time of their kingdom, when the transgressors are come to the full, a king of fierce countenance, and understanding dark sentences, shall stand up (10).

This scripture speaks of the latter time of their kingdom (The Kingdom of Greece) when the transgressors have become morally rotten and corrupt to the greatest degree, an angry king with great intelligence and shrewdness shall rise to power.

> Daniel 8:24-25: And his power will be mighty, but not by his own power, and he will destroy to an extraordinary degree and prosper and perform his will; he will destroy mighty men and holy people. And through his shrewdness, he will cause deceit to succeed by his influence; and he will magnify himself in his heart, and he will destroy many while they are at ease. He will even oppose the Prince of princes, . . . (12)

The supernatural power given to the king, in Daniel 9:23, is the same power given to the Beast described in Revelation 13:2-4. This fierce king or Beast will destroy mighty men and holy people, and even oppose the Prince of princes, which is Jesus Christ.

Antiochus Epiphanes in 168 BC was definitely a forerunner of the Beast described in Daniel 8, when he defiled the temple and slaughtered the Jews (19). However, he does not fulfill all that was written in Daniel 8, especially that pertaining to the time of the end. Daniel in 8:26 is told to keep the vision he had seen secret, for it pertains to many days in the future, indicating the time of the end.

In Daniel 12:9, Daniel is told to seal up the words until the time of the end. Many theologians believed that the words Daniel was told to seal is the book of the seven seals, which were to be opened at the time of the end as revealed in the Book of Revelation. (32, 33, 34)

Summary:

1. Revelation 17:8 shows that an angelic prince of Satan that once ruled a previous kingdom, will rule the seventh kingdom at the time of the end. Scripture says the Beast that was, is not, shall ascend out of the bottomless pit and goes into perdition. Only fallen angels come out of the bottomless pit.

2. Daniel 8 teaches that a fierce king will come out of the kingdom of Greece at the time of the end.

3. Revelation 17:10 shows that the prince of Rome, the sixth kingdom of iron was in power, when John was writing the Book of Revelation. The prince of the seventh kingdom was described as a prince that was, is not and will come. The angelic prince of Rome, ruling at the time John was writing the Book of Revelation, will not be the angelic prince of the seventh kingdom of iron and clay. This shows that the sixth kingdom and the seventh kingdom of Rome is not one continuous kingdom but two separate kingdoms.

4. Daniel 7 speaks of four beasts, the lion, the bear, the leopard and an unidentified beast as coming out of the sea (i.e. from among the people). Yet, each

beast was symbolic of an earthly kingdom: Babylon, Medo-Persia, Greece and Rome. Daniel 10 shows that a prince of Satan is over each of these kingdoms.

5. The Beast, in Revelation 13:1-2, is described as a composite with the main body being a leopard. The unidentified beast with ten horns in Daniel 7 had iron teeth and bronze claws. Iron and bronze represent the Roman and Grecian Empires.

Since,

1. Revelation 17:8, 10-11 shows that the angelic prince of Rome at the first coming of Christ, is not the angelic prince of Rome at the time of the end,

2. and since Daniel 8 speaks of a king coming out of a Grecian Kingdom at the time of the end, and the composite Beast with a body of a leopard that comes out of the sea in Revelation 13:1 is a symbol of Greece, and the bronze claws of the unidentified Beast represent Greece, it appears that the Beast or the Little Horn of the ten-nation federation will arise out of Greece to become the head of the seventh kingdom of iron and clay.

The term, "Beast" is used interchangeably for the angelic prince that ascended out of the bottomless pit and for the man who will be the head of the ten-nation federation. The angelic prince of Greece will be the prince that was, is not and shall come, who ascends out of the bottomless pit to enter into the son of perdition to become the eighth head in the body of the seventh head that was fatally wounded.

The angelic prince of Greece, who ruled the fifth kingdom (bronze) at the time of Alexander the Great, will also be the prince of the seventh kingdom (iron and clay).

Dake in his "Annotated Reference Bible" called the prince that comes out of the bottomless pit, in Revelation 17:8,10, "the prince of Greece" (35).

Scripture teaches that he will be a mighty ruler from Greece.

Has the Roman Empire continued from the time of Christ in the Roman Catholic Church?

Some biblical scholars believe that the Roman Empire at the time of Christ and the Roman Kingdom at the time of the end when the Lord returns are one continuous kingdom. A few Bible scholars have gone to great pains to prove that the torch of the Roman Empire, after its fall, was picked up and carried by the Roman Catholic Church and will continue until the kingdom of iron and clay comes into existence. The Encyclopedia Britannica (XIV Edition) says,

> The Roman Empire was and always continued to be ideally one and indivisible. There were two emperors but one Empire - two persons but one power. The point is of great importance for understanding of the middle ages. There only is and can be one Empire. (69)

This statement is not true. The seven-headed dragon is symbolic of the seven world kingdoms. The kingdom of iron is the sixth kingdom while the kingdom of iron and clay is the seventh kingdom. The kingdom of iron, and the kingdom of iron and clay are two different kingdoms as shown by the fact that they are ruled by two different angelic princes of darkness (Revelation 17:8, 10).

The kingdom of iron ended with the fall of the Roman Empire. The kingdom of iron and clay is another kingdom at the time of the end. If they are two different kingdoms i.e. the sixth and the seventh heads of the seven-headed dragon and are ruled by two different angelic princes, how can there be one continuous kingdom from the time of Christ until the time of the end.

The Prince of Rome – the Prince of the Seventh Kingdom of Iron and Clay

Gordon Lindsay called the beast of Daniel 7 and the beast of Daniel 8 one of the most puzzling and difficult questions for biblical scholars.

Is the Little Horn of Daniel 7 and 8, "the Prince that shall come" of Daniel 9:26-27 and the "Willful King" of Daniel 11:36-45 all one and the same?

The Little Horn or Beast in Daniel 7 is shown to be the prince of Rome. The Little Horn or Beast in Daniel 8 is shown to come out of Greece.

Daniel 9:27 shows that the seventieth week of Daniel begins, when the prince of the people that destroyed Jerusalem, makes a covenant with Israel for seven years. The people that destroyed Jerusalem after Christ were the Roman people in 68 to 70 AD. (13)

How can the Beast come out of Greece and be the Prince of the Roman people?

The answer to this question is very simple. Since Greece was part of the Roman Kingdom at the time of Christ and will probably be part of the ten-nation federation at the time of the end, it is possible for a man from Greece to be the head of the Roman Empire. If a man from Greece is over this ten-nation federation, he will be the prince of the Roman people.

Some students of prophecy believe that the Beast in Daniel 8 will be the False Prophet described in Revelation 13:11-17. However, the Beast in Daniel 8 is described as a king, having too much power to be the False Prophet. The False Prophet is not a king.

Who is the Little Horn and how does he come to power?

At this point, we are simply speculating, for no one knows how the Beast will come into power. Daniel 7:19, 8:23-26, Revelation 13:1 and 17:8, 10 show that the Beast or the Little Horn will come out of Greece or the Grecian Empire. The ten-nation federation will be in existence before the little horn moves in and takes over. This is shown by the unidentified beast in Daniel 7 having ten horns before the Little Horn appears uprooting three large horns. We see from Daniel 7 and Revelation 17:12 that the Little Horn is not one of the ten large horns.

> Revelation 17:12: And the ten horns which you saw are the ten kings, who have not received a kingdom, but they receive authority as kings with the beast for one hour (12).

The Little Horn or the Beast will have to have a military base in order to take over three nations. This man will probably be a military leader in Greece. He will somehow, by force, take over the government of Greece. The people of other nations will not interfere saying, "Oh, just an internal struggle for power."

The Beast, being a composite of the kingdoms of Babylon, Medo-Persia and Greece, will be a military genius exhibiting the outstanding features of Nebuchadnezzar, Alexander the Great, Genghis Khan and Napoleon. He will be a super-human gifted with charisma, intelligence, wisdom, knowledge and understanding.

Greece will be the first of the three nations conquered by the Beast. Shortly after taking over Greece, the Beast will move swiftly and take over Italy and Rome, the governing center of the ten-nation federation. It will be over before the people know what happened. One of the eight remaining nations will resist the Beast taking over

Rome and assuming a leadership role over them. The Beast will move quickly and defeat the third nation. The other seven nations will submit to the Beast. They will say, "Who is like the Beast? Who can make war with him?"

Some theologians believe the Beast will come out of Syria or another part of the Grecian Empire. This is highly unlikely, as the Beast has to have a military base to operate from. It would be difficult for Syria or another nation, outside the ten-nation federation, to take over three nations. Again if an outside nation took over, there would be eleven nations involved instead of ten nations.

In a very short period of time, the Beast will rise from obscurity to the most powerful, most feared figure in the world. Because of the ease with which the Beast overpowers three nations and takes over ten nations, the people will say, "Who is like the Beast? Who is able to wage war with him?" At this time the world will be in a chaotic turmoil. The people will be looking for a world leader, who can restore order and peace. The Beast, a super-human genius will be looked upon to restore order and peace.

The Beast will make a covenant with many for one week.

Scripture says the Beast will make a covenant with many for one week (Daniel 9:27). Many nations of the world will be anxious to make a covenant with the Beast for peace and protection.

The Kingdom of Iron and Kingdom of Clay

Scripture says the kingdom of iron and the kingdom of clay will come together in the seeds of men, but will not adhere to one another. The kingdom of clay is probably Russia and her allies, as discussed earlier in the book. The kingdom of clay, having great respect for the Beast, will make a covenant with the Beast and the ten nations of iron to become one kingdom.

Covenant with Israel is a covenant with death. This covenant marks the beginning of the seventieth week of Daniel.

Israel, a small nation, is being hemmed in and threatened by the nations of the north as well as the nations around Israel and the Palestinians, who want to take possession of the land and destroy the Jews. Because of this, Israel will make a covenant with the Beast, the prince of the Roman Empire, for seven years in exchange for peace and protection. Isaiah called this covenant "a covenant with death" (Isaiah 28:15). The minute this covenant is made will be the beginning of the seventieth week of Daniel (Daniel 9:27). The first three and one-half years will be peace.

A fierce king understanding dark sentences shall come.

> Daniel 8:23-25: And at the latter end of their kingdom, when the transgressors have reached the fullness, a king of fierce countenance and understanding dark trickery and craftiness, shall stand up. And his power shall be mighty, but not by his own power; and he shall corrupt and destroy astonishingly, and shall prosper, and do his own pleasure, and he shall corrupt and destroy the mighty men and the holy people - the people of the saints. And through his policy he shall cause trickery to prosper in his hand; he shall magnify himself in his heart and mind, and in their security he will corrupt and destroy many. He shall also stand up against the Prince of princes, . . . (59)

The Beast from Greece will be a fierce and ruthless king who understands dark sentences. His power will come from Satan. He will cause trade and craft to prosper. He will use trickery and deceit to take advantage of others. He will make war with the saints and wear out the holy people of God.

Daniel 8:25 says the Beast by peace shall destroy many.

Some translations say that while the people are living in security, the Beast through stealth or deceit will destroy many. The King James Version says that by peace the Beast will destroy many. The New American Standard says he will destroy to an extraordinary degree. He will destroy the mighty men and holy people of God while they are at ease. He will even oppose the prince of princes, Jesus Christ.

What is the meaning of the verse "by peace shall destroy many?" Israel will make a covenant of peace for seven years. Though Israel is at peace, the Beast will break the covenant and will begin the greatest holocaust the world has ever known. The Beast, with the help of the False Prophet has complete freedom in Israel and will begin killing those who will not bow down to worship him or his image and take his mark. Through peace, the Beast will destroy many. This is the reason Isaiah called this covenant, a covenant with death.

Daniel 11:1-34 speaks of Greece and the four divided kingdoms of Greece before the time of Christ. However, Daniel 11:35-45 leaps forward to the time of the end just prior to the return of the Lord (70).

The Beast will magnify himself above God.

> Daniel 11:36: Then the king will do as he pleases, and he will exalt and magnify himself above every god, and will speak monstrous things against the God of gods; and he will prosper until the indignation is finished, for that which is decreed will be done. (12)

> II Thessalonians 2:4: who opposes and exalts himself above every so-called god or object of worship, so that he takes his seat in the temple of God, displaying himself as being God (12).

He will not honor the god of his fathers.

> Daniel 11:37: He shall not regard the gods of his fathers or Him (to whom) women desire or any other god, for he shall magnify himself above all (59).

Many theologians believe the Beast will be a Jew because the scripture says he does not honor the gods of his fathers.

St. Hippolytus (170-236) said just as Christ came from the Hebrews, the Antichrist would also rise from the Jews. He said Moses spoke of Dan, as a lion whelp clearly showing the tribe from which the Antichrist would rise. Dan is one of the two tribes that is not listed or mentioned with the other tribes in the Book of Revelation. Jacob spoke, in Genesis 49, of what was going to happen in the days to come:

> Genesis 49:17: Let Dan be a serpent by the roadside, a horned viper by the path, that bite the horse's heel, so that the rider tumbles backward.

The beast will prohibit the celebration of the Holy Sacrifice of the Mass. The Lord's Supper will have to be celebrated underground in the forests and secret places, as it was in the first days of Christianity. The Antichrist will build the temple of stone in Jerusalem. (68)

St. Methodius of Olympus, who lived in 3rd century, stated that the Son of Perdition will be of the tribe of Dan according to the prophecy of Jacob. Judas Iscariot was also reported to be from the tribe of Dan (68).

St. John Chrysostom (347- 407), a prominent doctor of the Church, reported the Antichrist will be an illegitimate son of a Jewish woman and be possessed by Satan (68).

Adso, The Monk, in the 10th century stated that the Antichrist would be born of Jewish parents of the tribe of Dan (68).

St. Hildegard (1098-1179) stated the Antichrist would be a descendant of the tribe of Dan, born of an ungodly woman involved in the occult. She will live with perverse men and conceive the Son of Perdition without knowing who his father is (68).

St. Bridget of Sweden (1303 -1373) stated that as Christ was born of the highest of woman, the Antichrist will be born of the lowest (prostitute). The Antichrist's mother will be an accursed woman pretending to be well-informed in spiritual matters. (68)

St. Irenaeus (125-202) stated that the Antichrist would sit in the temple of God as if he were Christ. The Jews will be deceived to an extent that they will accept him as the Messiah and worship him (68).

St. Methodius of Olymus, who lived in 3rd century, said the Son of Perdition will perform many false miracles causing the blind to see, lame to walk and the deaf to hear. He deceives many, even the elect (68).

St. John Chrysostom, (347- 407) a prominent doctor of the Church, reported that the Antichrist will be an illegitimate son of a Jewish woman and be possessed by Satan. He is born of fornication and is brought up unnoticed: but all of a sudden he rises up, revolts and rules. When he gains complete control, he persecutes the Church of God and reveals all his wickedness. "And he shall come in signs and lying wonders" – sham ones and not real – and he shall seduce those whose intention rests on a rotten and unstable foundation and make them abandon the living God, "in as much as to scandalize (if possible) even the elect". (68)

St. John Damascene, (676-754), said the Antichrist would heal the sick, the blind, the deaf, the dumb, cause and claim storms, make trees blossom and wither at his word. He will rebuild the temple of Jerusalem (68).

St. Vincent Ferrer said, if you do not wish to be deceived, place your whole faith and trust in the name of Jesus Christ and refuse to acknowledge any miracle unless it was worked in his name (17).

The Beast speaks great blasphemies against God and wages war against the people of God for forty-two months.

> Apocalypse 13:5-7: And there was given to it a mouth speaking great things and blasphemies; and there was given to it authority to work for forty-two months. And it opened its mouth for blasphemies against God, to blaspheme his name and his tabernacle, and those who dwell in heaven. And it was allowed to wage war with the saints and to overcome them. . . . (9)

> Daniel 7:25: And he will speak out against the Most High and wear down the saints of the Highest One, and he will intend to make alternations in times and in law; and they will be given into his hand for time, times and half a time (42 months). (12)

The Beast will not only open his mouth against God and His people, he will make changes in time and law.

Many people believe that there will be seven years of tribulation. How can this be when the Beast is given power for only 42 months (3 1/2 years) to wage war with the people of God? The Beast will certainly be in power longer than forty-two months. He will actually be in power for at least seven years or longer. He will be over the ten-nation federation before he makes his covenant with Israel. The minute the Beast makes his covenant with Israel that will be the beginning of the seventieth week of Daniel, which is seven years. The scripture says the Beast will break the covenant in the middle of the week with the abomination and desolation of the temple (Daniel 9:27, Matthew 24:15). The breaking of the covenant is the beginning of the Great Tribulation. When the covenant is broken in the middle of the week, there are only three and one-half years (42 months) left for the Beast to wage war against the saints and those who will not take his mark. Apocalypse 13:6 above, speaks of blasphemies against the tabernacle or the temple.

At the end of the forty-two months, when the Lord Jesus Christ returns, the Beast and the False Prophet will be captured and thrown alive into the Lake of Fire (Revelation 19:20). The first part of the last forty-two months will be the Great Tribulation. The last part of the forty-two months will be the Wrath of God (Refer to Table 3 in Chapter 6).

Will the Beast control the whole earth?

> Apocalypse 13:7-8: . . . And there was given to it (Beast) authority over every tribe, and people, and tongue, and nation. And all the inhabitants of the earth will worship it whose names have not been written in the book of life of the Lamb who has been slain from the foundation of the world. (9)

Gordon Lindsay said we have to be careful about making scripture say what isn't intended (26).

1. When the New Testament refers to the entire world, it often refers to the Roman world. Such was the case, in Luke 2:1, when Augustus Caesar was referring

to the Roman world not the whole earth. Scripture, in Daniel 2:38-39, speaks of Nebuchadnezzar of Babylon and the Kingdom of Greece, respectively, ruling all the earth. However, these kingdoms did not rule North and South America, all of Africa or Asia.

2. Revelation 6:8 speaks of the wild beasts under the fourth horseman having authority over one-fourth of the earth. The wild beasts are the lieutenants under the Beast or the Antichrist. This scripture shows that the Antichrist will only control one-fourth of the earth.

3. Daniel 7:7-8 and Revelation 17:17-18 show that the Beast will control the territory of the ten kings.

4. Daniel 11:41 shows that the Beast will not have control of the land of Edom, Moab and Amman, which are parts of the country of Jordan. Edom is southeast of the Dead Sea. Moab is east of the Dead Sea. Amman is east of Israel from the Jordan River. These countries will be a place of refuge for the saints, i.e. the Jews and Christians in Israel, who heed the Lord's warning, in Matthew 24:15-22, and leave immediately before all means of escape are cut off.

5. Ezekiel 38:13 speaks of Sheba, Dedan and the merchants of Tarshish with all the young lions questioning the invasion of Israel at the time of the end. Many Bible scholars believe that the merchants of Tarshish represent England; while the young lions are the English-speaking nations.

6. Daniel 11:40 shows the king of the South coming against the Beast. Daniel 11:44-45 states that the countries in the North and East will make war with the Beast. The scripture in Revelation 16:12-16 speaks of all nations of the world gathering together in Israel

for the battle of Armageddon. Gordon Lindsay believes that the king of the South will be the English-speaking nations since all nations of the world will be gathered together for battle.

7. The English-speaking nations could not come into Israel from the west as that is the strong hold of the Beast. They could not come in through the north, as this is the territory of Russia and her allies. The English speaking nations couldn't come in through the east as this will be the gateway of the king of the East (believed to be China and other Far East nations). The only way for the English-speaking nations to come into Israel is through the south.

Nevertheless, it can be seen that the Beast does not have complete control of the world (26).

United Nations becomes a global police as national boundaries run together under a one world order.

John Leary received the following words, which indicate that America and most of the world will be under the control of the Antichrist.

> During the coming days you will see the UN become a global police as national boundaries will run together. Soon your laws will become subject to the laws of the one world order. This will set up the conditions for the Antichrist to command the whole world with his influence. This evil time will be stressful but your hope is that it will not last long. When I come in glory to put aside the evil one and his evil men, the earth will be free from his clutches for a millennium. Once you witness this peace, you will see that your

suffering was short and that it was well-worth waiting for this new era of Mine to dawn on you. Keep My love in your heart and remain faithful. Then you will witness your reward and see how much I have protected you. 5/10/94 (45)

John Leary had a vision of crowns falling to the ground and many golden chairs falling over backward. Jesus said:

My people, you will see many of the leaders of your nations falling from their places of power. As the Antichrist comes at the tribulation, he will assume full authority over all the nations. He will be allowed a length of time in history to test man. I will be with you at that time protecting you, but your faith must be strong at that time. I will allow My mother to crush the head of Satan with her foot as our triumphs over him will soon come to pass. Rejoice, all of mankind, for your Lord will come in glory thereafter. 12/12/96 (46)

Mr. Leary had a vision of bright lights and barbed wire fence.

You are seeing detention centers where political and religious prisoners will be kept. America in its decadence will be sliding into oblivion much like the Roman Empire. It will go from persecuting the unborn and the aged on to those who are openly religious and those who do not believe in the workings of the government. As the citizens are selected and tortured, all will be suspect eventually, thus degrading your democracy into a blatant tyranny of dictators. This chaos will cause revolutions and the last state of your nation will be worse than the first. As you take Me out of your life as a partner in forming your government, you are inviting the control of the Anti-Christ and disaster. Pray My people to endure this trial. 10/26/94 (43)

John Leary had a vision of a convoy of covered army trucks. He also could see many strands of barbed wire at a detention center. Jesus said:

> . . . You are seeing these vehicles, which will be carrying those captured. Those who refuse to take the mark of the beast or are not giving allegiance to the Antichrist will be among the captured. These trucks are taking their prisoners to the detention centers which are being readied even now. I am showing you these things, not to despair in fright, but to be forewarned to leave your homes for hiding as these signs I have given come about. Have full trust in Me that I will lead you to the refuges and safe havens I have prepared for you. Do not be afraid to proclaim these messages of warning, but pray for the strength to continue speaking, even if it may endanger your life. I will bring you My Holy Spirit to defend you against the attacks of the evil ones . . . 11/17/96 (46)

God gives a special command – if any one has ears, let him hear.

Revelation 13:9: If anyone has an ear, let him hear (12).

Seiss says that God has given a special admonition and command similar to the emphasis that was placed on the vital points of the gospel. Christians have a great need to study and understand what has been foreshown. This phase emphasizes something of intense urgency and importance, not only for theologians and biblical scholars, but also for all people who have an ear for learning the divine truth. (48)

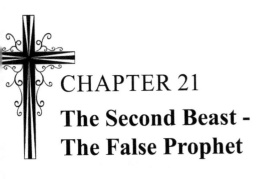

CHAPTER 21

The Second Beast - The False Prophet

The Beast comes out of the earth

> Revelation 13:11: Then I saw another beast, coming out of the earth. He had two horns like a lamb, but he spoke as a dragon (7).

The second Beast that rises up out of the earth is a man like the first Beast that rises out of the sea. They both come from among the people. The second Beast comes as a lamb. Jesus warns us about false prophets coming to us in sheep's clothing.

> Matthew 7:15: Beware of the false prophets, who come to you in sheep's clothing, but inwardly are ravenous wolves (12).

The second Beast comes as a gentle lamb having two horns. Horns are a symbol of power but these horns do not have crowns; therefore, political sovereignty or military power is out of the question. The Beast, coming as a lamb and a man of peace, will be a false prophet and a spiritual leader, not a king or a military leader. (47)

The first Beast comes out of the sea which is spoken of as a multitude of people of different nations, races and tongues (Revelation 17:15). The second Beast is a false prophet that comes from the earth. The False Prophet will speak as a dragon, i.e. he will speak with lies and deceptions.

> Revelation 13:12-14: He exercised all the authority of
> the first beast on his behalf, and made the earth and its
> inhabitants worship the first beast, whose fatal wound
> had been healed. And he performed great and miracu-
> lous signs, even causing fire to come down from heav-
> en to earth in full view of men. Because of the signs he
> was given power to do on behalf of the first beast, he
> deceived the inhabitants of the earth. . . . (7)

It was by God's supernatural power that Moses performed signs and wonders before Pharaoh and all of Egypt, to convince Pharaoh to let God's people go. In the days of the false prophets of Baal, it was by calling fire down from heaven that Elijah demonstrated that the God of Abraham, Isaac and Jacob was the God of Israel. It was by supernatural signs and wonders that Jesus showed that he was the Son of God.

Yet, the False Prophet will have his day. He will posses super-natural power to perform great miracles in the sight of the beast and men, so as to deceive those that dwell on earth. He will mislead even the elect, if possible.

> Matthew 24:24: For false Christs and false prophets
> will appear and perform great signs and miracles to
> deceive even the elect - if that were possible (7).

The False Prophet will be the counterfeit to the two witnesses who will also have power to perform signs and wonders in heaven and on earth, even calling fire down to consume their enemies.

A black Impostor Pope will be the False Prophet of Revelation 13.

A number of visionaries and locutionists through the centu-ries have reported the coming of the imposter, Anti-Pope, who will cause a great schism in the Church ushering in the apostate church just prior to the coming of the Antichrist and the return of the Lord Jesus Christ. Below are some of prophecies pertaining to the false Pope from different visionaries and locutionists that were written in the Catholic Prophecy Update, July / August 1997. (71)

St. Hildegard (1098 -1179) stated that just prior to the coming of the Antichrist that an Anti-Pope will come into power and lead two-thirds of the Christians with him. Jane Le Royer, 1798, Sister of the Nativity reported that as the Second Coming of Christ approaches, a bad priest would do much to harm the Church.

Julia of Yugoslavia, on February 28, 1976, in a conversation with the Lord about the false pope was told:

> "The false Pope has not yet come! One day, when the false shepherd rules he will spread a false doctrine and will persecute the Church. You will recognize him by the persecution of the Church. He will not have much time at his disposal. His rule will be short but strong. The good Christians and My true servants will have to hide themselves. . . Once the false Peter is in, he will persecute My Church and My Flock will be dispersed."

Joanne Kriva on June 25, 1992 received a message from the Lord, that a cardinal, who works seditiously to destroy what Pope John Paul II, his chosen Vicar, seeks to affirm as the revealed truth of his Word, is a son of Satan. This son of Satan, whose plotting and scheming will usher in the apostate church, and his cohorts, who stand poised to step into the shoes of the Fisherman, is not our Lord's successor, but a usurper and not the legitimate heir to the throne of Peter. In this apostate church every aberration will be condoned, every blasphemy permitted. This abomination is the church of Satan. The desecration of our Lord's holy temple will be complete. The true sacrifice and the living Eucharistic Presence will disappear from His Churches.

Sadie Jaramillo, on June 16, 1996, in a vision, saw a man, dressed in black pontifical robes, with a black miter, the type the Pope wears. I felt nothing but evil looking at this man. Then she was told,

> "This man exists and awaits his moment to take the seat of Vicar of Christ, though he, along with many others are wolves in sheep clothing. . . ."

On October 19, 1996 Sadie Jaramillo saw in a vision an empty chair and then heard the Lord says,

> "Weep bitter tears child, for they will soon come and pillage My sanctuaries and the Chair of Peter will soon be vacant of My chosen Vicar". (71)

According to the numerous prophetic messages received by John Leary, a demon possessed bishop will take over as a black, impostor pope, who is spoken of as the little horn of the apocalypse. (The little horn of the apocalypse (Revelation) is the False Prophet while the little horn of Daniel 8 is the Antichrist) He will cause a great schism in the Church. He will change the laws so that the Masses will no longer be valid. The black pope will come into power before the Antichrist. He and the Antichrist will reign together. He will cause all to worship the Antichrist. (72)

> . . . All manner of blasphemy and contradiction will come from this black pope and Satan will then cause a schism in My Church. It will be at this time, that My faithful remnant will be split away from those willing to follow the worldly ways of the black pope. The evil pope will be cunning and powerful in misleading the

people. Do not follow his decrees, but follow those things taught by the old fathers of My Church. Your faith will indeed be tested, but follow My warning and gather separately in your prayer groups, where you will find consolation. Pray for My help and I will lead you what to do. Have faith in Me and your reward will be found in heaven. 11/11/95 (44)

John Leary had a vision of a beautiful banquet table, which broke in the middle and fell to the floor with the wine and hosts falling as well. Jesus said,

My people, you can recognize the meaning of this broken table as the beginning of a great schism in My Church. This is the age of apostasy and when you see the impostor pope take his position, this time of trial will begin. All abomination and heresy will spew from his mouth. He will mislead many in My Church by his cunning and his lies. Many will not realize the changes he will bring, but My faithful will discern his erring spirit, as your traditions will be so corrupted that the mass will no longer be valid under his direction. Many of My remnants will then seek underground services to preserve My True Presence. This will be another sign to you of the coming tribulation. This black pope will then be in league with the Anti-Christ in an attempt to destroy all of mankind by conquering their souls for evil. Be not afraid, My people. I will be with you for your protection. Pray to Me and I will come to your need. Continue your prayers to strengthen yourselves for this time. 3/4/96 (44)

Some predicted that John Paul II would be the last of the good pope. Those making these predictions were wrong about Pope Benedict XVI as he was definitely a good and holy pope. There are many predictions that the pope after Pope Benedict XVI will be an evil pope. The messages below indicate that Pope Francis will be a strong holy pope in the manner of John Paul II and Pope Benedict XVI. A message below supposedly from the Blessed Mother stated that Pope Francis will move the Papacy to Jerusalem.

Benedict - A Bridge between Popes

Jesus - February 19, 2013

> Only the just man would be patient and faithful. Such is Pope Benedict, a pope after my own heart whom I have chosen as my Vicar. Now he has completed the course. He is the bridge between the two great popes. He provided the needed time of transition from one to the other. Now that Benedict's time is completed, I can raise up the one who will complement Pope John Paul II, who saw his mission but knew the pope would not live to see its fulfillment.

> What remains to be done to bring the Church into the third millennium? Certainly, the world is in the third millennium and Pope John Paul II was the pope to open that millennium. However, the Church has not yet found its way. In spite of these two great popes, John Paul and Benedict, the Church is slipping behind and not keeping pace. I must give the Church a new role, a surprising role, so that the whole world will see that the Church does not follow the world but is far ahead of the world. This can happen only by the intervening power of God in world events. (73)

The Gifts of the Two Popes - A Bridge between Popes

Jesus February 20, 2013

People look for reasons of why the Pope will resign. They should look into my Sacred Heart. He will resign because it is my will that he step down. He correctly sees himself as my instrument. I took him into my holy hands and used him for these years to guide my Church. He has brought to the Church his light and his intellect. He has constantly offered clear explanations of its truth and, most important, has tried to shine the light of faith upon every conceivable question. He lives by that light and has tried to cast that light upon every issue. He has laid an intellectual foundation. All who want to search his writings will find clarity and reason.

Now, I must bring another pope to the Chair of Peter. He will have a different goal, one that Benedict truly shares and deeply believes in. As I placed a great light of learning in Benedict, so I have placed the great light of my mother in the new pope. His heart is filled with Mary. He lives in her and, literally, breathes in her. Her name is always on his lips. She is the one who has prepared and chosen him from the beginning. Like Benedict, he will bring to the Chair of Peter exactly what I have placed in his heart. He will not see himself bringing his own talents. He knows they are too little. He carries Fatima in his heart. That will be his first gift. He also carries Jerusalem in his heart. That is his second gift. When he has given those two gifts to the Church, his papacy will be completed, just as Benedict's is now complete. (73)

The Pope of Fatima

Mary

> What am I to say when that moment is about to be fulfilled, the moment that I have waited for and planned for.? I am about to raise to the Chair of Peter the pope of Fatima, the pope who will consecrate Russia but will do so much more. He will bathe the Church in devotion to me. My name will always be on his lips. I will be lifted up as never before in the history of the Church. Through the pope, the Church will breathe in me. Every breath will give new life. He will not bring his own gifts because the gifts I have given him are so much greater. All will see the changes and blessings that occur. (73)

A Pope for All Nations

Jesus - February 26, 2013

> Because I open my heart to all nations, to all cultures and to all peoples, I will raise up a pope for all the nations. All will see in him a hope for salvation and a deliverance from the worldwide darkness that will soon envelope the earth, a darkness of confusion, doubt and, at times, even of hysteria and self-destruction. These will be the forces that will soon be unleashed. Before that happens, I will set in place a pope who will speak my word and release the powers of the kingdom. He will not teach in his own name nor bring forth human wisdom. He will speak my word, exactly as I have trained him to do. (73)

Mary

Now that the time is so close I will reveal the deep secrets of my heart, kept hidden for so long. I have prepared this pope by the greatest of graces. I have fashioned him in the darkness of my womb and soon, so very soon, I will bring him into the light of day. Upon him shall be the anointing of Jerusalem, because that is where he will go and there he will end his days in the papacy.

He already knows my plan and will fulfill it just as I have laid it out before him. He will not swerve, to the left or to the right. He will discern all the world events, for himself and for the Church. He will raise his voice like no other pope because the Spirit of the Lord is upon him. When the years of his short papacy are completed, the seeds of new life will be planted. His papacy will prepare the Church for all that will follow in this third millennium. (73)

The Messenger Pope – A Prophet to the Nations.

Jesus - February 27, 2013

How much time has been lost. The gifts of God set aside. So many times I have spoken to my servants, the prophets. I have given them heavenly messages for all the world to hear. . . . . The need for my prophetic word is too pressing. I can no longer just send messengers. I must send a pope who himself is the messenger. To him I will speak, directly, heart to heart, even face to face. All the world will know that this pope is a prophet to the nations. (73)

Mary –

> For so long I have kept this future pope in my bosom,
> hidden from the nations, yet called to be their light.
> I have trained him in my word and he has frequently
> brought it forth. He is no stranger to prophecy. He
> understands the gift. He is familiar with my voice.
> Know that I am raising up much more than just a
> pope. I am lifting up a prophet to the nations. All
> the world will listen because he will not just speak a
> word of wisdom but a clear prophetic word. He is not
> shy or bashful. He will not hide the gift. He will not
> be lifted up to place the lamp under a bushel basket.
> He knows where my word belongs.
>
> Suddenly, a new light will shine forth, a surprise, a
> new help for my children who are so confused by
> the darkness of the world. I will raise up this pope
> and prophet for my little ones who believe that I can
> speak directly to them. (73)

The Pope after Pope Benedict XVI cannot be the false prophet. There are 24 prophecies of saints, venerables, blesseds from many different countries from 4th century to the present time who have foretold the coming of a Holy Roman Catholic King of France who will conquer Europe and the Middle East who will be anointed a Holy Roman Emperor by a saintly pope prior to the coming of the Antichrist. It was foretold that this king will go to Jerusalem to die. It is interesting that one of the messages above stated that the next pope will move the Papacy office to Jerusalem. This is discussed in Chapter 27.

The worship of the image of the Beast

> Revelation 13:14: . . He ordered them to set up an image in honor of the beast who was wounded by the sword and yet lived. He was given power to give breath to the image of the first beast, so that it could speak and caused all who refused to worship the image to be killed. (7)

According to St. Vincent Ferrer, the Antichrist will cause both images (statues) and babes, one month old, to speak. The followers of the Antichrist will question these images and babes and will receive words that the Antichrist (the Beast) is their savior. The devil will move their lips and form the words they utter declaring the Antichrist to be the savior of the world. The Antichrist will cause the destruction of many souls. (17)

The worship of images as idols is not common in America, but very prevalent in other areas of the world as in Africa, the East and Far East. The worship of images of wood, silver, gold and stones was common throughout the Old Testament and New Testament.

The images of Nebuchadnezzar

The forced worship of images is found in the Book of Daniel. Nebuchadnezzar made an image of himself in gold that was ninety feet high and nine feet wide. It was set up in the Plain of Dura in the province of Babylon. Nebuchadnezzar invited everyone to come to the dedication of this statue. After all the officials and the people had gathered around the statue, they were told that after certain sounds, they were to bow down and worship the golden image of Nebuchadnezzar.

A large furnace was built near the golden image. The officials and the people were told that if they did not fall down and worship the golden image, they would be thrown into the blazing furnace to be burned alive. (Daniel 3)

This will also happen when the False Prophet places the image of the first Beast in the temple, bringing about the abomination of desolation, spoken of by Jesus, Daniel the prophet, and Paul. He will, by supernatural power, give the image a breath of life to become a living and speaking thing.

Moses, in the presence of Pharaoh, threw his rod or shaft on the floor and commanded it to become a living snake. The magicians of Pharaoh also did the same thing; however, Moses' snake ate the snakes of the magicians. Afterward, Moses' snake became his rod or shaft again.

The image, which the False Prophet commands to become a living thing, will cause all who do not bow down to the Beast or his image to be killed. When the abomination takes place, the believing Jews and Christians in Israel will have a very short time to flee before the roads and airports are closed and all means of escape are cut off.

> Matthew 24:15-21: So when you see standing in the holy place "the abomination that causes desolation" spoken of through the prophet Daniel - let the reader understand - then let those who are in Judea flee to the mountains. Let no one on the roof of his house go down to take anything out of the house. Let no one in the field go back to get his cloak. How dreadful it will be in those days for pregnant women and nursing mothers! Pray that your flight will not take place in winter or on the Sabbath. For then there will be great distress, unequaled from the beginning of the world until now - and never to be equaled again. (7)

THE SECOND BEAST - THE FALSE PROPHET

The mark of the Beast

> Revelation 13:16-17: He also forces everyone, small and great, rich and poor, free and slave, to receive a mark on his right hand or on his forehead, so that no one could buy or sell unless he had the mark, which is the name of the beast or the number of his name. (7)

The Beast will force everyone in the countries he controls to take his mark either on their right hand or forehead. Without this mark, people will not be able to buy or sell. The people will not be able to buy food or any of the necessities of life. All that is necessary to receive the mark is to bow down and worship the Beast or his image.

St. Vincent Ferrer, a Dominican priest who lived in the 14th century, was healed of a serious illness when the Lord appeared to him and touched him, leaving a permanent mark on his face. He was commanded by the Lord to preach on the coming judgment. St. Vincent Ferrer, known as the Angel of Judgment, preached throughout Europe on the coming of the Antichrist and a period of persecution and darkness, unprecedented in human history. This would be a time when the Lord's light would not shine, His Word would not be preached or heard, and the mentioning of the name of Jesus would not be tolerated. St. Vincent Ferrer stated that no Christian will be able to purchase the necessities of life except at the cost of denying Christ. They will be driven to hide in the deserts, eating grass for their food. The scriptures say that the Beast will have control of all the gold, silver and riches in the world. To keep from losing their dominion, rulers, kings and princes will follow the Antichrist. In like manner, many prelates, priests, and religious, for the fear of losing their dignities and to gain honor and riches will forsake the faith of Christ and adhere to the Antichrist. (17)

Many people, being fearful for their lives or the loss of their comfort or possessions and not wanting to see their children or loved ones killed or starved to death, will bow down to worship the Beast. They will say in their hearts, "God knows I am being forced to do this against my will and God will not hold this against me." The scriptures say otherwise.

> Revelation 14:9-12: . . . If anyone worships the beast and his image and receives his mark on the fore-head or on the hand, he, too, will drink of the wine of God's fury, which has been poured full strength into the cup of his wrath. He will be tormented with burning sulfur in the presence of the holy angels and of the Lamb. And the smoke of their torment rises forever and ever. There is no rest day or night, for those who worship the beast and his image, or for anyone who receives the mark of his name. This calls for patient endurance on the part of the saints who obey God's commandments and remain faithful to Jesus. (7)

It is far better to try to escape and die than to take the mark of the Beast.

Not everyone in the world will be forced to take the mark of the Beast. Scriptures speak of people from all the nations of the world coming to Jerusalem to worship the Messiah during the millennium (Zechariah 14:16-19). These people will not have taken the mark of the Beast as scriptures speak of those that took the mark of the Beast as being destroyed at the Lord's coming after the battle of Armageddon (Revelation 19:20-21). The people living in the countries controlled by the Beast will have a very short time to escape.

Some say that no man would do the things attributed to the Beast. All we have to do is look at Hitler's Germany and Idi Amin of Uganda in Africa in our own lifetime to know that this can happen. Laurinda Keys quotes Robert Munger as saying that there were more Christians killed under Idi Amin than in ancient Rome (74).

St. Irenaeus of Lyons wrote

> But when this Antichrist shall have devastated all things in this world, he will reign for forty-two months, and sit in the temple at Jerusalem; and then the Lord will come... sending this man and those who follow him into the lake of fire; but bring in for the righteous the times of the kingdom, that is, the rest, the hallowed seventh day; restoring to Abraham the promise inheritance, in which kingdom the Lord declared, that many coming from east and from the west should sit down with Abraham, Isaac and Jacob. (75)

When the Antichrist comes, he will reign for three and one-half years. He will sit in the temple in Jerusalem as God destroying those who do not worship him. Then the Lord will come and throw the Beast and those who worship him into the Lake of Fire.

The Number of the Beast

> Revelation 13:18: Here is wisdom. Let him who has understanding calculate the number of the beast, for the number is that of a man; and his number is six-hundred sixty-six (12).

Scripture says, "Let him who has wisdom, count the number of the Beast, for his number is 666."

We need to review some of the facts in regard to numbers in the scriptures. In the English language, the alphabets and numbers

273

have two separate units of identification. In the Greek or Hebrew language, the alphabets are used both for letters and numbers. The number value of each Greek or Hebrew letter can be found in the Webster dictionary. (76, 77)

The number 666 in Greek translation of the Book of Revelation consists of three letters. The first letter has a value of 600. The second and third letter has a value of 60 and 6, respectively. The three letters added together equal 666.

Fascinating discoveries in regard to numbers in the scripture

There have been some fascinating discoveries made in the last few years in regard to numbers in the scriptures. Jerry Lucas and Del Washburn have demonstrated that God created a deep, complex, mathematical design within the scriptures.

Each Greek or Hebrew letter has a mathematical value, and all the letters in a word or phrase or complete sentence can be added up. The Greek letters in the name Jesus, add up to 888. Lucas and Washburn have shown that all the letters in any verse of scripture, whether the main word, phrase or complete sentence that has to do with Jesus, can be added up and divided by 111 or 37 to give a whole number. For example, 888 divided by 37 equal 24 or 888 divided by 111 equal 8. The sum of all verses that have to do with Jesus can also be divided evenly by 37 or 111 to give a whole number, no fraction.

Lucas and Washburn asked some professional statisticians to determine the odds of thirty-two scripture verses, having to do with Jesus, being divided evenly by 111. The statisticians determined that the odds of this happening by chance were 1 in 31,608,834,580,00 0,000,000,000,000 chances. This is one chance in thirty-one septillion, six hundred eight sextillion, eight hundred thirty-four quintillion, five hundred eighty quadrillion.

This number is unrealistic. This is equivalent to 1 second in 1,002,312,743,880,010 years. That is one second in one-quadrillion, two trillion, three-hundred twelve billion, seven-hundred forty-three million, eight-hundred eighty thousand and ten years. The earth is estimated by certain scientists to be 4.5 billion years old. As old as the earth is, there would have to be 22,273 times 4.5 billion years to have enough seconds that one second would be equivalent to the odds that thirty-two verses of scriptures, having to do with Jesus, could be divided evenly by 111.

These are the odds for thirty-two verses of scriptures. There are many, many more scripture verses, dealing with Jesus, in which all can be divided evenly by 37 or 111, making the odds of this happening by chance reaching into eternity.

That is not all. Washburn has uncovered many other common denominators in the scriptures, which are discussed in his books. He has found that words and phrases, which have related spiritual meaning, will be divisible by a common multiple. (76, 77)

The Greek language has 26 characters, which consist of both vowels and consonants, while the Hebrew language has 22 characters, which are all consonants. Though Greek and Hebrew are two different languages, related scriptures in both languages are divisible by the same common denominator.

The total numerical value of every main word, phrase or sentence having to do with Satan, dragon, hell, law, flesh, etc. can be divided evenly by 276. The following related scriptures can be divided by the following number:

Fisher of men	-	153
Bride of Christ	-	144
Creation	-	425
The Beast	-	616

The odds of this happening once, much less numerous times in the scriptures, is more than just a coincidence. (76,77)

The Number of the Beast – 666 or 616?

Washburn believes that the number of the Beast in the original manuscript was 616 instead of 666. A copy of the manuscript from the second century shows 616. Washburn states that St. Irenaeus (140 - 205 A.D.) knew about the 616 but did not adopt it while St. Jerome did accept it. St. Irenaeus was a disciple of Polycarp, who was a disciple of John, while St. Jerome is called a Doctor of the Church.

Washburn found that scriptures pertaining to the Beast, discussed in Revelation 13, are divisible by 616 but not 666. He also found numerous scriptures in both the Old and the New Testament that are divisible by 616, leading him to believe that 616 was the original number instead of 666. (77) Father John Dietzen also wrote that several ancient scripture manuscripts and writings have the number 616 instead of 666. (4)

Not one letter of the law shall pass away.

> Matthew 5:18: Of this much I assure you: until heaven and earth pass away, not the smallest letter of the law, not the smallest part of a letter, shall be done away with until it all comes true (60).

The words of Jesus, in Matthew 5:18 take on a very significant meaning, in the light of what we have just discussed. If one letter were missing, the total numerical value of the scripture verses would not divide evenly. If the number of the alphabets were changed, the numbers would not divide evenly. It is absolutely amazing and difficult to comprehend how the Bible, a collection of the oldest books known to civilization, written by primitive men of different backgrounds, cultures, times and languages, covering a span of at least

1600 years from the writing of the first book to the last book, survived many primitive copying, and yet, every scriptural verse that is spiritually related is divisible by a common multiple.

There is no other book in the world, even those written by the most learned men in our advanced age of computers, satellites, nuclear physics and chemistry that has any of these features of the most complex mathematical design just described. Though the scriptures say that you can find and please God only through faith, it is difficult to comprehend how any one could not be overwhelmed by this question. How did primitive men of different cultures, languages and backgrounds, covering a span of at least 1600 years, unwittingly write books containing a complex mathematical design, discovered 1900 to 3500 years after the books were written through which all books can be interrelated by spiritually related scriptures which are divisible by a common multiple? All of this is difficult to comprehend, unless every letter and word that these men wrote was guided by the hand of a living God.

The complex math hidden in the scriptures shows that the Lord intends for those with wisdom to be able to calculate the number of the Beast, for it is a number of a man, and his number will be either 666 or 616.

> Revelation 13:18: Here is (room for) discernment - a call for wisdom (of interpretation); let any one who has intelligence (penetration and insight enough) calculate the number of the beast, for it is a human number - the number of a certain man; his number is six hundred and sixty-six. (59)

The Beast will be from Greece

We have shown that the scriptures teach that the Beast will come out of Greece. The Greek alphabet is the same today, as it was 2000 years ago. If the man who comes out of Greece has a Greek name, there will be no problem adding up the numbers in each letter in his name.

Some theologians believe that the Beast will not be a man but a system since the Greek language does not have articles such as "a" and reads "It is the number of man" not "of a man". Even though some theologians believe that the Beast will be a system instead of a man, the system would have to be run by men.

It is difficult to believe that the Beast will be a system instead of a man because the scriptures teach:

1. The Beast will speak blasphemy against God.
2. The Beast will be allowed to wage war with the saints and overcome them. (Daniel 7:21, 25).
3. The Beast will be mortally wounded and live (Revelation 13:3). The world will marvel after the Beast. There is no way the term mortally wounded and lives could feasibly be applied to a system.
4. The False Prophet commands an image of the Beast to breathe, live and speak. This is an image of a man not a system.
5. At the end of the seventieth week of Daniel, when the Lord comes, the Beast and the False Prophet are taken and thrown alive into the "Lake of Fire. The Lord would not throw a system into a Lake of Fire to be physically tormented.

6. At the end of 1000 years, the Beast and the False Prophet are still alive in the Lake of Fire. Therefore the Beast is a man, not a system. (67)

What is the mark of the Beast that is given to the people?

Revelation 13:16-17: He also forced everyone, small and great, rich and poor, free and slave, to receive a mark on his right hand or on his forehead, so that no one could buy or sell unless he had the mark, which is the name of the beast or the number of his name. (7)

The mark of the Beast is either the name of the Beast or the sum total numerical value of the letters of his name, which add to 616 or 666. The mark of the Beast is not a social security number or any other number. Scripture says either the name of the Beast or the number of his name will be placed on the right hand or on their forehead.

Gordon Lindsay said, "The mark of the beast is like a cattle brand which shows ownership by the beast" (67).

What must one do to receive this mark?

Revelation 13:15: . . . cause all who refused to worship the image to be killed (7).

All one must do to receive the mark of the Beast is to bow down and worship the Beast or the image of the Beast. Those who refuse to worship the Beast or his image will be killed.

After the man-child is taken up to heaven, Satan and his angels are driven from heaven to the earth (Revelation 12:9, 12-13). Satan knows his time is short. He is angry and full of fury.

The Beast who was wounded to death and lives will be furious and angry over the assassination attempt. He is now ready to vent his rage on the world. The Beast will begin this rage with the abomination of desolation of the temple spoken of by Daniel the prophet. He will proclaim himself to be God. Because of the miracles and

279

wonders performed by the False Prophet in the presence of the Beast, most people will be deceived into believing that he is God. Jesus said in Matthew 24:24 that even the elect, if possible, will be deceived.

The Beast will issue a decree that unless you bow down and worship him or his image and take his mark, you will not be able to buy or sell in the countries he controls. Those who do not take the mark will be put to death. The Beast will have a military or police state in which he controls everything.

Jesus said,

> Matthew 24:21: for then there will be great tribulation, such as has not occurred since the beginning of the world until now, nor ever shall (12).

When we think of the horrible holocaust in Hitler's Germany, it is difficult to imagine anything worse. There were over six million Jews killed in concentration camps (42). A Polish friend of mine who spent three years in the Auschwitz concentration camp said there were as many Polish people killed as there were Jews. This does not include the millions of people killed as a result of World War II. The following quotation in the Air and Space Museum of the Smithsonian Institute in Washington, D.C. stated that more than thirty-five million people lost their lives in World War II, which started in Germany.

> World War II, which began on September 1, 1939 and ended on August 15, 1945, was the largest and most destructive war in history. More than 35,000,000 people lost their lives during this conflict. Confined to Europe for two years, it spread throughout the Pacific with the Japanese attack on Pearl Harbor on December 7, 1941.

The only way the Great Tribulation could be worse is in the sheer number of people killed.

Hitler shipped the people in boxcars to concentration camps to secretly do away with them. There were so many people killed that they had trouble disposing of the bodies. Many bodies were thrown into furnaces to be burned before they were completely dead. The insensitive, senseless, and satanic cruelty in the concentration camps was and is unimaginable.

Though the Beast will probably have concentration camps, he will probably be more open, having public torture and execution as an example to the people, who refuse to worship him or his image or take his mark. This is what Nebuchadnezzar, the King of Babylon, did when he invited everyone to come to the dedication of his statue. A furnace was built near the statue to take care of the people who refused to bow down to his image.

Because of the miracles performed by the False Prophet, most of the people will believe that the Beast is God. The Beast will be very popular as he causes everyone to prosper through his trade and craft. Because of his wisdom, knowledge, intelligence, military strength, charisma and popularity especially after being fatally wounded, yet now alive, will be able to sway the majority of the people into believing that anyone who does not take his mark should be killed.

There are enough crazy, satanic people in the world that would enjoy the sport of killing people as the Romans did in the crucifixion of the 6,000 slaves along the Appian Way (78) or as Nero and his people did when the Christians were fed to hungry lions in the Roman Coliseum.

With Satan and his angels driven from heaven to the earth, this will be the greatest concentration of evil on earth the world has ever seen. This is Satan's final hour of glory and moment of revenge until the end of the millennium. The Beast will have a very short time after the abomination of desolation of the temple to make the Great Tribulation, the greatest holocaust the world has ever seen. Though the Beast will be given unlimited power for forty-two months after the abomination of desolation of the temple, the Great Tribulation will cover only the first part of the forty-two months, i.e. the opening of the first five seals. When the sixth seal is opened, the Great Tribulation will be over. The Wrath of God, which covers the last part of the forty-two months, begins with the opening of the seventh seal. The seventh seal includes the seven trumpets judgments and seven vials judgments.

Though the Great Tribulation and the Wrath of God will cover forty-two months, no one knows what part of the time will be the Great Tribulation and what part will be the Wrath of God. Scripture speaks of men being tormented for five months during the fifth trumpet. In the sixth trumpet, scripture speaks of four angels being prepared for a year, a month, a day and an hour to kill a third of mankind. We do not know if scripture means that the angels will be killing men on earth for this length of time or if this will be the moment of time they will be called on to kill one-third of mankind.

The Beast, with the help of his lieutenants and the people who take the mark of the Beast, will make the Great Tribulation the greatest holocaust the world has ever seen.

There is much talk about a cashless society where all transactions are controlled by computers and social security numbers. The Beast will definitely have all the advancements of science at his fingertips. Though the social security number or a number may be a tool of the Beast, it will not be the mark of the Beast. Scripture says the mark of the Beast is either the name of the Beast or the number of his name.

The procedure, the Beast will use in controlling those who buy or sell, will be very simple. Bow down and worship the Beast or his image and take his mark or be killed. The marked public will openly participate in the Beast's dirty work by killing unmarked people in front of stores, supermarkets and in the streets when they attempt to buy or sell without the mark.

Today we depend on supermarkets and stores to provide food and other necessities of life. It would be difficult for most people to go beyond two weeks without having to go to the store. In a very short period of time, the people would be forced to either take the mark of the Beast or be killed. Those that are destined to die will have no choice but to give their lives or suffer the consequences of an eternal death in the Lake of Fire and brimstone.

The computer chip

The Antichrist will control the people through buying and selling. According to the prophecies received by John Leary, the groundwork for this take-over will start with smart cards, which have a computer chip, which enable people to buy without cash. Since smart cards can easily be misplaced, lost or stolen, people will be encouraged to have the computer chip injected into their right hand for safety. An electronic scanner will be used to read the computer chip. This computer chip will be used by the Beast, not only to control buying and selling, but to control the people and their movements. The agents of the Antichrist will encourage the people to voluntarily take the chips. Later, people will be forced to take the chip to be able to buy or sell. When this happens, Jesus tells the people not to take the chip but to go into hiding. As the time of the Great Tribulation draws closer, the Lord is giving His people more details and a clearer understanding of what to expect and what He wants them to do.

> Amos 3:7: Indeed the Lord does nothing without revealing his plan to his servants, the prophets (24).

Below are some of the many prophecies received by John Leary.

> The electronic cards called "debit cards" as you heard today will gain increasing acceptance for handling all financial transactions. It is through these means that the Anti-Christ will control or attempt to control your lives. Each stage pushed under the guise for your protection from theft. In reality, it is their means to gain control of the money of the world. Once you are forced to accept a mark on your hand or forehead for doing transactions, do not accept it. This will be the mark of the beast which I have told you to shun. For those who accept this, accept the devil's world and not Me. You must seek Me first no matter at what cost in order to save your soul. 5/31/94 (45)

Mr. Leary had a vision of people receiving a chip implant in their hand. Jesus said:

> You are indeed seeing preparations being made by Antichrist agents for world takeover by the U.N. Many forces of different nations will be secretly in your country under the auspices of the U.N. You will soon see a call for all people to receive this computer chip so they can be registered with the world computer the "Beast". This will be hailed as a means for more efficient buying and selling, but in actually it will be the Antichrist means to control the people.

When you see people applying for this chip, know that it is the time to go into hiding in some safe haven or refuge. After an initial grace period to sign voluntarily, the agents will then come looking for those who did not sign up and force them to take the chip. This is the mark of the beast you should avoid at all costs. Refuse this even under pain of death or you will not be written in the Book of Life. It will be at this time you will need a heavy trust in Me to take care of you. I will do it, if you ask My help in prayer since I told you I would protect your soul. This warning will come before a transition of power so you will truly know that you will be choosing either Me or Satan. Keep together for safety in numbers and I will watch over you. 8/23/94 (43)

Someone asked if debit cards were considered smart cards? Smart and debit cards are explained by Joe Hunt and how they can be used to control the people.

Smart cards have a foil-contact section that allows a reader-machine to alter the balance of money on the card and/or your bank account. A simple debit card may or may not be a smartcard, according to the technology used. If you buy a card that holds a certain value, like $10, $25, or $50, like for telephone long distance use, it is a smart card, but a very basic chip.

On the more advanced chips planned for release soon, a "lot" of information can be placed on it about you, -- everything from your politics to your medical & criminal records. It is interactive with your bank account, subtracting and adding dollar amounts easily. Once the society is forced to use smartcards, the government can constantly keep track of your whereabouts by your using it.

They can either capture you when you use it or just disable your account, making it impossible for you to buy food, gasoline, pay bills, tolls or even drive a car. In short, it is a "dream" for governments to have this much control over its citizens, turning them into vassals who can survive only at the pleasure of the state.

Fail to pay a parking ticket? Your smartcard won't work unless you first use it to pay the ticket. That's already planned. And since this will be automatic, nothing can stop even city councils from upping the cost of a $10 parking citation to $100, or even $500. After all, if they don't get their money first, you can't buy food or gasoline....

Any government officer or clerk who doesn't like you or wants to neutralize you, places an 'eat' order onto the SWIFT computer system: you put your card into a purchasing reader anywhere on the planet, and the machine eats your card, leaving you stranded financially. You'd be lucky at the time if you turned around and didn't see an arriving UN arrest team hopping out of an APC just after the machine ate your card. (Internet)

What is not known is that LEO (Low Earth-Orbit) satellites can track the person on the ground anywhere on the planet, and the chips can be used to modify the victim's behavior. 12/15/97 (72)

Even if one does not have a bank account and pay for everything in cash, a computer chip will be required to be able to buy or sell.

Digital angel – a digital transceiver – implantable in human

A U.S. Patent Number 5,629,678 was granted on May 13, 1997 for a "personal tracking and recovery system," consisting of a miniature digital transceiver – implantable in humans – with a built-in, electromechanical power supply and actuation system. This digital transceiver sends and receives data, which can be continuously tracked by Global Positioning Satellites for years without maintenance.

On December 10, 1999, Applied Digital Solutions, Inc. acquired the patent rights to this technology, which the company calls the "Digital Angel". This transceiver can be implanted just under the skin or hidden on or within valuable personal belongings and priceless works of art. This device can locate individuals, including children, who are lost or who have been abducted, track and locate military, diplomatic and other essential government personnel; determine the location of valuable property or track the whereabouts of individuals in the wilderness. (79)

This device will be used by the Antichrist to control the people by monitoring everyone's coming and going.

The Antichrist will perform miracles

Scripture speaks of the Antichrist calling fire down out of heaven. John Leary had a vision of huge blotches of pink lightning flashing across the sky. Jesus said:

> When you see this phenomenon of pink lightning,
> know that it is the time of the Antichrist. He will call
> this form of lightning to the ground as if bringing fire
> out of the sky. This will so mesmerize some with his

power that he will convert many nonbelievers to his side. His wonders and powers will be a new reign of principalities and powers which will overcome those souls who are weak and not full of My grace. He will lead them as a Pied Piper to a deception of his lies such that they will do everything he says. They will seek out Christians for him to persecute. They will be acting as robots under his complete control. This is why I tell you, My people, to build up your spiritual strength now since the evil one will test even My elect to the breaking point. But reach out to Me, My children, and I will protect you. Have faith in Me always no matter what the odds and you will have a peace which no other creature can give you. 11/1/94 (43)

Hiding

The Lord tells His people to prepare to go into hiding, primarily underground to prevent detection by the Antichrist and for protection against the plagues He will send to the earth to persecute those who have taken the mark of the Beast. The Lord will send His angels to guide and protect His people.

My children, when the time of your trial arrives, put all your faith and trust in Me. Call on Me. Call on Me to help you and lead you and I will send My angel to show you the way to safety. While you are in hiding, My angel will advise you where to go to be free from your persecutors. In Exodus My angel led the people in the desert. Even now, this protection will soon be available to you when you need it most, so do not fear as I have told you, but have faith that I will take care of you. Pray often for your future strength to remain faithful to Me even when things look helpless in your eyes. Many miracles await you in answer to your prayers, if you would just ask at that time. 11/6/94 (43)

My people, I will always be watching over you even during the tribulation. Once the warning comes, be forewarned to make ready your preparation for hiding from the Anti-Christ and his agents. One of your necessities will be a shovel for areas where you can dig out a house or tunnel. You must be below ground to avoid detection from helicopters and satellites who will be looking for My faithful. This also will serve as good protection from bombs or other chastisements. Be hopeful My people. You may suffer a short time, but your quest of heaven will be your reward. Pray much for My graces to help you through this time. 11/24/94 (43)

My people, you think you are secure now, but I tell you, your life will be turned upside down in this evil age. Soon the evil one will control all jobs and money in the factories. To survive, you must seek the countryside to live off the land, and what I will provide for you. Do not worry what you are to bring, since I will make up the difference of what you need. It is sufficient, My children, not to take the mark of the beast and put your trust wholly in My help. Pray for the help I will send My faithful through their angels. You will be led to safety away from evil men. Be willing to give up everything you have, and you will save your soul, for no one can be written in the Book of Life, unless he comes to Me and denies his self and the things of the world. Be attentive to your prayer life, and protect yourself spiritually from the coming evil trial. 10/13/96 (46)

When you go into hiding, My people, pray to your guardian angel to direct you. They will then lead you to safe places in such way, that no evil men will find you. Even if they should try to find you with their electronic devices, I will confuse their instruments. If they should sends out tracking dogs for you, I will go to great length to protect those who pray for My help. Seek Me at all times, and you will find My love and peace. All this I keep telling you so you will not lose heart but see this power of having full faith and trust in Me. Pray for discernment in your problem and I will help you in any of your concerns. 10/31/95 (44)

The Lord will protect His people

John Leary had a vision of some people climbing a mountain, while others were seeking to hide in the woods. Jesus said:

My people, you are seeing how you must flee the Antichrist's agents to avoid being placed in detention centers. I am reminding you that they will search for you with satellites and helicopters, using many electrical sensing devices. You must pray to Me and your angels that we will block their finding you. Those who are faithful to Me, I will protect from all of these demonic forces. You will see My power will overshadow anything that Satan will devise. Even though you think it impossible to avoid these evil forces, I will perform miracles to protect you. Take hope, My children, I will be watching over you in spiritual and physical matter. Even amidst evil men, I will thwart their designs on you. I will only allow those intended by My will to be martyred. The rest will be miraculously cared for. You will not have seen such open protection, since the days I helped My people in the Exodus. This purification time will be shown to be a battle of good and evil that has been destined for centuries. 10/29/96 (46)

CHAPTER 22
The 144,000

The 144,000 on Mount Zion

Revelation 14:1-5: Then I looked and lo, the Lamb stood on Mount Zion, and with Him a hundred and forty-four thousand who had His name and His Father's name inscribed on their foreheads. And I heard a voice from heaven like the sound of great waters and like the rumbling of mighty thunder; the voice I heard of harpists accompanying themselves on their harps. And they sing a new song before the throne (of God) and before the four living creatures and before the elders. No one could learn that song except the hundred and forty-four thousand who had been ransomed (purchased, redeemed) from the earth. These are they who have not defiled themselves by relations with women, for they are (pure as) virgins. These are they who follow the Lamb wherever He goes. These are they who have been ransomed (purchased, redeemed) from among men as the first fruits for God and the Lamb. No lie was found to be upon their lips, for they are blameless - spotless, untainted, without blemish - before the throne of God. (59)

Is Mount Zion in Revelation 14:1 in heaven or on earth?

Some people believe that the Mount Zion in Revelation 14:1 is on earth. However, the scriptural evidence seems to show that this

Mount Zion is the heavenly Mount Zion which Paul talked about.

Hebrews 12:22: But you have come to Mount Zion and to the city of the living God, the heavenly Jerusalem, and to myriads of angels (12).

1. In Revelation 14:1, Christ stands on Mount Zion; yet Christ does not return to the earth until the end of the seventieth week of Daniel at the battle of Armageddon. Zechariah 14:4 teaches that the Lord's feet will first touch the Mount of Olives.

2. Revelation 14:3 -5 shows that the 144,000 are standing before the throne of God and before the elders and four living creatures. The elders and four living creatures were mentioned as being before the heavenly throne in Revelation 4 and 5. This throne is the heavenly throne as there is no throne on earth during the Great Tribulation.

3. The 144,000 are standing before the throne singing a song that no one could sing except the 144,000, who had been redeemed from the earth. This shows that the 144,000 are not on earth, as they have been redeemed from the earth.

4. Revelation 14:9-11 shows that the Great Tribulation is on by the warning given to the people not to take the mark of the Beast. Jesus does not come to the earth before or during the Great Tribulation. When the rapture occurs, Jesus meets the saints in the air.

These scriptures indicate that Mount Zion in Revelation 14:1 is the heavenly Mount Zion mentioned in Hebrews 12:22. (61)

Who are the 144,000?

1. They are standing on heavenly Mount Zion before the throne of God.
2. They are in the presence of the elders and four living creatures.
3. They have Jesus' name and the Father's name written on their foreheads. This shows they belong to Jesus and the Father; while those with the mark of the Beast belong to the Beast.
4. They have been redeemed from the earth.
5. They sing a new song before the throne that only the redeemed from the earth can sing.
6. They are pure virgins. No deceit or lies were found on their lips. They are blameless.
7. They are the first fruits to God and to the Lamb. They follow the Lamb wherever He goes.

What is the difference between the 144,000 in Revelation 14 and the 144,000 in Revelation 7?

> Revelation 14:3: . . . the hundred and forty-four thousand who had been ransomed (purchased, redeemed) from the earth (59).

1. This group is the first fruits to God and the Lamb. If they are the first fruits to God and the Lamb, they would have gone up when the door was open in heaven in Revelation 4.

2. The scriptures below show that this group in Revelation 14 is in heaven before and while the Great Tribulation is going on.

Revelation 14:3: And they sang a new song before the throne and before the four living creatures and elders; . . . (12).

Revelation 14:9-10: . . . If anyone worships the beast and his image, and receives a mark on his forehead or upon his hand, he also will drink of the wine of the wrath of God, . . . (12).

The four living creatures and the elders are standing before the throne in heaven before the Great Tribulation begins as shown in Revelation 4. This group of 144,000 is standing before the throne of God before the elders and the four living creatures at the beginning of Revelation 14. Later in Revelation 14:9, 10 a warning is given not to take the mark of the Beast, which shows that the Great Tribulation is on, while the 144,000 first fruits are standing before the throne in heaven.

3. These people are overcomers. They have been redeemed from the earth. Gordon Lindsay said that if anyone will look up the word "earth" in a concordance, he will find that it refers to the entire world and is never localized to Israel. This shows that the 144,000 in Revelation 14 consist of people of all nations of the earth, not just the Jews, as in Revelation 7.

4. This group follows the Lamb wherever He goes. This is the characteristic of the bride. The bride follows her husband wherever He goes.

5. These people, the 144,000 in Revelation 14, are part of the overcomers. They will rule nations with a rod of iron during the millennium (61).

Revelation 7 – the 144,000 Israelites

> Revelation 7:4: . . . one hundred and forty-four thousand sealed from every tribe of the sons of Israel: (12)

1. This group consists of Israelites from the twelve tribes of Israel.
2. This group is not sealed until after the opening of the seventh seal. The Great Tribulation is over with the opening of the sixth seal (Matthew 24:29-30, Revelation 6:12-16). The Christians, who went through the Great Tribulation and have made reparation for their sins, are taken up to heaven before the opening of the seventh seal. The 144,000 Israelites are not sealed until after the opening of the seventh seal.
3. This group goes through the Wrath of God. They are sealed and protected so that nothing can hurt them (Revelation 9:4).
4. This group will be on the earth when the Lord returns to set up His earthly kingdom and to sit on the throne of His father, David for a thousand years.

> Proverbs 2:21-22: For the upright will dwell in the land, the honest will remain in it; But the wicked will be cut off from the land, the faithless will be rooted out of it (24).

It can be seen from the scriptures, and looking at Table 5 in Chapter 16, that the 144,000 in Revelation 14 is a different group from the 144,000 in Revelation 7.

What are the qualifications for the 144,000 first fruits?

Gordon Lindsay has probably given more serious thought to the 144,000 first fruits standing before the throne in Revelation 14 than anyone. He said this question must be approached humbly and prayerfully as sectarianism, prejudice and tradition have too often entered into the discussion of this subject. The qualifications of the 144,000 first fruits can be answered only in the light of what the Bible teaches. (61)

1. No guile was found in their mouth.

    Revelation 14:5: And in their mouth was found no guile: for they are without fault before the throne of God (10).

A second translation says,

    On their lips no deceit has been found; they are indeed without flaw (60).

Another translation says,

    No lie was found to be upon their lips, for they are blameless - spotless, untainted, without blemish - before the throne of God (59).

Guile means cunning, deceitfulness, slyness, trickery, shrewd and deceptive. There are many Christians, who are shrewd businessmen. What they do is not exactly wrong, but neither is it right, i.e. trickery and deception.

The scriptures speak of restraining the tongue.

    James 3:2, 6: All of us fall short in many respects. If a person is without fault in speech he is a man in the fullest sense, because he can control his entire body. . . . The tongue is such a flame. It exists among our members as a whole universe of malice. The tongue defiles the entire body. Its flames encircle our course from birth, and its fire is kindled by hell. (60)

Jesus, in Matthew 5:37, said to let your speech be "yes, yes; no, no; and whatever is beyond these comes from the evil one."

There are very few Christians that can be called blameless, spotless and without flaw, without deceit in their mouth. Yet, the 144,000 first fruits, standing before the thrones, are blameless without deceit or flaw.

2. The 144,000 first fruits are called virgins.

Revelation 14:4: These are they who have not defiled themselves by relations with women, for they are (pure as) virgins. . . . (59).

Does this means that it is a sin or wrong to be married?

No, for God ordained the sacrament of marriage.

Genesis 2:18, 24: . . . It is not good for man to be alone. . . . For this reason a man will leave his father and mother and be united to his wife, and they will become one flesh (7).

Hebrews 13:4: Marriage should be honored by all, and the marriage bed kept pure, for God will judge the adulterer and all sexually immoral (7).

Obviously, the defilement, in Revelation 14:4, does not refer to sex in marriage, but to sexual acts outside of marriage. Virgin does not mean that they were never married on earth. Paul, in talking to the Corinthians, was certainly talking to some married people when he said,

2 Corinthians 11:2: I am jealous for you with a godly jealousy. I promise you to one husband, to Christ, so that I might present you as a pure virgin to him (7).

298

Virgins mean pure, holy and Christ-like.

Gordon Lindsay referred to virgins as being separated from the world.

The scriptures in James speak of spiritual adultery.

> James 4:4-5: You adulterous people, don't you know that friendship with the world is hatred toward God? Anyone who chooses to be a friend of the world becomes an enemy of God. Or do you think Scripture says without reason that the spirit he caused to live in us tends toward envy, but he gives us more grace? (7)

Spiritual adultery has nothing to do with sex, but involves friendship with the world. Paul says in the very next verse,

> II Corinthians 11:3: But I am fearful lest that even as the serpent beguiled Eve by his cunning, so your minds may be corrupted and seduced from wholehearted and sincere and pure devotion to Christ. (59)

The attractions and desires of the world have tarnished many Christians. Yet, the 144,000 first fruits were spoken of as pure virgins without blemish or flaw.

3. The 144,000 first fruits follow the Lamb wherever He goes (Revelation 14:4). This obviously is the characteristic of the bride. The bride follows her husband wherever He goes.

Gordon Lindsay says,

> If this company follows Christ wherever He goes in heaven, it is obvious that they learned to follow Him in His footsteps here on earth. . . . Those who would

be the Bride of Christ, the First-fruits unto God will follow Christ in His sufferings, His temptations, His labor of love for the lost, His prayer life, in His concentration to the will of the Father. As Christ came down from heaven only to do the will of the Father, so we should be willing to forsake all that we might win Christ. As Christ came to this world to be a missionary to redeem lost humanity, so we too must consider the supreme work of our life is helping to get the gospel out to the nations.

4. The "Bride of Christ" will be those that respond to His call.

    Ephesians 5:25-27,28-32 . . . just as Christ loved the Church and gave himself up for her to make her holy, cleansing her by the washing with water through the word, and to present her to himself as a radiant church, without stain or wrinkle or any other blemish, but holy and blameless. . . . ". . . He who loves his wife loves himself. After all, no one ever hated his own body, but he feeds and cares for it, just as Christ does the church - for we are members of his body. For this reason a man will leave his father and mother and be united to his wife, and the two will become one flesh. This is a profound mystery - but I am talking about Christ and the church." (7)

The call of the bride is seen in Psalm 45:11-12

Hear, O daughter, and see; turn your ear, forget your people and your father's house. So shall the king desire your beauty; for he is your lord, and you must worship him. (24A)

The scriptures call for the bride to worship the Lord and King. The scriptures would not ask one to worship anyone except the Lord God. This shows that Psalm 45 is speaking of the Lord's bride.

Gordon Lindsay says,

> The true bride will be those who respond to this call. There is something for the bride to do. She is willing to forget her own people. As Rebekah of old, she says, "I will go" (61).

5. We must realize that there is a prize to be won. The possibility of being among the first fruits unto the lamb and to follow Him for all eternity would be a glorious honor. We must do as Paul says,
    Philippians 3:13-14: . . . forgetting those things which are behind, and reaching forth unto those things which are before, I press toward the mark for the prize of the high calling of God in Christ Jesus. (10)

Gordon Lindsay says,

> We must have some realization that there is a prize to be won. The attitude of some Christians seems to be merely to hold out to the end. They desire to escape hell, but have little vision or understanding of the prize to be won, or the glories that are to be revealed. The First-fruits saints realize these things and plunge into the race. They put all they have into the battle and to winning the contest; they become the first part of the harvest. The First-fruits are not a company, reserved for people who have attained unusual prominence, but will consist of those who in their concentration have earnestly sought God's plan for their life, whether it

will be a humble walk, or whether it be in the lime-light, and have dedicated themselves once and for all to the absolute will of God. We must remember that Elijah, who is a type of the First-fruits was a man of like passions such as we (James 5). It is faithfulness to God's Word that counts. (61)

The first fruits are prayer warriors. They will spend time each day in concentrated prayer. Prayer will be a way of life, as they go about their daily work. Prayer is a life-line to the Lord. If we will make a sincere effort to spend time in prayer, study God's Word and deal with the sins in our life, with God's help, we can strive to run the race that Paul ran with all his might with our reward being for all eternity.

Are the 144,000 first fruits, the bride of Christ?

Gordon Lindsay says,

> There is every indication that they are part of the Bride of Christ, but they are not the only ones that are in the Bride. The Apostle John was not a member of the 144,000 and who will say that he was not in the Bride? It is best for us not to press our curios-ity too far. It is enough for us to know that there is an opportunity for all who will strive for the prize. Time will reveal those who won it. Paul said he had not yet apprehended nor was already made perfect, but he pressed forward to the prize. We believe he at length won it. For his testimony at the end was: "I have fought a good fight, I have finished my course, I have kept the faith: Henceforth there is laid up for me a crown of righteousness, which the Lord, the righ-teous judge, shall give me at that day: and not to me

only, but unto all them also that love his appearing."
(II Timothy 4:7-8) (61)

Many Christians probably feel that they are too sinful and de-filed to run the race for the prize of the high calling. We must re-member that Paul said he was the chief of sinners (I Timothy 1:15). He was in charge of the persecutions of the Christians. Paul looked on, approving the stoning of Steven to death. Yet, Paul ran this race with all his might. Paul said that he had not yet been made perfect, still he pushed forward for the prize. The Lord accepts us wherever we are and begins the cleansing process. Dealing with the sins in our life and being made perfect is an ongoing, lifetime process.

God is not a respecter of persons (Acts 10:34). Those of us that have serious sins in our lives need to repent. Turning from sin is a decision. It is like turning on a light bulb. It is a decision that clicks in our mind to turn away from people, places, thoughts or occasions that will lead us to sin or temptation to sin. If we make this decision to turn away from sin, the Lord will help us.

Jesus said that if we would confess our sins, He is faithful and just to forgive us our sins and that He would take our sins and throw them into the depth of the sea, never to be remembered anymore (I John 1:9, Micah 7:19, Isaiah 43:25). If you will confess and turn away from your sins, you will be a new creature with a new heart, a new walk and a new goal, to strive to win the prize of the high call-ing - which is Jesus Christ.

The scripture in I Corinthians 2:9 says,

> . . . Eye has not seen, ear has not heard, nor has it so much as dawned on man what God has prepared for those who love him (60).

The kingdom of heaven is a place of indescribable love, joy, beauty, peace and pleasure beyond our wildest imagination and understanding. I can think of no joy greater than to be with the Lord, the saints and united with parents, grandparents, brothers, sisters and love ones who have gone on before us.

How many will go up in the Man-child Rapture?

The Man-child rapture appears to be numbered, while the Harvest Rapture is without number, i.e. too numerous to count (Revelation 14:1, 7:9). The Man-child rapture was the prize of the high-calling of which Paul was running a race in an effort to win.

1. After the man-child is taken up to heaven, and the sun-clothed woman flees into the wilderness, the dragon (Satan) makes war with the rest of her children who keep the commandments of God and have the testimony of Jesus Christ.
   We have shown that the sun-clothed woman is the symbolic mother of God's people. If the man-child represents a company of people, then the rest of her children would represent a much larger group of people.

2. If the ten virgins in the story of the ten virgins represent the Body of Christ and the Bridegroom took half of them, then this would imply that half of the people would go up in the Man-child rapture. However, if half of the people went up in the Man-child rapture, why would Paul have a hard time running a race in an effort to be a part of the Man-child resurrection?

The Man-child rapture appears to be numbered (small) in comparison to the Harvest Rapture which is too numerous to count.

Is the 144,000 literally a number?

Gordon Lindsay says,

> There certainly is a company of First-fruits which will number 144,000. This is not all the First-fruits. The twenty-four Elders who are Kings and priests unto God are not included in the number. There may be many hundreds of thousands or even millions of others in the First-fruits. We do not know. We should understand that there are different orders among the redeemed. In the resurrection, the righteous shall differ one from another as "one star differed from another star in glory" (I Corinthians 15:41). There will be many positions and offices of varying importance and honor, among God's people in the resurrection. The 144,000 on Mount Zion are the First-fruits unto God, and they will be with Christ and follow Him throughout eternity as one of the highest orders in heaven. They are, however, not all the First-fruits and it is a definite fallacy to hold that only 144,000 will go up in the rapture (Man-child).

It is best that we do not speculate on how many are going up in the Man-child rapture, but know that God is no respecter of persons, and we have the opportunity to run the race for the prize of the high calling as Paul did (61).

The fact that the 144,000 are standing before the throne in heaven, before and while the Great Tribulation is going on, supports the fact that the Man-child rapture takes place before the Great Tribulation begins.

The contrast between the Man-child and the Harvest Rapture

Man-child Rapture	Harvest Rapture
1. Occurs before the Great Tribulation.	Occurs after the Great Tribulation
2. This group is numbered i.e. able to be counted.	Too numerous to count.
3. Occurs at the midnight hour while everyone is asleep (Matthew 25:6).	Every eye shall see Him (Matthew 24:29-31).
4. Shall follow the Lamb wherever He goes. This is the characteristic of a bride. A bride follows her husband wherever he goes (Revelation 14:4).	Will be guests at the marriage feast of the Lamb (Revelation 19:9).
5. Shall rule nations with a rod of iron. These saints will be kings, leaders and rulers over nations, cities and communities helping the Lord run the government (Revelation 12:5; 2:27 and Luke 12:42-44).	Shall serve Him day and night in the temple. The duties of those in the Harvest Rapture will be as servants (Revelation 7:15).

CHAPTER 23

The Three Angels Flying Through The Air

The first angel flies through the air proclaiming the Gospel

> Apocalypse 14:6, 7: And I saw another angel flying in midheaven, having an everlasting gospel to preach to those who dwell upon the earth and to every nation and tribe and tongue and people, saying with a loud voice, "Fear God and give him honor, for the hour of his judgment has come; and worship him who made the heaven and the earth, the sea and fountains of waters." (9)

An angel flies through the air preaching the everlasting Gospel to all that dwell on earth. This is a drastic change from the commission the Lord gave to the apostles whereby men were in charge of preaching the Gospel.

> Matthew 24:14: And this gospel of the kingdom shall be preached in the whole world for a witness to all the nations, and then the end shall come (12).

The preaching of the Gospel by the angel finishes the commission that the Lord gave to the apostles. Angels have always been used as messengers of the Lord throughout the Old and New Testaments. However, during the Great Tribulation, they will preach the Gospel. Many theologians believe that the 144,000 Jews from the twelve tribes of Israel are the ones that preach the Gospel; however, we have shown that these 144,000 are not sealed until after the Great Tribulation and rapture is over.

The angel will warn the people of all nations of the world to turn to the Lord for the judgment of God is at hand. At this time, the opportunity to win the prize of the high calling has passed. All that people can do is to save themselves. (61)

The second angel proclaims that Babylon has fallen.

> Revelation 14:8: A second angel followed and said, "Fallen! Fallen is Babylon the Great, which made all nations drink the maddening wine of her adulteries (7).

Jeremiah spoke of Babylon as a golden cup in the Lord's hand that made all nations drunk with her wine.

> Jeremiah 51:7: Babylon was a gold cup in the Lord's hand; she made the whole earth drunk. The nations drank her wine; therefore they have now gone mad (7).

The maddening wine of her adulteries is overindulging in spiritual adulteries, i.e., friendship with the world and its idols: gold, silver and material wealth.

> Jeremiah 50:38: A drought on her waters, and they will be dried up! For it is a land of idols, and they are mad over fearsome idols (12).

The final destruction of Babylon is described in Revelation 17 and 18 that occurs during the seventh bowl (61).

The third angel warns the people not to worship the Beast.

> Revelation 14:9-11: And another angel, a third one, followed them, saying with a loud voice, "If any one worships the beast and his image, and receives a mark on his forehead or upon his hand, he also will drink of the wine of the wrath of God, which is mixed in full strength in the cup of His anger; and he will be tormented with fire and brimstone in the presence of the holy angels and in the presence of the Lamb. And the smoke of their torment goes up forever and ever; and they have no rest day or night, those who worship the beast and his image, and whoever receives the mark of his name." (12)

The Great Tribulation is on. The angel gives a solemn warning to the inhabitants of the earth not to worship the Beast or take his mark. There is no excuse for any to worship the Beast and take his mark, for they were forewarned by the angel and the two witnesses. Though the False Prophet will deceive many by his miraculous signs and wonders, the people are obligated to search the scriptures for the truth because of the teachings of the angel and the two witnesses. Many people will be forced to either worship the Beast or his image or face death. Their decision will be the difference between life and death for all eternity.

Those who take the course of least resistance and worship the Beast, commit the unforgivable sin. The scripture says fire and brimstone will torment them day and night for all eternity (61).

Blessed are the saints that are martyred.

Revelation 14:12-13: Here is the perseverance of the saints who keep the commandments of God and their faith in Jesus. And I heard a voice from heaven, saying, "Write, 'Blessed are the dead who die in the Lord from now on!'" "Yes," says the Spirit, "that they may rest from their labors, for their deeds follow with them. (12)

A voice comes from heaven saying, "blessed are those that die from this point in the Lord for they shall have rest." Those that take the mark of the Beast will not have any rest or peace for the smoke of their torment shall go up forever. Many people make decisions in this life as if they are going to live forever with no thought about death or life thereafter.

Most of the saints, living in the countries controlled by the Beast will have no choice but to give their life during the Great Tribulation in order to enter the kingdom of heaven.

The Son of Man on a cloud with a golden crown on his head.

> Revelation 14:14: And I looked, and behold, a white cloud, and sitting on the cloud was one like a son of man, having a golden crown on His head, and a sharp sickle in His hand (12).

> Matthew 24:29-30: But immediately after the tribulation of those days the sun will be darkened, and the moon will not give its light, and the stars will fall from the sky, and the powers of the heavens will be shaken, and then the sign of the Son of Man will appear in the sky, and then all the tribes of the earth will mourn, and they will see the Son of Man coming on the clouds of the sky with power and great glory. (12)

The Son of Man is seen coming in a cloud immediately after the Great Tribulation, in Matthew 24:29-30 and Revelation 14:14.

When did the Son of Man receive the golden crown?

Daniel 7:13 shows the Son of Man coming before the Ancient

of Days to receive a kingdom. When one receives a kingdom a crown is also given. This is similar to the scene described in Revelation 4 and 5 before the judgment of God and the beginning of the Great Tribulation. In Revelation 6:2, the rider of the white horse received a crown, as he goes forth conquering and to conquer. We have shown that the rider of the white horse is Christ. Therefore the crown the Son of Man has on in Revelation 14:14 was received in Revelation 6:2. (61)

The Son of Man has a sharp sickle in his hand – the Harvest Rapture

> Revelation 14:15-16: And another angel came out of the temple, crying out with a loud voice to Him who sat on the cloud, "Put in your sickle and reap, because the hour to reap has come, because the harvest of the earth is ripe." And He who sat on the cloud swung His sickle over the earth: and the earth was reaped. (12)

An angel cries in a loud voice to the Son of Man, sitting on a cloud, to put in His sickle and reap for the harvest of the earth is ripe.

The gathering of the harvest is spoken of in many places in the scripture. In Matthew 9:37 and Luke 10:2, the Lord refers to the harvest being great, but the laborers are few.

In Matthew 13:37-43, the Lord explained the parable of the weeds in the field of wheat. The Son of Man sows the good seeds. The field is the world. The weeds are the sons of the evil one. The harvest is at the end of the age. The harvesters are the angels. The weeds are gathered and thrown into the fire, where there will be weeping and gnashing of teeth. The righteous will shine like the sun.

The harvest of the earth, spoken of in Revelation 14:15-16 is also seen in Matthew 24:31 and Revelation 7:9, 14, and takes place immediately after the Great Tribulation.

> Matthew 24:31: And He will send forth His angels with a great trumpet and they will gather together His elect from the four winds, from one end of the sky to the other (12).

> Revelation 7:9, 14: After these things I looked, and behold, a great multitude, which no one could count, from every nation and all tribes and people and tongues, standing before the throne and before the Lamb, clothed in white robes, and palm branches were in their hands; . . . These are the ones who come out of the Great Tribulation, and they have washed their robes and made them white in the blood of the Lamb. (12)

Some people think the harvest spoken of in Revelation 14:15-16 refers to the wicked. However, this cannot be, for the next verse, Revelation 14:17-20, refers to the wicked.

The wicked are cast into the wine press of the Wrath of God.

> Revelation 14:17-20: And another angel came out of the temple which is in heaven, and he also had a sharp sickle. And another angel, the one who has power over fire, came out from the altar; and he called with a loud voice to him who had the sharp sickle, saying, "Put in your sharp sickle and gather the clusters from the vine of the earth, because her grapes are ripe." And the angel swung his sickle to the earth, and gathered the clusters from the vine of the earth, and threw them into the great wine press

of the wrath of God. And the wine press was trodden outside the city, and blood came out from the wine press, up to the horses' bridles, for a distance of two hundred miles. (12)

Who is the angel with a sharp sickle who gathers the grapes and cast them into the wine press of the Wrath of God?

In Revelation 14:14, the Son of Man was the One with the sickle, Who harvested the earth. The angel who comes out of the temple in heaven must be Christ, for Isaiah says the Lord is the one that treads the winepress of the Wrath of God.

> Isaiah 63:2-4, 6: Why is Your apparel red, and Your garments like one who treads in the winepress? I have trodden the wine trough alone, . . . I also trod them in My anger, and trampled them in My wrath; and their life blood is sprinkled on My garments, and I stained all My raiment. For the day of vengeance was in My heart, and My year of redemption has come. . . . And I trod down the peoples in My anger, and made them drunk in My wrath, and I poured out their life blood on the earth. (12)

Revelation 19 speaks of the Lord as the one that treads the wine press and that His robe is stained with blood.

> Revelation 19:13, 15: And He is clothed with a robe dipped in blood; and His name is called the Word of God. . . . and He treads the winepress of the fierce wrath of God, the Almighty (12).

If the Lord is revealed throughout the Book of Revelation as different characters such as the Lamb of God, the rider of the white horse, One with eyes as a flame of fire and the Mighty Angel; then there is no reason why He cannot be seen as the Angel with the sickle to gather the grapes of His wrath. (80)

What does the scripture "the wine press was trodden outside the city, and blood came out from the wine press up to the horses bridles for a distance of two hundred miles" mean?

The city refers to Jerusalem. The winepress is trodden outside the city. The trodden of the winepress actually takes place north of the city in the plains of Megiddo where the battle of Armageddon will be fought. All the kings of the earth with their armies are gathered together for the great battle of the Lord (Revelation 16:13-14, 16) (80, 81)). The slaughter will be so great that blood will be up to the horses' bridles and will flow two hundred miles.

It is difficult to comprehend blood flowing two hundred miles, since all water within Israel flows into the Dead Sea, which is the lowest spot on earth (1286 feet below sea level). The distance from Megiddo to the Dead Sea is not more than 70 miles. It is interesting that the distance between the Sea of Galilee and the Dead Sea is 65.7 miles, yet the Jordan River takes a winding course of over two hundred miles (82). This is a possible explanation of how blood may flow two hundred miles.

Joel, the prophet, speaks of the harvest of the wrath of God.

> Joel 3:12-16: Let the nations be aroused and come up to the valley of Jehoshaphat, for there I will sit to judge all the surrounding nations. Put in the sickle, for the harvest is ripe. Come, tread, for the wine press is full; the vats overflow, for their wickedness is great. Multitudes, multitudes in the valley of decision! For the day of the Lord is near in the valley of decision. The sun and moon grow dark, and the stars lose their brightness. And the Lord roars from Zion

314

and utters His voice from Jerusalem, and the heavens
and earth tremble. But the Lord is a refuge for His
people and a stronghold to the sons of Israel. (12)

Joel, the prophet, speaks of the Lord gathering the nations into
the valley of Jehoshaphat for judgment. The winepress is full and
overflowing for wickedness of the people is great (80).

CHAPTER 24

The Seventh Trumpet -
The Third Woe - The Seven Plagues

What is the third woe?

The first and second woes are described in the text after the sounding of the fifth and sixth trumpets. In Revelation 11:14-15, the scriptures say the second woe is passed and the third woe comes with the sounding of the seventh trumpet. After the sounding of the seventh trumpet the scriptures say, "The kingdom of the world has become the kingdom of our Lord and of His Christ, and He will reign forever and ever." However, the third woe is not discussed. Revelation 15 tells what the third woe is. (80)

> Revelation 15:1: I saw in heaven another great and marvelous sign: seven angels with the seven last plagues - last, because with them God's wrath is completed (7).

The third woe is the seven plagues. Revelation 15:1 says that the wrath of God is finished with the seven plagues.

If the seventh trumpet, the third woe, is mentioned in Revelation 11 but not discussed until Revelation 15, what about Revelation 12, 13 and 14?

Revelation 12, 13 and 14 start back at the beginning of the Great Tribulation, describing in detail the things not covered in Revelation 4 through 11. Table 6 shows the order of events from Revelation 12 through 14 and how it parallels the Great Tribulation, the Harvest Rapture, and the Wrath of God.

The song of Moses and the song of the Lamb

> Revelation 15:2-3: And I saw, as it were, a sea of glass mixed with fire, and those who had come off victorious from the beast and from his image and from the number of his name, standing on the sea of glass, holding harps of God. And they sang the song of Moses the bond-servant of God and the song of the Lamb, saying,

> Great and marvelous are Thy works, O Lord God, the Almighty; Righteous and true are Thy ways, Thou King of the nations (12).

The "Song of Moses" is the victory dance after crossing the Red Sea with victory over Pharaoh and the Egyptians. The "Song of the Lamb" is one of victory and triumph over Satan, the Beast, the False Prophet, and death (81).

The temple of the tabernacle opened in heaven.

> Revelation 15:5: After these things I looked, and the temple of the tabernacle of testimony in heaven was opened (12).

The temple in heaven was opened in Revelation 11:19 after the seventh trumpet was sounded. The opening of the temple in heaven in Revelation 11:19 and 15:5 confirms that Revelation 15 picks up where Revelation 11 left off. The seventh trumpet is the third woe which consists of the seven plagues or the seven bowls of the wrath of God.

TABLE 6 SHOWS THE ORDER OF EVENTS FROM REVELATION 12 THROUGH 14

	GREAT TRIBULATION	SIXTH SEAL	WRATH OF GOD
	3 1/2 YEARS		

CHAPTER 12
(1) Man-Child Rapture (Prize of the High Calling) – The Overcomers.
(2) Woman Flees into the wilderness for three and one-half years.
(3) Satan and his angels are driven to the earth.

CHAPTER 13
(4) The beast and the false prophet.

CHAPTER 14
(5) The 144,000 first-fruit standing before the throne of God (part of the Man-Child Rapture).
(6) First angel flies through the air preaching the gospel.
(7) Second angel proclaimed the fall of Babaylon (Revelation 17 and 18).
(8) Third angel warns the people not to worship the beast or his image or take his mark.

(9) Lord on the cloud – The Great Tribulation is over. Harvest Rapture
(Mat. 24:29-31, Rev 6:12-17, Rev. 7:9-17, Rev. 14:14-16)

(10) Harvest of the grapes (the wicked) – cast into the wine press of the wrath of God
(Rev. 14:17-20)

The seven angels with the seven plagues

> Revelation 15:6-7: . . . and the seven angels who had the seven plagues came out of the temple, clothed in linen, clean and bright, and girded around their breasts with golden girdles. And one of the four living creatures gave to the seven angels seven golden bowls full of the wrath of God, who lives forever and ever. (12)

The seven angels pouring out the seven bowls is the judgment of God on those who took the mark of the Beast and are destroying the earth.

Who are the seven angels?

> Revelation 17:1-2: And one of the seven angels who had the seven bowls came and spoke with me, saying "Come here, I shall show you the judgments of the great harlot who sits on many waters, with whom the kings of the earth committed acts of immorality, . . ." (12)

> Revelation 21:9: And one of the seven angels who had the seven bowls full of the last plagues, came and spoke with me, saying, "Come here, I shall show you the bride, the wife of the Lamb" (12).

> Revelation 19:9-10: And he said to me, "Write, 'Blessed are those who are invited to the marriage supper of the Lamb.'" . . . And I fell at his feet to worship him. And he said to me, "Do not do that; I am a fellow servant of yours and your brethren who hold the testimony of Jesus; worship God." . . . (12)

> Revelation 22:8-9: And I, John, am the one who heard and saw these things. And when I heard and

saw, I fell down to worship at the feet of the angel who showed me these things. And he said to me, "Do not do that; I am a fellow servant of yours and of your brethren the prophets and of those who heed the words of this book; worship God." (12)

It can be seen from the scriptures mentioned above that one of the seven angels who had the seven bowls was talking to John. John fell down to worship him. The angel told John not to do this for he was a fellow servant, brethren, and prophet like him. A brethren is a human or man like John.

The seven angels are saints that have been redeemed from the earth. Men will be involved in God's judgment on earth.

I Corinthians 6:2-3: Do you not know that the saints will judge the world? . . . Do you not know that we will judge angels? . . . (7).

The temple was filled with smoke.

Revelation 15:8: And the temple was filled with smoke from the glory of God and from His power; and no one was able to enter the temple until the seven plagues of the seven angels were finished (12).

This is similar to the scene in Isaiah 6:1-4, which shows the Lord sitting on a throne, lofty and exalted with the train of His robe filling the temple. As the angels cried out "Holy, holy, holy is the Lord Almighty; the whole earth is full of His glory," the door posts and the foundation of the temple shake, while the temple is filled with smoke.

The temple in heaven was filled with smoke from the mighty presence and power of the Lord. In the Old Testament, the Lord dwelt in the temple on earth. The temple was where one worshiped the Lord, and received atonement for one's sins. However, at this time, there is no mercy, the temple is spewing out God's wrath on those who dwell on earth. (80)

> Revelation 16:1: And I heard a loud voice from the temple, saying to the seven angels, "Go and pour out the seven bowls of the wrath of God into the earth" (12).

In the five of the first six trumpets only one-third of everything on earth was affected, while in the seventh trumpet, which is the bowls or vial judgment, everything is affected.

1. First trumpet - one-third of the trees and earth burned up.
2. Second trumpet - one-third of sea turned to blood, destroying a third of the ships and creatures in the sea.
3. Third trumpet - a blazing star fell from heaven, poisoning one-third of the rivers and fountain of water.
4. Fourth trumpet – affected one-third of the sun, moon and stars so that one third of the day and one-third of the night was without light.
5. Fifth trumpet – men, without the seal of God, were tormented
6. Sixth trumpet – one third of man kind was killed by the three plagues
7. Seventh trumpet – (seven bowls) everything is affected.

First bowl – cancerous sores

> Revelation 16:2: And the first angel went and poured out his bowl into the earth; and it became a loathsome and malignant sore upon the men who had the mark of the beast and who worshiped his image (12).

The pouring out of the first bowl helps to differentiate between the Great Tribulation and the Wrath of God. The fact that the people with the mark of the Beast are receiving incurable sores shows that the Great Tribulation is over. This is the time of God's wrath on those that took the mark of the Beast.

The first bowl is similar to God's judgment on the Egyptians.

> Exodus 9:8-9: Then the Lord said to Moses and Aaron, "Take for yourselves handfuls of soot from a kiln, and let Moses throw it toward the sky in the sight of Pharaoh. And it will become fine dust over all the land of Egypt, and will become boils breaking out with sores on man and beast through all the land of Egypt." (12)

Moses took soot and threw it into the sky in the presence of Pharaoh, causing sores and boils to break out on all Egyptians and their animals. Pharaoh's magicians could not stand in the presence of Moses because of the sores.

Moses told the Israelites that if they did not obey the Lord and follow all of his commandments, the curses of Egypt would come upon them.

> Deuteronomy 28:15: But it shall come about, if you will not obey the Lord your God, to observe to do all His commandments and His statutes which I charge you today, that all these curses shall come upon you and overtake you. (12)

One of the curses Moses foretold was:

> Deuteronomy 28:35: The Lord will strike you on the knees and legs with sore boils, from which you

cannot be healed, from the sole of your foot to the crown of your head (12).

This prophecy of incurable sores will be manifested with the pouring out of the first bowl. The people who have the mark of the Beast will come down with incurable sores (80, 81).

Second bowl - sea of blood

Revelation 16:3: And the second angel poured out his bowl into the sea, and it became blood like that of a dead man; and every living thing in the sea died (12).

This event is similar to the second trumpet, which affected one-third of the sea. The second bowl appears to affect all seas, killing all life in the sea. This curse is similar to one of the plagues of Egypt, whereby Moses smote the water, and the river turned to blood. Blood was all through the land of Egypt.

Third bowl – rivers and springs of water became as blood.

Revelation 16:4-7: And the third angel poured out his bowl into the rivers and springs of waters; and they became blood. And I heard the angel of the waters saying, "Righteous art Thou, who art and who wast, O Holy One, because Thou didst judge these things; for they poured out the blood of saints and prophets, and Thou hast given them blood to drink. They deserve it." And I heard the altar saying, "Yes, O Lord God, the Almighty, true and righteous are Thy judgments." (12)

Gordon Lindsay said,

The worshipers of the beast had taken a sadistic delight in shedding the blood of the prophets and the saints. Now they are judged and punished in their own coin - they are given blood to drink. Having rejected the water of life, freely offered, they now must drink blood.

This plague is similar to the third trumpet in that it affects the water. However, the third trumpet affected only one-third of the fresh water. This plague affects all waters in the rivers and in the springs of the earth. After the second and third bowls, the water supply of the whole world will have turned to blood. (80)

Fourth bowl – the sun scorched men with fire.

> Revelation 16:8-9: And the fourth angel poured out his bowl upon the sun; and it was given to it to scorch men with fire. And men were scorched with fierce heat; and they blasphemed the name of God who has the power over these plagues; and they did not repent, so as to give Him glory. (12)

With the fourth trumpet, one-third of the sun is darkened, while with the fourth bowl, the heat of the sun is increased causing men to be scorched. Men will blaspheme the name of the Lord because of the plagues.

Moses, Malachi and Isaiah foretold the days in which men would be tormented with burning heat.

> Deuteronomy 32:24: they shall be wasted with hunger and devoured with burning heat and poisonous pestilence; . . . (31).

> Malachi 4:1: For behold, the day comes that shall burn as an oven; and all the proud and arrogant, yes and all that do wickedly and are lawless shall be

stubble; the day that comes shall burn them up, says
the Lord of hosts, so that it will leave them neither
root nor branch. (59)

Isaiah 24:5-6: The earth is defiled by its people; . . .
Therefore earth's inhabitants are burned up, and very
few are left (7).

Though men were scorched by this fierce heat, they did not repent but continued to blaspheme his name (80, 81).

Fifth bowl – Kingdom of the Beast was darkened

Revelation 16:10-11: And the fifth angel poured
out his bowl upon the throne of the beast; and his
kingdom became darkened; and they gnawed their
tongues because of pain, and they blasphemed the
God of heaven because of their pains and their sores;
and they did not repent of their deeds. (12)

These grievous sores came upon those with the mark of the
Beast during the first bowl. In the fifth bowl, these sores were still
there. With the second and third bowls, all the water turned to blood.
With the fourth bowl, they were scorched with a fierce heat. Now, a
thick darkness covers the kingdom of the Beast. Men did not repent.
Because of their pain, they gnawed their tongues and blasphemed
God. (80, 81)

This darkness that came upon the Beast and his kingdom is similar to the plague of darkness that Moses called down on the Egyptians.

Exodus 10:21-23: Then the Lord said to Moses,
"Stretch out your hand toward the sky, that there
may be darkness over the land of Egypt, even a darkness which may be felt." So Moses stretched out his

hand toward the sky, and there was thick darkness in all the land of Egypt for three days. They did not see one another, nor did anyone rise from his place for three days, but all the sons of Israel had light in their dwellings. (12)

Isaiah 13:9-13: Behold, the day of the Lord is comes! Fierce, with wrath and raging anger, to make the land and the whole earth a desolation, and to destroy out of it its sinners. For the stars of heavens and their constellations will not give their light; the sun will be darkened at it rising, and the moon will not shed its light. And I, the Lord, will punish the world for its evil and the wicked for their guilt and iniquity; I will cause the arrogance of the proud to cease, and will lay low the haughtiness of the terrible and boasting of the violent and ruthless. I will make man more rare than fine gold, and mankind scarcer than the pure gold of Ophir. Therefore I will make the heavens tremble, and the earth will be shaken out of its place at the wrath of the Lord of hosts in the day of His fierce anger. (59)

Blessed Anna-Maria Taigi (19th century, Italy) revelation about three days of darkness:

There shall come over the whole earth an intense darkness lasting three days and three nights. Nothing can be seen, and the air will be laden with pestilence which will claim mainly, but not only, the enemies of religion. It will be impossible to use any man-made lighting during this darkness, except blessed candles. He, who out of curiosity, opens his window to look out, or leaves his home, will fall dead on the spot. During these three days, people should remain in their homes, pray the Rosary and beg God for mercy." (84)

John Leary had a number of visions pertaining to three days of darkness.

The three days of darkness will probably occurs during the fifth bowl of the seventh trumpet of the Wrath of God.

You are seeing how I will separate the evil men from the faithful during the three days of darkness. All My faithful will be marked with a cross on their foreheads, while those evil men and women will be marked with the sign of the beast. I will send My angels to mark My faithful to be protected so that they will be passed over for purification much like the Hebrews were protected with the lamb's blood on their lintels. The devil and his angels will be allowed to take those unprotected souls. At that time, all unworthy souls and demons will be sent to hell to purify the earth. Then all the living souls and those faithful who died during the tribulation will be sent to a safe place. I will renew the earth. Then those worthy will be brought back to the heaven on earth to enjoy the fruits of My Mother's triumph for an era of peace. This will give hope to all My faithful to pray and keep close to Me since your reward is not far off. 8/28/94 (43)

Fear not, My people, during this hour, for the time of final chastisement will cleanse all evil from the earth. It will be much like when the angel of death

327

came and the first-born of all Egyptians were slain. When you are enclosed in your room with burning blessed candles and closed windows, you will be as the Hebrews were with death all around them. Pray to your heavenly Father that you will be saved from this evil age. For if you truly follow My commands and My will, you will know your salvation. Once the earth is cleansed of evil I will renew the earth as at creation. Man will once again enjoy all that I had intended for him before the fall. You will live for that glorious day when I invite you into the new heaven on earth. 10/15/94 (43)

My son, you are seeing a massive volcanic eruption in this vision where dark smoke was evolving. It is true that you will continue to see volcanic eruptions increase, but this one will occur as the comet strikes the earth. There will be a tremendous distortion of the earth's crust which will give rise to many such volcanoes. It will be a combination of these eruptions and comet's debris that will give rise to the three days of darkness. . . . It is during these three days of darkness that a cave or underground dwelling will afford you the best protection from the cold and the sulfur in the air depleting the oxygen for a short duration. Pray, my people, and listen to My instructions, and I will direct you where to go and how I will feed you with My Heavenly Bread. 7/23/96 (41)

Sixth bowl – Euphrates River dries up so the kings of the East may cross over on dry shod.

Revelation 16:12: The sixth angel poured out his bowl on the great river Euphrates, and its water was dried up to prepare the way for the kings from the East (7).

The great river Euphrates rises in the mountains of Turkey and flows 1780 miles into the Persian Gulf. Most of the river is from 10 to 30 feet deep and from 1000 feet to one mile wide. Through the centuries, the Euphrates River has been the dividing line between the East and the West, as the river was almost impassable by large armies. This is not true today. However, during the sixth bowl, the Euphrates River will dry up, so the kings from the east with their armies can cross over dry shod. The scripture teaches that the two witnesses have the power to shut up the sky, so it doesn't rain during the three and one-half years of their prophecies. If it doesn't rain, the rivers will dry up.

Unclean spirits like frogs

> Revelation 16:13-14: Then I saw three evil spirits that looked like frogs; they came out of the mouth of the dragon, out of the mouth of the beast and out of the mouth of the false prophet. They are spirits of demons performing miraculous signs, and they go out to the kings of the whole world, to gather them for the battle on the great day of God Almighty. (7)

Three evil spirits will come out of the mouths of the dragon (Satan), the Beast and the False Prophet to go throughout the world performing miraculous signs and lying wonders to deceive the kings of the earth to come to Israel for a great battle.

The kings of the earth will be deceived in a similar manner as King Ahab was in the Old Testament. King Ahab was deceived by his prophets into believing he could defeat the Syrian army to take Ramoth Gilead. The true prophet of the Lord - Micah said,

> I Kings 22:19-23: . . . Therefore hear the word of the Lord: I saw the Lord sitting on his throne with all the

host of heaven standing around him on his right and on his left. And the Lord said, "Who will lure Ahab into attacking Ramoth Gilead and going to his death there?" One suggested this, another that. Finally, a spirit came forward, stood before Lord and said, 'I will lure him.' 'By what means?' the Lord asked. I will go out and be a lying spirit in the mouths of all his prophets.' he said. "You will succeed in luring him," said the Lord. "Go and do it." So now the Lord has put a lying spirit in the mouths of all these prophets of yours. The Lord has decreed disaster for you. (7)

King Ahab was killed in the battle with the Syrian army. The lying spirit spoke through the mouth of his prophets to deceive King Ahab into thinking he would win the battle. In a similar manner, the lying spirits will come out of the mouths of the dragon, the Beast, and the False Prophet to perform lying wonders and gather all nations of the world to Israel for battle. Exactly how these lying spirits will deceive all nations of the world to come to Jerusalem to battle, no one knows. (80, 81)

In Zechariah, the Lord speaks of gathering all nations of the world to Jerusalem to battle.

> Zechariah 14:2: I will gather all nations to Jerusalem to fight against it; the city will be captured, the houses ransacked, and the woman raped. Half of the city will go into exile, but the rest of the people will not be taken from the city. (7)

The Lord will put hooks into their jaws.

In Ezekiel when the Lord was talking to the nations of the north, He spoke of putting hooks into their jaws and bringing them down to the unwalled nation, Israel, after they have been re-gathered from exile from all the nations of the world. Israel became a nation in 1948 after 2500 years in exile. Israel was not an independent nation at the time of Christ as it was under the Roman Kingdom.

> Ezekiel 38:4, 10-13: And I will turn you back, and put hooks into your jaws, and I will bring you forth and all your army, . . . At the same time thoughts shall come into your mind, and you will devise an evil plan. And you will say, I will go up against an open country - the land of unwalled villages; I will fall upon those who are at rest, who dwell securely, all of them dwelling without walls and having neither bars nor gates, to take spoil and prey; to turn your hand upon the desolate places now inhabited, and assail the people gathered out of the nations, who have obtained livestock and goods, who dwell at the center of the earth (Palestine). Sheba and Dedan and the merchants of Tarshish, with all their young lion-like cubs shall say to you, have you come to take a spoil? Have you gathered your hosts to take the prey? To carry away silver and gold, to take away livestock and goods, to take a great spoil? (59)

The evil thoughts that come into the minds of the leaders of the nations of the north, to take a spoil in the land of Israel, will be put there by evil spirits that will come out of the mouths of the dragon, the Beast, and the False Prophet. Russia took over nine nations during and after World War II. Russia has long coveted the land of Israel. She has given the Arab nations military supplies and equipment in an effort to wipe Israel off the map. Russia, under a godless communism, has made no secret of the fact that she intends to take over the whole world.

331

Though the cold war seems to be over, and there is peace and religious freedom, all of this is just temporary. We have shown in Chapter 5 that the nations of the north are the kingdom of clay. At the appropriate time, Russia and nine other nations will be united to form the kingdom of clay. This kingdom of clay, after making a covenant with the Beast and his ten nations of the kingdom of iron, will break the covenant and invade Israel. The Beast, being furious with the nations of the north, will come to Israel to fight. Up to this time, while the kingdom of iron and clay are united, the Beast Kingdom will be the most powerful, most feared and the most hated kingdom on earth. When the Beast Kingdom becomes divided, this will be an opportunity for other nations of the world to try to defeat the Beast.

When the nations of the north invade Israel, there is going to be some opposition as the scripture shows Sheba, Dedan, and the merchants of Tarshish with the young lions questioning the invasion of Israel. These nations will probably come to Israel's aid. Some nations will come in an effort to defeat the Beast. One way or another, the evil spirits will gather all nations of the world to Jerusalem for the great battle of the Almighty God.

The events of the first six bowls will probably take place over a short period of time. However, there is probably a lapse of time between the sixth and the seventh bowls, as time is required for the evil spirits to go all over the world and gather all nations of the world to Jerusalem for battle. This battle will be the final showdown, as the Lord will fight for Israel in this battle. The Lord will go forth to fight after Jerusalem has been taken and half of the city led into exile (Zechariah 14:2).

Blessed is he, who stays awake.

> Revelation 16:15: Behold, I come like a thief! Blessed is he who stays awake and keeps his clothes

with him, so that he may not go naked and be shamefully exposed (7).

The Lord is giving a warning to the people who have not taken the mark of the Beast to not be caught naked and defiled with sin. They are to stay awake, be alert, and watch for His coming (80).

Seventh bowl – the Battle of Armageddon

Revelation 16:16-17: Then they gathered the kings together to the place that in Hebrew is called Armageddon. The seventh angel poured out his bowl into the air, and out of the temple came a loud voice from the throne, saying, "It is done!" (7)

When the seventh angel sounded his trumpet, there were loud voices in heaven saying:

Revelation 11:15: . . . The kingdom of the world has become the kingdom of our Lord and His Christ: and He will reign forever and ever (12).

When the seven bowls of the seventh trumpet is over, it is finished. The kingdom of this world becomes the kingdom of our Lord Jesus.

Lightning, thunder, earthquake and hail

Revelation 16:18-20: Then there came flashes of lightning, rumblings, peals of thunder and a severe earthquake. No earthquake like it has ever occurred since man has been on earth, so tremendous was the quake. The great city split into three parts, and the cities of nations collapsed. God remembered Babylon the Great and gave her the cup filled with the wine of the fury of his wrath. Every island fled away and the mountains could not be found. From the sky huge hailstones of about a hundred pounds each fell upon men. And they cursed God on account of the plague of hail, because the plague was so terrible. (7)

Revelation 11 also speaks of the judgment of the seventh bowl.

Revelation 11:19: And the temple of God which is in heaven was opened; and the ark of His covenant appeared in His temple, and there were flashes of lightning and sounds and peals of thunder and an earthquake and a great hailstorm. (12)

The thunder, lightning, earthquake, and hail are all events of the seventh bowl, which is part of the battle of Armageddon.

After Jerusalem is taken, the women raped, half of the city is exiled, then the Lord will go forth to fight.

After the Lord gathers all nations of the world to Jerusalem to battle and Jerusalem is taken, the women are raped, their homes ransacked, then the Lord will go forth to fight for Israel.

Zechariah 14:2-4: I will gather all the nations to Jerusalem to fight against it; the city will be captured, the houses ransacked, and the women raped. Half of the city will go into exile, but the rest of the people will not be taken from the city. Then the Lord will go out and fight against those nations, as he fights in the day of battle. On that day his feet will stand on the Mount of Olives, east of Jerusalem, and the Mount of Olives will be split in two from east to west, forming a great valley, with half of the mountain moving north and half moving south. (7)

The Mount of Olives, splitting into two sections, will probably be due to the great earthquake that occurs, when the Lord's feet touch the Mount of Olives.

Nuclear warfare

> Zechariah 14:12-13, 15: This is the plague with which the Lord will strike all the nations that fought against Jerusalem: Their flesh will rot while they are still standing on their feet, their eyes will rot in their sockets, and their tongues will rot in their mouths. On that day men will be stricken by the Lord with great panic. Each man will seize the hand of another, and they will attack each other. . . . A similar plague will strike the horses and mules, the camels and donkeys and all the animals in those camps. (7)

The eyes, tongues, and flesh of men and animals rotting, while they are standing on their feet, are the symptoms of a nuclear explosion.

Rome, the city of the Beast, also called the city of Babylon, is destroyed in an hour.

It is during the seventh bowl that the city of Rome, the city of Babylon, is destroyed in one hour.

> Revelation 18:9-10: When the kings of the earth who committed adultery with her and shared her luxury see the smoke of her burning, they will weep and mourn over her. Terrified at her torment, they will stand far off and cry: 'Woe! Woe, O great city, O Babylon, city of power! In one hour your doom has come!" (7)

The kings of the earth will stand far off, terrified of the torment that destroyed the great city in one hour. This is a description of a nuclear explosion. The kings of the earth and the merchants are terrified of nuclear radiation and fallout.

Huge hailstones

From the sky, huge hailstones of about one hundred pounds will fall upon the earth. The people will curse God because the hail is so terrible.

When the atomic bomb was dropped on Marshall Island, large dents were noticed on the heavy armor on the ship. The officials were puzzled as to how these dents got on the heavy armor. Movies of the nuclear explosion showed that the ships were hit by very large hailstones that were created by the air turbulence in the nuclear explosion. (83)

There seems to be no question that nuclear warfare is involved in the battle of Armageddon and in the destruction of the city of Rome. The giant hail may be the result of nuclear explosions.

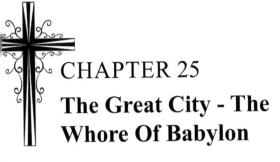

CHAPTER 25

The Great City - The Whore Of Babylon

The great harlot – the Whore of Babylon

Revelation 17:1-7: One of the seven angels who had the seven bowls came and said to me, "Come, I will show you the punishment of the great prostitute, who sits on many waters. With her the kings of the earth committed adultery and the inhabitants of the earth were intoxicated with the wine of her adulteries. Then the angel carried me away in the Spirit into a desert. There I saw a woman sitting on a scarlet beast that was covered with blasphemous names and had seven heads and ten horns. The woman was dressed in purple and scarlet, and was glittering with gold, precious stones and pearls. She held a golden cup in her hand, filled with abominable things and the filth of her adulteries. The title was written on her forehead:

Mystery
Babylon the Great
the mother of prostitutes
and of the abominations of the earth

I saw that the woman was drunk with the blood of saints, the blood of those who bore testimony to

Jesus. When I saw her, I was greatly astonished. Then the angel said to me: "Why are you astonished? I will explain to you the mystery of the woman and of the beast she rides, which has the seven heads and ten horns." (7)

What is the seven-headed beast with ten horns that the woman rides?

Revelation 17:9-10, 12: Here is the mind which has wisdom. The seven heads are the seven mountains on which the woman sits, and they are seven kings; five have fallen, one is, the other has not yet come: . . . And the ten horns which you saw are ten kings, who have not yet received a kingdom, but they receive authority as kings with the beast for one hour. (12)

Revelation 12 shows that the seven-headed beast is Satan. The seven heads represent the seven world kingdoms of Satan that have existed throughout history. Daniel discussed five of the seven kingdoms, as two of the kingdoms had already passed. These kingdoms are:

1. Egypt
2. Assyria
3. Babylon
4. Medo-Persia
5. Greece
6. Roman Kingdom at the first coming of Christ
7. Roman Kingdom at the time of the end

The ten horns represent the ten kings of the ten kingdoms of the seventh head of the beast. This was discussed earlier in Chapter 17.

The woman that rides the seven-headed beast

Since the seven-headed beast is a sign that represents Satan and his worldly kingdoms throughout history, then the woman that rides the beast must have been in existence an equal amount of time. The woman that rides the seven-headed beast is called the Whore of Babylon. She is a religious symbol, representing the mother of all abominations and evil on earth. She is opposite the Sun-clothed woman, who is the mother of God's people.

Who is the woman that is the Whore of Babylon?

> Revelation 17:18: The woman you saw is the great city that rules over the kings of the earth (7).

John called the woman the great city. The American College Dictionary says the term "the" refers to a definite article when used before a noun as opposed to an indefinite article like "a" or "an". "The" means a specific city. (85) John used the term "the great city" several times in the Book of Revelation. They must all refer to the same city.

What is the great city?

> Revelation 11:8: And their dead bodies will lie in the street of the great city which mystically is called Sodom and Egypt, where also their Lord was crucified (12).

The great city where our Lord was crucified was Jerusalem. Yet, John called this city mystical Sodom and Egypt. Mystical Sodom and Egypt is just another name for Mystery Babylon the Great.

The third place, where John used the term "the great city" is when Jerusalem was split into three parts by a great earthquake. It is interesting that the next verse says Babylon was remembered by God.

339

> Revelation 16:18-19: . . . and there was a great earth-
> quake, such as there had not been since man came to
> be upon earth, so great an earthquake was it, and so
> mighty. And the great city was split into three parts,
> and the cities of nations fell. And Babylon the great
> was remembered before God, to give her the cup of
> the wine of His fierce wrath. (12)

Zechariah gives further teaching on Jerusalem being divided by
a great earthquake.

> Zechariah 14:4: And in that day His feet will stand on
> the Mount of Olives, which is in front of Jerusalem
> on the east; and the Mount of Olives will be split in
> its middle from east to west by a very large valley, so
> that half of the mountain will move toward the north
> and the other half toward the south. (12)

The Mount of Olives and Jerusalem will be split by an earthquake. Two thirds of Jerusalem will perish.

> Zechariah 13:1, 8-9: In that day a fountain will be
> opened for the house of David and for the inhabit-
> ants of Jerusalem, for sin and for impurity. . . . "And
> it will come about in all the land," declares the Lord,
> "That two parts in it will be cut off and perish; But
> the third will be left in it. "And I will bring the third
> part through fire, refine them as silver is refined, and
> test them as gold is tested. . . ." (12)

The fountain, mentioned in verse 1, is the living water de-
scribed in Zechariah 14:8 and Ezekiel 47 that will flow out of
Jerusalem into the eastern sea (Dead Sea) and into the western sea
(Mediterranean Sea).

The scriptures in Zechariah 13:1, 8-9 and 14:4 show that a great earthquake will divide Jerusalem and the Mount of Olives. Revelation 16:18-19 confirms that the great city, Jerusalem, will be divided by a great earthquake.

Oliver Greene and Gordon Lindsay both wrote that the great city that was split by an earthquake in Revelation 16:18-19, was Jerusalem. (80, 81)

If the Book of Revelation was written by one man, and he called the great city in Revelation 11:8 and 16:18-19 Jerusalem, then it would be logical that the great city, the whore of Babylon, in Revelation 17:18 would also be Jerusalem. It is interesting that when Jerusalem was destroyed by an earthquake in Revelation 16:18-19 that the next verse says," Babylon was remembered by God."

The great whore sits on many waters.

> Revelation 17:15: Then the angel said to me, "The waters you saw, where the prostitute sits, are peoples, multitudes, nations and languages (7).

The great whore is a city of people of many different nations and languages.

Jerusalem is a city of many nations and languages.

The Lord has re-gathered His people, the Jews from every nation on earth. The people of Jerusalem speak the language of every nation from which they came. There are three main languages in Jerusalem: Hebrew, Arabic and English. Jerusalem is truly a city of many people, nations, and languages.

The Beast and the ten kings will destroy the Whore of Babylon.

> Revelation 17:16-17: The beast and the ten horns you saw will hate the prostitute. They will bring her

341

to ruin and leave her naked; they will eat her flesh and burn her with fire. For God has put it into their hearts to accomplish his purpose by agreeing to give the beast their power to rule, until God's words are fulfilled. (7)

We must remember that the woman is the great city Jerusalem. The Beast started destroying the woman with the abomination of desolation of the temple, proclaiming that he is God. The Beast has slowly destroyed the city and its inhabitants throughout the three and one-half years of the Great Tribulation and the Wrath of God.

Jerusalem is portrayed as a woman, a city and a harlot.

The New International Version of the Bible called the sixteenth chapter of Ezekiel an allegory of unfaithful Jerusalem. Jerusalem is depicted as a woman, a city and a harlot. Notice how the scriptures below compare with Revelation 17:16-17.

> Ezekiel 16:2, 35-51: Son of man, make known to Jerusalem her abominations . . . Therefore, O harlot, hear the word of the Lord. Thus says the Lord God, "Because your lewdness was poured out and your nakedness uncovered through your harlotries with your lovers and with all your detestable idols, and because of the blood of your sons which you gave to idols, therefore, behold I shall gather all your lovers with whom you took pleasure, even all those whom you loved and all those whom you hated. So I shall gather them against you from every direction and ex-pose your nakedness to them that they may see all your nakedness.
>
> Thus I shall judge you, like women who commit adultery or shed blood are judged; and I shall bring

on you the blood of wrath and jealousy. I shall also give you into the hands of your lovers, and they will tear down your shrines, demolish your high places, strip you of your clothing, take away your jewels, and will leave you naked and bare. They will incite a crowd against you, and they will stone you and cut you to pieces with their swords. And they will burn your houses with fire and execute judgments on you in the sight of many women. Then I shall stop you from playing the harlot, and you will also no longer pay your lovers.

So I shall calm My fury against you, and My jealousy will depart from you, and I shall be pacified and angry no more. Because you have not remembered the days of your youth but have enraged Me by all these things, behold, I in turn will bring your conduct down on your own head," declares the Lord God, "so that you will not commit this lewdness on top of all your other abominations." "Behold, every one who quotes proverbs will quote this proverb concerning you, saying 'Like mother, like daughter.' "You are the daughter of your mother, who loathed her husband and children. You are also the sister of your sisters, who loathed their husbands and children. Your mother was a Hittite and your father was an Amorite.

Now your older sister is Samaria, who lives north of you with her daughters; and your younger sister, who lives south of you, is Sodom with her daughters. Yet you have not merely walked in their ways or done according to their abominations; but, as if that were too little, you acted more corruptly in all your conduct than they. "As I live," declares the Lord God, "Sodom, your sister, and her daughters, have not done as you and your daughters have done." Behold, this was the guilt of your sister Sodom: she and her daughters had arrogance, abundant food, and careless ease, but she did not help the poor and needy. Thus they were haughty and committed abominations before Me. Therefore I removed them when I saw it. Furthermore, Samaria did not commit half of your sins, for you have multiplied your abominations more than they. Thus you have made your sisters appear righteous by all your abominations which you have committed. (12)

In Revelation 17:16-17, the prostitute, the great city will be stripped naked. They will eat her flesh and burn her with fire. In Ezekiel, the Lord called Jerusalem a woman, a city and a harlot, saying that her sins were worse than the sins of her sisters, Sodom and Samaria. In both Ezekiel and Revelation, the Lord said to Jerusalem, you will be stripped of your clothing and jewels and left naked. You will be cut to pieces with the sword and your houses burned with fire.

Isaiah calls Jerusalem a harlot.

Isaiah 1:21-26: See how the faithful city has become a harlot! She once was full of justice; righteousness used to dwell in her but now murders! . . . Your rulers are rebels, companions of thieves; they all love bribes and chase after gifts. They do not defend the cause of the fatherless; the widow's case does not come before them. Therefore the Lord, the Lord Almighty, the Mighty One of Israel, declares: "Ah, I will get relief from my foes and avenge myself on my enemies. I will turn my hand against you; I will thoroughly purge away your dross and remove your impurities. I will restore your judges as in the day of old, your counselors as at the beginning. Afterward you will be called the City of Righteousness, the Faithful City." (7)

Though the Lord called Jerusalem a harlot, He said he was going to purge her and remove her impurities and restore her as "The Faithful City."

The woman (Jerusalem) was drunk with the blood of the saints.

Revelation 17:6 I saw that the woman was drunk with the blood of the saints, the blood of those who bore testimony to Jesus. . . . (7).

Jerusalem is a city known for murdering her saints and prophets, including Jesus Christ, the Son of God and the greatest of the prophets. Zechariah the prophet was murdered in the temple between the sanctuary and the altar (Matthew 23:35).

Matthew 23:37: O Jerusalem, Jerusalem, who kills the prophets and stones those who are sent to her! . . . (12)

How can Jerusalem be the city of the living God and the Whore of Babylon?

Jeremiah tells why Jerusalem will be destroyed.

Jeremiah 22:8-9: People from many nations will pass by this city and will ask one another, "Why has the Lord done such a thing to this great city?" And the answer will be: "Because they have forsaken the covenant of the Lord their God and have worshiped and served other gods." (7)

When the Jews rejected the Lord and started worshiping other gods, Jerusalem was no longer the city of the Living God but became as Sodom and Egypt, the abomination of the earth. Jerusalem is the great city, mystically Sodom and Egypt called Mystery Babylon the Great.

The great city, the whore of Babylon, reigns over the kings of the earth.

The seven heads of the dragon represent the seven kingdoms throughout history. The woman, the whore of Babylon, has reigns over the seven kingdoms. We need to remember that the woman, the Whore of Babylon, is the mother of all abominations of the earth. This woman, that rides the seven-headed dragon (Satan), is a sign or symbol like the dragon and the sun-clothed woman. Just as the sun-clothed woman is the symbolic mother of God's people, the Whore of Babylon is the symbolic mother of all evil. Just as Satan is the unseen ruler of the world forces of darkness, the woman represents a symbolic spiritual or religious reign of evil.

Jerusalem, a sacred city of Jewish, Christian, and Moslem faiths, is the religious center of the world. At this time, Jerusalem is under control of the Satanic trinity: Satan, the Beast, and the False Prophet. The False Prophet is the spiritual religious leader that deceived the world by miracles. Jerusalem is the city where the Beast defiles the temple by proclaiming that he is God.

Both Isaiah and Ezekiel called Jerusalem a prostitute, saying her sins were worse than her sisters, Sodom and Samaria. This is because God's chosen people knew the Lord and chose to sin. The scriptures say that it is better to have never known the Lord than to know the Lord and reject him (Hebrews 6:4-6; 10:26-31). This is what Jerusalem did. Jerusalem, once the city of God, is now the Whore of Babylon under the control of the Satanic trinity because

God's people rejected him.

The reign of Jerusalem over the kings of the earth is a spiritual reign. Revelation 16:13-14 shows three unclean spirits coming out of the mouths of Satan, the Beast, and the False Prophet to go throughout the world to persuade the kings of the earth to come to Jerusalem for the great battle of Armageddon. This is the spiritual reign of the woman, the Whore of Babylon. This happens prior to the end of the seventieth week of Daniel, just before the battle of Armageddon,

The woman has been reigning over the kingdoms and cities of the Beast and evil throughout history. This is shown by the fact that she is riding the seven-headed dragon. The climax of her rule is at the time of the end when Jerusalem, once the city of God, is under the control of the satanic trinity: Satan, the Beast, and the False Prophet. This is her last great thrust against God, when she gathers the kings of the earth to Jerusalem for battle. It is at this time that Jerusalem reigns over the kings of the earth, just before the Lord returns to destroy Jerusalem and take possession of the earth.

Ezekiel speaks of a vision he saw of the Lord, when He came to destroy the city Jerusalem, the whore of Babylon. This occurs when Jesus' feet touches the Mount of Olives. Revelation 16:19 says that the Lord remembers Babylon the Great and gives her the cup, filled with the wine of the fury of His wrath.

> Ezekiel 43:3: . . like the vision which I saw when He came to destroy the city (12).

The Beast and the ten kings have been slowly destroying Jerusalem since the abomination in the temple. The final destruction of Jerusalem by an earthquake occurs when the Lord returns. At this time Jerusalem is split by a great earthquake and two-thirds of the people perish. After Jerusalem is destroyed, the next verse says, "Babylon came up in remembrance before the Lord" (Revelation 16:19).

> Revelation 16:19: And the great city was split into three parts, and the cities of nations fell. And Babylon the great was remembered before God, to give her the cup of the wine of His fierce wrath (12).

Jerusalem, the whore of Babylon, the city of many nations and languages received the cup of the Lord's fierce wrath.

Is Rome, the city of seven hills or is the Catholic Church the Whore of Babylon?

Many biblical scholars have tried to show that the seven heads of the Beast represent the Seven Hills of Rome (86, 87). However, scriptures call the seven heads, the seven mountains represented by seven kings. As discussed earlier in Chapter 17 and 20, a mountain is often used in scripture to denote a kingdom. How could the Seven Hills of Rome represent Satan's seven kingdoms throughout history? The Seven Hills of Rome do not represent any king or kingdom.

Some Bible scholars think the Catholic Church or Rome is the Whore of Babylon (86, 87). The Catholic Church has been in existence less than 2000 years, while the woman, the Whore of Babylon that rides the seven-headed dragon, has been in existence throughout the history of the world. The Catholic Church or Rome has never reigned over the kings of the whole earth. The continents of Asia, Africa, North and South America have never been under the rule of Rome or the Catholic Church. There has never been a literal city that ruled the whole earth.

Scripture says that the waters, where the harlot sits, is a city of a multitude of people from many nations and languages. This city is an international city. Though Rome has ruled over a few nations and the papacy is the spiritual leader of Roman Catholics in many nations,

Rome is not an international city. Rome is not a city of many nations and languages. Rome is a city of Italians that speaks Italian.

Jerusalem is an international city.

The Jews have been re-gathered from all nations of the world. They speak the languages of countries from where they came. Jerusalem is a city of three main languages: Hebrew, Arabic and English. Jerusalem is truly the international city identified by scriptures as the great city of the Bible that is called the Whore of Babylon. Jesus destroys the city by an earthquake, as His feet touch the Mount of Olives, fulfilling the vision Ezekiel saw in Ezekiel 43:3.

Since the Whore of Babylon was shown to be the city of Jerusalem, is the sun-clothed woman a city?

Since the Whore of Babylon, the mother of all abominations of the earth is a symbol representing the city of Jerusalem, then the Sun-clothed woman must also be a city.

The Sun-clothed woman in Revelation 12 is the mother of the Man-child, who was taken up to heaven before the Great Tribulation began. When the dragon was unable to get the Man-child and the woman, he makes war with the rest of the woman's children, the Christians and the Jews, who were on earth after the Great Tribulation began.

> Revelation 12:17: . . . the dragon was furious (enraged) at the woman, he went away to wage war on the remainder of her descendants, who obey God's commandments and who have the testimony of Jesus Christ . . . (59)

The Sun-clothed woman is the symbolic mother of God's people.

Isaiah 66 speaks of a woman giving birth to a male child and also having other children just as the Sun-clothed woman did.

Who is the woman in Isaiah 66?

The following scripture shows that the woman, in Isaiah 66, is the city, Jerusalem.

> Isaiah 66:7-13: Before she travailed, she brought forth; Before her pain came, she gave birth to a boy. . . . As soon as Zion travailed, she brought forth her sons. . . . Be joyful with Jerusalem and rejoice for her, all you who love her; Be exceedingly glad with her, all who mourn over her, that you may nurse and be satisfied with her comforting breasts, that you may suck and be delighted with her bountiful bosom. For thus says the Lord, "Behold, I extend peace to her like a river, and the glory of the nations like an overflowing stream; and you shall be nursed, you shall be carried on the hip and fondled on the knees. As one whom his mother comforts, so I will comfort you. And you shall be comforted in Jerusalem. (12)

> Isaiah 66:7 in the "Good News for Modern Man" says, "My holy city is like a woman, who suddenly gives birth to a child, without ever going into labor" (88). Since the woman, in Isaiah 66, is the mother of God's people and is called Jerusalem, then the Sun-clothed woman must also be Jerusalem.

How can the Sun-clothed woman and the Whore of Babylon both be Jerusalem?

This is a paradox. There are obviously two different cities of Jerusalem. Galatians speaks of two different Jerusalems: An earthly Jerusalem and a heavenly Jerusalem.

Galatians 4:22-26: It says that Abraham had two sons, one by a slave woman, the other by a free woman. His son by the slave woman was born in the usual way, but his son by the free woman was born as a result of God's promise. These things can be understood as a figure: the two women represent two covenants. The one whose children are born in slavery is Hagar, and she represents the covenant made at Mt. Sinai. Hagar, who stands for Mt. Sinai in Arabia, is a figure of the present city of Jerusalem, in slavery with all its people. But the heavenly Jerusalem is free, and she is our mother. (88)

The present city of earthly Jerusalem is compared to Hagar who represents slavery, bondage and sin. The Whore of Babylon, the mother of all abominations of the earth, who correlates to slavery, bondage and sin, is earthly Jerusalem. The Sun-clothed woman correlates to the heavenly Jerusalem, the mother of all of God's people.

Hebrews and Revelation both speak of the city of heavenly Jerusalem.

Hebrews 12:22: Instead, you have come to Mount Zion and to the city of the living God, heavenly Jerusalem with its thousands of angels (88).

Revelation 21:2: And I saw the Holy City, the new Jerusalem, coming down out of heaven from God, prepared and ready, like a bride dressed to meet her husband (88).

The Sun-clothed woman, the symbolic mother of God's people, is the city of heavenly Jerusalem, which comes down from heaven.

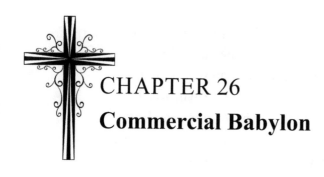

CHAPTER 26
Commercial Babylon

The two Babylons – two different cities

Revelation 17 dealts with a woman that was called the Whore of Babylon and a city. The woman, the mother of all abominations and evil, is a religious symbol opposite the Sun-clothed woman, which was the symbolic mother of all God's people. This chapter utilizes symbols, which were all explained in the text.

Revelation 18 also deals with a city called Babylon. However, this city is commercial Babylon. This chapter is interpreted literally.

Dake and Lindsay both pointed out the similarities and the contrasts of the two Babylons (34,86).

Similarities of the two Babylons:

1. Both Babylons commit fornication with the kings of the earth; one in a religious way, while the other in a commercial way (Revelation 17:2; 18:3,9: 19:2).
2. Both Babylons shed the blood of the prophets and the saints (Revelation 17:6;18:24).
3. Both have a cup of abominations (Revelation 17:4; 18:6).
4. Both Babylons are called a city (Revelation 17:18; 18:10,16,18-21).
5. Both are called "Babylon the Great."

At first, it appears that both Babylons are the same. However, upon closer examination, there is a great contrast.

The differences between the two Babylons

1. The woman and the Beast in the seventeenth chapter of Revelation are symbolic while the eighteenth chapter is interpreted literally. The symbols are explained in the seventeenth chapter while no explanation is needed for the eighteenth chapter.
2. No merchants become rich by the commerce of the first Babylon, while they become rich with the commerce of the second.
3. The ten kings rejoice over the destruction of the woman, the Whore of Babylon (Revelation 17:16-17), while they mourn over the destruction of the commercial city, Babylon (Revelation 18:9-10).
4. A period of time is required for the destruction of the woman Babylon in Revelation 17, while commercial Babylon, in Revelation 18, is destroyed in one hour.
5. The merchants and the kings stand far off in fear in the destruction of commercial Babylon, but not in the destruction of the Whore of Babylon.
6. The ten kings and the Beast are involved in destroying the Whore of Babylon. They did not destroy commercial Babylon as they wept over its destruction.
7. Merchandise is described in commercial Babylon, but not in religious Babylon.

There is no question concerning the great contrast between the two Babylons. The first Babylon was a spiritual religious system, shown to be Jerusalem. The second Babylon is a commercial system.

Will the ancient Babylon on the Euphrates River be rebuilt?

There are reports that Iraq is pouring millions of dollars into the rebuilding of Babylon on the Euphrates River. However, the Babylon on the Euphrates River will not be the Babylon of Revelation 18 (89).

Reasons why Babylon on the Euphrates River will not be the Babylon of Revelation 18.

1. God said Babylon, after being destroyed by Medo-Persia, would not be inhabited again.

   Isaiah 13:17,19-21 Behold, I am going to stir up the Medes against them, . . . And Babylon, the beauty of kingdoms, the glory of the Chaldeans' pride, will be as when God overthrew Sodom and Gomorrah. It will never be inhabited or lived in from generation to generation; nor will the Arab pitch his tent there, nor will shepherds make their flocks lie down there. But desert creatures will lie down there, and their houses will be full of owls, ostriches also will live there, and shaggy goats will frolic there. (12)

2. The ancient city Babylon has been desolate since its destruction by Medo-Persia. God said it would never be inhabited again.

3. Babylon of Revelation 18 is readily accessible to all merchants who trade by sea. Babylon on the Euphrates River is not easily accessible to trade by sea.

4. Babylon, of Revelation 18, when destroyed is mourned by every sea captain and sailor who made their living by sea and had become rich through her wealth.

5. Babylon on the Euphrates River is not the Babylon of Revelation 18, as the Euphrates River dries up during

the sixth bowl. If the Babylon on the Euphrates River were the Babylon of Revelation 18, the merchants would have groaned long before its destruction during the seventh bowl, as ships would not be able to travel up the Euphrates River after it dried up during the sixth bowl.

6. If the Babylon on the Euphrates River were the Babylon of Revelation 18, the merchants and sailors would not be able to witness its destruction from the sea, as Babylon on the Euphrates River is too far inland from the Persian Gulf (more than 300 miles inland).

7. When God destroyed Babylon on the Euphrates River, a large millstone was thrown into the Euphrates River (Jeremiah 51:63-64). When God destroys Babylon in Revelation 18, the millstone will be thrown into the sea.

Revelation 18:21: And a strong angel took up a stone like a great millstone and threw it into the sea, saying, "Thus will Babylon, the great city, be thrown down with violence, and will not be found any longer". (12)

8. The Babylon on the Euphrates River is 300 miles from the sea; therefore it is not close to a sea. This shows that Babylon on the Euphrates River and the Babylon of Revelation 18 are two different Babylons in two different locations.

9. The Beast causes all nations to prosper. The scriptures show that the Roman nation (Italy), probably the city of Rome, will be the Beast's headquarters. The Babylon on the Euphrates is over eighteen hundred miles from Rome by air and over five thousand miles by sea (90). Why would the Beast, with his headquarters in Italy,

cause Babylon on the Euphrates River to be responsible for the wealth of all nations, instead of his own
city where he (the Beast) is situated?

10. Italy is easily accessible by sea for trade by all nations
especially the ten nations under the Beast. Babylon
on the Euphrates River is not close to the sea and is
not easily accessible to trade by all nations. It is too
far out of the way. Ships will have to travel five thousand miles around Saudi Arabia to reach Babylon on
the Euphrates River. (90)

The name, Babylon, probably had its beginning immediately
after the flood at the tower of Babel, which was more than 2,000
years before Christ. Scripture speaks of an Israelite family coveting
a Babylonian garment after the fall of Jericho (Joshua 7:21). This
was approximately 1,500 years before Christ.

When the Jews went into Babylonian captivity, this was the
kingdom of Babylon, which was represented by the third head of
the seven-headed dragon. The kingdom of Babylon existed a little
over 500 years before the coming of Christ. Starting in the Book of
Genesis, the name Babel and Babylon are mentioned throughout the
Bible. The term, Babylon, was used long before the city Babylon
on the Euphrates River came into existence. The name, Babylon, is
applied to two different cities in Revelation, which are destroyed at
the time of the end.

The woman who rides the seven-headed beast is the Whore of
Babylon, the mother of all abomination and evil on earth. The seven
heads of the beast (dragon, Satan) represent her seven world kingdoms throughout history. The capital city of each kingdom, at its
moment in history, can justly be called the city of Babylon because
of the woman, the Whore of Babylon that rides the seven-headed

beast. The woman, the Whore of Babylon, was a mother to each of the kingdoms.

Jerusalem was called Sodom and Egypt and the Whore of Babylon because of her sins. Jerusalem, being called Sodom and Egypt, shows that Jerusalem, the Whore of Babylon, represents both a city and a kingdom.

The commercial city of Babylon in Revelation 18, which causes all nations to prosper by her trade, will be the headquarters of the Beast. Babylon on the Euphrates River is not within the boundaries of the seventh Beast kingdom.

Since the woman, the Whore of Babylon, rides the seven-headed dragon (Satan), there is no reason why the host city of the Beast, the last of the seven kingdoms of the dragon cannot be called the city of Babylon. Since the scriptures speak of the prince of the Roman people as the Beast of the seventh kingdom, the commercial city of Babylon will probably be Rome.

CHAPTER 27

Scene In Heaven

The Marriage Feast Of The Lamb And The Battle Of Armageddon

Hallelujah! God has judged the harlot and avenged the blood of His saints

> Revelation 19:1-4: After this I heard what sounded like the roar of a great multitude in heaven shouting: "Hallelujah! Salvation and glory and power belong to our God, for true and just are his judgments. He has condemned the great prostitute who corrupted the earth by her adulteries. He has avenged on her the blood of his servants." And again they shouted: "Hallelujah! The smoke from her goes up for ever and ever." The twenty-four elders and the four living creatures fell down and worshiped God, who was seated on the throne. And they cried: "Amen, Hallelujah!" (7)

There is great joy in heaven. God has brought judgment on the great prostitute, the mother of all abomination, the whore of Babylon, the rider of the seven-headed dragon, and avenged the blood of His saints. The great prostitute was shown to be the city of Jerusalem.

Revelation 19:5-6: Then a voice came from the throne, saying: Praise our God, all you his servants, you who fear him, both small and great!' Then I heard what sounded like a great multitude, like the roar of rushing waters and like loud peals of thunder, shouting: "Hallelujah! For our Lord God Almighty reigns." (7)

This is the same scene seen in Revelation 11:15-18, where the scriptures say that when the seventh trumpet sounded, the kingdom of the world becomes the kingdom of our Lord, and He shall reign forever. The twenty-four elders fell on their faces to worship and praise God.

The marriage of the Lamb

In Revelation 19:5-6, the roar of a great multitude comes from the throne as thunder shouting: Hallelujah! For the reign of our Lord has come. The time for the marriage of the Lamb has come.

Revelation 19:7-8: Let us rejoice and be glad and give him glory! For the wedding of the Lamb has come, and his bride has made herself ready. Fine linen, bright and clean, was given her to wear" (7).

When does this Marriage take place?

"After this" and "then" in Revelation 19:1,5 show that the marriage of the Lamb takes place in heaven after the judgment of the prostitute, but before the Lord returns to the earth (Revelation 19:11-21).

Revelation 19:9: Then the angel said to me, "Write: 'Blessed are those who are invited to the wedding supper of the Lamb!'" And he added, "These are the true words of God" (7).

Who are the guests that are invited to the marriage feast of the Lamb?

Whoever is invited to the marriage feast is already in heaven as the marriage takes place before the Lord returns to the earth. The bride is not invited as she naturally has a place reserved for her (34). We will get some understanding who the guests are from Psalm 45.

Nuptial ode for the Messianic King

The New American Bible called Psalm 45 a "Nuptial Ode for the Messianic King."

> Psalm 45:7, 10-12, 15: Your throne, O God, stands for ever and ever;
>
> . . . The daughters of kings come to meet you; the queen takes her place at your right hand in gold of Ophir. Hear, O daughter, and see; turn your ear, forget your people and your father's house. So shall the king desire your beauty; for he is your lord, and you must worship him. . . . In embroidered apparel she is borne in to the king; behind her the virgins of her train are brought to you. (60)

Seiss says the 45th Psalm unmistakably refers to the marriage of the Messiah.

The qualities and doings of the kings, coming forth from ivory palaces, are described with great vigor and animation. There is also the Queen, the King's Bride, standing on His right hand, in gold of Ophir, and all glorious within. It is said of her, "She shall be brought unto the king in raiment of needlework." But beside the Queen, the King's Bride, there is another blessed company, who are to enter with rejoicing into the King's palace, and to share the light of His countenance. They are called "virgins," the companions, associates

360

and bosom friends of the Queen, but plainly distinct from the Queen herself. They do not go with her when she is taken but "follow her" - come after her - and are "brought unto the king" at a subsequent time, and in quite another capacity than that of the Queen or Bride. All of them are made forever happy in their Lord their King. But the Queen is one class, and the virgins, her companions that follow her, are another class. (48)

The 45th Psalm refers to the marriage of the Messiah. The queen stands at the right hand of the King (Psalm 45:10). In Psalm 45:15, the queen is presented in embroidered apparel to the King. The virgins follow after the queen. Psalm 45 shows that the queen, the bride, is attended to by the virgins. This indicates that the whole church will not be the bride of Christ. The King is the Lord, the Messiah, for Psalm 45:12 give the command to worship Him.

John the Baptist said that he was just a friend to the Bridegroom and was not a part of the bride.

> John 3:27-29: To this John replied, ". . . You your-selves can testify that I said, 'I am not the Christ but am sent ahead of him.' The bride belongs to the bridegroom. The friend who attends the bridegroom waits and listens for him, and is full of joy when he hears the bridegroom's voice. That joy is mine, and it is now complete. (7)

John the Baptist said he was just a friend of the Bridegroom. The guests and friends will include all those in heaven, that is, the Old Testament saints and the Christians that did not win the race for the prize of the high-calling. This is discussed more fully in Chapter 37.

Honors and awards

Seiss says,

> It is also the common doctrine of scriptures that there
> are great diversities in the portions awarded to saints.
> There are some greatest and some least in the king-
> dom of heaven. There are some who shall be first
> and some who shall be last. There are some who get
> crowns, and there are some who get none. There are
> some who are assigned dominion over ten cities,
> some five, and some who lose all reward, and are
> saved only "so as by fire." (48)

Lay up for yourself rewards in heaven.

> Matthew 6:19-21: Do not lay up for yourselves trea-
> sures upon earth, where moth and rust destroy, and
> where thieves break in and steal. But lay up for your-
> selves treasures in heaven, where neither moth nor
> rust destroys, and where thieves do not break in or
> steal; for where your treasure is, there will your heart
> be also. (12)

Our rewards are like treasures stored in heaven, never forgotten
by God Almighty and become a part of man's glory for all eternity.

As discussed in Chapter 18, the bride of Christ is the prize of the
high-calling that Paul ran a race for with all of his might. The same
opportunity is there for everyone. The scriptures encourage us to
study the Word so that we will know the truth and the truth will set
us free. It is essential that we study Revelation and the other books
of the Bible so that we may know what God's plans are, and realize
that there is a prize to be won. It is to our advantage to run this race
with all our might.

The rider on the white horse

> Revelation 19:11-12: I saw heaven standing open and there before me was a white horse, whose rider is called Faithful and True. With justice he judges and makes war. His eyes are like blazing fire and on his head are many crowns. (7)

After the marriage and wedding feast of the Lamb, the door of heaven opens. The Lord is on a white horse just as He was when the first seal of the book was opened, and He went forth conquering and to conquer.

> Revelation 6:2: . . . a white horse, and he who sat on it had a bow, and a crown was given to him; and he went out conquering, and to conquer (12).

The Lord continues in Revelation 19 going forth to judge and wage war. This is similar to the scene in Thessalonians where the Lord is revealed in blazing fire, taking vengeance on those that do not know the Lord:

> 2 Thessalonians 1:7-8: . . . This will happen when the Lord Jesus is revealed from heaven in blazing fire with his powerful angels. He will punish those who do not know God and do not obey the gospel of our Lord Jesus. (7)

Christ has many crowns. When did Christ receive these crowns?

When the first seal was opened, Christ, the rider of the white horse, received a crown. He went forth conquering and to conquer (Revelation 6:1-2). Immediately after the Great Tribulation, the Lord is seen on a cloud with a crown on His head (Revelation 14:14). Yet, in Revelation 19:12, the Lord has many crowns on His head. When did He receive these crowns? The only time the Lord could have received these crowns is after the judgment of the prostitute (the whore of Babylon) when there was great rejoicing in heaven, prior to the marriage of the Lamb. (62) The kings will rule the nations of the world when the Lord is sitting on the throne in Jerusalem. All kings have a crown. The many crowns show that Jesus is the King of kings.

The King of kings and Lord of lords

> Revelation 19:12-16: . . . and He has a name written upon Him which no one knows except Himself. And He is clothed with a robe dipped in blood: and His name is called The Word of God. And the armies which are in heaven, clothed in fine linen, white and clean, were following Him on white horses. And from His mouth comes a sharp sword, so that with it He may smite the nations; and He will rule them with a rod of iron; and He treads the wine press of the fierce wrath of God, the Almighty. And on His robe and on His thigh He has a name written, "KING OF KINGS, AND LORD OF LORDS. (12)

The battle of Armageddon – the great supper of the Lord God

> Revelation 19:17-21: And I saw an angel standing in the sun; and he cried out with a loud voice, saying to all the birds which fly in mid-heaven, "Come, assemble for the great supper of God; in order that you may eat the flesh of kings and the flesh of commanders and the flesh of mighty men and the flesh of horses and of those who sit on them and the flesh of all men, both free and slaves, small and great." And I saw the beast and the kings of the earth and their armies, assembled to make war against Him who sat upon the horse and against His army. And

the beast was seized, and with him the false prophet
who performed the signs in his presence, by which
he deceived those who had received the mark of
the beast and those who worshiped his image; these
two were thrown alive into the lake of fire which
burns with brimstone. And the rest were killed with
the sword which came from the mouth of Him who
sat upon the horse and all the birds were filled with
their flesh. (12)

This is the battle of Armageddon. The sixth bowl in Revelation
16:12-16 speaks of gathering the kings of the earth to a place called
Armageddon. The battle of Armageddon takes place when the Lord
returns to the earth with His army to fight against the Beast, the
False Prophet, and the kings of the earth.

The Book of Jude speaks of Enoch prophesying the return of the
Lord to the earth with His saints:

Jude 14-15: . . . Behold, the Lord came with many
thousands of His holy ones, to execute judgment
upon all, and to convict all the ungodly of all their
ungodly deeds which they have done in an ungodly
way, and of all the harsh things which ungodly sinners have spoken against Him. (12)

The great supper of our Lord is described in Ezekiel:

Ezekiel 39:4: . . . I will give you as food to all kinds
of carrion birds and to the wild animals (7).

**It was shown in Chapter 5 that the invasion of Israel by the nations
of the north and battle of Armageddon was one and the same.**

When the Nations of the North invade Israel to take a great spoil,

Ezekiel 38 speaks of the people of Israel dwelling securely in villages without walls.

Today, Israel does not dwell securely and in peace without walls as foretold by Ezekiel. Hezbollah, Hamas, Palestinians, and other terrorists are constantly shooting rockets and sending suicide bombers into Israel. The Israelites are building a 403 mile wall at some point 20 feet high to protect themselves from Palestinian terrorists. At the time of the invasion by the Nations of the North, the Israelites are living peacefully and secure with no walls. (91)

What are the possible explanations of Israelites dwelling peacefully and securely in unwalled villages when the Nations of the North invade Israel?

Psalm 83 speaks of the Arab nations declaring war with Israel with the intent to wipe Israel off the map. Since the Arab countries are not mentioned in Ezekiel when the Nations of the North invade Israel, it is believed that Israel will have defeated the Arab nations as foretold by Scriptures. The battle between Israel and the Arab countries will take place long before the invasion of Israel by the Nations of the North. (91)

Three groups of ten nation's federation against Israel

The Beast or Anti-Christ kingdom, the Nations of the North and the Arabs will all have ten nations each. The Beast kingdom is the kingdom of iron while Russia and her allies will be the kingdom of clay as discussed in Chapter 5. Russia captured and took over nine nations after World War II. This group broke up when the cold war ended.

Bill Salus points out that there are two groups within the ten nations' federations which he calls the inner circle and the outer circle. The inner circle consists of ten Arab nations on Israel's border mentioned in Psalms 83. The outer circle is Russia and her allies which do not border Israel. They are mentioned in Ezekiel 38 as attacking Israel. The outer circle of nations is the kingdom of clay. The Antichrist will make a covenant with the Nations of the North to form one kingdom. Scripture says that they will come together in the seed of men but will not adhere to each other. Toward the end of the seventieth week of Daniel, the Nations of the North will break relationship with the Beast kingdom and invade Israel. This will precipitate the battle of Armageddon. The inner circle of Arabs nations are not mentioned in Ezekiel when the Nations of the North invade Israel. An explanation could be that they have already been defeated by Israel. (91)

Psalms 83 speaks of Arab nations conspiring to wipe Israel off the map.

> Psalms 83:2-9: God, do not be silent; God, be not still and unmoved! See how your enemies rage; your foe proudly raise their heads. They conspire against your people, plot against those you protect. They say, "Come, let us wipe out their nation; let Israel's name be mentioned no more!" They scheme with one mind, in league against you: The tents of Ishmael and Edom, the people of Moab and Hager, Gebal, Ammon, and Amalek, Philistia and the inhabitants of Tyre. Assyria, too in league with them gives aid to the descendants of Lot. (24A)

The inner circle of nations bordering Israel

1. Edom – descendants of Esau, – Southern Jordan and Palestinian refugees
2. Ishmaelites – descendants of Ishmael, - Saudi Arabia and Palestinian refugees

3. Moab – descendants of Lot – Central Jordan and Palestinian refugees
4. Hagrites – Egypt
5. Gebal – Northern Lebanon
6. Ammon – descendants of Lot – Northern Jordan and Palestinian refugees
7. Amalek – The Negev and Sinai Peninsula areas
8. Philistia – Gaza Strip and Hamas
9. Tyre – Southern Lebanon and Hezbollah
10. Assyria – Syria and northern Iraq

The outer circle of nations is the Nations of the North, which are mentioned in Ezekiel.

Ezekiel 38:1- 15: And the word of the Lord came into me: Son of man, set your face against Gog, of the land of Magog, the prince of Meshech, and Tubal, and prophesy against him. And say, Thus says the Lord God: Behold, I am against you, O Gog, chief prince (or ruler) of Rosh, of Meshech and Tubal. And I will turn you back, and put hooks into your jaws, and I will bring you forth and all your army, horses and horsemen, all of them clothed in full armor, a great company with buckler and shield, all of them handling swords; Persia, Cush, and Put or Libya with them; all of them with shield and helmet; Gomer and all his hordes; the house of Togarmah in the ut-termost parts of the north, and all his hordes; many people are with you. You, (Gog) be prepared; yes, prepare yourself, you and all your companies that are assembled about you, and you be a guard and a commander for them. After many days you shall be visited and mustered (for service); in the latter years you shall go against the land that is restored from ravages of the sword, where people are gathered out of many nations upon the mountains of Israel, which had been a continual waste; but its (people) are brought forth out of the nations, and they shall dwell securely, all of them. You shall ascend and come like a cloud to cover the land, you and all your hosts, and many people with you. . . . You will say, I will go up against an open country – the land of un- walled villages; I will fall upon those who are at rest, who dwell securely, all of them dwelling without bars nor gates. To take spoil and prey; to turn your hand upon the desolate places now inhabited, and as- sail the people gathered out of the nations, who have obtained livestock and goods, who dwell at the cen- ter of the earth (Palestine). Sheba and Dedan and the merchants of Tarish, with all their lion-like cubs shall say to you, have you gathered your hosts to take the prey? To carry away livestock and goods, to take a great spoil? Therefore, son of man, prophesy and say to Gog, Thus says the Lord God: In that day when My people Israel dwell securely, will you not know it and be aroused? And you will come from your place out of the uttermost parts of the north, you and many peoples with you, all of them ridding on horses, a great host, a mighty army. (59)

The outer ten nation's federation which is the kingdom of clay will come from the following nations mentioned in Ezekiel 38. The area of some of the names below will consist of two nations today. We will not know the exact current names of the countries until the invasion takes place. Since there are ten nations in the kingdom of iron, we know that there will be ten nations in the kingdom of clay as there are ten toes which is a mixture of clay and iron.

1. Rosh	5. Gomer	9. Togarmah
2. Gog	6. Cush	10. ?
3. Meshech	7. Put or Libya	
4. Persia	8. Tubal	

The Arab's nations of the inner circle surrounding Israel are not mention in Ezekiel when the outer circle Nations of the North invades Israel indicating that they were defeated by the mighty Israeli army.

Jeremiah 48 and 49 speaks of the destruction of the Moab, Ammonite, Edom and the city of Damascus. Isaiah also speaks of the city of Damascus being destroyed.

Isaiah 17:1 Damascus will cease to be a city, and will become a heap of ruins.

There are a number of Scriptures which speaks of Arab nations being defeated and Israel taking possession of the land the Lord promised to Abraham.

Obadiah 1:17- 19: . . . And the house of Jacob shall take possession of those that dispossessed them. The house of Jacob shall be a fire, and the house of a flame; the house of Esau shall be stubble, and they shall set them ablaze and devour them; then none shall survive of the house of Esau, for the Lord has spoken. They shall occupy the Negeb, the mount of Esau, and the foothills of the Philistines; (60)

With the defeat of the inner circle of nations, Israel will greatly expand its territory. Since the Arab countries are not mentioned in Ezekiel when the nations of the north invade Israel, it is believed that the battle between Israel and the Arab countries will take place long before Israel is invaded by the nations of the north. (91)

A Great French Catholic king

Another possible explanation of peace in the Middle East is the coming of a great French Catholic king and an era of peace prior to the coming of the Anti-Christ and the battle of Armageddon.

Desmond A Birch did an elaborate study of prophecies concerning a powerful, holy, French Catholic king who will supposedly come into power prior to the coming of the Anti-Christ. This king has been predicted to defeat the Russian, Prussian, Arab or Middle Eastern forces. He will be anointed Holy Roman Emperor by a saintly pope.

Mr. Birch quoted prophesies from following saints, venerables, blesseds and others from the 4th Century to the present time who foretold the coming a great Catholic king in France: St. Methodius, 4th Century; St. Remigius, 5th Century; St. Caesar of Arles, Father of the Church, 6th Century; St. Catald(us), 7th Century; Rabanus Maurus, 9th Century; Mark Adso(n), 10th Century; St. Thomas a'Becket, 12th Century; St. Hildegard, 12th Century; Werdin D'Otrante, 13th Century; John of Vatiguerro, 13th Century; St. Vincent Ferrer, 14th Century; St. Bridget of Sweden, 14th Century; St. Francis of Paula, 15th Century; Venerable Bartholomew Holzhauser, 17th Century; Rudolph Gekner, 17th Century; Capuchin Friar, 18th Century; Fr. Nectou, 18th Century; Brother Louis Rocco, 19 Century; Nursing Nun of Belay, 19th Century; St. John Vianney, The Cure of Ars, 19th Century; Abbe Souffrand, 19th Century; Sister Marianne, 19th Century; The Ecstatic of Tours, 19th Century; Blessed Ann-Maria Taigi , 19th Century. (3)

The following prophecy by Holzhauser of the 17th century is one of many prophecies concerning the coming of the French King.

371

The Powerful Monarch, who will be sent by God, will uproot every Republic. He will submit everything to his authority, and he will show great zeal for the true Church of Christ. The empire of the Mohammedans will be broken up, and this Monarch will reign in the East as well as in the West. All nations will come to worship God in the true Catholic and Roman faith. There will be many Saints and Doctors (of the Church) on earth. Peace will reign over the whole earth because God will bind Satan for a number of years until the days of the Son of Perdition. No one will be able to pervert the word of God since, during the sixth period, there will be an ecumenical council which will be the greatest of all councils. By the grace of God, by the power of the Great Monarch, by the authority of the Holy Pontiff, and by the union of all the most devout princes, atheism and every heresy will be banished from the earth. The Council will define the true sense of Holy Scripture, and this will be believed and accepted by everyone.

The sixth period of the Church will begin with the powerful Monarch and the Holy Pontiff, as mentioned previously, and it will last until the revelation of Antichrist. In this period, God will console His Holy Church for the affliction and great tribulation which she has endured during the fifth period. All nations will become Catholic. Vocations will be abundant as never before, and all men will seek only the Kingdom of God and His justice. Men will live in peace, and this will be granted because people will make their peace with God. They will live under the protection of the Great Monarch and his successors.

St. Hildgegard of Germany of the 12th century prophesies:

> Peace will return to the world when the White Flower again takes possession of the throne of France. During this period of peace, people will be used for making agricultural implements and tools. Also during this period, the land will be very productive, and many Jews, heathens, and heretics will join the Church.

Werdin D'Otrante of Italy – 13th Century foretold the coming of Great Monarch:

> The Great Monarch and the great pope will precede the Antichrist. The nations will be at war for four years and a great part of the world will be destroyed. The pope will go over the sea carrying the sign of Redemption on his forehead. The Great Monarch will come to restore peace and the pope will share in the victory. Peace will reign on earth.

This king will bring an era of peace prior to the coming of the Antichrist. There will be a large conversion of Muslims to the Catholic faith. This could be a possible explanation why the Israelites are dwelling in peace and in security in unwalled villages at the time Israel is invaded by the nations of the north.

The prophecies of these saints from different nations of Europe and Middle East over the centuries indicate that the coming of the Anti-Christ of the Book of Revelation is further down the road as this great French king has not yet come into power. (3)

The coming of the Son of Man

> Luke 17:26-30: And just as it happened in the days
> of Noah, so it shall be also in the days of the Son of
> Man: they were eating, they were drinking, they were
> marrying, they were being given in marriage, until the
> day that Noah entered the ark, and the flood came and
> destroyed them all. It was the same as happened in the
> days of Lot: they were eating, they were drinking, they
> were buying, they were selling, they were planting,
> they were building; but on the day that Lot went out
> from Sodom it rained fire and brimstone from heaven
> and destroyed them all. It will be just the same on the
> day that the Son of Man is revealed. (12)

Scripture says as it was in the days of Noah and Lot so shall it be
with the coming of the Son of Man.

What was going on in the days of Noah and Lot?

Scripture says the people were eating, drinking, buying, selling,
building, planting, and marrying. These are the every day activities
of life. It was just another day when all of a sudden the flood came,
or when Sodom was destroyed. It will be another day of normal activities when the Son of Man comes.

> Luke 17:31-36: On that day, let not the one who is
> on the housetop and whose goods are in the house go
> down to take them away; and likewise let not the one
> who is in the field turn back. Remember Lot's wife.
> Whoever seeks to keep his life shall lose it, whoever
> loses his life shall preserve it alive. I tell you, on that
> night there will be two men in one bed; one will be
> taken, and the other will be left. There will be two
> women grinding at the same place; one will be taken

and the other will be left. Two men will be in the field, one will be taken and the other will be left. (12)

Who was taken in the days of Noah and Lot?

Noah and Lot were saved from destruction, but they were not taken. They were left on earth. The wicked were the ones that were taken in the days of Noah and Lot. So shall it be with the coming of the Son of Man.

The Great Supper of our Lord

> Luke 17:37: And answering they said to Him, "Where, Lord?" And He said to them, "Where the body is, there also will the vultures be gathered" (12).

What is the body and the vultures?

The body is the wicked that were taken as they were in the days of Noah and Lot. The vultures are the birds that were invited to the great supper of the Lord to feed on the rich men, the captains, the kings, and all the wicked that were killed at the battle of Armageddon, or by the sword that came out of the mouth of the Lord.

The wicked are consumed by the sword that comes out of the mouth of the Lord.

> Revelation 19:21: And the rest were killed with the sword which came from the mouth of Him who sat upon the horse, and all the birds were filled with their flesh (12).

Those that were not killed at the battle of Armageddon were killed wherever they were throughout the world by the sword (The Word) that came out of the mouth of the Lord. The righteous will be on earth when the Lord returns to begin His earthly reign on the throne of David for a thousand years.

The righteous shall inherit the land. The wicked shall be rooted out of the earth.

> Proverbs 2:21-22: For the upright shall dwell in the land, and the men of integrity, blameless and complete, shall remain in it; But the wicked shall be cut off from the earth, and the treacherous shall be rooted out of it. (59)

The righteous who inherit the land will be the Jews, Christians and Gentiles who did not go up in the Man-child or Harvest Raptures and survived the Great Tribulation and the Wrath of God without taking the mark of the Beast.

The Beast and the False Prophet are cast alive into the Lake of Fire.

> Revelation 19:19-20: And I saw the beast and the kings of the earth and their armies, assembled to make war against Him who sat upon the horse and against His army. And the beast was seized, and with him the false prophet who performed the signs in his presence, by which he deceived those who had received the mark of the beast and those who worshiped his image; these two were thrown alive into the lake of fire which burns with brimstone. (12)

The Beast and the False Prophet are thrown alive into the Lake of Fire at the end of the seventieth week of Daniel. The meaning of this scripture is not clear as Daniel speaks of the Beast being slain and his body being cast into the fire to be burnt up.

> Daniel 7: 11: . . . I watched, then, from the first of the arrogant words which the horn spoke, until the beast was slain and its body thrown into the fire to be burnt up (24).

376

There are two or three possible explanations to what appears to be a conflict in scriptures. Dake, in "Dake's Annotated Reference Bible," expressed the belief that the Beast and the False Prophet are killed then resurrected and cast into the Lake of Fire (34).

We have shown that Revelation 13:3 and 17:8, 11 teach that the Beast (man), the ruler of the seventh kingdom, is mortally wounded. At that moment, a prince of darkness ascends from the bottomless pit and enters into the Beast's body to become the eighth head in the body of the seventh head. The little horn (the Beast) is really slain but his body is not cast into the fire until the end of the seventieth week of Daniel.

Another possible explanation is: In Daniel, the Beast is symbolic of a kingdom while the little horn is symbolic of a ruler. In Revelation, the Beast is symbolic of a ruler while the horn is symbolic of a kingdom. In this case, the destruction of the Beast in Daniel is speaking of a destruction of a kingdom and not necessarily the ruler (the little horn).

> Daniel 7:11-12: As I watched, the brutal fourth animal was killed and its body handed over to be burned because of its arrogance against Almighty God, and the boasting of its little horn. As for the other three animals, their kingdoms were taken from them, but they were allowed to live a short time longer. (64)

Dake states, "The beasts or kingdoms preceding the little horn will each reign for a season and a time, then pass away, allowing a succeeding one to come until the little horn comes, whose kingdom is the 8th and the last kingdom before the second advent of Christ . . ." (35)

Gordon Lindsay believed that the Beast and the False Prophet are angelic spirit beings that will come up from the bottomless pit and enter into two human bodies (Revelation 13:1,11; 17:8,11). These angelic spirits, being fallen angels, have already been judged, and will be cast alive into the Lake of Fire. (67)

The wicked dead will be judged at the great white throne judgment.

Satan is bound for a thousand years.

> Revelation 20:1-3: And I saw an angel coming down from heaven, having the key of the abyss and a great chain in his hand. And he laid hold of the dragon, the serpent of old, who is the devil and Satan, and bound him for a thousand years, and threw him into the abyss, and shut it and sealed it over him, so that he should not deceive the nations any longer, until the thousand years were completed; after these things he must be released for a short time. (12)

The Lord is taking double precautions to keep Satan from escaping during the millennium. Satan is chained with a spiritual chain and sealed in the abyss to prevent him from having the freedom of trying to escape (67).

The abodes of the wicked

The abyss or bottomless pit, Hades, and the Lake of Fire are all mentioned in the Book of Revelation (67).

1. The bottomless pit is a place of confinement for the wicked angels. Revelation 17:8 speaks of the Beast ascending out of the abyss or bottomless pit. This is where Satan will be chained for a thousand years.

2. Hades or hell is the place where the wicked human dead are confined until judgment. In Luke 16:19-31, Jesus told about the rich man in Hades. The rich man showed no concern for Lazarus, the beggar, during his life on earth. When Lazarus died, he was carried to Abraham's bosom in Hades. When the rich man died, he also went to Hades. However, there was a big gulf between Lazarus and the rich man. The rich man looked up and begged Abraham to send Lazarus with water to cool his tongue for he was a man most miserable. Abraham told the rich man there was no way for Lazarus to cross the wide gulf between them. It is interesting that the rich man could see, recognize, talk, hear, and feel (in torment) in Hades. He also had great concern for his brothers on earth because he wanted Abraham to send Lazarus back to the earth to warn his brothers. Abraham told him that if his brothers would not listen to Moses and the prophets, they would not listen to anyone raised from the dead.

3. The Lake of Fire and sulfur is where the wicked angels and people will be thrown after the great white throne judgment. The Beast and the False Prophet will be cast into the Lake of Fire before the millennium begins. A thousand years later, Satan and his angels and the wicked people will be thrown into the Lake of Fire and brimstone.

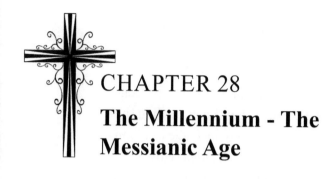

CHAPTER 28

The Millennium - The Messianic Age

The Millennium – a thousand Years

The thousand years are mentioned six times in Revelation 20. Three of the times have to do with Satan, while two of the times speak of Christ reigning a thousand years. The sixth has to do with the resurrection of the deads.

The Second Coming of the Messiah

The Jews missed the first coming of the Messiah because they were looking for a king as the scriptures foretold. Today, many people think that when the Lord Jesus Christ comes, we will meet Him in the air and go to heaven. They do not believe that the Lord will return to the earth with His saints and reign over an earthly kingdom. People with this belief are being deceived just as the Jews were deceived at the first coming of the Messiah. This belief is contrary to the teaching of the scriptures. Even the disciples believed that Jesus was going to restore the kingdom to Israel (Acts 1:6).

The millennium, or the thousand year reign of Christ on earth, was accepted and taught by the early Fathers of the Church.

The early Church's Fathers: Papias, St. Justin Martyr, St Ireanaeus of Lyons, Tertullia, Hippolytus of Rome, St. Methodius of Olympus, Lactantius, all living in the first three centuries, believed and taught that Christ would dwell on earth and reign in Jerusalem for 1000 years. The Teachings of the Catholic Church published in 1952 and has the seal of the Church, stated that it is not contrary to Catholic teaching to believe in some mighty triumph of Christ on earth before the final consummation of all things. Many in the Church today do not believe in a physical reign of Christ on earth with His resurrected saints. (2) This is contrary to the teachings of the scripture.

Prophecy - Know that the 1,000 years referred to in the Book of Revelation means just that.

> To My children on earth, know that prophecies contained in the **Book of Daniel** and the **Book of Revelation still have to take place. Know that the 1,000 years referred to in the Book of Revelation means just that.** If it was meant to be something different then it would have been given a different time. **My Church, the Catholic Church, has not declared their beliefs because they have not done this yet.** My Remnant Church, the remaining tendrils of My Catholic Church on earth will understand the true meaning of My Era of Peace on earth. **You are in the end times but the earth will be renewed.** I call out to all of you, My sacred servants. My voice is hoarse as I beg you to respond to My Holy Call from Heaven. (92)

> My prayer partner and I, while praying, asked the Lord if He had any comment about people being skeptical concerning His physical return to reign on earth. There was a vision of the Lord riding a mighty, frisky, white stallion that was snorting with vapors coming out of its nostrils. The Lord said,

381

Let my Word speak for itself.

The Lord's words below and those in the manuscript clearly speak of His physical return and reign on earth.

In Luke 1:30-33, the angel told Mary that she would have a son and that He would sit on the throne of His father, David. This is an earthly throne. In Acts 1:6-7, 11, the Apostle asked the Lord, when He was going to set up His earthly kingdom. Jesus did not deny an earthly kingdom. He replied that only the Father knew the time this would take place. After Jesus ascended up to heaven, two angels told the disciples that Jesus would return to the earth the same way He left. Zechariah 14:4 states that Jesus' foot would touch Mount Olives, and it would split into a large valley. Zechariah 14:9 says on that day the Lord will be king over the whole earth.

In Ezekiel 43:1-7, the Lord said that His throne would be in the sanctuary (temple in Jerusalem), and He would dwell there among the Israelites. Zechariah 6:12-13 shows that the Lord will build the temple, and His throne will be in the temple. He will sit and rule on His throne. This is the Millennium Temple, as there is no temple after the Millennium (Revelation 21:22).

> Revelation 21:22: And I saw no temple in it, for the
> Lord God, the Almighty, and the Lamb, are its temple.

Jude 14-15, Enoch, the seventh from Adam, prophesied that the Lord is coming with thousands upon thousands of his Holy ones to judge everyone.

The book of Jeremiah says in verses 23:5-6 and 33:15-16 that the Lord will reign as King and will execute justice and righteous on earth. Isaiah 24:23 speaks of the Lord reigning on Mount Zion and in Jerusalem. Both Isaiah 30:19-20 and Ezekiel 39:28-29 state that the Lord will no longer hide His face but will be visible to the people. Isaiah 2:2-3 speaks of Jerusalem as a world capital.

Ezekiel 48:9 teaches that the Lord would receive an allotment of land just as the 12 tribes of Israel. Revelation 20 speaks of the Lord reigning with resurrected saints for a thousand years. When the thousand years are up, Satan will be released from prison to go out and deceive the nations of the world. Then fire will come down from heaven to destroy those who are attacking the saints. The scriptures clearly teach that the Lord will return and reign on earth as the King of kings.

The three titles of Christ

We will discuss the three titles of Jesus and prophecies concerning His Second Coming and reign during the millennium. The three offices of Christ are prophet, priest, and king of the order of Melchizedek. Melchizedek was the only man on earth to hold all three titles. During the time the children of Israel dwelled in the Promised Land, the three offices were held by separate men. Jesus, being of the order of Melchizedek, holds all three titles.

Prophet

> Hebrews 1:1-2: God, after He spoke long ago to the fathers in the prophets in many portions and in many ways, in these last days has spoken to us in His Son, whom He appointed heir of all things, through whom also He made the world. (12)

> Acts 3:22-23: Moses said, "The Lord God shall raise up for you a prophet like me from your brethren; to Him you shall give heed in everything He says to you. And it shall be that every soul that does not heed that prophet shall be utterly destroyed from among the people." (12)

High priest

Hebrews 3:1: Therefore, holy brethren, partakers of a heavenly calling, consider Jesus, the Apostle and High Priest of our confession (12).

Hebrews 4:14-15: Since then we have a great high priest who has passed through the heavens, Jesus the Son of God, let us hold fast our confession. For we do not have a high priest who cannot sympathize with our weaknesses, but one who has been tempted in all things as we are, yet without sin. (12)

Hebrews 5:6: . . . Thou art a priest forever according to the order of Melchizedek (12).

Hebrews 6:20: . . . where Jesus has entered as a fore-runner for us, having become a high priest forever according to the order of Melchizedek (12).

King - Jesus is the Lord of lords and the King of kings, and He will sit on the earthly throne of His earthly father, David. He will rule over all nations of the earth.

Isaiah 9:6-7: For a child will be born to us, a son will be given to us; and the government will rest on His shoulders; and His name will be called Wonderful Counselor, Mighty God, Eternal Father, Prince of Peace. There will be no end to the increase of His government or of peace, on the throne of David and over his kingdom, to establish it and to uphold it with justice and righteous from then on and forevermore. The zeal of the Lord of hosts will accomplish this. (12)

The son given to us is the Lord Jesus Christ as scripture calls Him the Mighty God. He will sit on the throne of David. The throne of David is an earthly throne. The government of the world will rest on the Lord's shoulders.

In Luke, the angel tells Mary that she will have a son and that He will be called the Son of the Most High and He will sit on the throne of His father, David.

> Luke 1:30-31: And the angel said to her, "Do not be afraid, Mary; for you have found favor with God. And behold, you will conceive in your womb, and bear a son, and you shall name Him Jesus. He will be great, and will be called the Son of the Most High; and the Lord God will give Him the throne of His father David;" (12)

> Isaiah 9:7: . . . He will rule with perfect fairness and justice from the throne of His father David. He will bring true justice and peace to all the nations of the world. . . . (64).

> Psalm 72:8-9, 11: He will rule from sea to sea and from the River to the ends of the earth. . . . All kings will bow down to him and all nations will serve him. (7)

> Psalm 98:9: Before the Lord who comes, who comes to govern the earth, to govern the world with justice and people with fairness (24A).

If the first part of this scripture has been fulfilled, then the second part has to also be fulfilled (31). Jesus sitting on the earthly throne of His father, David, has not scripturally come to pass.

Daniel speaks of the Son of Man receiving a kingdom.

> Daniel 7:13-14: I kept looking in the night visions, and behold, with the clouds of heaven one like a Son

of Man was coming, and He came up to the Ancient of Days and was presented before Him. And to Him was given dominion, glory and a kingdom that all the peoples, nations and men of every language might serve Him. His dominion is an everlasting dominion which will not pass away; and His kingdom is one which will not be destroyed. (12)

Here the Son of Man received a kingdom. Scripture says that all the people of all nations and languages might serve Him. This is an earthly kingdom, since nations are not found in heaven.

The Lord returns to the earth the same way He left.

Acts 1:6-7, 9-11: And so when they had come together, they were asking Him, saying, "Lord, is it at this time You are restoring the kingdom to Israel?" He said to them, "It is not for you to know times or epochs which the Father has fixed by His own authority;" . . . And after He said these things, He was lifted up while they were looking on, and a cloud received Him out of their sight. And as they were gazing intently into the sky while He was departing, behold, two men in white clothing stood beside them; and they also said, "Men of Galilee, why do you stand looking into the sky? This Jesus, who has been taken up from you into heaven, will come in just the same way as you have watched Him go into heaven." (12)

Scripture shows that the apostles believed that the Lord was going to set up an earthly kingdom. The angels said He would return to the earth the same way He left.

Zechariah teaches that Jesus will first touch the Mount of Olives, the same mountain He ascended from.

> Zechariah 14:4-5, 9: And in that day His feet will stand on the Mount of Olives, which is in front of Jerusalem on the east; and the Mount of Olives will be split in its middle from east to west by a very large valley, so that half of the mountain will move toward the north and the other half toward the south. . . . Then the Lord, my God, will come and all of the holy ones with Him! . . . And the Lord will be king over all the earth; . . . (12)

When the Lord returns, His feet will first touch the Mount of Olives and He will bring all His saints with Him. On that day, He will be king over all the earth.

The Scriptures teach that Jesus will be King over all the earth.

> Revelation 1:5: . . . Jesus Christ, the faithful witness, the first born of the dead, and ruler of the kings of the earth. . . . (12).

> Jesus is the King of kings and will rule over the kings of the earth.

> Revelation 11:15: . . . The kingdom of the world has become the kingdom of our Lord, and of His Christ; and He will reign forever and ever. (12)

If everyone were to go heaven and Jesus did not return to the earth, there would be no way for the kingdom of this world to become the kingdom of our Lord Jesus Christ. The kingdom of this world is not a kingdom in heaven. Jesus will return to the earth, and sit on the throne of His father, David. He will rule over the kings of the earth.

Jesus will be both a king and a priest

> Zechariah 6:12-13: . . . Thus says the Lord of hosts, "Behold, a man whose name is Branch, for He will branch out from where He is; and He will build the temple of the Lord. "Yes, it is He who will build the temple of the Lord, and He will bear the honor and sit and rule on His throne. Thus, He will be a priest on His throne, and the counsel of peace will be between the two offices. " (12)

The following scriptures show that the Branch is Jesus Christ, the Son of David. He will be both king and priest during the millennium.

> Zechariah 3:8: . . . I am going to bring in My Servant the Branch (12).

> Isaiah 4:2: In that day the Branch of the Lord will be beautiful and glorious, and the fruit of the earth will be the pride and the adornment of the survivors of Israel (12).

> Isaiah 11:1: Then a shoot will spring from the stem of Jesse, and a branch from his roots will bear fruit (12).

> Jeremiah 23:5-6: "Behold, the days are coming, "declares the Lord, "When I shall raise up for David a righteous Branch; and He will reign as king and act wisely and do justice and righteousness in the land. In His day Judah will be saved, and Israel will dwell securely; and this is His name by which He will be called, the Lord our righteousness (12).

> Jeremiah 33:15-16: In those days and at that time I will cause a righteous Branch of David to spring

forth and He shall execute justice and righteousness on the earth (12).

These scriptures show that Jesus Christ will be both High Priest and King and that His kingdom will be on earth during the millennium.

Saints will return to the earth with the Lord

Enoch foretold that the Lord would return to the earth with His saints.

> Jude 14-15: And about these also Enoch, in the seventh generation from Adam, prophesied, saying, "Behold, the Lord came with many thousands of His holy ones, to execute judgment upon all, and to convict all the ungodly of all their ungodly deeds . . . (12)

Zechariah speaks of the Lord returning with His holy ones.

> Zechariah 14:4-5: And in that day His feet will stand on the Mount of Olives, which is in front of Jerusalem on the east; the Mount of Olives will be split in its middle from east to west by a very large valley, so that half of the mountain will move toward the north and the other half toward the south . . . Then the Lord my God, will come, and all the holy ones with Him! (12)

Saints shall rule nations.

The scriptures say Jesus Christ is the Ruler of the kings of the earth. Jesus promised the saints who overcame and prevailed until the end that He would give them authority to rule over nations. The saints will be kings and priests who will rule the earth with a rod of iron. The Scriptures do not speak of nations in heaven. I cannot imagine or visualize a loving God ruling His people in heaven with a rod of iron. Ruling with an iron rod pertains to rebellious people who are born, live, and die on earth in the millennium.

> Revelation 2:26-28: And he who overcomes, and he who keeps My deeds until the end, to him I will give authority over the nations; and he shall rule them with a rod of iron, as the vessels of the potter are broken to pieces, as I also have received authority from My Father; and I will give him the morning star. (12)

> Revelation 5:10: You have made them to be a kingdom and priests to serve our God, and they will reign on the earth (7).

This scripture says upon earth. The saints would have to return with the Lord to reign upon the earth.

> Revelation 12:5: And she gave birth to a son, a male child, who is to rule all the nations with a rod of iron; and her child was caught up to God and to His throne (12).

The male child is made up of the saints who overcame and will rule nations with a rod of iron. The saints will return with the Lord and reign with Him for a thousand years.

> Wisdom 3:1-8: But the souls of the just are in the hand of God, and no torment shall touch them. They seemed, in the view of the foolish, to be dead; and their passing away was judged an affliction and their going forth from us, utter destruction. But they are in peace. For if before men, indeed, they be punished, yet is their hope full of immorality; chastised a little, they shall be greatly blessed, because God tried them and

found them worthy of himself. As gold in the furnace, he proved them, and as sacrificial offerings he took them to himself. In time of their visitation they shall shine and shall dart about as sparks through stubble; they shall judge nations and rule over peoples, and the Lord shall be their King forever. (24)

The world speaks of the souls of the just who have passed on as dead and foolish. Yet, the Lord says they are as gold that was tested and purified in the fire of the furnace. They are blessed and at peace. They shall shine and dart as sparkle through stubble. With the Lord Jesus Christ as their King, they shall judge nations and rule over the people of the earth.

The first resurrection

Revelation 20:4-6: . . . And I saw the souls of those who had been beheaded because of the testimony of Jesus and because of the word of God, and those who had not worshiped the beast or his image, and had not received the mark upon their forehead and upon their hand; and they came to life and reigned with Christ for a thousand years. The rest of the dead did not come to life until the thousand years were completed. This is the first resurrection. Blessed and holy is the one who has a part in the first resurrection; over these the second death has no power, but they will be priests of God and of Christ and reign with Him for a thousand years. (12)

The scriptures teach that there are two resurrections, which are a thousand years apart. Blessed are those who have part in the first resurrection for they shall reign with Christ for a thousand years before the wicked dead are raised to life for judgment.

The first resurrection includes several resurrections: the resurrection of the first fruit of the Old Testament saints when Jesus rose from the dead (Matthew 27:52); the Man-child resurrection (Revelation 12, 14:1-4); the Harvest Rapture (Matthew 24:31; Revelation 7:9-16; 14:14-16) and the two witnesses (Revelation 11:12).

Daniel foretold that the saints will receive a kingdom.

> Daniel 2:44: And in the days of those kings the God of heaven will set up a kingdom which will never be destroyed, and that kingdom will not be left for another people; it will crush and put an end to all these kingdoms, but it will itself endure forever. (12)

> Daniel 7:18, 27: But the saints of the Highest One will receive the kingdom and posses the kingdom forever, for all ages to come. . . . Then the sovereignty, the dominion, and the greatness of all the kingdoms under the whole heaven will be given to the people of the saints of the Highest One; His kingdom will be an everlasting kingdom, and all dominions will serve and obey Him. (12)

The kingdom under the heaven is obviously an earthly kingdom, which will be given to the saints.

Romans and Timothy teach that we are heirs with Christ and we shall reign with Him.

> Romans 8:17: . . . and if children, heirs also, heirs of God and fellow-heirs with Christ, if indeed we suffer with Him in order that we may also be glorified with Him (12).

> II Timothy 2:12: If we endure, we shall also reign

with Him; . . . (12).

The Saints are to sit on the thrones.

Matthew 19:28: And Jesus said to them, "Truly I say to you, that you who have followed Me, in the regeneration when the Son of Man will sit on His glorious throne, you also shall sit upon twelve thrones, judging the twelve tribes of Israel. (12)

Revelation 3:21: He who overcomes, I will grant to him to sit down with Me on My throne, as I also overcame and sat down with My Father on His throne (12).

Revelation 20:4: And I saw thrones, and they sat upon them, and judgment was given to them. . . . (12).

I Corinthians 6:2-3: Or do you not know that the saints will judge the world? And if the world is judged by you, are you not competent to constitute the smallest law courts? Do you not know that we shall judge angels? How much more, matters of this life? (12)

Hebrews 12:28: Therefore, since we receive a kingdom which cannot be shaken, let us show gratitude, by which we may offer to God an acceptable service with reverence and awe; . . . (12).

Psalm 149:6-9: Let the high praises of God be in their mouth, and a two-edged sword in their hand, to execute vengeance on the nations, and punishment on the peoples; to bind their kings with chains, and their nobles with fetters of iron; to execute on them the judgment written; this is an honor for all His godly ones. Praise the Lord! (12)

These scriptures show that the saints will sit on thrones judging not only the wicked people but the wicked angels as well.

CHAPTER 29

The Lord Reigns On Earth

The Lord's throne will be in the temple.

> Ezekiel 43:1-7: Then he led me to the gate, the gate facing toward the east; and behold, the glory of God of Israel was coming from the way of the east. And His voice was like the sound of many waters; and the earth shone with His glory. And it was like the appearance of the vision which I saw, like the vision which I saw when He came to destroy the city. . . . I fell on my face. And the glory of the Lord came into the house by the way of the gate facing toward the east. And the Spirit lifted me up and brought me into the inner court; and behold, the glory of the Lord filled the house. Then I heard one speaking to me from the house, while a man was standing beside me. And He said to me, "Son of man, this is the place of My throne and the place of the soles of My feet, where I will dwell among the sons of Israel forever. . . ." (12)

Ezekiel teaches that the glory of the Lord came through the east gate and went into the inner court of the temple, where the Lord said, "Son of man, this is the place of My throne and the place of the soles of My feet, where I will dwell among the sons of Israel forever." This shows that the throne will be in the temple in Jerusalem during the millennium, as there is no temple after the millennium.

The city that Ezekiel saw being destroyed was Jerusalem, the city of Babylon. This happens when Jesus' feet touch the Mount of Olives, causing a severe earthquake.

The Lord will reign on Mount Zion in Jerusalem.

Isaiah shows that the Lord will reign on Mount Zion in Jerusalem.

> Isaiah 24:23: Then the moon will be abashed and the sun ashamed, for the Lord of hosts will reign on Mount Zion and in Jerusalem and His glory will be before His elders (12).

The Lord will be visible to the people on earth.

> Isaiah 30:19-20: O people in Zion, inhabitant in Jerusalem, you will weep no longer. . . . He, your Teacher will no longer hide Himself, but your eyes will behold your Teacher (12).

> Ezekiel 39:28-29: Then they will know that I am the Lord their God, for though I sent them into exile among the nations, I will gather them to their own land, not leaving any behind. I will no longer hide my face from them, for I will pour out my Spirit on the house of Israel, declares the Sovereign Lord. (7)

This verse speaks of the Lord re-gathering His people from the nations of the world and bringing them back to their home, Israel. This is happening now. The Lord said He will be visible to the people living on earth, and He will teach them.

The Lord shall build His temple.

> Zechariah 6:12-13 : . . . Behold, a man whose name is Branch, for He will branch out from where He is; and He will build the temple of the Lord. Yes, it is He

who will build the temple of the Lord, and He will bear the honor and sit and rule on His throne. Thus, He will be a priest on His throne, and the counsel of peace will be between the two offices. (12)

Zechariah teaches that the Lord will build the temple and His throne will be in the temple. The Lord will be both priest and king, sitting on His throne in the temple. This is the millennium, since there is no temple after the millennium (Revelation 21:22).

People from other nations will help the Lord build the temple and the walls during the millennium.

Zechariah and Isaiah show that people from other nations will help the Lord build the temple and the walls.

> Zechariah 6:15: And those who are far off will come and build the temple of the Lord. . . . (12).

> Isaiah 60:10-11: And foreigners will build up your walls, and their kings will minister to you; for in My wrath I struck you, and in My favor I have had compassion on you. And your gates will be open continually; they will not be closed day or night, so that men may bring to you the wealth of the nations, with their kings led in procession. (12)

The saints shall serve the Lord before the throne in the temple.

The saints shall serve the Lord day and night before the throne. Scripture teaches that the throne is in the temple.

> Revelation 7:15-17: For this reason, they are before the throne of God: and they serve Him day and night in His temple: and He who sits on the throne shall spread His tabernacle over them. They shall hunger

no more, neither thirst any more; neither shall the sun beat down on them, nor any heat; for the Lamb in the center of the throne shall be their shepherd, and shall guide them to springs of water of life; and God shall wipe every tear from their eyes. (12)

This group, to whom the Lord is speaking in Revelation 7:15-17, went up in the Harvest Rapture. They are called servants since they serve Him day and night in the temple.

The Man-Child Rapture, in Revelation 12:5, and those standing before the throne in Revelation 14, are different from the servants. These are they who rule nations with a rod of iron and follow the Lamb wherever He goes.

Jerusalem will be the world capital. All nations of the world will stream toward Jerusalem and the temple which is the house of the Lord.

The scripture below speaks of the temple in Jerusalem in the last days when all nations will stream to it. This scripture speaks of Jerusalem being lifted up on a mountain while Zechariah 14:10: in the next chapter speaks of surrounding area around Jerusalem being made into a plain. This is the millennium when the Lord is sitting on His throne. This has not come yet to pass.

> Isaiah 2:2-3: In the last days the mountain of the Lord's temple will be established as chief among mountains; it will be raised above the hills, and all nations will stream to it. Many peoples will come and say, "Come, let us go up to the mountain of the Lord, to the house of the God of Jacob. He will teach us his ways, so that we may walk in his paths." The law will go out from Zion, the word of the Lord from Jerusalem. (7)

The Lord will rule nations from Jerusalem. He will teach the people His ways and how to walk in His path.

> Hebrew 8:10-12: For this is the covenant that I will make with the house of Israel after those days, says the Lord: I will put My laws into their minds, and I will write them upon their hearts. And I will be their God, and they shall be My people. And they shall not teach everyone his fellow-citizen, and every one brother, saying, "Know the Lord," for all shall know Me, from the least to the greatest of them. For I will be merciful to their iniquities, and I will remember their sins no more. (12)

All of Israel will be saved.

> Romans 11:26 speaks of all Israel being saved. This will happen in the era of peace in the millennium when Lord Jesus Christ is sitting on the throne of His father David in the temple in Jerusalem. The Israelites saved will be from the 144,000 of the twelve tribes that are sealed for protection during the wrath of God.

Yet, there is another scripture Romans 9:27 which quote Isaiah 10:22, that says though the sons of Israel will be as numerous as the sands of the seashore, only a remnant will be saved. Throughout history most of the Israelites have rebelled and disobeyed the Lord

Weapons of war will be no more.

> Isaiah 2:4: And He will judge between nations, and will render decisions for many peoples; and they will hammer their swords into plowshares, and their spears into pruning hooks. Nation will not lift

399

up sword against nation, and never again will they
learn war. (12)

As in the days of Solomon, the Lord will settle disputes between
peoples and nations. Never again will there be war. Weapons of war
will be forged into implements of peace.

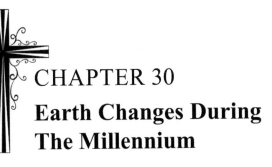

CHAPTER 30

Earth Changes During
The Millennium

Many changes will take place on earth during the millennium.

Jerusalem will be on a mountain surrounded by a plain.

Jerusalem is on the highest mountain in the hill country. During the millennium the hill country around Jerusalem will be a plain.

> Zechariah 14:10: All the land will be changed into a plain from Geba to Rimmon south of Jerusalem; but Jerusalem will rise and remain in its site . . . (12).

The mountainous hill country around Jerusalem will turn into a plain. A great earthquake during the seventh bowl will level the mountains of Israel. When the millennium begins, Jerusalem will be lifted up to be a holy mountain, surrounded by a plain.

Isaiah speaks of Jerusalem being forgiven for her sins and the hills and valleys leveled to make a plain.

> Isaiah 40:1-5: Comfort, give comfort to my people, says your God. Speak tenderly to Jerusalem, and proclaim to her that her service is at an end, her guilt is expiated; indeed, she has received from the hand of the Lord double for all her sins. A voice cries out: In the desert prepare the way of the Lord! Make straight in the wasteland a highway for our

God! Every valley shall be filled in, every mountain and hill shall be made low; the rugged land shall be made a plain, the rough country, a broad valley. Then the glory of the Lord shall be revealed, and all mankind shall see it together; for the mouth of the Lord has spoken. (60)

Baruch 5:7: For God has decreed the flattening of each high mountain, of the everlasting hills, the filling of the valleys to make the ground level so that Israel can walk in safety under the glory of God (57).

Luke 3:5: Every valley shall be filled in, every mountain and hill be laid low, winding ways will be straightened and rough roads made smooth (57).

Though the voice in the desert or wilderness refers to John the Baptist, this prophecy goes beyond the time of John the Baptist. Jerusalem is not forgiven of her sins until the Lord returns to the earth. It is at this time that the hills and the valleys will be made level.

John Leary received words of changes on the earth. Jesus said:

My people, have faith and be patient, for not much longer and you will see the prophecies of Isaiah will be fulfilled. Recognize the signs of the end times that are around you. Those who believe things will continue as they are, will be suddenly shaken. I will be a shepherd guarding My flock through the coming tribulation. Soon you will see the mountains made low and path made straight as I renew the earth to its former glory. Rejoice, My faithful, for My victory is close at hand. 12/10/96 (46)

The broad plains of the earth

When the millennium is over, Satan will be set free. Satan will deceive and gather people from all nations of the world for battle against the Lord and His saints. This army will surround the camp of the saints and the beloved city, Jerusalem, in an area called the broad plain of the earth.

> Revelation 20:7-9: And when the thousand years are completed, Satan will be released from his prison, and will come out to deceive the nations which are in the four corners of the earth, Gog and Magog, to gather them together for the war; the number of them is like the sand of the seashore. And they came up on the broad plain of the earth and surrounded the camp of the saints and the beloved city, and fire came down from heaven and devoured them. (12)

This scripture further confirms that the hill country around Jerusalem will become a plain.

Desert will blossom.

> Isaiah 35:1-2: The desert and the parched land will be glad; the wilderness will rejoice and blossom. Like the crocus, it will burst into bloom; it will rejoice greatly and shout for joy. . . . (7).

> Isaiah 35:6-7: . . . Water will gush forth in the wilderness and streams in the desert. The burning sand will become a pool, the thirsty ground bubbling springs. In the haunts where jackals once lay, grass and reeds and papyrus will grow. (7)

> Isaiah 41:18-19: I will make rivers flow on barren heights, and springs within the valleys. I will turn

403

the desert into pools of water and the parched ground into springs. I will put in the desert the cedar and the acacia, the myrtle and the olive. I will set pines in the wasteland, the fir and cypress together, . . . (7)

Isaiah 55:13: Instead of the thornbush will grow the pine tree, and instead of briers the myrtle will grow (7).

Isaiah 51:3: . . . Her deserts he shall make like Eden, her wasteland like the garden of the Lord; . . . (60).

The scriptures show that the desert will blossom and become like a fertile green valley. Trees and plants that do not grow in a desert will grow there.

Day and night will change

The moon will be like the sun. The sun will be seven times brighter.

Isaiah 30:20,26: . . . He, your Teacher will no longer hide Himself, but your eyes will behold your Teacher. . . . And the light of the moon will be as the light of the sun, the light of the sun will be seven times brighter, like the light of seven days, on the day the Lord binds up the fracture of His people and heals the bruise He has inflicted. (12)

The Dead Sea becomes a living sea.

Water shall flow out of the temple into the Dead Sea.

Ezekiel 47:1-5, 8: Then he brought me back to the entrance of the temple, and I saw water flowing out from beneath the threshold of the temple toward the east, for the facade of the temple was toward the east;

the water flowed down from the southern side of the temple, south of the altar. He led me outside the north gate, and around to the outer gate facing the east, where I saw water trickling from the southern side. Then when he had walked off to the east with a measuring cord in his hand, he measured off a thousand cubits and had me wade through the water, which was ankle-deep. He measured off another thousand and once more had me wade through the water, which was now knee-deep. Again he measured off a thousand and had me wade; the water was up to my waist. Once more he measured off a thousand, but there was now a river through which I could not wade; for the water had risen so high it had become a river that could not be crossed except by swimming. . . . He said to me, "This water flows into the eastern district down upon the Arabah, and empties into the sea, the salt waters, which it makes fresh. (60)

The Dead Sea becomes alive with fish.

Ezekiel 47:9-10: Wherever the river flows, every sort of living creature that can multiply shall live, and there shall be abundant fish, for wherever this water comes the sea shall be made fresh. Fishermen shall be standing along it from En-gedi to En-eglaim, spreading their nets there. Its kinds of fish shall be like those of the Great Sea, very numerous. (60)

The water that flows from the sanctuary in the temple will turn the Dead Sea into a living sea. En-gedi and En-eglaim are located on the Dead Sea. Fishermen will make a living casting their nets for fish in the sea that was once dead.

Salt will be obtained from marshes and swamps.

> Ezekiel 47:11: Only its marshes and swamps shall
> not be made fresh; they shall be left for salt (60).

Since the Dead Sea has become a living sea, there will be no
more salt in the Dead Sea. The scriptures say that salt will be found
in the marshes and swampland.

**Water will flow from Jerusalem into the Dead Sea and the
Mediterranean Sea.**

> Zechariah 14:8: On that day, living water shall flow
> from Jerusalem, half to the eastern sea, and half to
> the western sea, and it shall be so in summer and in
> winter (60).

The water from the sanctuary turns into a river, in which half of
the water flows into the Dead Sea and half into the Mediterranean
Sea. The Dead Sea becomes a living sea full of fish. Notice that the
seasons will change as the scripture mentions summer and winter.

**Fruit trees will bear fruit every month of the year. Tree leaves
will serve as medicine for the healing of the people.**

> Ezekiel 47:12: Along both banks of the river, fruit
> trees of every kind shall grow; their leaves shall not
> fade, nor their fruit fall. Every month they shall bear
> fresh fruit, for they shall be watered by the flow from
> the sanctuary. Their fruit shall serve for food, their
> leaves for medicine. (60)

During the millennium, the messianic age, fruit trees will bear
fruit every month of the year. The leaves will never fade. This means
the leaves will not have to be raked up as they will never fall from the
trees. The leaves (herbs) will serve as medicine for the healing of the

people. Even though the Lord is sitting on the throne in Jerusalem, there is still sickness among the people as this scripture show there is a need for medicine.

Wild animals will become tame.

> Ezekiel 34:24-25: And I, the Lord, will be their God, and My servant David will be prince among them; I, the Lord have spoken. And I will make a covenant of peace with them and eliminate harmful beasts from the land, so that they may live securely in the wilderness and sleep in the woods. (12)

> Ezekiel 34:28: And they will no longer be a prey to the nations, and the beast of the earth will not devour them; but they will live securely, and no one will make them afraid (12).

The nature of wild animals will change and they will become tame. People will be able to live and sleep in the wilderness without fear.

The lion will eat straw like an ox.

> Isaiah 11:6-7: And the wolf will dwell with the lamb, and the leopard will lie down with the kid, and the calf and the young lion and the fatling together; and a little boy will lead them. Also the cow and the bear will graze; their young will lie down together; and the lion will eat straw like the ox. (12)

> Isaiah 65:25: "The wolf and the lamb shall graze together, and the lion shall eat straw like the ox; and dust shall be the serpent's foods. They shall do no evil or harm in all My holy mountain," says the Lord (12).

Carnivorous animals like the wolf, leopard, and lion will no longer kill other animals. Their nature will be changed to eating straw like the ox. The wolf and the lamb, the leopard and the kid, the cow and the bear, and the lion and the calf will all live together in peace.

A baby will play by the hole of a cobra.

> Isaiah 11:8-9: And the nursing child will play by the hole of the cobra, and the weaned child will put his hand on the viper's den. They will not hurt or destroy in all My holy mountain, for the earth will be full of the knowledge of the Lord as the waters cover the sea. (12)

A child can play with a cobra with no fear. Animals will no longer kill or hurt in all the earth because the Lord makes a covenant with the creatures of the earth.

> Hosea 2:18-20: In that day I will also make a covenant for them with the beasts of the field, the birds of the sky, and the creeping things of the ground. And I will abolish the bow, the sword, and war from the land, and will make them lie down in safety. And I will betroth you to Me forever; yes, I will betroth you to Me in righteousness and in justice, in loving kindness and in compassion, and I will betroth you to Me in faithfulness. Then you will know the Lord. (12)

John Leary had a vision of some tigers and other animals with a golden light on all of them. Jesus said:

> My people, you are seeing again how My loving hand will touch the animal kingdom with My coming return. The wild animals will become tame and neither will require food from lower levels. Man will

also be in harmony with the animals. This vision is to show the extent of the beauty of the renewal, I will bring both for man and nature. I have shown you the enrichment of your knowledge of the plants and vegetation in the era of peace. Now, you are seeing that same touch on the animals as well. Much like I preserved the animals in Noah's time, you will see again how I will protect the animals, even through the fire of the tribulation. This again is to give you hope in seeing the results of My purification of the earth in all respects. 11/7/96 (46)

CHAPTER 31

As The Years Of A Tree So Shall The Years Of My People Be.

People will live as long as trees.

People will live as long as trees during the millennium.

> Isaiah 65:20 No longer shall there be in it an infant who lives but a few days, or an old man who does not round out his full lifetime; he dies a mere youth who reaches but a hundred years, and he who fails of a hundred shall be thought accursed. (59)

> Zechariah 8:4: Thus says the Lord of hosts, "Old men and old women will again sit in the streets of Jerusalem, each man with his staff in his hand because of age (12).

> Isaiah 65:22 : . . . For as the lifetime of a tree, so shall be the days of My people, . . . (12).

As the years of a tree, so shall the years of my people be. Scripture speaks of people living over 900 years before the flood.

How do we know if the years before the flood are the same as our years?

The Lord did not intend for us to be ignorant on the number of days in a year and how long people lived before and during the flood. It is not a coincidence that Noah's age and specific dates of various events of the flood are recorded in scripture. Genesis gives us an understanding of the number of days in a year during the flood.

Some biblical scholars say that there are two different accounts of the flood, written by two different authors. Whether this is true or not, the Bible is inspired and this does not contradict the events of the flood.

Noah's age and dates of the events during the flood are:

Genesis Events Noah's Age Month Day

Genesis	Events	Noah's Age	Month	Day
7:1-4	Noah entered ark	600	2	10
7:11	Flood began	600	2	17
7:17	Rain stop	600	3	27
8:3-4	Ark rests on Mt. Ararat	600	7	17
8:5	Top of the mountain seen	600	10	1
8:6-7	Bird is released	600	11	10
8:10	Dove sent out second time	600	11	17
8:12	Dove sent out last time	600	11	24
8:13	Covering of ark removed	601	1	1
8:14	Noah leaves the ark	601	2	27

Scripture says that Noah was 600 years old, when the flood began. The flood began on the 17th day of the second month. Genesis 8:3-4 speaks of the ark coming to rest on Mount Ararat on the 17th day of the seventh month, 150 days after the flood began. From the 17th day of the second month to the 17th day of the seventh month is five months of 150 days. Five months of 150 days is 30 days per month.

$$\frac{150 \text{ days}}{5 \text{ months}} = 30 \text{ days per month}$$

Thirty days per month for five months show that there were 360 days in a year during the flood. Thirty days per month or 360 days per year confirms to the number of days in a month or year in the Books of Daniel and Revelation. Time, times and half a time or 3 1/2 years or 42 months or 1260 days are all equal to the same length of time (Revelation 12:6, 14; 13:5).

$$\frac{1260 \text{ days in } 3\ 1/2 \text{ years}}{3\ 1/2 \text{ years}} = 360 \text{ days per year}$$

$$\frac{360 \text{ days per year}}{12 \text{ months per year}} = 30 \text{ days per month}$$

$$\frac{1260 \text{ days in } 3\ 1/2 \text{ years}}{42 \text{ months in } 3\ 1/2 \text{ years}} = 30 \text{ days per month}$$

A year of 360 days gives a perfect 30 days per month. There is nothing perfect about our present year of 365 1/4 days. (14)

Noah was 601 years old when he got off the ark on the 27th day of the second month. Noah spent one year and seventeen days on the ark. The detailed documentation of Noah's age, the date and months of the events during the flood are within five and one-fourth days of our year. Noah was 600 years old when the flood began. He got off the ark one year and seventeen days later at the age of 601 years. This shows that people did live to be over 900 years before the flood. There is no reason why people should not live this long again during the millennium. As the scripture says, "As the years of a tree so shall the years of my people be."

The earth will be as it was before the sin of Adam.

John Leary received following words:

> My people, I wish to share with you in this vision of the era of peace, and some descriptions of things then. This is an age when all men will experience the time before Adam's sin on a renewed earth. This will

be a time when the aging process will cease in your thirties. Older people will be strengthened to look younger, and the children will mature in their thirties. The animals and man will be in perfect harmony, as you will all grow in perfection at that time. You will be able to call on Me and I will answer you at any time. You will be exposed to full knowledge of My universe. You will live to an old age and many will live to the end of this age. You will experience My love and peace, so you will be as heaven on earth. You will see in this age how I intended the world to be without the influence of evil. When you are truly faced with the glory of My creation, you will choose to please Me in every facet of your life. Time will continue, but there will be no wars, as you will love your neighbor as you love Me. Only My faithful will be brought back to life with glorified bodies. You will have time to adore Me and serve Me every day. You will be giving Me thanks continually that you have been graced to be present in this age. This is a message of hope I am showing you, so that My faithful, who have been purified, will enjoy their reward in My splendor of My kingdom. 10/6/96 (46)

My people, you are witnessing a mountaintop experience when I come again in triumph to defeat Satan. After My triumph, I will usher in an era of peace that has been promised even in My scriptures. . . . Those who have died and are resurrected will have glorified bodies and will live to the end of this era. Those, who are faithful and live through the tribulation, will have their reward also in My era of peace. These will have

413

their bodies rejuvenated and will live long lives. It is only some of these people who may see death before the end of this era. Do not be concerned over the details of how My will intends things. It is My keeping with scripture and My promises that are more important. Be joyful in My gifts to you and do not doubt over anything I have given you. I give you all reason to be joyful and your thanks should be ever in your prayer. 10/7/96 (46)

Why were there 360 days in a year before the flood and during the flood, and there are 365 ¼ days now?

Genesis 1:14: Then God said, "Let there be lights in the expanse of the heavens to separate the day from the night, and let them be for signs, and for seasons; and for days and years; (12)

God created the days and nights to divide seasons, days and years. God created everything perfect. A year of 360 days is perfect. There is nothing perfect about 365 1/4 days. When the flood came, the earth was shaken off its foundation and course. Psalm 82:5 speaks of the foundation of the earth being shaken. The King James translation says that the foundation of the earth is out of course. When the millennium comes, the earth will be greatly shaken and restored to its original foundation. The people again will live as long as trees, as before the flood. (14)

Comet will change the earth orbit and the magnetic poles.

On July 23, 1996, John Leary received the following words which spoke of a comet striking the earth, changing the positions of the magnetic poles and pushing its orbit off course, away from the sun. This event occurs during the Wrath of God.

My son, you are seeing a massive volcanic eruption in this vision where dark smoke was evolving. It is true that you will continue to see volcanic eruptions increase, but this one will occur as the comet strikes the earth. There will be tremendous distortion of the earth's crust which will give rise to many such volcanoes. It will be a combination of these eruptions and the comet's own debris that will give rise to three days of darkness. Other repercussions will be a changing of the magnetic poles from their present position, and a brief change in earth's orbit away from the sun. The gravity of the sun will correct this change in orbit, but for a while the earth will be colder. It is during these three days of darkness that a cave or underground dwelling will afford you the best protection from the cold and the sulfur in the air depleting the oxygen for a short duration. Pray, My people, and listen to My instructions, and I will direct you where to go and how I will feed you with My Heavenly Bread. (41)

People will build their own houses and raise their own food.

Isaiah 65:21-24: They shall live in houses they build, and eat the fruit of the vineyards they plant. They shall not build houses for others to live in, or plant for others to eat. As the years of a tree, so the years of my people; and my chosen ones shall long enjoy the produce of their hands. They shall not toil in vain, nor beget children for sudden destruction; for a race blessed by the Lord are they and their offspring. Before they call, I will answer; while they are yet speaking, I will hearken to them. (60)

The earth during the millennium or the Messianic age will be very similar to the Garden of Eden. The animals will not be wild. They will be tame and eat straw like an ox. There will be no poisonous snakes as they will be harmless and eat dirt for their food. The climate will be ideal, neither hot nor cold as fruit trees will bear fruit every month of the year. People will live as long as trees. Each family will build its own home. It will not be as it is today, where builders and contractors build homes and people buy them. People will plant and eat their own food. There will not be any commercial farming, where one person plants and another eats, as it is today. People will enjoy the fruit of their labor, and take pride in the work of their own hands. They will live in the home they build, and eat the food they raise. The children will be protected. They will not be aborted or destroyed.

Universal knowledge of the Lord

> Isaiah 11:9: They will not hurt or destroy in all My holy mountain, for the earth will be full of the knowledge of the Lord as the waters cover the sea (12).

> Jeremiah 31:33-34: "But this is the covenant which I will make with the house of Israel after those days," declares the Lord, "I will put My law within them, and on their heart I will write it; and I will be their God, and they shall be My people. And they shall not teach again, each man his neighbor and each man his brother, saying, "Know the Lord," for they shall all know Me, from the least of them to the greatest of them," declares the Lord, . . . (12)

> Zechariah 8:22-23: So many people and mighty nations will come to seek the Lord of hosts in Jerusalem and to entreat the favor of the Lord. Thus says the

Lord of hosts, "In those days ten men from the nations of every language will grasp the garment of a Jew saying, "Let us go with you, for we have heard that God is with you." (12)

People of all nations will ask a Jew to take him to Jerusalem to meet the Lord. The whole earth will be full of the knowledge of the Lord.

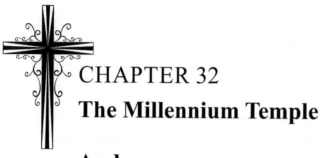

CHAPTER 32

The Millennium Temple

And

The Israelites After 2000 Years Of Christianity

How do we know that the temple, described in Ezekiel 40 to 48, is the millennium temple?

1. Both Ezekiel 43:7 and Zechariah 6:12-13 speaks of the Lord's throne being in the temple. The Lord told Ezekiel that His throne would be in the temple and that the soles of His feet would dwell there among the Israelites forever.

2. Ezekiel 47 described a stream of water that flows from the sanctuary of the temple. This stream as it leaves the temple turns into a river, which flows into the Dead Sea.

3. The water from the temple turns the Dead Sea into a living sea. All kinds of fish will live in the Dead Sea. Fishermen will make a living fishing in this sea.

4. Fruit trees of all kinds will grow by the bank of this river. These trees will bear fruit every month of the year. The leaves of these trees will serve as medicine

for the healing of the people.

5. The Lord Himself will receive an allotment of land
    just as each of the tribes of Israel (Ezekiel 48:9).

These prophecies, which have not yet been fulfilled, will be fulfilled during the reign of the Messiah, during the millennium. The scriptures say there will be no temple in the new Jerusalem, which comes down out of heaven, after the millennium, and the great white throne judgment.

> Revelation 21:2, 22: And I saw the holy city, new Jerusalem, coming down out of heaven from God, made ready as a bride adorned for her husband, . . And I saw no temple in it, for the Lord God, the Almighty, and the Lamb, are its temple. (12)

The fact that there is no temple after the millennium and the great white throne judgment shows that the temple in which the Lord sits on in Ezekiel 43:7 is the millennium temple.

Land will be allotted to the twelve tribes of Israel during the millennium.

When Jacob was on his deathbed, he blessed Joseph's two sons, Ephraim and Manasseh, giving them equal status with the other tribes of Israel. Ephraim and Manasseh are half-tribes but are listed as tribes along with all thirteen receiving an allotment of land during the millennium.

Tribes:

1. Dan
2. Asher
3. Naphtali
4. Manasseh - son of Joseph
5. Ephraim - son of Joseph

6. Reuben
7. Judah
8. Simeon
9. Issacar
10. Zebulun
11. Gad
12. Benjamin
13. Levi

When the children of Israel came into the Promised Land, an allotment of land was given to twelve of the thirteen tribes except for the tribes of Levi. The tribe of Levi did not receive any allotment of land, as they were priests who were living among the twelve tribes, ministering to them.

In Revelation 7, the tribes of Dan and Ephraim were not included among the twelve tribes sealed by the Lord for protection during the Wrath of God. The tribes of Dan and Ephraim were probably not listed because they were responsible for leading Israel into idolatry (Judges 18; I Kings 12:13; Hosea). Joseph and his son Manasseh were listed as tribes in place of Dan and Ephraim to give a total of twelve tribes.

During the millennium, all thirteen tribes are listed as tribes in Ezekiel 48 and are given allotments of land.

The Lord receives an allotment of land during the millennium.

The Lord told Ezekiel in 43:6-7 that His throne would be in the sanctuary and He would dwell there among the Israelites. The following scripture shows that the Lord will receive an allotment of land, just as the thirteen tribes receive an allotment of land during the millennium.

> Ezekiel 48:9-12: The tract that you set aside for the
> Lord shall be twenty-five thousand cubits across by

twenty thousand north and south. In this sacred tract the priests shall have twenty-five thousand cubits on the north, ten thousand on the west, ten thousand on the east, and twenty-five thousand on the south; and the sanctuary of the Lord shall be in its center. The consecrated priests, the Zadokites, who fulfilled my service and did not stray along with the Israelites as the Levites did, shall have within this tract of land their own sacred domain, next to the territory of the Levites. (60)

The Lord will receive an allotment of land with the sanctuary in the middle. The descendants of Zadok, who were faithful to the Lord during the time of idolatry before the Assyrian and Babylonian captivity, will minister to the Lord in the sanctuary, while the other Levites will not. The consecrated priests, descendants of Zadok will live on the land allotted to the Lord. Notice that the Levite tribe will have a separate allotment of land next to the Lord.

Ezekiel 48:13: The Levites shall have a territory corresponding to that of the priests, twenty-five thousand cubits by ten thousand. The whole tract shall be twenty-five thousand cubits across and twenty thousand north and south. (60)

In the Old Testament, the Levites lived among the different tribes and did not have an allotment of land. While in the millennium, they will have allotment of land as the other tribes.

How will we know the descendants of Zadok after 2500 years? How do we know which of the Jews belong to each of the tribes?

Only the Lord knows who the descendants of Zadok are, or which of the Jews belong to each of the tribes.

The Israelites after 2,000 years of Christianity

The twelve tribes of Israel are mentioned in Revelation 7 and Ezekiel 48. Revelation 7 speaks of the twelve tribes being sealed with the seal of the living God for protection during the Wrath of God. Ezekiel 48 shows the twelve or thirteen tribes of Israel receiving allotments of land during the millennium. The events in Revelation 7 and Ezekiel 48 take place after 2000 years of Christianity.

Are there any scriptures that speak of the Lord re-gathering His people after 2,000 years of Christianity?

We need to review the promises the Lord made to the Israelites. The Lord promised to bless the Jews above all people and nations, if they would keep His commandments and listen to His voice (Deuteronomy 26:16-19; 28:1-15). However, if they did not obey Him, He would curse them and scatter them among all nations of the world.

> Deuteronomy 28:64: Moreover, the Lord will scatter you among all peoples, from one end of the earth to the other end of the earth; . . . (12).

Approximately one thousand years later, at the time of the Assyrian and Babylonian captivity, Israel was divided into two kingdoms, the northern kingdom and the southern kingdom. The northern kingdom consisted of ten tribes while the southern kingdom consisted of two tribes. Because of idolatry, the Israelites were taken into captivity. The northern kingdom went into Assyrian captivity, one hundred years before the southern kingdom went into Babylonian captivity. The northern kingdom never came back from the Assyrian captivity. Jeremiah, the prophet, prophesied that the southern kingdom would spend seventy years in Babylonian captivity before coming back to Israel (Jeremiah 25:11). The Messiah was born from this remnant that came back to Israel. Within forty years, after the Jews rejected and crucified the Messiah, they were taken captive by the Romans and sold into slavery and dispersed throughout the world.

The Lord foretold that He would re-gather His people from all nations.

> Deuteronomy 30:1-5: So it shall become when all of these things have come upon you, the blessing and the curse which I have set before you, and you call them to mind in all nations where the Lord your God has banished you, and you return to the Lord your God and obey Him with all your heart and soul according to all that I command you today, you and your sons, then the Lord your God will restore you from captivity, and have compassion on you, and will gather you again from all the peoples where the Lord your God has scattered you. If your outcasts are at the ends of the earth, from there the Lord your God will gather you, and from there He will bring you back. And the Lord your God will bring you into the land which your fathers possessed and you shall posses it; and He will prosper you and multiply you more than your fathers. (12)

In the Book of Deuteronomy, the Lord foretold that He would bless the Israelites if they obeyed Him, and curse them and scatter them to all nations of the world if they did not obey. In the same book, He also said He would re-gather them from all nations of the world. This prophecy is being fulfilled today, 3,500 years after it was spoken by Moses, the prophet, and after 2,000 years of Christianity. The Jews have returned to Israel from all nations of the world.

Isaiah prophesied that the Lord would re-gather His people a second time.

> Isaiah 11:11-12: Then it will happen on that day that the Lord will again recover the second time with His hand the remnant of His people, who will remain, from Assyria, Egypt, Pathros, Cush, Elam, Shinar, Hamath, and from the Islands of the sea. And He will lift up a standard for the nations, and will assemble the banished ones of Israel, and will gather the dispersed of Judah from the four corners of the earth. (12)

Isaiah prophesied that the Lord would re-gather His people for a second time. This was foretold two hundred years before the Babylonian captivity before the Lord had re-gathered His people for the first time. The second time, He re-gathered them from all nations of the world. This prophecy has been fulfilled today, 2,500 years after the Babylonian captivity. Isaiah foretold that Israel would be a nation and have a flag. Israel has not been a nation since before the Babylonian captivity. At the time of Christ, they were under the Roman Empire. The Jews needed permission of the Roman governor, Pontius Pilate, to crucify the Lord.

Israel became a nation on May 14, 1948 after the United Nations voted to declare Israel a nation on November 29, 1947 (13).

Though the Jews have been dispersed and scattered among all nations of the world, they have maintained their Jewish heritage separate from the gentiles. They have not intermarriage with the gentiles. After 2,500 years in exile, they have returned to their homeland from all nations of the world as Jews. This is why Jerusalem is a city of people of many nations and languages.

Our family took a trip to the Holy Land in 1973. Our Jewish

guide explained that the Jordan River is fresh water and the Sea of Galilee is salt water. Though the Sea of Galilee is 5 to 6 miles wide and 13 miles long, the fresh water from the Jordan River passes through the Sea of Galilee into the Jordan River on the other side as fresh water. The fresh water does not mix with the salt water. The guide said the fresh water of the Jordan River is like a Jew. The Jews have gone all over the world but have not intermarried with the gentiles. They have come back to their homeland as Jews.

Ezekiel speaks of the Israelites from all the nations of the world.

Ezekiel speaks of the nations of the north attacking the people of Israel who have been re-gathered from all nations of the world

> Ezekiel 38:11-12: You will have said, "Israel is an unprotected land of unwalled villages! I will march against her and destroy these people living in such confidence! I will go to those once-desolate cities that are now filled with people again - those who have returned from all the nations - and I will capture vast booty and many slaves. For the people are rich with cattle now, and the whole earth revolves around them!" (64)

> Ezekiel 36:24, 28: For I will take you away from among the nations, gather you from all foreign lands, and bring you back to your own land. - - You shall live in the land I gave your fathers; you shall be my people, and I will be your God. (60)

> Baruch 5:5: Arise, Jerusalem, stand on the heights and turn your eyes to the east; see your sons reassembled from west and east at the command of the Holy One, jubilant that God has remembered them (57).

The Lord has re-gathered His people Israelites from all the nations of the world, as He foretold that He would. The Lord is still dealing with Israel. He will be their earthly king during the millennium. The Catholic Church is not the new Israel as St. Augustine taught and many believe. God is still dealing with the Jewish people and Israel. If the Lord is no longer dealing with Israel, why will He seal the 144,000 Jews from the twelve tribes of Israel in Revelation 7 for protection during the Wrath of God?

CHAPTER 33
Bloody Sacrifices

Sacrifices have always been a way of worshiping and appeasing the Lord. When Adam and Eve sinned, God committed the first sacrifice in the shedding of blood to provide skins as clothing for Adam and Eve (Genesis 3:21). Abel and Cain, the sons of Adam and Eve made sacrificial offerings to the Lord (Genesis 4:1-5). Abraham, Isaac, and Jacob all offered sacrifices to the Lord (Genesis 22:13, 31:54, 46:1).

Under the Law of Moses, bulls, goats, and lambs were sacrificed and burned as an offering to the Lord to make atonement for the sins of the people. These sacrifices did not take away sins, only covered them.

> Hebrews 10:3-4: But through those sacrifices there came only a yearly recalling of sins, because it is impossible for the blood of bulls and goats to take sins away (60).

The shedding of blood and taking a life was necessary to make atonement for the sins of the people. These sacrifices serve to emphasize the seriousness of sin.

Sin is a serious offense against God. After Adam and Eve sinned, God said He would have to send His Son into the world, as a man, to be offered as a sacrifice before man's sins could be forgiven. Jesus emptied Himself of His divine nature as God and became like man in every respect except sin

> Philippians 2:6-8: Who, though he was in the form
> of God, did not regard equality with God something
> to be grasped. Rather, he emptied himself, taking
> the form of a slave, coming in human likeness; he
> humbled himself, becoming obedient to death, even
> death on a cross. (24A)

God's love

The following scriptures show that God loves us so much that
He willingly sent His Son into the world to be offered as a sacrifice
for our sins, so that we can be reconciled with Him.

> John 3:16-17: For God so loved the world, that He
> gave His only begotten Son, that whoever believes in
> Him should not perish, but have eternal life. For God
> did not send the Son into the world to judge the world;
> but that the world should be saved through Him. (12)

> Romans 5:8-10: But God demonstrates His own love
> toward us, in that while we were yet sinners, Christ
> died for us. Much more then, having now been justi-
> fied by His blood, we shall be saved from the wrath
> of God through Him. For if while we were enemies,
> we were reconciled to God through the death of His
> Son, much more, having been reconciled, we shall be
> saved by His life. (12)

> Ephesians 1:7-8: It is in Christ and through his blood
> that we have been redeemed and our sins forgiven,
> so immeasurably generous is God's favor to us (60).

> I John 4:9: By this the love of God was manifested in
> us, that God has sent His only begotten Son into the

world so that we might live through Him (12).

Jesus is the Paschal Lamb

Jesus offered Himself as the Paschal Lamb for our sins.

> Isaiah 53:4-8, 12: Yet it was our infirmities that he bore, our sufferings that he endured, . . . But he was pierced for our offenses, crushed for our sins, upon him was the chastisement that makes us whole, by his stripes we were healed. We had all gone astray like sheep, each following his own way; but the Lord laid upon him the guilt of us all. Though he was harshly treated, he submitted and opened not his mouth; like a lamb led to the slaughter or a sheep before a shearer, he was silent and opened not his mouth. Oppressed and condemned, he was taken away, . . . When he was cut off from the land of the living, and smitten for the sin of his people, . . . Because he surrendered himself to death. . . . he shall take away the sins of many, and win pardon for their offenses. (60)

> Hebrews 9:26, 28: . . . But now he has appeared at the end of the ages to take away sins once for all by his sacrifice. . . . so Christ was offered up once to take away the sins of many; . . . (60).

> Hebrews 10:10-12: By this will, we have been sanctified through the offering of the body of Jesus Christ once for all. Every other priest stands ministering day by day, and offering again and again those same sacrifices which can never take away sins. But Jesus offered one sacrifice for sins and took his seat forever at the right hand of God: (60)

These scriptures show that Jesus offered Himself up as a sacrifice for our sins.

The Last Supper is a reminder of Jesus' sacrifice on the cross

Jesus asks us to partake of His Body and Blood in remembrance of His sacrifice.

> Matthew 26:26-28: And while they were eating, Jesus took some bread, and after a blessing, He broke it and gave it to the disciples, and said, "Take, eat; this is My body." And He took a cup and gave thanks, and gave it to them, saying, "Drink from it, all of you; for this is My blood of the covenant, which is to be shed on behalf of many for forgiveness of sins. (12)

> Mark 14:22-24: And while they were eating, He took some bread, and after a blessing He broke it; and gave it to them, and said, "Take it; this is My body." And He took a cup, and when He had given thanks, He gave it to them; and they all drank from it. And He said to them, "This is My blood of the covenant, which is to be shed on behalf of many." (12)

> Luke 22:19-20: And having taken some bread, when He had given thanks, He broke it, and gave it to them, saying, "This is My body which is given for you; do this in remembrance of Me. And in the same way He took the cup after they had eaten, saying, "This cup which is poured out for you is the new covenant in My blood." (12)

At the Last Supper, while celebrating the Feast of the Passover, the Lord took bread and wine and blessed (consecrated) them and said, "This is My Body and My Blood. Do this in remembrance of Me." The Lord gave the command that we are to celebrate the Lord's Supper in remembrance of His death on the cross.

The Lord's death is to be proclaimed until He comes again.

> I Corinthians 11:23-26: For I received from the Lord that which I also delivered to you, that the Lord Jesus in the night in which He was betrayed took bread; and when He had given thanks, He broke it, and said, "This is My body, which is for you; do this in remembrance of Me." In the same way He took the cup also, after supper, saying, "This cup is the new covenant in My blood; do this, as often as you drink it, in remembrance of Me." For as often as you eat this bread and drink the cup, you proclaim the Lord's death until He comes. (12)

The sacrifices in the Old Testament were only preparation for the true and perfect sacrifice of our Lord on the cross. After His crucifixion, the bloody sacrifices of the Old Testament were done away with.

In the new covenant, Christ offered His Body and Blood as a constant reminder of His bloody sacrifice on the cross. Every time we partake of the Lord's Supper, we proclaim the Lord's death until He comes. Instead of the bloody sacrifices of bulls and goats as a constant reminder of our sins, we have the unbloody sacrifice of our Lord every time we partake of His Body and Blood. This is the new covenant the Lord made with His people.

Jesus said, "I am the Bread of Life."

> John 6:33, 35: For the bread of God is that which comes down out of heaven, and gives life to the world. . . . Jesus said to them, "I am the bread of life;

he who comes to Me shall not hunger, and he who believes in Me shall never thirst." (12)

Is the bread and wine symbolic or the real body and blood of the Lord?

The Jews were grumbling because Jesus said, "I am the bread that came down out of heaven (John 6:41)

> John 6:51: I am the living bread that came down out of heaven; if any one eats of this bread, he shall live forever; and the bread also which I shall give for the life of the world is My flesh (12).

Jesus said this bread was His flesh.

When the bread and wine are lifted up and consecrated (blessed), does it become the real body and blood of our Lord?

Many of us are probably like the Jews. The Jews really question how this man (Jesus) could give us His flesh and blood.

> John 6:52: The Jews therefore began to argue with one another, saying, "How can this man give us His flesh to eat?" (12).

Jesus said, "Unless you eat His Flesh and drink His Blood you will not have life".

> John 6:53-54: Jesus therefore said to them, "Truly, truly, I say to you, unless you eat the flesh of the Son of Man and drink His blood, you have no life in yourselves. He who eats My flesh and drinks My blood has eternal life; and I will raise him up on the last day. (12)

Did Jesus say that the bread and wine was symbolic of His body and blood?

No! Jesus said,

> John 6:55-58: For My flesh is true food, and My blood is true drink. He who eats My flesh and drinks My blood abides in Me, and I in him. As the living Father sent Me, and I live because of the Father, so he who eats Me, he also shall live because of Me. This is the bread which came down out of heaven; not as the fathers ate, and died, he who eats this bread shall live forever. (12)

Jesus said that the bread and wine when consecrated become His real body and blood (Matthew 26:26-28, Mark 14:22-24, Luke 22:19-20, I Corinthians 11:23-26). This is a mystery that we have to accept on faith. The scriptures say that without faith you cannot please God (Hebrews 11:6).

Do we believe that the bread and wine, when consecrated become His Body and Blood, or are we like the disciples that walked away?

> John 6:60-61: Many therefore of His disciples, when they heard this said, "This is a difficult statement; who can listen to it?" But Jesus, conscious that His disciples grumbled at this, said to them, "Does this cause you to stumble?" (12)

Because Jesus said this bread and wine was truly His Flesh and Blood, many of His disciples left Him.

> John 6:66-68: As a result of this many of His disciples withdrew, and were not walking with Him anymore. Jesus said therefore to the twelve, "You do

not want to go away also, do you?" Simon Peter answered Him, "Lord, to whom shall we go? You have words of eternal life." (12)

Jesus did not say to the disciples who were leaving, "Hey, wait a minute, come back, I was just kidding, the bread and wine are just were symbols of my Body and Blood." No! He said, "It is My Body and Blood". This statement caused division among His disciples. If we say the bread and wine are only symbols of His Body and Blood then we are like the disciples that grumbled at that statement and left Him.

His Body and Blood give us life.

Jesus said if we do not eat His body and drink His blood, we shall not have life within us. How can we eat and drink His body and blood and have life, if we believe that the bread and wine are symbols?

It is the Spirit that changes the bread and wine into His body and blood. Scripture says that some of you do not believe this.

When the bread and wine is consecrated, it is the Holy Spirit that changes the bread and wine into the Body and Blood of Christ. Though the Body and Blood may look and tastes like bread and wine, it is truly the Body and Blood of Christ.

> John 6:63-64: It is the Spirit who gives life; the flesh profits nothing; the words that I have spoken to you are spirit and are life. But there are some of you who do not believe. . . . (12).

The Lord said that many do not believe that the bread and wine are actually His Body and Blood.

Jesus speaking to Louise Starr Tomkiel said:

My child, I began to speak to you at Mass tonight,

at the consecration. The bread and wine is truly My Body and Blood. Far too many of My children do not believe this miracle actually takes place at every Mass around your world. The faith of many religious and lay people is weak. It truly is your Jesus of Mercy and Love that comes to you in the sacrament of the Eucharist. I have given you My Body and Blood to nourish and to strengthen you. You should receive this life-giving Bread and Wine frequently. It is imperative that you pray and receive Me frequently. **I am the food for strength. I am the food for life.** Pray before the Eucharist, which is Me, Body, Mind, Soul and Divinity and thank Me for giving you salvation and hope for everlasting life in Heaven, that was opened to all sinners, because of My death for your sins.

The night before My death, at the Last Supper, with My Apostles, I gave them bread and wine and transformed it into My Body and Blood. I instituted the Eucharist. It is My Gift for all mankind. Here is your strength in sickness, health and now at the hour of your earthly distress. Eat of this Bread and drink of this Wine to have the strength and nourishment to fight off Satan and his evil helpers all the days of your life. Remain in the State of Grace. Live in My Love and do for Me all the days of your life until we meet in Heaven, face to face, in everlasting peace. (93)

Bread and wine becomes flesh and blood.

There are numerous instances throughout the history of the Church, where the consecrated bread and wine actually physically became Flesh and Blood. Bob and Penny Lord described many of these circumstances in their two books (93, 94). One incident

435

occurred at Cebrero, a village in Spain in the year 1300. Juan Santin, a peasant from Barjamayor, a village near Cebrero had a great devotion and attended Mass as often as he could. He came to Mass one bitter cold day. The priest was frustrated at having to say Mass for one person. The priest said, "Why do you come just to get a piece of bread?" The priest actually had doubts about the real presence of Jesus in the consecrated bread and wine. At the consecration, the bread and wine physically became Flesh and Blood before the eyes of the priest. The priest broke down in tears, as he knew this was meant for him (94).

In Trani, Italy around 1,000 A.D., there was a Jewish witch with a strong hatred against the Catholics. She managed to get a hold of a consecrated Host that she intended to desecrate by burning to prove that it was nothing but bread. She prepared a skillet with oil and waited until the oil was boiling. She threw the Host into the skillet. To her surprise the Host turned into Flesh and started bleeding profusely overflowing over the skillet onto the stove and onto the floor. She started screaming and panicking, realizing that this was truly the Body and Blood of Jesus. Bob and Penny Lord discuss many other events, where the consecrated bread and wine turned into Flesh and Blood (94).

Partaking of the Body and Blood of the Lord unworthily

If the bread and wine are symbols of the Body and Blood of the Lord, how can anyone partake of this bread and wine unworthily and be guilty of the Body and Blood of the Lord?

> I Corinthians 11:27-30: Therefore whoever eats the bread or drinks the cup of the Lord in an unworthy manner, shall be guilty of the body and the blood of the Lord. But let a man examine himself, and so let him eat of the bread and drink of the cup. For he who

eats and drinks, eats and drinks judgment to himself, if he does not judge the body rightly. For this reason many among you are weak and sick, and a number sleep. (12)

The scriptures say that we are to examine ourselves before we partake of the Lord's Supper. Many people become weak, sick and even die, because they failed to prepare themselves to receive the Lord's Body and Blood. If the bread and wine are symbolic, why would people become sick and even die from eating a piece of bread and drinking some wine. The scriptures teach that the bread and wine, when consecrated, truly become the Body and Blood of the Lord.

As often as we eat this bread and drink this wine, we are to proclaim the Lord's death until He comes.

> I Corinthians 11:26: For as often as you eat this bread and drink the cup, you proclaim the Lord's death until He comes (12).

Every time we partake of the Body and Blood of the Lord, we are to remember His sacrifice and death on the cross.

Early Christians broke bread daily

The early Christians participated in the Lord's Supper by breaking bread daily.

> Acts 2:42, 46: And they were continually devoting themselves to the apostles' teaching and to fellowship, to the breaking of the bread and to prayer. . . . And day by day continuing with one mind in the temple, and breaking bread from house to house, . . . (12)

The early Christians broke bread daily, participating in the unbloody sacrifice of the Last Supper, proclaiming the Lord's death. We are to do this until He comes again. The Body and Blood of Christ gives life (John 6:53-54). We should receive His Body and Blood as often as possible, just as the early Christians broke bread daily.

Man is different from any other creature in that he has a soul, a spirit and a body. The soul is our intellectual mind. The spirit is the part of the body that is like God and the angels, and cannot be seen. Each part is different and yet, each is interrelated. Each part must be fed and nourished properly. We need to read and hear the Word (scriptures) daily, to receive nourishment for our soul to make us strong Christians and soldiers for Jesus Christ. We need to partake of the Lord's Body and Blood for spiritual nourishment, just as we need to eat the proper food for our physical body.

Christ said that His Body and Blood would give us life. Though the Body and Blood is primarily nourishment for our spiritual body, it also gives life to our soul and physical body. This is shown by the fact that if we partake of the Body and Blood of the Lord unworthily, scripture says many become weak, sick and even die. If anything happens to one part of the body, then the other parts will also be affected.

Partaking of the Lord's Body and Blood worthily and reading the scriptures daily, rightly dividing the word of truth will make us strong and healthy Christians. This will help to keep us from being polluted with the world and sets us free from any bondage to sin.

After the Lord returns to the earth, will there be bloody sacrifices during the millennium, when He is sitting on the throne?

Zechariah described the events on earth after the Lord returns. Zechariah 14:16-19 shows that the people of all nations will come to Jerusalem to worship the King, the Lord of hosts, to celebrate the Feast of the Tabernacle. The Feast of the Tabernacle involves bloody and burnt sacrifices. Zechariah 14:21 mentions this sacrifice. Bloody sacrifices are described in detail in the discussion of the Millennium Temple in Ezekiel 40 to 48.

If the temple described in Ezekiel 40 to 48 is the Millennium Temple, and the Lord is sitting on the throne in the temple, why will there be bloody sacrifice and grain offerings to the Lord?

Bloody sacrifices have always been a way of worshiping and appeasing the Lord. In the Old Testament, the sacrifice of bulls and goats did not take away sin. The purpose of the bloody sacrifice during the millennium will be to serve as a reminder to the participants of what the Lord went through, as the Passover Lamb, to redeem them from their sins.

Levites will be earthly priests in the temple during the millennium.

Isaiah 65 and 66 described some of the events on earth during the millennium. Isaiah speaks of people from all nations coming to Jerusalem to bring offerings to the Lord. The Levites will be priests during this time.

> Isaiah 66:18-21: I come to gather nations of every language; they shall come and see my glory. I will set a sign among them; from them I will send fugitives to the nations: to Tarshish, Put and Lud, Mosoch, Tubal and Javan, to the distant coastlands that have never heard of my fame or seen my glory; and they shall proclaim my glory among the nations. They shall bring all your brethren from all the nations as an offering to the Lord, on horses and in chariots, in carts, upon mules and dromedaries, to Jerusalem, my holy mountain, says the Lord, just as the Israelites bring

their offerings to the house of the Lord in clean vessels. Some of these I will take as priests and Levites, says the Lord. (60)

Ezekiel speaks of the Levites ministering to the Lord in the temple.

Ezekiel 43:19: Give a young bull as a sin offering to the priests, the Levites who are of the line of Zadok, who draw near to me to minister to me, says the Lord God (60).

Sacrificial rituals in the Millennium Temple

Ezekiel described the rituals for the purification of the temple and offering sacrifices during the millennium.

Ezekiel 43:18-27: . . . Son of man, thus says the Lord God: These are the statues for the altar when it is set up for the offering of the holocausts upon it and for the sprinkling of blood against it. Give a young bull as a sin offering to the priests, the Levites who are of the line of Zadok, who draw near me to minister to me, says the Lord God. Take some of its blood and put it on the four horns of the altar, and on the four corners of the ledge, and on the rim all around. Thus you shall purify it and make atonement for it. Then take the bull of the sin offering, which is to be burnt in a designated part of the temple, outside the sanctuary. On the second day present an unblemished he-goat as a sin offering, to purify the altar as was done with the bull. When you have finished the purification, bring an unblemished young bull and an unblemished ram from the flock, and present them before the Lord; the priests shall strew salt on them and offer them to the Lord as holocausts. Daily for seven days you shall offer a he-goat as a sin offering, and a young bull and a ram from the flock, all unblemished, shall be offered for seven days. Thus atonement shall be made for the altar, and it shall be purified and dedicated. And when these days are over, from the eighth day on, the priests shall offer your holocausts and peace offering on the altar. Then I will accept you, says the Lord God. (60)

Sabbath days and feast days

Holocausts, cereal, and peace offerings will be offered on Sabbath days, the new moons, and the different feast days of the year.

> Ezekiel 45:17: It shall be the duty of the prince to provide the holocausts, cereal offerings, and libations on the feasts, new moons, and sabbaths, on all the festivals of the house of Israel. He shall offer the sin offering, cereal offerings, holocaust and peace offerings, to make atonement on behalf of the house of Israel. (60)

The Passover

Ezekiel shows that the feast of the Passover will be celebrated during the millennium.

> Ezekiel 45:21: On the fourteenth day of the first month you shall observe the feast of the Passover; for seven days unleavened bread is to be eaten (60).

When did the Lord say He would celebrate the Passover again with His disciples?

> Luke 22:15-16: And He said to them, "I have earnestly desired to eat this Passover with you before I

suffer; for I say to you, I shall never again eat it until it is fulfilled in the Kingdom of God" (12).

At the Last Supper, the Lord said He would not eat and drink at the Passover until it is fulfilled in the kingdom of God. The Lord did eat with His disciples after His resurrection, but He did not celebrate the Passover, since this occurs only once a year. This shows that the Passover will be celebrated in His kingdom during the millennium.

When did the Lord say He would partake of the bread and wine, which He had consecrated into his Body and Blood?

> Luke 22:17-20: And having taken a cup, when He had given thanks, He said, "Take this and share it among yourselves; for I say to you, I will not drink of the fruit of the vine from now on until the kingdom of God comes." And having taken some bread, when He had given thanks, He broke it, and gave it to them, saying, "This is My body which is given for you; do this in remembrance of Me. And in the same way He took the cup after they had eaten, saying, "This cup which is poured out for you is the new covenant in My blood." (12)

During the Passover meal, the night before He died, the Lord instituted the Eucharist by consecrating the bread and wine into His Body and Blood. The Lord said He would not eat His Body or drink His Blood until He celebrated it (Passover) anew in His kingdom. This shows that the Lord will celebrate the Last Supper in His kingdom during the millennium.

The feast of the tabernacle

The feast of the tabernacle will also be celebrated during the millennium (Ezekiel 45:25). This scripture shows that the Lord will be sitting on the throne in Jerusalem as the families of different nations are required to go to Jerusalem to worship the Lord, the King. If they do not go and worship the Lord, they will not receive any rain for their crops.

> Zechariah 14:16-21: Then it will come about that any who are left of all the nations that went against Jerusalem will go up from year to year to worship the king, the Lord of hosts, and to celebrate the Feast of the Booths. And it will be that whichever of the families of the earth does not go up to Jerusalem to worship the King, the Lord of hosts, there will be no rain on them. And if the family of Egypt does not go up or enter, then no rain will fall on them; it will be the plague with which the Lord smites the nations who do not go up to celebrate the Feast of Booths. This will be the punishment of Egypt, and the punishment of all the nations who do not go up to celebrate the Feast of Booths. In that day there will be inscribed on the bells of horses, "HOLY TO THE LORD." And the cooking pots in the Lord's house will be like the bowls before the altar. And every cooking pot in Jerusalem and in Judah will be holy to the Lord of hosts; and all who sacrifice will come and take of them and boil in them. . . . (12)

The Feast of the Booths is another name for the Feast of the Tabernacle. In the Old Testament, it was the Jews who celebrated the Feast of the Tabernacle. During the millennium, people of all nations will go to Jerusalem every year to worship the Lord and to celebrate the Feast of the Tabernacle.

Foreigners will worship the Lord, offering sacrifices.

> Isaiah 56:6-7: Also the foreigners who join them-
> selves to the Lord, to minister to Him, and to love the
> name of the Lord, to be His servants, every one who
> keeps from profaning the sabbath, and hold fast My
> covenant; even those I will bring to My holy moun-
> tain, and make them joyful in My house of prayer.
> Their burnt offering and their sacrifice will be ac-
> ceptable on My altar; For My house will be called a
> house of prayer for all the peoples. (12)

Foreigners will be servants, ministering to the Lord and offering burnt sacrifices to the Lord. In the Old Testament, foreigners
were considered unclean and they were not allowed to come into the
temple or to offer sacrifice. The Lord is accepting the sacrifices of
both Jews and Gentiles during the millennium.

> Isaiah 66:19-20: I will set a sign among them; from
> them I will send fugitives to the nations: to Tarshish,
> Put and Lud, Mosoch, Tubal and Javan, to the distant
> coastlands that have never heard of my fame, or seen
> my glory; and they shall proclaim my glory among
> the nations. They shall bring all your brethren from
> all the nations as an offering to the Lord, on horses
> and in chariots, in carts, upon mules and dromedar-
> ies, to Jerusalem, my holy mountain, says the Lord,
> just as the Israelites bring their offering to the house
> of the Lord in clean vessels. (60)

**The bloody sacrifice of the Old Testament and the Lord's
Supper will be combined during the millennium.**

The bloody sacrifice of the Old Testament and the partaking of
the Lord's Body and Blood of the New Testament will be celebrated

during the millennium, in remembrance of our Lord's crucifixion and death on the cross. Though the Sabbath days and the feast days, such as the Feast of the Passover and the Feast of the Tabernacle, are memorial events, none are as significant and precious as the crucifixion, death and resurrection of our Lord Jesus Christ. The bloody sacrifice and the partaking of the Lord's Body and Blood will greatly dramatize and emphasize the significance of our Lord's crucifixion, and death that saved us from our sins and united us with him forever.

Sin during the millennium

Though Satan will be chained for a thousand years, and will not be allowed to tempt people to sin, people will sin during the millennium; that is, people living on earth, not the redeemed saints reigning with Christ. An example of temptation and sin is: If an attractive, scantly clothed woman walks by, a man may be tempted to lust in his heart after her. Jesus said, "If a man lusts in his heart after a woman, he has already committed adultery" (Matthew 5:28). If a man does not cultivate these thoughts, even though he is tempted, he does not commit a sin. If a properly clothed woman walks by and a man cultivates lustful thoughts in his heart, even though he was not tempted, he commits a sin.

Though Satan is chained and will not be allowed to put thoughts of temptation in the minds of the people, people will sin through their own will. Scripture teaches that the plagues of Egypt will come on the nations that do not go up each year to worship the Lord. The plagues of Egypt are curses from the Lord. To disobey the command of the Lord to come to Jerusalem to worship him each year is a sin (Zechariah 14:16-21).

People will live for long periods of time during the millennium, as they did before the flood. If a child dies at the age of one hundred, it will be considered a curse. Today, very few people reach the age of one hundred. Yet, during the millennium, it will be considered a curse if a person does not live well beyond the age of one hundred.

> Isaiah 65:19-20, 22: I will rejoice in Jerusalem and exult in my people. No longer shall the sound of weeping be heard there, or the sound of crying; no longer shall there be in it an infant who lives but a few days, or an old man who does not round out his full lifetime; he dies a mere youth who reaches but a hundred years, and he who fails of a hundred shall be thought accursed. . . . As the years of a tree, so the years of my people; . . . (60)

The plagues of Egypt and the curse of a child reaching only the age of one hundred shows that sin will exist during the millennium.

Though Jesus will reign as King of the world during the millennium, the world will not be pure, sinless, or perfect. Only the government (theocracy) governed by Jesus Christ and His resurrected saints will be righteous and without fault. Sin and death will continue through the millennium and will not be destroyed until after the millennium.

CHAPTER 34
Satan Is Set Free

Satan is released from prison when the thousand years are up.

> Revelation 20:7-9: And when the thousand years are completed, Satan will be released from his prison, and will come out to deceive the nations which are in the four corners of the earth, Gog and Magog, to gather them together for the war; the number of them is like the sand of the seashore. And they came up on the broad plain of the earth and surrounded the camp of the saints and the beloved city, and fire came down from heaven and devoured them. (12)

Why was Satan chained for a thousand years and then released?

To understand this question, we need to review the history of creation. Scripture says that in the beginning God was. God created the angels, gave them a free will, and put them before His throne without testing them. Satan, known as Lucifer, the most beautiful of all angels was placed in command of all the angels. Scripture says that pride entered the heart of Lucifer, and he desired to sit on the throne of God (Isaiah 14:13-14). Satan would never have attempted to overthrow the Lord unless he thought he could succeed. He thought he could succeed by getting the majority of the angels on his side. When the final count was made, scripture says he only had one-third of the angels on his side. Satan and his angels were kicked out of heaven by Michael and his angels(Revelation 12:4-9).

After Satan and his angels rebelled against God, God apparently decided to never again create a spirit and put him before the throne without first testing him. Under this plan, God made man. He made man under a veil of secrecy. God could see man and knew all his thoughts, but man could not see God. God used Satan in his plan to tempt and test man. When Adam and Eve sinned, man lost the right to enter the kingdom of heaven. All men have been tempted and tested to determine their faithfulness to the Lord.

People can sin during the millennium, even though Satan and his angels will not be allowed to tempt the people. A lot of people will be born during the thousand years while the Lord is sitting on the throne in Jerusalem. These people have never been tempted and tested. After the thousand years are up, Satan and his angels are released from prison to tempt and test these people before the Lord will allow them to come into His eternal kingdom. It is interesting that the number of people that gathered on the great plain of the earth to rebel against the Lord and His saints were as numerous as the sand on the seashore.

How does Satan deceive the people?

The scripture says the saints shall rule nations with a rod of iron. Many of the people will want out from this rule. Satan, after being set free, will tempt the people and deceive them into thinking that they can overthrow the Lord and His saints. It is interesting that those who are tempted and deceived will be as numerous as the sand of the seashore. They will come together from all nations to battle against the Lord and His saints on the broad plains of Jerusalem. At this moment, fire will come down from heaven and consume them.

> Revelation 20:8-9: the number of them is like the sand of the seashore. And they came up on the broad plain of the earth and surrounded the camp of the

saints and the beloved city, and fire came down from heaven and devoured them. (12)

Why will the people, who have first-hand knowledge of the Lord, rebel against Him?

It is hard to believe that these people who have first-hand knowledge of the Lord would rebel against Him. However, when we consider the miracles the Lord performed through Moses against Pharaoh in Egypt, the parting of the Red Sea, and the miracles performed in the wilderness, still these Israelites rebelled against the Lord. Judas, who was with Jesus for three years, witnessing all the miracles and wonders He performed, then betrayed Him. Knowing this, it is understandable why the people living during the millennium will also rebel against the Lord.

Satan and his angels are thrown into the Lake of Fire.

Revelation 20:10: And the devil who deceived them was thrown into the lake of fire and brimstone, where the Beast and the False Prophet are also; and they will be tormented day and night forever and ever (12).

When the Lord has no more use for Satan, he and his angels will be thrown into the Lake of Fire in punishment for their rebellion against God.

Will the angels that are thrown into the Lake of Fire be destroyed or tormented forever and ever?

The Beast and the False Prophet were still alive in the Lake of Fire after a thousand years. Life will not be destroyed, but will be tormented forever.

Jesus said,

Mark 9:47-48: If your eye is your downfall, tear

it out! Better for you to enter the kingdom of God with one eye than to be thrown with both eyes into Gehenna, where the worm dies not and the fire is never extinguished (60).

People who are thrown into the Lake of Fire will be tormented forever and ever.

Hebrews 10:31: It is a fearful thing to fall into the hands of the living God (60).

CHAPTER 35
The White Throne Judgment

The books will be opened

The books will be opened and everyone's deeds will be revealed. Those whose names are not found written in the book of life will be thrown into the Lake of Fire.

> Revelation 20:11-15: And I saw a great white throne and Him who sat upon it, from whose presence earth and heaven fled away, and no place was found for them. And I saw the dead, the great and the small, standing before the throne, and books were opened; another book was opened, which is the book of life; and the dead were judged from the things which were written in the books, according to their deeds. And the sea gave up the dead which were in it, and death and Hades gave up the dead which were in them; and they were judged, every one of them according to their deeds. And death and Hades were thrown into the lake of fire. This is the second death, the lake of fire. And if anyone's name was not found written in the book of life, he was thrown into the lake of fire. (12)

The white throne judgment is the awesome judgment of the wicked dead. This moment is so serious and solemn that scripture says that heaven and earth fled away from the presence of the Lord. Those that did not partake in the first resurrection, or lived and were not saved during the millennium, will have nothing to look forward to except the second resurrection and the judgment of the Almighty God. (96)

Everyone will be held accountable for every idle word.

Scripture says that the books will be opened, revealing everyone's deeds. The Lord will be able to show an audio-video tape of each person's life, and everything that person has ever said and done.

> Luke 12:2-3: But there is nothing covered up that will not be revealed, and hidden that will not be known. Accordingly, whatever you have said in the dark shall be heard in the light, and what you have whispered in the inner rooms shall be proclaimed upon the housetops. (12)

Jesus said that a person will be held accountable for every idle word he has spoken.

> Matthew 12:36-37: But I tell you that men will have to give account on the day of judgment for every careless word they have spoken. For by your word you will be acquitted, and by your words you will be condemned. (7)

Every person whose name was not written in the Book of Life will stand before the white throne judgment. There will not be anyone missing. Everyone that ever lived will be accounted for. Their deeds are recorded. There shall be no escape. (96)

Jesus said, "What you did to the least of My brothers, you have done to Me."

Jesus spoke of the last judgment in Matthew.

Matthew 25:31-46: But when the Son of Man comes in His glory, and all the angels with Him, then He will sit on His glorious throne. And all the nations will be gathered before Him; and He will separate them from one another, as the shepherd separates the sheep from the goats; and He will put the sheep on His right, and goats on the left. Then the King will say to those on His right, "Come, you who are blessed of My Father, inherit the kingdom prepared for you from the foundation of the world. For I was hungry, and you gave Me something to eat; I was thirsty, and you gave Me drink; I was a stranger, and you invited Me in; naked, and you clothed Me; I was sick, and you visited Me; I was in prison, and you came to Me. Then the righteous will answer Him, saying, "Lord when did we see You hungry, and feed You, or thirsty, and give You drink? And when did we see You a stranger, and invite You in, or naked, and clothe You? And when did we see You sick, or in prison, and come to You?" And the King will answer and say to them, "Truly I say to you, to the extent that you did it to one of these brothers of Mine, even the least of them, you did it to Me." Then He will also say to those on His left, "Depart from Me, accursed ones, into the eternal fire which has been prepared for the devil and his angels; for I was hungry, and you gave Me nothing to eat; I was thirsty, and you gave Me nothing to drink; I was a stranger, and you did not invite Me in; naked, and you did not clothe Me; sick, and in prison, and you did not visit Me." Then they themselves also will answer, saying, "Lord when did we see You hungry, or thirsty, or a stranger, or naked, or sick, or in prison, and did not take care of You?" Then He will answer them, saying, "Truly I say to you, to the extent that you did not do it to one of the least of these, you did not do it to Me." And these will go away into eternal punishment, but the righteous into eternal life. (12)

Jesus said, "What you have done to the least of My brethren, you have done to Me." Those that obtained, performed or supported abortion, the Lord will say,

"You killed Me in My mother's womb" (97).

Those not found written in the book of life are cast into the Lake of Fire where there will be weeping and gnashing of teeth.

Revelation 21:6-8: And He said to me, "It is done. I am the Alpha and the Omega, the beginning and the end. I will give to the one who thirsts from the spring of water of life without cost. He who overcomes shall inherit these things, and I will be his God and he will be My son. But for the cowardly and unbelieving and abominable and murderer and immoral persons and sorcerers and idolaters and all liars, their part will be in the lake that burns with fire and brimstone, which is the second death." (12)

CHAPTER 36

A New Heaven And A New Earth

Revelation 21:1: And I saw a new heaven and a new earth; for the first heaven and the first earth passed away, . . . (12).

Peter speaks of a day coming when heaven and earth will be renewed by fire, and godless people will be destroyed. The scripture in Hebrew speaks of created things passing away.

II Peter 3:7, 10, 12-13: The present heavens and earth are reserved by God's word for fire; they are kept for the day of judgment, the day when godless men will be destroyed. . . . The day of the Lord will come like a thief, and on that day the heavens will vanish with a roar; the elements will be destroyed by fire, and the earth and all its deeds will be made manifest. . . . the heavens will be destroyed in flames and the elements will melt away in a blaze. What we await are new heavens and a new earth where, according to his promise, the justice of God will reside. (60)

Hebrews 1:10-12: And, "Thou, Lord, in the beginning didst lay the foundation of the earth, and the heavens are the work of thy hands; they will perish, but Thou remainest: and they all will become old as a garment, and as a mantle Thou wilt roll them up; as a garment they will also be changed. But Thou art the same, and Thy years will not come to an end." (12)

Hebrews 12:25-29: Do not refuse to hear him who speaks. For if the Israelites did not escape punishment when they refused to listen as God spoke to them on earth, how much greater punishment will be ours if we turn away from him who speaks from heaven! His voice then shook the earth, but now he has promised, "I will once more shake not only earth but heaven!" And that "once more" shows that shaken, created things will pass away, so that only what is unshaken may remain. Wherefore, we who are receiving the unshakable kingdom should hold fast to God's grace, through which we may offer worship acceptable to him in reverence and awe. For our God is a consuming fire. (60)

Isaiah 65:17-19: For behold, I create new heavens and a new earth; and the former things shall not be remembered or come to mind. But be glad and rejoice forever in what I create; for behold, I create Jerusalem for rejoicing and her people for gladness. I will also rejoice in Jerusalem, and be glad in My people; . . . (12)

Scripture, in Hebrews speaks, of the earth being shaken once more. The earth was renewed by water when it was shaken the first time by the great flood. Since the earth did not pass away when it was shaken the first time, it probably will not pass away, when it is shaken the second time. The earth will probably be renewed by fire when it is shaken the second time just as it was renewed by water when it was shaken the first time. Ecclesiastes speaks of the earth remaining forever.

Ecclesiastes 1:4: A generation goes and a generation comes but the earth remains forever (12).

The earth will probably be renewed with fire, burning all the elements to purify the earth (96).

The sea is no more.

Revelation 21:1: . . . and there is no longer any sea (12).

Over three-fourths of the earth is covered by water. After the millennium and the white throne judgment the sea will be no more on earth.

God, the Father, will dwell among His people.

Revelation 21:3: And I heard a loud voice from the throne, saying, "Behold the tabernacle of God is among men, and He shall dwell among them, and they shall be His people, and God Himself shall be among them, (12)

Revelation 22:3-4: . . . and the throne of God and of the Lamb shall be in it, and His bond-servants shall serve Him; and they shall see His face, and His name shall be on their foreheads (12).

During the millennium, Jesus will be visible to the people, since He rules from the throne of His father, David, in Jerusalem. God the Father will not be visible until after the millennium. God the Father and Jesus will live among the people after the white throne judgment, and the people shall see the Father and the Son face to face.

Crying, pain, and death, will be no more

Revelation 21:4: and He shall wipe away every tear from their eyes; and there shall no longer be any death; there shall no longer be any mourning, or crying, or pain; the first things have passed away (12).

Isaiah 65:17: . . . the former things shall not be remembered or come to mind (12).

The Lord will heal all hurts and pain, and death will be no more.

The new Jerusalem

Revelation 21:2: And I saw the holy city, new Jerusalem, coming down out of heaven from God, made ready as a bride adorned for her husband (12).

Revelation 21:9-11: And one of the seven angels who had the seven bowls full of the seven last plagues, came and spoke with me, saying, "Come here, I shall show you the bride, the wife of the Lamb." And he carried me away in the Spirit to a great and high mountain, and showed me the holy city, Jerusalem, coming down out of heaven from God, having the glory of God. Her brilliance was like a very costly stone, as a stone of crystal-clear jasper. (12)

Earthly Jerusalem has been portrayed as a woman, a harlot, a city and the whore of Babylon, the mother of all abomination of the earth.

Heavenly Jerusalem is portrayed as a woman, a mother, and a city. The sun-clothed woman, the symbolic mother of God's people was shown to be the new heavenly Jerusalem. The sun-clothed woman, fleeing into the wilderness after the birth of the man-child, was symbolic of a warning to the remnant of her children to flee into the wilderness immediately after the abomination of the temple to escape persecution. Now, the new Jerusalem, coming down out of heaven, is portrayed as the Lord's bride coming to meet her husband.

The new Jerusalem is literally a city, where the Lamb and His bride will live. The new Jerusalem is like a beautiful bride, adorned with radiant jewelry and precious stones reflecting the glory of God.

Description of the new Jerusalem

The new city, which comes down from heaven, was described as being 1500 miles long, 1500 miles wide and 1500 miles high. The city was pure gold like clear glass, while its walls were made of jasper. The foundation of the city walls was decorated with all kinds of precious stones. The streets of the city were made of pure transparent gold. There were twelve gates, three on each side of the city, which were named for the twelve tribes of Israel. The walls had twelve foundation stones, which were named for the twelve apostles (Revelation 21:9-21).

The temple is no more.

In the Old Testament God dwelt in the sanctuary in the temple. During the Church age God dwelt in the temple of the people.

> I Corinthians 3:16-17: Do you not know that you are a temple of God, and that the Spirit of God dwells in you? If any man destroys the temple of God, God will destroy him, for the temple of God is holy, and that is what you are. (12)

During the millennium Jesus will dwell in the temple in Jerusalem. After the millennium and the great white throne judgment, the temple will be no more for the Lord God, the Almighty Father, and the Lamb are its temple.

> Revelation 21:22: And I saw no temple in it, for the Lord God, the Almighty, and the Lamb, are its temple (12).

The city has no need of the sun or moon for the Lamb will be its light.

> Revelation 21:23-27: And the city has no need of the sun or of the moon to shine upon it, for the glory of God has illumined it, and its lamp is the Lamb. And the nations shall walk by its light, and the kings of the earth shall bring their glory into it. And in day-time (for there shall be no night there) its gates shall never be closed; and they shall bring the glory and the honor of the nations into it; and nothing unclean and no one who practices abomination and lying, shall ever come into it, but only those whose names are written in the Lamb's book of life. (12)

> Revelation 22:5: And there shall no longer be any night; and they shall not have need of the light of a lamp nor the light of the sun, because the Lord God shall illumine them; and they shall reign forever and ever (12).

Only the city of Jerusalem will not need the sun or the moon. The sun and the moon will shine on earth forever as shown in Psalm 89 and Jeremiah 31.

> Psalm 89:34-37: My covenant I will not violate, nor will I alter the utterance of My lips. Once I have sworn by My holiness; I will not lie to David. His descendants shall endure forever, and his throne as the sun before Me. It shall be established forever like the moon, and the witness in the sky is faithful. (12)

> Jeremiah 31:35-36: Thus says the Lord, Who gives the sun for light by day, and the fixed order of the

moon and the stars for light by night, . . . "If this fixed order departs from before Me," declares the Lord, "Then the offspring of Israel also shall cease from being a nation before Me forever." (12)

Psalm 89 and Jeremiah 31 show that the sun and moon will last forever. Only the city of Jerusalem has no need of the sun or moon, for the glory of the Lord will illuminate the city twenty-four hours a day (34).

The Tree of Life

Revelation 22:1-2: And he showed me a river of the water of life, clear as crystal, coming from the throne of God and of the Lamb, . . . And on either side of the river was the tree of life, bearing twelve kinds of fruit, yielding its fruit every month; and the leaves of the tree were for the healing of the nations. (12)

Revelation 22:14: Blessed are those who wash their robes, that they may have the right to the tree of life, and may enter by the gates into the city (12).

In Genesis, the Lord spoke of two trees, the tree of life and the tree of knowledge of good and evil.

Genesis 2:9: And out of the ground the Lord God caused to grow every tree that is pleasing to the sight and good for food; the tree of life also in the midst of the garden, and the tree of knowledge of good and evil (12).

Adam and Eve could partake of the fruit of any tree in the garden except for the fruit of the tree of knowledge of good and evil. If they had not eaten the fruit of the tree of knowledge of good and evil, they would have eventually found the tree of life and eaten the fruit of it. However, when Adam and Eve sinned, the Lord sent cherubim with flaming sword to guard the tree of life.

> Genesis 3:24: So He drove the man out; and at the east of the garden of Eden He stationed the cherubim, and the flaming sword, which turned every direction, to guard the way to the tree of life (12).

Why did the Lord send cherubim to guard the tree of life after Adam and Eve sinned?

Partaking of the tree of life will enable one to live forever. To live forever in a sinful and unforgiving state would be very tormenting (96).

What would have happened if Adam and Eve had not sinned?

After a period of testing, they would have found the tree of life and eaten its fruits. Then they would have been taken up to heaven like Enoch (98).

> Genesis 5:24: Then Enoch walked with God, and he was no longer here, for God took him (60).

> Hebrews 11:5: By faith Enoch was taken up so that he should not see death; and he was not found because God took him up; for he obtained the witness that before his being taken up he was pleasing to God. (12)

The tree of life, which was available to Adam and Eve in the beginning, will be available to the saints at the time of the end. The Lord promised the overcomers in the Church of Ephesus that He would give them the right to eat from the tree of life, which is in the paradise of God (Revelation 2:7). Scripture says that those that wash their robes and make them white by the Blood of the Lamb will be allowed to partake of the tree of life and to enter the city.

Trees bear fruits and leaves for the healing of nations.

Resurrected saints will reign with Jesus on earth for one thousand years.

> Revelation 20:4-6: . . . and they came to life and reigned with Christ for a thousand years. The rest of the dead did not come to life until the thousand years were completed. This is the first resurrection. Blessed and holy is the one who has a part in the first resurrection; over these the second death has no power, but they will be priests of God and of Christ and reign with Him for a thousand years. (12)

On that day, Jesus will be King over all the earth.

> Zechariah 14:4-5, 9: And in that day His feet will stand on the Mount of Olives, which is in front of Jerusalem on the east; . . . Then the Lord, my God, will come and all of the holy ones with Him! . . . And the Lord will be king over all the earth; (12)

Leaves will be for the healing of the people during the millennium.

The temple described in Ezekiel is the millennium temple. Jesus' throne will be in this temple (Ezekiel 43:7). The water will flow from the sanctuary of the temple and turns into a river. Fruit trees grow on both sides of the river providing food for the people, while leaves will be for the healing of the people. With the exception of the resurrected saints, people living in the millennium will have mortal bodies. They will at times need physical healing. We know this is the millennium temple as the scripture says this structure temple will be no more after the millennium as God the Father and Jesus are the temple (Revelation 21:22).

> Ezekiel 47:12: And by the river on its bank, on one side and on the other, will grow all kinds of trees for food. Their leaves will not wither, and their fruit will not fail. They will bear every month because their water flows from the sanctuary, and their fruit will be for food and their leaves for healing. (12)

The trees in Revelation 22:2 are called the "trees of life." Though the leaves from the trees in Ezekiel are for healing of the people, the trees in Ezekiel are not called the "trees of life." You cannot partake of the "tree of life" until you are in heaven. People in Ezekiel have mortal bodies. People will be born, live, and die in the millennium. As the years of a tree so shall the years of my people be. If a child dies at the age of 100 years, it will be considered a curse.

Leaves from the "trees of life" will be used to heal people after they enter heaven.

In Revelation 22, the millennium is over. There is a new heaven and a new earth. God the Father and the Lamb are living among the people. Yet, Revelation 22:2 speaks of leaves for the healing of nations or healing of the people.

> Revelation 22:1-2: And he showed me a river of the water of life, clear as crystal, coming from the throne of God and of the Lamb, in the middle of its street. And on either side of the river was the tree of life, bearing twelve kinds of fruit, yielding its fruit every month; and the leaves of the tree were for the healing of the nations. (12)

Why would people with resurrected or glorified bodies need

healing in the new heaven and new earth when God the Father and the Lamb is living among the people? Apparently the answer to this question is that everyone will not be perfected when they enter the kingdom. Example: I received understanding from the Lord that even though my aunt and uncle were in heaven they were in bondage. I said, "Lord, I do not understand how they can be in heaven and be in bondage." The Lord said it was something they were taught on earth that was not of Him. When I prayed for the bondage to be broken, there was a vision of my aunt receiving the Body of the Lord at communion. The minute the Body of Jesus in the form of bread was placed in her hand, Jesus appeared in her hand. She recognized the real presence of Jesus in the Eucharist and the bondage was broken. The same thing happened for my uncle. I do not know what my aunt and uncle were taught on earth, but it appears that they had doubts about the real presence of Jesus in the Eucharist. Obviously, healing can come from Jesus' Body.

My prayer partner received understanding that after his mother and dad had entered the kingdom of heaven, the Lord sent them to school so they could learn some things.

People on earth receive teachings or understandings that are not of the Lord. People are still learning and being perfected after they enter the kingdom. I do not understand the words "healing of nations" as only people can eat leaves. Somehow the leaves from the "tree of life" play a role in the healing of nations or the healing of people. As the people are healed, the nations are healed.

Adam and Eve were prevented from eating of the tree of life in Genesis since they would have been sealed and tormented for life in a sinful state. There are many levels and honors in the kingdom of heaven. Those that had a closer walk with the Lord on earth will know more of the nature of God than those that are just within the door of the kingdom. The Lord will give everyone who overcomes the right to eat from the tree of life. Obviously, something will happen to a person when he partakes of the "tree of life."

Jesus is coming with his rewards.

> Revelation 22:12-13: Behold, I am coming quickly, and My reward is with Me, to render to every man according to what he has done. I am the Alpha and the Omega, the first and the last, the beginning and the end. (12)

Jesus is coming to reward each man according to his works and deeds. Salvation is a gift from God and cannot be earned. However, there are prizes to be won. Paul spoke of the prize of the high-calling, for which he ran a race for with all of his might. Some will be the bride of Christ and will follow Him, wherever He goes. Others will be servants and will serve Him day and night. Some will receive a crown. Some will receive many crowns. The scriptures speak of several crowns: the crown of righteousness (II Timothy 4:8), the crown of life (James 1:12), and the crown of glory (I Peter 5:4). In Revelation 19:12, Jesus is seen wearing many crowns.

Jesus is spoken of as the Lord of lords and the King of kings. Jesus will rule the earth from Jerusalem. Some of the saints will be kings ruling over a nation. Some will be priests. Some will be rulers over ten cities. Some will be rulers over five cities. Some will shine brightly as stars for all eternity. Some will just barely make it into the kingdom. Others will lose their reward, but they will be saved by fire.

Daniel and Matthew speak of the righteous saints shining brightly as the stars and the sun for all eternity.

> Daniel 12:3: And those who have insight will shine brightly like the brightness of the expanse of heaven,

and those who lead the many to righteousness, like the stars forever and ever (12).

Matthew 13:43: The righteous will shine forth as the sun in the kingdom of their Father (12).

In the resurrection there are different orders among the redeemed. The righteous shall differ one from another just as "one star will differeth from another star in glory" (I Corinthians 15:41). (61)

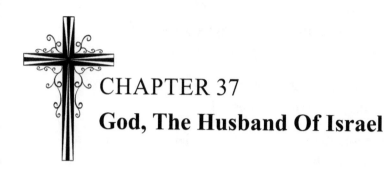

CHAPTER 37

God, The Husband Of Israel

The Old Testament speaks of God as a husband married to Israel. For some time, thoughts have been passing through my mind about God, the husband of Israel. I did not intend to write on this subject, as I did not have an understanding of this relationship. A prayer partner confirmed that I was to write about God the Father, the husband of Israel. The Lord asked me to review the scriptures pertaining to the bride of Jesus, and an understanding, which was previously overlooked, would come forth.

We need to remember there is one God but three persons in God: God the Father, God the Son and God the Holy Spirit. This is a mystery we have to accept in faith. Israel is the bride of God the Father. Jesus' bride will come from His Body, the Church. The Blessed Mother is the spouse of the Holy Spirit.

The parallel of the marriage covenant and God's covenant with His people Israel.

To understand the covenant God made with His people, Israel, we need to understand the depth and seriousness of the covenant of marriage. The marriage covenant is the most serious, most sacred, most honored, most profound, and highest level of commitment two people can make to each other before God. The marriage vow is a lifetime binding commitment to be loyal and faithful to each other regardless of the circumstances they may encounter in their journey through life.

The seriousness with which a person takes his marriage vows will reflect the seriousness of his relationship with God. The attitude of our society toward the sacredness of marriage is a reflection of our society's relationship with God. This, in turn, reflects the character, honor, and strength of our nation. The marriage covenant is the same covenant that God made with Israel.

Ezekiel 16 shows God making a covenant with Jerusalem and taking her as His bride.

> Ezekiel 16:3, 8: . . ., Thus saith the Lord God unto Jerusalem . . . Now when I passed by thee, and looked upon thee, behold, thy time was the time of love; and I spread my skirt over thee, and covered thy nakedness: yea, I sware unto thee, and entered into a covenant with thee, saith the Lord God, and thou becamest mine. (10)

God is a husband married to Israel.

The following scriptures show God is a husband and is married to Israel. However, God's people, Israel, did not keep the covenant and played the harlot.

> Jeremiah 3:14, 20: Turn, O backsliding children, saith the Lord, for I am married unto you. . . . Surely as a wife treacherously departeth from her husband, so have ye dealt treacherously with me, O house of Israel, saith the Lord. (10)

> Jeremiah 31:32: . . . My covenant which they broke although I was their Husband, says the Lord (59).

God divorces Israel. God gives Israel a certificate of divorce.

> Jeremiah 3:6-8: . . . the Lord said to me, "Have you seen what faithless Israel has done? She has gone

up on every high hill and under every spreading tree and has committed adultery there. I thought that after she had done all this she would return to me but she did not, and her unfaithful sister Judah saw it. I gave faithless Israel her certificate of divorce and sent her away because of all her adulteries." (7)

God gave the Israelites a certificate of divorce and scattered them to all nations of the world because they broke their covenant with Him.

God forgives Israel.

Isaiah 54:4-8: Fear not, for you shall not be ashamed; neither be confounded and depressed, for you shall not be put to shame; for you shall forget the shame of your youth, and you shall not remember the reproach of your widowhood any more. For your Maker is your husband, the Lord of hosts is His name; and the Holy One of Israel is your Redeemer, the God of the whole earth He is called. For the Lord has called you like a woman forsaken, grieved in spirit and heartsore, even a wife (wooed and won) in youth, when she is later refused and scorned, says your God. For a brief moment I forsook you, but with great compassion and mercies I gather you to Me again. In a little burst of wrath I hid My face from you for a moment, but with age-enduring love and kindness I will have compassion and mercy on you, says the Lord, your Redeemer. (59)

The Lord God promises to take Israel back and to enter into another covenant with her, to take her as His bride and wife.

Jeremiah 31:31-32: Behold, the days are coming says the Lord, when I will make a new covenant with the house of Israel and with the house of Judah. Not according to the covenant which I made with their fathers in the day when I took them by hand to bring them out of the land of Egypt, My covenant which they broke although I was their Husband, says the Lord. (59)

Hosea 2:19-20: And I will betroth you to Me for ever; yes, I will betroth you to Me in righteousness and justice, and in steadfast love, and in mercies. I will even betroth you to Me in stability and in faithfulness, and you shall know - recognize, be acquainted with, appreciate, give heed to and cherish - the Lord. (59)

Both Jeremiah and Hosea show God making a covenant with Israel to be His bride and wife.

The Old Testament speaks of God as the husband of Israel while the New Testament speaks of Jesus as the Bridegroom. Who is the bride of Jesus? Is the Church the bride of Jesus? Let's see what the scriptures say.

John the Baptist said the bride belongs to Jesus. He, himself, was just a friend to the bridegroom and was not a part of the bride.

John 3:26-29: They came to John and said to him, "Rabbi, that man who was with you on the other side of the Jordan - the one you testified about - well, he is baptizing, and everyone is going to him." To this John replied, "A man can receive only what is given him from heaven. You yourselves can testify that I said, 'I am not the Christ but am sent ahead of him.' The bride belongs to the bridegroom. The friend who attends the bridegroom waits and listens for him, and is full of joy when he hears the bridegroom's voice.

That joy is mine, and it is now complete. (7)

Another translation says:

> John 3:29: He who has the bride is the bridegroom; but the groomsman, who stands by and listens to him rejoices greatly and heartily on account of the bride-groom's voice. This then is my pleasure and joy, and it is now complete. (59)

Though Jesus identifies Himself as the Bridegroom, He did not call His disciples or followers the bride. Jesus said they were His wedding guests or attendants. Why?

Jesus called his disciples his wedding guests.

> Mark 2:18-20: The disciples of John and of the Pharisees were accustomed to fast. People came to Jesus and objected,

> "Why do the disciples of John and the disciples of the Pharisees fast, but your disciples do not fast?"

Jesus answered them,

> "Can the wedding guests fast while the bridegroom is with them? As long as they have the bridegroom with them they cannot fast. But the days will come when the bridegroom is taken away from them, and then they will fast on that day. . . ." (24A)

> Matthew 9:14-15: Then the disciples of John ap-proached him and said, "Why do we and the Pharisees fast but your disciples do not fast? Jesus answered them, "Can the wedding guests mourn as long as the bridegroom is with them? The days will come when

the bridegroom is taken away from them, and then they will fast. (24A)

Luke 5:33-35: And they said to him, "The disciples of John fast often and offer prayers, and the disciples of the Pharisees do the same; but yours eat and drink." Jesus answered them, "Can you make the wedding guests fast while the bridegroom is with them? But the days will come, and when the bridegroom is taken away from them, then they will fast in those days." (24A)

Obviously, these are the scriptures to which the Lord was referring when he told my friend and me, while in prayer, to review the scriptures pertaining to the bride of Christ and an understanding that was overlooked would come forth. John the Baptist said the bride belongs to Jesus, but he did not say that those with Jesus were the bride. Though Jesus identified Himself as the Bridegroom, He did not call His disciples the bride. Why? Jesus said that His disciples were His wedding guests or attendants. This shows that all Christians and followers of Jesus are not the bride of Christ. This does not mean that the disciples are not a part of the bride of Christ. It means that at that point in time they had not yet finished the course and won the race for the prize of the high-calling to be a part of the bride of Christ of which Paul spoke.

Is the Church the bride?

Ephesians 5:22-32 compares the relationship between a husband and a wife with Christ and the Church. A husband should love and care for his wife just as Christ loves and cares for His Church. However, this scripture does not say the Church is the bride of Christ.

Ephesians 5:30 teaches that the Church is the Body of Christ, but there are no scriptures that say the Church is the bride of Christ. Eve was taken from the rib of Adam, but the whole body of Adam was not used to make Eve. The bride of Christ will come from the Body of Christ (the Church), but the whole Body of Christ (the Church) will not be the bride.

Paul told the Corinthians that he wanted to present them as a pure virgin to Christ.

> 2 Corinthians 11:2: I am jealous for you with a godly jealousy. I promised you to one husband, to Christ, so that I might present you as a pure virgin to him. But I am afraid that just as Eve was deceived by the serpent's cunning, your minds may somehow be led astray from your sincere and pure devotion to Christ. (7)

The following scripture in Ephesians speaks of the Lord Jesus Christ giving His life, so that He may receive a radiant and holy Church that has been purified by washing with water and a cleansing through the word, without any stain, blemish or defect.

> Ephesians 5:25-27: Husbands, love your wives, just as Christ loved the church and gave himself up for her to make her holy, cleansing her by the washing with water through the word, and to present her to himself as a radiant church, without stain or wrinkle or any other blemish, but holy and blameless. (7)

The emphasis is on a virgin or a church who is pure and holy with no stain, blemish, or defect.

Revelation 14 speaks of 144,000 first fruits unto the Lamb. They were called virgins that were holy and blameless without defilement.

Revelation 14:4-5: . . . These are they who follow the Lamb wherever He goes. These are they who have been ransomed (purchased, redeemed) from among men as the first fruits for God and the Lamb. No lie was found to be upon their lips, for they are blameless - spotless, untainted, without blemish, (59)

The first fruits to God and the Lamb are pure virgins without defilement. They follow the Lamb wherever He goes. This is the characteristic of the bride. The bride follows her husband wherever He goes.

The first fruits to God and the Lamb are obviously Christians who had a close walk with the Lord while they were on earth. They purged themselves of their sins, and were sensitive to the anointing, prompting, and guidance of His Spirit. There are very few Christians, if any, (the scripture indicates that there are some) that have purged themselves to the point where they are pure, blameless, spotless, without blemish, or defilement. Repenting and turning from sin and striving for perfection is a goal for which every one should strive. This is an on-going, life-long process. I want to emphasize that I do not fall into this category. Nonetheless, with God's help, I am going to do my best to respond to the prompting of the Holy Spirit to deal with each of my sins and to try to turn away from them.

The relationship between God (the Father) and His bride and Jesus and His bride.

Since I did not have an understanding of the relationship of God and His bride or of Jesus and His bride, I asked a friend to pray with me to ask the Lord for an enlightenment and understanding of this relationship. The first question I asked was:

Will John the Baptist have an opportunity to become a part of the bride of Christ?

I was putting my friend to a test as he and I prayed because he was not aware of the scripture in which John said that he was only a friend of the Bridegroom. My friend said he received knowledge that John was not a part of the bride of Christ. This is what the scriptures teach, which indicates that the Old Testament saints are not a part of the bride of Christ. As we prayed for more understanding, the following revelation and knowledge came to us.

> The bride of God - includes all of those, whom Christ has reconciled to God. All of those that accept the Bridegroom and believe in His name will be God's bride.

> The bride of Christ - will be glorified with more blessings. The bride of Christ includes those who have accepted His name, have walked in faith, are prayer warriors, are diligent workers for Christ's sake, and have brought many into His kingdom. God's judgment will determine who these are.

> Revelation on John the Baptist - John is included in a special habitation within God's kingdom. He is classified as a messenger for God. He had a special anointing from God before he was even born. John is labeled the bride of God like some of the Old Testament saints who were brought up to heaven.

> The bride of Christ will occupy a higher level of external existence and will know more about God's nature than the rest who are just within the door of the kingdom of God.

My friend and I were praying, seeking the Lord about the meaning of the phrase "like some of the Old Testament saints." The Lord revealed that John the Baptist was like Elijah. The scriptures teach that John went forth in the spirit of Elijah. The Lord also said John was like the Old Testament saints that walked the streets of Jerusalem. Matthew 27:52-53 teaches that many of the Old Testament saints walked the streets of Jerusalem after Christ's resurrection. As we continued to pray, seeking the meaning of the word "some" the Lord showed us a golden box with a lock on it. He told us to stop praying and not to try to open the box because there are some things that are not to be revealed at this time. However, John was like some of the Old Testament saints because all of the Old Testament saints have not yet been raised from the dead.

The Lord gives an insight into the relationship between Jesus and the bride of God. These words were written just as they were spoken.

> A man marries a woman. Later, a son is born. The son is actually a part of the man before he is born as his seed was in his father. The son is also a part of woman, but not in a concentrated relationship.

> God and his people are the same way. God's Son, Jesus, is of God. God's former bride was the people of Israel. Jesus is God's Son through the people Israel. Since Jesus had not yet come into the world, the people of Israel were not married to Jesus Christ.

> We are all God's children physically in respect to our physical birth. Spiritual birth is something else. If we accept Christ, we are spiritually reborn with God and our seed is planted to grow eternally. God gave His Son so that sinners could become part of the bride

and be brought into his family.

The above words of knowledge, received in prayer, show that God married Israel to bring forth His Son to save man from his sins. God's wife, the people of Israel, broke her covenant with her husband, God. God gave her a certificate of divorce. He, then, forgave her and promised to marry her again. The new bride of God will include Jews, Christians, and everyone who makes it into the kingdom of heaven.

Jesus will take His bride from His Body, the Church, but the whole Church will not be the bride of Christ, just as Eve did not come from the whole body of Adam. The bride of Christ is the prize of the high calling that Paul ran a race for with all his might in an effort to be a part. It seems that Paul won the prize as he says:

> 2 Timothy 4:6-7: For I am already being poured out like a drink offering, and the time has come for my departure. I have fought the good fight, I have finished the race, I have kept the faith (7).

The words of knowledge, received in prayer, revealed that the bride of Christ will be those that:

1. have accepted His name,
2. have walked in faith,
3. are prayer warriors,
4. are diligent workers for Christ's sake,
5. and have brought many into the kingdom.

God's judgment will determine those who will be the bride of Christ.

The bride of Christ, the prize of the high calling, will include people from every walk of life from janitors, housewives, mechanics, doctors, and to evangelists, priests, nuns, and missionaries who are on the front lines bringing people to the Lord. These people will all have one thing in common: they will be prayer warriors. They spend considerable time in prayer. They bind the forces of darkness and pray to the Lord of harvest to send laborers into the field to gather the harvest. These prayer warriors also pray for the Lord to send ministering angels to convict people of their sins and turn them to the Lord. They will receive credit for the harvest the laborers gather, even though they were not physically involved in the actual labor of bringing people to the Lord.

The following scripture encourages us to pray without ceasing.

1 Thessalonians 5:16-23: Rejoice always, never cease praying, render constant thanks; such is God's will for you in Christ Jesus. Do not stifle the Spirit. Do not despise prophecies. Test everything; retain what is good. Avoid any semblance of evil. May the God of peace make you perfect in holiness. May he preserve you whole and entire, spirit, soul, and body, irreproachable at the coming of our Lord Jesus Christ. (60)

God the Father promises to marry Israel again.

The bride of God will include all of those that make it into the kingdom of heaven. This will include the Jews, the Christians, and everyone living before the millennium, as well as those that live during the millennium. The marriage of the Lamb will take place in heaven before the millennium begins, before the Lord Jesus Christ returns to the earth. The Jews and gentiles that live during the millennium will not have an opportunity to become a part of the bride of Christ, since Jesus will marry His bride before He returns to the earth. Jesus will be visible to the people living during the millennium, but God the Father will not be visible to the people until after the millennium. God the Father will probably marry His bride after the millennium, when He is visible to everyone.

To be great in the kingdom of heaven, one must first be a servant.

> Matthew 20:25-28: But Jesus called them to Himself, and said, "You know that the rulers of the Gentiles lord it over them, and their great men exercise authority over them. It is not so among you, but whoever wishes to become great among you shall be your servant, and whoever wishes to be first among you shall be your slave; just as the Son of Man did not come to be served, but to serve, and to give His life a ransom for many." (12)

Jesus asked His disciples what they were discussing as they walked along the way to Capernaum.

> Mark 9:34-35: But they kept silent, for on the way they had discussed with one another which of them was the greatest. And sitting down, He called the twelve and said to them, "If any one wants to be first, he shall be last of all, and servant of all." (12)

Jesus set an example by coming not to be served but to serve.

Salvation is a gift from God by faith and cannot be earned.

> Ephesians 2:8-10: For by grace you have been saved through faith; and that not of yourselves, it is the gift of God; not as a result of works, that no one should boast. For we are His workmanship, created in Christ Jesus for good works, which God prepared before hand, that we should walk in them. (12)

Another translation says:

Because of his kindness you have been saved through trusting Christ. And even trusting is not of yourselves; it too is a gift from God. Salvation is not a reward for good we have done so none of us can take any credit for it. It is God himself who has made us what we are and given us new lives from Christ Jesus; (64)

Scripture says that in the last days, whosoever shall call upon the name of the Lord shall be saved.

Acts 2:17, 21: And it shall be in the last days, God says . . . that every one who calls on the name of the Lord shall be saved (12).

A person can call upon the Lord at the moment of his death and be saved. There is nothing a person can do at the moment of his death to earn salvation. Salvation is a free gift from God through faith and is not a reward for good work.

Work, alone, will not get a person into the kingdom of heaven.

Matthew 7:21-23: Not every one who calls me "Lord, Lord," will enter into the kingdom of heaven, but only those who do what my Father in heaven wants them to do. When Judgment Day comes, many will say to me, "Lord, Lord! In your name we spoke God's message, by your name we drove out many demons and performed many miracles!" Then I will say to them, "I never knew you. Get away from me, you wicked people!" (88)

Good works alone will not get one into the kingdom of heaven. We must do what the Father wants us to do.

Jesus told His disciples to go and bear much fruit.

> John 15:14-16: And you are my friends, if you do what I command you. I do not call you servants any longer, because a servant does not know what his master is doing. Instead, I call you friends, because I have told you everything I heard from my Father. You did not choose me; I chose you, and appointed you to go and bear much fruit, the kind of fruit that endures. (88)

The fruit we bear will be part of our reward in heaven.

Rewards have to be earned.

Scripture speaks of laying up treasures in heaven where they cannot be stolen or destroyed.

> Matthew 6:19-21: Do not lay up for yourselves treasures upon earth, where moth and rust destroy, and where thieves break in and steal. But lay up for yourselves treasures in heaven, where neither moth nor rust destroys, and where thieves do not break in or steal; for where your treasure is, there will your heart be also. (12)

Unless a man works to put treasures in heaven, he will not have any.

> I Corinthians 3:11-15: For no man can lay a foundation other than the one which is laid, which is Jesus Christ. Now if any man builds upon the foundation with gold, silver, precious stones, wood, hay, straw, each man's work will become evident; for the day will show it, because it is to be revealed with fire; and the fire itself will test the quality of each man 's work. If any man's work which he has built upon it

remains, he shall receive a reward. If any man's work
is burned up, he shall suffer loss; but he himself shall
be saved, yet so as through fire. (12)

Jesus is seen, in Revelation 22:12, coming to reward each man according to the works or deeds he has done. There are many rewards, honors, and positions of authority within the kingdom of heaven, with the bride of Christ being the prize of the high-calling. Salvation is a free gift from God, but rewards are not. Rewards have to be earned in this life. Once we cross the line from time to eternity, our fate is sealed for all eternity. There is no climbing the ladder or advancement as there is in the military or business world today.

When one considers that life on earth is like a single grain of sand on the seashore or a drop of water in the ocean in contrast to eternity, it is essential that we take a look at ourselves and our relationship with God, to see where our niche is going to be for all eternity.

Are we going to make it into the kingdom? Are we going to be just within the door of the kingdom? Are we going to be among those that are kings, priests, and rulers or are we going to be servants? Are we making an effort to run the race for the prize of the high-calling to be a part of the bride of Christ, with the privilege of following Him wherever He goes for all eternity?

The manner in which we spend time in prayer, developing a relationship with God, reading and studying His word, and being sensitive to knowing and doing His will, will determine our rewards, honor, and place in heaven for all eternity. There is nothing more important in this life than our relationship with Jesus Christ. If we do not learn to follow Him in this life, how can we be among those that will follow Him wherever He goes for all eternity?

Purification

While in prayer early one morning, I saw a picture of a beautiful wedding ring. The ring was gold with decorative silver inlaid in the middle. Through prayer, it was discerned that the Lord wanted me to review the scriptures pertaining to the marriage at Cana.

It is interesting that Jesus, who began His ministry at the marriage at Cana, will climax His career with His own wedding and feast in heaven. Jesus began His ministry by changing the water that was placed into six purification jars into wine. The purification jars were used by the Jewish people to clean themselves before eating, according to the tradition of the elders (Mark 7:4). It was only appropriate that purification jars were used to hold the wine, which was the fruit of the wedding at the marriage of Cana. If we hope to participate, share and enjoy the full fruit of the wedding at the marriage of the Lamb, we must begin with our own purification process. The act of purification is an ongoing, lifetime process of dealing with the sins in our life and turning from them.

The one hundred and forty-four thousand, in Revelation 14, are spoken of as being among the first fruits unto the Lamb. They are pure, holy and blameless without any stain, blemish, or defect. They are among those who follow the Lamb, wherever He goes. This is the characteristic of the bride. The bride follows her husband wherever He goes.

While in prayer with a prayer partner, we received the following knowledge and understanding:

> The children of the Lamb are those who have been washed in the Blood of the Lamb.

> The bride of the Lamb is those who undertake the purification process in an effort to win the prize of the high-calling.

484

If we desire to attain the call the prize of the high-calling, we have to run the race that Paul spoke of which is the purification process. We cannot be lax or passive in purging and cleansing ourselves. Our thought-life, which is related to our spiritual life, must be purified. Everything that is sinful has to be dealt with, such as pride (getting our feelings hurt), anger, bitterness, unforgiveness, unbelief, lust, greed, envy, jealousy, lying, stealing, disobedience, rebellion, gossip, etc. This purification comes through the study of God's Word. God's Word convicts us of how impure, imperfect, and sinful we really are. The scriptures teach that if we study His word, we will know the truth, and the truth will set us free.

> Psalm 119:11 says, "I have hidden your word in my heart that I might not sin against you." (7)

Not only do we need to deal with the obvious sins in our life, we need to study and know God's word so that we will not unknowingly sin against Him.

Those who hope to attain the prize of the high-calling, to be a part of the bride of Christ, with the privilege of wearing this beautiful wedding ring and to follow Him wherever He goes, must undergo this purification process to become pure, holy and blameless without any stain, blemish, or deceit, just as the one hundred and forty-four thousand in Revelation 14. We cannot do this on our own. Just saying the words, that we are sorry for our sins, does not change a person's heart. Only with God's help can a person's heart be changed and purified.

Though the children of the Lamb and the guests will attend and share in the joy of the Lamb and His bride at their wedding feast, they will not be able to participate and share in the intimacy and joy that only a bride can have with her husband.

The race for the prize of the high calling is not difficult.

While in prayer, a prayer partner and I received knowledge that running the race for the prize of the high-calling is not difficult. What is difficult is making and keeping the commitment to run the race. We can run a long and hard race, but if we stop just before we reach the finish line, we will not finish or complete the race. I have been spending two to three hours a day in prayer. For years the Lord had been waking me up, in the middle of the night, to spend an hour or two in prayer. Recently, I had been sick, tired and fatigued, and had not been consistent in my prayer time for about two weeks. Even though I have been going to Mass daily, the Lord spoke to me one morning and said, "Are you going to be ready, when I come?" I responded, "I hope to be." I knew the Lord was encouraging me to be faithful in my prayer time and to continue running the race without stopping, so that I will be ready to cross the finish line just before He calls me home.

In running the race for the prize of the high calling, we can be in the race running real hard, but if we stop before crossing the finish line, we will not finish the race. To win we must run continuously.

The bride will help the Lord govern the earth in the millennium

Those who make the Man-child rapture will rule nations with a rod of iron.

> Revelation 2:26-27: And he who overcomes, and who keeps My deeds until the end, to him I will give authority over the nations and he shall rule them with a rod of iron (12).

> Revelation 5:10: And hast made us unto our God kings and priests: And we shall reign on the earth (10).

> Revelation 12:5: And she gave birth to a son, a male child, who is to rule all nations with a rod of iron; and

her child was caught up to God and to His throne (12).

The Man-child will help the Lord to govern the nations and cities of the world. Those involved in the Harvest Rapture or the general resurrection are not involved in governing the cities and nations of the world as they are called servants.

Vision of two large white books with green letters – A to L on one and M to Z on the other

These books list those who have been washed with the Blood of My Son. These are those whose names will be called first. They are without stain or blemish. These are My earthly warriors. They pray and work every quadrant of the spirit. They do not stop. They have given up all for Me. They come to Me exhausted from their race, each has won. Each has Me as their center. They lived in this world but are not of it. They are Mine.

Since my understanding is that the number winning the race for the prize of the high-calling is limited, I said, "Lord, these two large books certainly contain far more than 144,000 names?" My prayer partner then received knowledge that these two books contained the life history of each person that had won the race for the prize of the high-calling. The words flow with beauty.

Wedding invitation

I heard a voice, which said, "Send out the wedding invitations." The Lord said:

My invitations are ready to be sent out. Yet, I know many will not come to the banquet feast of My Son. Yet, they will be given one more invitation and for most, it will be their last. Pain and suffering must come for those who are at the door when it has been shut. Yet, those who will be there will forever rejoice at My coming. You have been given the joy of announcing My coming in the spirit to all those who are listening for My voice. Continue to pray and intercede for those who do not know Me. You are My joy.

The Monarch butterfly

I had a picture of a Monarch butterfly during my prayer time. My friend received the following words, while in prayer.

> The butterfly is a delicate and beautiful creation. So easily could you crush it, yet it has the power to rise up and fly hundreds of miles. It is indeed a wonder of My creation. Yet, you are so much more than a butterfly. You have the strength to endure far more than you can ever know. Endurance begins with your determination to end the race at the finish line. Keep the frail butterfly in your sight. When you feel to fall aside, remember its endurance and pick yourself up and continue your journey.

The Monarch butterflies fly up to 2,000 miles from Canada and the northern states to Angangueo, a mountainous area in central Mexico to spend the winter. El Rosario is a mountainous preserve that shelters some 300 millions butterflies after their fall migration. In the spring, these delicate creatures begin their trek northward, eventually reaching the northern states and Canada (99).

Many are invited to the marriage feast of the Lamb.

> Revelation 19:9: And he said to me, "Write, 'Blessed are those who are invited to the marriage supper of the Lamb' (12).

The Spirit and the bride give an invitation for others to come and drink of the life-giving water.

> Revelation 22:16-17: . . . I am the root and offspring of David, the bright morning star. The Spirit and the bride say, "Come." Let the one who thirsts come forward, and the one who wants it receive the gift of life-giving water. (24A)

The bride is never invited to her wedding or marriage feast. She is the one that does the inviting. Who are the guests that are invited to the marriage feast of the Lamb, if everyone is the bride? Psalm 45, Mark 2:18-20, Matthew 9:14-15, Luke 5:33-35, and Revelation 22:16-17 show that everyone is not the bride of Christ.

CHAPTER 38
Bride Of Christ

This chapter is a summary and review of scriptures and personal revelations pertaining to the bride of Christ.

The midnight hour rapture

In 1973, I had a dream in which my wife and I woke up at the midnight hour and walked out onto the porch with our two oldest sons, who were 8 and 9 years old. There was an unusual light or glow coming down from above. I could not see directly up as we were under the porch. I had knowledge that this was the midnight hour rapture and the Lord was coming for His bride. There was a tremendous feeling of excitement. The Scripture that came to me was the story of the ten virgins waiting to meet the Bridegroom.

I was puzzled why our son, who was two years old, was not with us.

Later, I received understanding that the bride of Christ is the prize of the high-calling for which Paul ran a race for with all of his might. A two-year-old child is not capable of running a race for the prize of the high-calling. I do not wish to imply that I or any of my family has won the race of which Paul spoke of. The Lord put a strong desire in my heart to study and learn about Revelation and the end times.

While in prayer the Lord told me to review the Scriptures pertaining to the bride of Christ. An understanding that was overlooked would come forth.

Though Jesus identified Himself as the Bridegroom and John the Baptist said the bride belongs to Jesus, neither Jesus nor John the Baptist called Jesus' disciples the bride. Jesus said that His disciples were His wedding guests or attendants.

> Mark 2:18-20: The disciples of John and of the Pharisees were accustomed to fast. People came to Jesus and objected,
>
> "Why do the disciples of John and the disciples of the Pharisees fast, but your disciples do not fast?"
>
> Jesus answered them,
>
> "Can the wedding guests fast while the bridegroom is with them? As long as they have the bridegroom with them they cannot fast. But the days will come when the bridegroom is taken from them, and then they will fast on that day. . . ."   (24A)
>
> Matthew 9:14-15: Then the disciples of John approached him and said, "Why do we and the Pharisees fast but your disciples do not fast? Jesus answered them, "Can the wedding guests mourn as long as the bridegroom is with them? The days will come when the bridegroom is taken away from them, and then they will fast. (24A)
>
> Luke 5:33-35: And they said to him, "The disciples of John fast often and offer prayers, and the disciples of the Pharisees do the same; but yours eat and

drink." Jesus answered them, "Can you make the wedding guests fast while the bridegroom is with them? But the days will come, and when the bridegroom is taken away from them, then they will fast in those days." (24A)

If Jesus did not call His disciples the bride, how can the Church be the bride?

This does not mean that the disciples and many in the Church won't be the bride of Christ. It is that at this point in time, the disciples or some in the Church had not yet run and completed the race for which Paul had run for with all his might and won. The bride of Christ is a prize for which to strive and win. It is only after the race is won at the finish line that one becomes the bride.

Paul said that he hoped to make the resurrection.

Paul emphasizes in six verses that he hopes to attain the resurrection of the dead.

Philippians 3:11: if somehow I may attain the resurrection of the dead.

1. It is not that I have already reached it (the resurrection of the dead),
2. or have already finished my course.
3. I am racing to grasp the prize (resurrection of the dead) if possible.
4. I do not think of myself as having reached the finish line (resurrection of the dead), for
5. My entire attention is on the finish line (resurrection of the dead).
6. I run toward the prize (resurrection of the dead) to which God calls me.

Paul was not talking about salvation. Paul knew he had salvation through the grace of Jesus Christ. The Scripture in Acts 2:21 says, "It shall come to pass, that whosoever shall call on the name of the Lord, shall be saved" (10). If Paul were talking about salvation, who could be saved? Paul was not talking about the general resurrection (the harvest rapture – Matthew 24:29-31), he was talking about the Man-child resurrection (the mid-night hour resurrection) that he was running a race in an effort to be a part of (60).

What was the prize of the resurrection?

> Philippians 3:14: My entire attention is on the finish line as I run toward the prize to which God calls me - life on high in Christ Jesus (60).

The very top prize is Jesus, i.e., being Jesus' bride and following Him, wherever He goes.

Second Thessalonians speaks of the Antichrist being restrained until one who restrains him is taken out of the way.

> 2 Thessalonians 2: 6-8: And you know what restrains him now, so that in his time he may be revealed. For the mystery of lawlessness is already at work; only he who now restrains will do so until he is taken out the way. And then that lawless one will be revealed whom the Lord will slay with the breath of His mouth and bring to an end by the appearance of His coming. (12)

Message from the Lord to Maurice Sklar, a Messianic Jew – 7/29/10

The Lord told Maurice Sklar that He was coming for His bride first.

I always thought that it was the Holy Spirit that was restraining the evil in the earth and keeping the anti-Messiah – that wicked world dictator that will be empowered by Satan during the last seven years – from taking over everything. But, the Lord corrected me and said to me:

"If I took My Spirit out of the earth, then no one would be able to come to Me in the last time. But many millions of souls will cry out to me and be saved during the final seven years. But they will pay with their lives for their faith in Me. No one can come to Me unless the Holy Spirit draws them. No! It is not My Spirit that will be taken out of the earth. **It is My Bride that will be taken out of the earth.** Who is My Bride? It is only those that choose to love Me, walk with Me, obey Me, serve Me, and choose Me over all else right now. It is those that choose to be overcomers and will endure to the end. **It is the prayers and the intercession of My Bride that are holding back the flood of evil and judgment soon to come upon the whole earth. It is to allow My grace to continue to reach out to the lost and the backslidden church just a little bit longer.** It is not My will that any perish in hell. "I am now at the door! All is now ready! I am ready to come for My beautiful Bride! How I long for her! But, only the Father knows the precise day and hour of My appearing. First I must APPEAR to take My Bride away. Then, I must RETURN to this earth as KING OF KINGS. She will return with me. Time has run out. There will be no stopping the judgments much longer from coming like birth pangs upon the earth.

"Nevertheless, tell My Bride that I have heard her cries, her prayers, and her intercessions. I have seen her tears. It has restrained much that would have already happened. My grace is abundant in this final hour! How I weep for those that refuse to repent and come to Me now! My heart is broken for them, for I know the terrible evils coming upon them. Satan is now gathering his full armies to devour and destroy the nations of the earth. Only you, My precious Bride, are holding him back through your prayers...for this I am pleased.

Stay with Me in the place of prayer now! Nothing else matters. Take up the mantle of intercession and prayer as never before. Pray in the supernatural languages I have given you through the Holy Spirit and let ME pray through you. This is your highest calling! I am sweeping through this earth in a final call of revival that will rapidly end the time of grace to the nations. Do not waste the precious time I have given you. You can never recover it again in the eternities to come! Great is the reward for those that take hold of the horns of the altar and go to war to restrain the evil storm clouds on the horizon. Many millions of souls are at stake, even now, My Beloved!

"The lines have been already drawn. I know who are Mine and who are not. All of heaven is now ready for the greatest party and celebration that has ever been in the eternities past! There is no more preparation for the Wedding Supper any longer. It is DONE! I am waiting to appear in the air to catch and take My Bride home. What a Wedding Day it will BE! But, Beloved, YOU must prepare yourself so that you can hear the call of the shofar. Many will not hear because they have lost their bridal veils and their crowns. Hold fast to what I have given you. Do not let Satan steal your heart from Me. "These are events that will soon come and will signal your departure from this earth, My Beloved: (100)

Maurice Sklar thought it was the Holy Spirit that was holding back the appearance of the anti-Christ.

The Lord told him, "No, it is His bride that is holding back the coming of the anti-Christ." The Lord said that if He took the Holy Spirit out of the earth, no one could be saved during the last seven years. **The Holy Spirit was needed to reach out to the lost and backslidden Church.** Many Bible scholars believed that the Church is raptured before the tribulation as they do not see the word Church mentioned in the Scripture after Revelation 3. Notice that the Lord uses the word "Church" in His message to Maurice Sklar - meaning that the Church is on earth and going through the tribulation.

Mid-night Rapture

When I had the dream of the mid-night rapture, the Lord revealed to me that He was coming for His Bride at the mid-night hour. The Lord asked me to review the scriptures on the bride of Christ. He said an understanding that was overlooked would come forth. The understanding is that Jesus did not call His disciples the bride; He called them wedding guests or attendants. The bride was the prize of the high-calling for which Paul ran a race for with all his might.

The 144,000 on Mount Zion – The First Fruits unto the Lamb

Revelation 14:1-5: Then I looked and lo, the Lamb stood on Mount Zion, and with Him a hundred and forty-four thousand who had His name and His Father's name inscribed on their foreheads. And I heard a voice from heaven like the sound of great waters and like the rumbling of mighty thunder; the voice I heard of harpists accompanying themselves on their harps. And they sing a new song before the throne (of God) and before the four living creatures and before the elders. No one could learn that song except the hundred and forty-four thousand who had been ransomed (purchased, redeemed) from the earth. These are they who have not defiled themselves by relations with women, for they are (pure as) virgins. These are they who follow the Lamb wherever He goes. These are they who have been ransomed (purchased, redeemed) from among men as the first fruits for God and the Lamb. No lie was found to be upon their lips, for they are blameless - spotless, untainted, without blemish - before the throne of God. (59)

The 144,000, the First Fruits unto the Lamb

In a dream the Lord revealed to me that He was coming for His bride at the mid-night hour. I learned that a two year old is not capable of running a race for the prize of the high-calling i.e. to be a bride of Christ. This means everyone will not be the bride of Christ.

Since the Lord told Maurice Sklar that He was coming for His bride first and that the 144,000 before the throne are called first fruits unto the Lamb, these 144,000 have to be the first fruits rapture as they are standing before the throne and before the elders in heaven while the tribulation is going on. They are singing a song that only those redeemed from the earth can sing. The only other rapture the Scriptures speak of is in Matthew 24:29 – 31. It takes place immediately after tribulation when the sun is darkened and the moon is turned blood-red with the opening of the sixth seal. This means that there is no such thing as a pre-tribulation rapture of the Church.

In Revelation 14 there is a multitude of 144,000 before the throne. This is a pre-tribulation rapture as Revelation 14 speaks of angels flying through the air preaching the Gospel warning people not to take the mark of the beast prior to the tribulation. The first fruits are pure and holy. These are they who follow the Lamb wherever He goes. It is the bride who follows the Lamb wherever He goes. These are they who have been ransomed (purchased, redeemed) from among men as the first fruits for God and the Lamb. No lie was found to be upon their lips, for they are blameless - spotless, untainted, without blemish - before the throne of God.

The Book of Daniel says the prince of the Roman people, the beast, will make a covenant with Israel for one week (seven years). Israel will accepts this covenant for peace and protection as it is being hemmed in and threatened by many nations that want to destroy it. Isaiah 28 calls this covenant, a covenant with death. The beast breaks this covenant in the middle of the week with the abomination and desolation of the temple.

Jesus said when you see the abomination and desolation of the temple spoken of by Daniel the Prophet, there shall be great tribulation like the world has never seen. When the covenant is broken, there are only 3 ½ years left in the 70th week of Daniel. The beast has authority to wage war against the Christians and Jews for 3 ½ years. When the 7th trumpet is blown in Revelation 11, the Scripture says it is finished as the kingdom of this world has becomes the kingdom of our Lord Jesus Christ. The 7th trumpet includes the seven bowls that begins in Revelation 15.

When we get to Revelation 12, Scripture says that the woman gives birth to the man-child and then flees into the wilderness for 3 ½ years. There cannot be an additional 3 ½ years after the 7th trumpet in Revelation 11, as the beast only has authority to wage war for 3 ½ years. This means that Revelation 12, 13, and 14 have to go back and overlap Revelation 4 to fit within the time frame of the 70th week of Daniel. Revelation 12, 13 and 14 are pre-tribulation. The great tribulation begins with the opening of the first seal and with the rider of the white horse going forth to conquer and to conquer. The woman flees into the wilderness immediately after the birth of the man-child which is the beginning of the great tribulation.

The man-child rapture is the mid-night hour rapture, the first fruits rapture and the pre-tribulation rapture.

The very moment the man-child is born and taken up to heaven, is the very moment that a door is opened in heaven in Revelation 4, and there is a multitude before throne. Revelation 14 calls this multitude before the throne the first fruits unto the Lamb. The first fruits follow the Lamb wherever He goes. This is the bride. The bride is the one who follows her husband wherever He goes.

The man-child rapture is the midnight hour rapture, which occurs when the Lord comes for His bride. Afterwards, Revelation 14:6 speaks of angels flying through the air preaching the Gospels and Revelation 14:9 warns the people not to take the mark of the beast. This shows that the man-child rapture takes place prior to the beginning of the great tribulation. The moment the woman flees into the wilderness is the beginning of the great tribulation.

The other resurrection, spoken of in Matthew 24:29-31, will occur in broad daylight when every eye shall see Him. The mid-night hour resurrection takes place, when the door is opened in heaven in Revelation 4:1. After this door is opened, there is immediately a multitude before the throne. This multitude is the first fruits unto the Lamb, which includes the 144,000 discussed in Revelation 14. The male child that is born in Revelation 12 rises to heaven, when this door is opened in Revelation 4.

Male-child – the midnight hour resurrection

The male child, which is the 144,000 spoken of in Revelation 14, is called the first fruits unto the Lamb. They were called virgins, as they were pure, holy, and blameless without blemish or defect.

> Revelation 14:4-5: . . . These are they who follow the Lamb wherever He goes. These are they who have been ransomed (purchased, redeemed) from among men as the first fruits for God and the Lamb. No lie

was found to be upon their lips, for they are blameless - spotless, untainted, without blemish, (59)

The first fruits to God and the Lamb are pure virgins without defilement. They follow the Lamb, wherever He goes. This is the characteristic of the bride. The bride follows her husband, wherever He goes. The 144,000 are definitely part of the bride of Christ, but this does not include the entire bride. There may be millions or more that are also part of the bride.

The first fruits to God and the Lamb are obviously Christians that had a close walk with the Lord, while they were on earth. They purged themselves of their sins and were sensitive to the anointing, prompting, and guidance of His Spirit. There are very few Christians, if any that have purged themselves to the point, where they are pure, blameless, spotless, without blemish, or defilement. (the Scripture indicates that there are some)

Virgin does not mean they were never married. Paul, in talking to the Corinthians, was certainly talking to some married people when he said in

2 Corinthians 11:2: I am jealous for you with a godly jealousy. I promise you to one husband, to Christ, so that I might present you as a pure virgin to him (7).

Virgin means pure, holy, and Christ-like.

When the door is opened in heaven in Revelation 4, there is immediately a multitude before the throne. This is the mid-night hour resurrection or rapture of the first fruits unto the Lamb that is discussed in Revelation 14. The mid-night hour resurrection is the bride of Christ. This takes place before the great tribulation begins. The Harvest Rapture in Matthew 24:29-31 takes place immediately after the great tribulation, but before the Wrath of God, which begins in Revelation 8.

Harvest Rapture or resurrection

Matthew 24:29 - 31 speaks of the great tribulation being over, when the sun is darkened and the moon does not give its light. The sun is darkened and the moon turns blood-red in Revelation 6 with the opening of the sixth seal. Harvest rapture or resurrection takes places immediately after the great tribulation. This includes the multitude standing before the throne in Revelation 7:9-17. Included are all nations, tribes, and tongues that are too numerous to count.

What is the duty of the Christians in the Harvest Rapture?

> Revelation 7:15: Therefore, they are before the throne of God and serve him day and night in his temple; ... (7).

The Christians in the Harvest Rapture are called tribulation saints. They are not the first fruits unto God, as those on Mount Zion mentioned in Revelation 14. They are not the highest order of the redeemed. They do not rule as kings or priests. They do not follow the Lamb wherever He goes. They are servants. They serve the Lord day and night in the temple. (40)

Vision of two large white books with green letters – A to L on one book and M to Z on the other book.

> The Lord said, "These books list those, who have been washed with the blood of My Son. These are those, whose names will be called first. They are without stain or blemish. These are my earthly warriors. They pray and work every quadrant of the Spirit. They do not stop. They have given up all for Me. They come to Me exhausted from their race each has won. Each has Me as the center. They lived in

this world, but are not of it. They are Mine."

Since my understanding is that the number winning the race for the prize of the high-calling is limited, I said, "Lord, these two large books certainly contain far more than 144,000 names?" My prayer partner then received knowledge that these two books contained the life history of each person that had won the race for the prize of the high-calling. The words of their life story flow with beauty.

Who will make up the Man-child company?

Gordon Lindsay believed the man-child will consist of people from all walks of life, from preachers who are fighting the battle on the front lines to janitors pushing a broom. However, those who make up the Man-child Company will have one thing in common; they will be "prayer warriors". They will have a disciplined prayer life. They will spend time in prayer. (61)

When my prayer partner and I prayed for an understanding about the bride of Christ, we received the following words:

> The bride of God includes all of those whom Christ has reconciled to God. All of those that accept the Bridegroom and believe in His name will be God's bride.

> The bride of Christ will be glorified with more blessings. The bride of Christ includes those who have accepted His name, have walked in faith, are prayer warriors, are diligent workers for Christ's sake and have brought many into His kingdom. God's judgment will determine who these are.

> The bride of Christ will occupy a higher level of external existence and will know more about God's

nature than the rest who are just within the door of the kingdom of God.

The bride of Christ is the prize of the high calling for which Paul ran a race for with all his might in an effort to be a part. It seems that Paul won the prize as he says:

> 2 Timothy 4:6-7: For I am already being poured out like a drink offering, and the time has come for my departure. I have fought the good fight, I have finished the race, I have kept the faith (7).

The words of knowledge, received in prayer, revealed that the bride of Christ will be those that:

1. have accepted His name,
2. have walked in faith,
3. are prayer warriors,
4. are diligent workers for Christ's sake,
5. and have brought many into the kingdom.

God's judgment will determine those who will be the bride of Christ.

The bride of Christ, the prize of the high calling, will include people from every walk of life from janitors, housewives, mechanics, and doctors to evangelists, priests, nuns, and missionaries who are on the front lines bringing people to the Lord. These people will all have one thing in common: they are prayer warriors. That is, they spend considerable time in prayer. They bind the forces of darkness and pray to the Lord of the harvest to send laborers into the field to gather the harvest. These prayer warriors also pray for the Lord to send ministering angels to convict people of their sins and turn them to the Lord. They will receive credit for the harvest the laborers gather, even though they were not physically involved in the actual labor of bringing people to the Lord. When we do not pray, the angels do not have ammunition to fight the power of darkness. Our prayers help the angels to get through the power of darkness and help the labors who are gathering the harvest.

In the following Scripture, Paul encourages us to pray without ceasing.

> 1 Thessalonians 5:16-23: Rejoice always, never cease praying, render constant thanks; such is God's will for you in Christ Jesus. Do not stifle the Spirit. Do not despise prophecies. Test everything; retain what is good. Avoid any semblance of evil. May the God of peace make you perfect in holiness. May he preserve you whole and entire, spirit, soul, and body, irreproachable at the coming of our Lord Jesus Christ. (60)

Words were spoken to me about Jesus being the Bridegroom, while His disciples were called wedding guests then the word – "storm" came to me.

> In praying for an understanding, Jesus' disciples could not become part of the bride until they had gone through the storm, of trials, tribulations, persecutions, fasting, sufferings, etc.

Purification

While in prayer early one morning, I saw a picture of a beautiful wedding ring. The ring was gold with decorative silver inlaid in the middle between the gold. Through prayer, I discerned that the Lord wanted me to review the Scriptures pertaining to the marriage at Cana.

It is interesting, that Jesus, who began His ministry at the marriage at Cana, will climax His career with His own wedding and feast in heaven. Jesus began His ministry by changing the water that was placed into six purification jars into wine. According to the tradition of the elders (Mark 7:4), the purification jars were used by the Jewish people to clean themselves before eating. It was only appropriate that purification jars were used to hold the wine, which was the fruit of the wedding at the marriage of Cana. If we hope to participate, share and enjoy the full fruit of the wedding at the marriage of the Lamb, we must begin with our own purification process. The act of purification is an ongoing, life-long process of dealing with the sins in our life and turning from them.

The 144,000 in Revelation 14 are spoken of as being among the first fruits unto the Lamb. They are pure, holy, and blameless without any deceit, stain, or blemish. They are among those who follow the Lamb, wherever He goes. This is the characteristic of the bride. The bride follows her husband wherever He goes.

While in prayer with a prayer partner, we received the following knowledge and understanding:

> **The children of the Lamb** are those who have been washed in the Blood of the Lamb.

> **The bride of the Lamb** is those who have undertaken the purification process in an effort to win the prize of the high-calling.

If we desire to attain the high-calling, we have to run the race that Paul spoke of which is the purification process. We cannot be lax or passive in purging and cleansing ourselves. Our thought-life, which is related to our spiritual life, must be purified. Everything that is sinful, has to be dealt with, such as pride (getting our feelings hurt), anger, bitterness, unforgiveness, unbelief, lust, greed, envy, jealousy, lying, stealing, disobedience, rebellion, gossip, etc. This purification comes through the study of God's word. God's word convicts us as to how impure, imperfect and sinful we really are. The Scriptures teach that if we study His word, we will know the truth, and the truth will set us free.

Psalm 119:11 says, "I have hidden your word in my heart that I might not sin against you." (7) Not only do we need to deal with the obvious sins in our life, we need to study and know God's word, so that we will not unknowingly sin against Him.

Those, who hope to attain the prize of the high-calling, to be a part of the bride of Christ, with the privilege of wearing this beautiful wedding ring and to follow Him wherever He goes, must undergo this purification process to become pure, holy and blameless without any stain, blemish, or deceit just as the 144,000 mentioned in Revelation 14. We cannot do this on our own. Just saying the words, that we are sorry for our sins, does not change a person's heart. Only with God's help, can a person's heart be changed and purified.

Though the children of the Lamb and the guests will attend and share in the joy of the Lamb and His bride at their wedding feast, they will not be able to participate and share in the intimacy and joy that only a bride can have with her husband.

The race for the prize of the high calling is not difficult.

While in prayer, a prayer partner and I received knowledge that running the race for the prize of the high-calling is not difficult. What is difficult is making and keeping the commitment to run the race. We can run a long and hard race, but if we stop just before we reach the finish line, we will not complete the race. I have been spending two to three hours a day in prayer. For years the Lord had been waking me in the middle of the night, to spend an hour or two in prayer. Recently, I was sick, tired and fatigued, and had not been consistent in my prayer time for about two weeks. Even though I have been going to Mass daily, the Lord spoke to me one morning and said, "Are you going to be ready, when I come?" I responded, "I hope to be." I knew the Lord was encouraging me to be faithful in my prayer time and to continue running the race without stopping, so that I will be ready to cross the finish line just before He calls me home. The Lord is encouraging me to spend time in prayer with Him.

In running the race for the prize of the high calling – we can be in the race running real hard but if we stop before crossing the finish line, we will not finish the race. To win we must run continuously.

The bride will help the Lord govern the earth in the millennium.

Those, that make the Man-child Rapture, will rule nations with a rod of iron.

> Revelation 2:26-27: And he who overcomes, and who keeps My deeds until the end, to him I will give authority over the nations and he shall rule them with a rod of iron, . . (12).

> Revelation 5:10: And hast made us unto our God kings and priests: And we shall reign on the earth (10).

> Revelation 12:5: And she gave birth to a son, a male child, who is to rule all nations with a rod of iron; and her child was caught up to God and to His throne (12).

The Man-child will help the Lord to govern the cities and nations of the world in the millennium. Ruling people with a rod iron is for rebellious people who are being born, living and dying on earth in the millennium. There will not be any rebellious people in heaven.

Many are invited to the marriage feast of the Lamb

> Revelation 19:9: And he said to me, "Write, 'Blessed are those who are invited to the marriage supper of the Lamb' (12).

The Spirit and the bride give an invitation for others to come and drink of the life-giving water.

> Revelation 22:16-17: . . . I am the root and offspring of David, the bright morning star. The Spirit and the bride say, "Come." . . . Let the one who thirsts come forward, and the one who wants it receive the gift of life-giving water. (24A)

The bride is never invited to her wedding or marriage feast. She is the one that does the inviting. Who are the guests that are invited to the marriage feast of the Lamb, if everyone is the bride? Psalm 45, Mark 2:18-20, Matthew 9:14-15, Luke 5:33-35, and Revelation 22:16-17 show that everyone is not the bride of Christ.

Question?

I was reluctant to ask the Lord this question. The question was – Am I doing what is necessary to be worthy to be a part of the bride of Christ?

> My son, My son, no man ever lived, who could do enough to deserve this.

> It is Mine to give, and I give it to whom I please.

Facts:

1. When the beast makes a covenant with Israel for one week (seven years) that will be the beginning of the 70th week of Daniel. Israel makes this covenant for peace and protection as Israel is being hemmed in by other nations that want to destroy it. Isaiah 28 calls this covenant a covenant with death.

2. Daniel foretold that this covenant would be broken in the middle of the week with the abomination and desolation of the temple. When this covenant is broken, there are 3 ½ years left in the 70th week of Daniel.

3. The beast has power to wage war and persecute the Jews and Christians for 3 ½ years.

4. Jesus said that, when you see the abomination and desolation spoken by Daniel the Prophet, there shall be great tribulation as the world had never seen.

5. The Book of Revelation is a book of seven seals, seven trumpets and seven bowls which covers a period of 3 ½ years which is the last half of the 70th week of Daniel.

6. When the 7th trumpet is blown in Revelation 11, Scripture says that the kingdom of this world becomes the kingdom of our Lord Jesus Christ.

7. In Revelation 12 the woman gives birth to the man-child and then flees into the wilderness for 3 ½ years. There cannot be an additional 3 ½ years after the 7th trumpet as the beast only has power to wage war for 3 ½ years.

8. This means that Revelation 12, 13 and 14 has to go back and overlap Revelation 4 to fit within the time frame of the 70th week of Daniel.

9. It can be seen that Revelation 12, 13 and 14 are pre-tribulation as the angels fly through the air preaching the Gospel and warning the people not to take the mark of the beast before the beginning of tribulation.

10. The tribulation begins with the opening of the first seal and the going forth of the rider on the white horse. The woman flees into the wilderness immediately after the birth of the man-child.

11. Matthew 24:29-31 says that the tribulation is over when the sun is darkened and the moon turned blood-red. The sun is darkened and the moon turns blood-red with the opening of the 6th seal.

12. The 7th seal marks the beginning of the wrath of God in Revelation 8 which includes the seven trumpets and seven bowls.

13. The tribulation is when the beast persecutes those who do not worship him and take his mark. The wrath of God is when the Lord torments those who took the mark of the beast. The wrath of God is where water is turned to blood, meteors, fire and hails fall from the sky, sun is darken, men are tormented by scorpions, etc.

14. The 144,000 in Revelation 14 are called the man-child rapture, the mid-night hour rapture and the first fruits unto the Lamb.

15. The minute the man-child is born, is the minute the door is opened in heaven in Revelation 4 and there is a multitude before the throne. Revelation 14 calls this multitude the first fruits into the Lamb. This is the first fruits rapture. This multitude follows the Lamb wherever He goes. It is the bride that follows the Lamb wherever He goes.

16. The first five seals is the tribulation. The tribulation is over with the opening of the sixth seal. The harvest rapture takes place with the opening of the sixth seal.

17. The harvest rapture (Matthew 24:29-31) takes place immediately after the tribulation when the sun is darkened and the moon is turned blood-red. The sun is darkened and the moon is turned blood-red with the opening of the 6th seal in Revelation 6.

18. The 144,000 in Revelation 7 are the twelve tribes of Israel. They are not sealed and protected until the tribulation is over. They are protected from the events that will occur during the wrath of God.

19. The 7th seal in Revelation 8 is the beginning of the wrath of God. The wrath of God involved the seven trumpets and seven bowls.

20. Table 3 on page 93 shows where the seven seals, seven trumpets and seven bowls occur during the 70th week of Daniel.

References

1. Alexander Roberts and James Donaldson, Ante-Nicene Fathers, Volume 1 *The Apostolic Fathers Justin Martyr, Irenaeus*, Chapters 80 and 81, Fourth Printing 2004, Hendrickson Publishers, Inc., P.O. Box 3473, Peabody, Massachusetts 01961-3473

2. Joseph Iannuzzi, OSJ, *The Triumph of God's Kingdom in the Millennium and End Times,* St. John the Evangelist Press, 222 S. Manoa Road, Havertown, PA 19083 1999.

3. Desmond A. Birch, *Trial, Tribulation & Triumph Before, During and After Antichrist,* 1996, Queenship Publishing Company, P.O.Box 220, Goleta, CA 93116

4. Father John Dietzen, Question Corner: "What exactly is a theologian?" Catholic News Service, Catholic East Texas Vol. XVIII No. 21 Diocese of Tyler September 2, 2005

5. *The World Book Encyclopedia*, Field Enterprises Educational Corporation, Chicago, Illinois, 1972.

6. *Catechism of the Catholic Church*, 1994, United States Catholic Conference, Inc. – Libreria Editrice Vaticana, Citta del Vaticano

7. *New International Version of the Holy Bible*, The Zondervan Corporation, Grand Rapids, Michigan 49506, 1978.

8. Gordon Lindsay, "The Seven Churches of Prophecy," *The Book of Revelation Made Easy Series*, Vol. 1, Christ For The Nations, Dallas, Texas 75224,1971.

9. *The Holy Bible, The Douay Version of the Old Testament - 1609, and The Confraterity Edition of the New Testament - 1826,* published by P. J. Kenedy & Sons, New York, April 10, 1950.

10. *The Holy Bible, Authorized King James Version,* The World Publishing Company, Cleveland and New York.

11. J. A. Seiss, *The Apocalypse,* Vol. I, Charles C. Cook, 47 Broadstreet, New York, N. Y., 1865 (1900).

12. *New American Standard Bible,* Foundation Press Publications, Box 277, La Habra, California 90631, 1960.

13. Gordon Lindsay, "Daniel's 70 Weeks," *The Prophecies of Daniel Series,* Vol. III, Christ For The Nations, Dallas, Texas 75224, 1969.

14. Gordon Lindsay, <u>*God's Plan of the Ages as Revealed in Bible Chronology,*</u> Christ For The Nations, Dallas, Texas 75224, 1971.

15. E. W. Bullinger, <u>*Number in Scripture,*</u> Kregel Publication, Grand Rapids, Michigan 49503, 1894.

16. Gordon Lindsay, "America, Russia and the Antichrist," *Prophecies of Daniel Series,* Vol. IV, Christ For The Nations, Dallas, Texas 75224, 1969.

17. S. M. C., *Angel of Judgment - a life of Vincent Ferrer,* Ave Maria Press, Notre Dame, Indiana, 1954.

18. Alexander Cruden, <u>*Cruden's Complete Concordance,*</u> Zondervan Publishing House, Grand Rapids, Michigan 49506.

19. John L. McKenzie, <u>*Dictionary of the Bible,*</u> The MacMillan Company, New York, New York, 1965.

20. Sami Awwad, *"The Holy Land in Colour,"* Sami Awwad, The Mount Scopus Hotel, P.O. Box 19702, Jerusalem.

21. Asher S. Kaufman, "Where the Ancient Temple of Jerusalem Stood," *Biblical Archaeology Review,* Vol. IX No. 2, Biblical Archaeology Society, 1317 F Street, Northwest, Washington D.C. 20004, March/April 1983.

22. Mike Evans *"The Temple Mount",* Called, Published by Jerusalem Prayer Team, P.O. Box 30000, Phoenix, AZ 85046 -0009 July 2013

23. Charles Duncombe, *"The World in Prophecies,"* Christ For The Nations, Vol. 34:11, Dallas, Texas 75224, February 1982.

24. *Saint Joseph Edition of the New American Bible*, Catholic Book Publishing Co., New York, 1970.

24A. *Saint Joseph Edition of the New American Bible*, Revised New Testament– 1986 and revised Psalms - 1991 Catholic Book Publishing Co., New York, 1970.

25. Gordon Lindsay, "The Story of Daniel," *Prophecies of Daniel Series*, Vol. I, Christ For The Nations, Dallas, Texas 75224, 1969.

26. Gordon Lindsay, "The Rise of the Antichrist," *The Book of Revelation Made Easy Series*, Vol. 9, Christ For The Nations, Dallas, Texas 75224, 1972.

27. Pat Robertson, Special Issue: "Prophetic insights for the Decade of Destiny," Pat Robertson's Perspective, Christian Broadcasting Network, Inc., Virginia Beach, Virginia 23463, February/ March 1980.

28. *Bible Reading for the Home Circle*, Southern Publishing Association, Nashville, Tennessee, 1914.

29. Gordon Lindsay, "The Antichrist Rise to Power," *End of the Age Series*, Vol. III, Christ For The Nations, Dallas, Texas 752245, 1973.

30. Bishop Fulton Sheen's Tape.

31. *The Bible - Revised Standard Version*, American Bible Society, New York.

32. Gordon Lindsay, "The Sun-Clothed Woman and The Man-child," *The Book of Revelation Made Easy Series*, Vol. 7, Christ For The Nations, Dallas, Texas 75224,1962.

33. Lehman Strauss, *The Book of Revelation*, Loizeaux Brothers, Neptune, New Jersey, 1964.

34. Gordon Lindsay, "The Judgment Throne and the Seven Seals," *The Book of Revelation Made Easy Series*, Vol. 3, Christ For The Nations, Dallas, Texas 75224,1962.

35. John Leary, *Prepare for the Great Tribulation and the Era of Peace*, Vol. 55, Queenship Publishing Co., P.O. 220, Goleta, CA 93116, April 12, 2009

36. Finis J. Dake, *Dake's Annotated Reference Bible*, The Holy Bible, Dake Bible Sales, Inc., P.O. Box 173, Lawrenceville, Georgia 30245, 1961.

37. Arthur Bloomfield, *All Things New,* Bethany Fellowship, 6820 Auto Club Road, Minneapolis 20, Minnesota, 1959.

38. William DeBurgh, *An Exposition of the Book of Revelation*, Richard Moore Tims, 85 Grafton, Street, Dublin, Samuel Bagster and Sons, London, MDCCCXXXIX (1939).

39. Moses Stuart, *Commentary on the Apocalypse,* Maclachlan Stuart & Co., University Press, 32 Thistle Street, Edinburgh, MDCCCXLVII (1847).

40. Gordon Lindsay, "The Great Day of the Lord," *The Book of Revelation Made Easy Series*, Vol. 4, Christ For The Nations, Dallas, Texas 75224, 1972.

41. John Leary, *Prepare for the Great Tribulation and the Era of Peace*, Vol. IV, Queenship Publishing Co., P.O. Box 42028, Santa Barbara, Ca. 93140

42. Lucys Dawidowicz, *The War Against The Jews 1933 - 1945*, Holt, Rhinehart and Winston, New York 1975.

43. John Leary, *Prepare for the Great Tribulation and the Era of Peace,* Vol. II, Queenship Publishing Co., P.O. Box 42028, S anta Barbara, Ca. 93140

44. John Leary, *Prepare for the Great Tribulation and the Era of Peace*, Vol. III, Queenship Publishing Co., P.O. Box 42028, Santa Barbara, Ca. 93140

45. John Leary, *Prepare for the Great Tribulation and the Era of Peace,* Vol. I, Queenship Publishing Co., P.O. Box 42028, Santa Barbara, Ca. 93140

46. John Leary, *Prepare for the Great Tribulation and the Era of Peace*, Vol. V, Queenship Publishing Co., P.O. Box 42028, Santa Barbara, Ca. 93140

47. Gordon Lindsay, "The Rapture and the Second Coming of Christ," *The Book of Revelation Made Easy Series*, Vol. 8, Christ For The Nations, Dallas, Texas 75224, 1972.

48. J. A. Seiss, *The Apocalypse*, Vol. II, Approved - Book Store, 1721-27 Spring Garden, Philadelphia, Pennsylvania, 1865.

49. Immanuel Velikonsky, *World in Collision,* Dell Publishing Co., Inc., 1 Dag Hammarskjold Plaza, New York, N.Y. 10017, 1967.

50. L. A. Kulik, "The Question of the Meteorite of June 30, 1908 in Central Siberia," Popular Astronomy 1937, pages 559-562.

51. John Baxter and Thomas Atkins, "The Fire came by - The Riddle of the Great Siberian Explosion," Reader Digest, Vol. 112 No. 670, February 1978, Pleasantville, New York 10570.

52. Rowe Findley and Steve Raymer, "The Mountain that was - and will be – Mount St. Helen's Aftermath," National Geographic Society, Washington D.C. 20013, Pages 713 -733, 198.

53. Gordon Lindsay, "The Tribulation Temple," *The Book of Revelation Made Easy Series*, Vol. 5, Christ For The Nations, Dallas, Texas 75224, 1961.

54. Gordon Lindsay, "The Two Witnesses," *The Book of Revelation Made Easy Series*, Vol. 6, Christ For The Nations, Dallas, Texas 75224, 1961.

55. St. Augustine, "The City of God," Book XX, Chapter 29, Encyclopaedia Britannica, Inc., Chicago, London, Toronto.

56. R. E. Brown, J. A. Fitzmyer and R. E. Murphy, *The Jerome Biblical Commentary*, Prentice-Hall, Inc., Englewood Cliffs, New Jersey, 1968.

57. *The Jerusalem Bible*, Doubleday & Company, Inc., Garden City, N.Y., 1966.

58. Reginald Fuller, Leonard Johnston and Conleth Kearns, *A New Catholic Commentary on Holy Scripture*, Thomas Nelson, Inc., Publishers, Nashville and New York, 1953.

59. *The Amplified Bible*, Zondervan Publishing House, Grand Rapids, Michigan, 1965.

60. Holy Bible -*The New American Bible,* Catholic Edition, Thomas Nelson, Publishers, Nashville – Camden – New York, 1970

61. Gordon Lindsay, "The 144,000," *The Book of Revelation Made Easy Series,* Vol. 11, Christ For The Nations, Dallas, Texas 75224, 1962.

62. Gordon Lindsay, "Armageddon," *The Book of Revelation Made Easy Series*, Vol. 14, Christ For The Nations, Dallas, Texas 75224, 1972.

63. *Lectionary For Mass*, The Liturgical Press, Collegeville, Minnesota 2002

64. *The Living Bible*, Tyndale House Publishers, Wheaton, Illinois, 1971.

65. "The Spirit of Israel - 25 th Anniversity," Life - Special Report, Times, Inc., 229 Park Avenue South, New York, N.Y. 10003, 1973.

66. Louise Tomkiel – June 9, 2004 joycelist2@yahoogroups.com
67. Gordon Lindsay, "The Beast from the Bottomless Pit," *The Book of Revelation Made Easy Series*, Vol. 10, Christ For The Nations, Dallas, Texas 75224, 1962.

68. Catholic Prophecy – http://myweb.tiscali.co.uk/praeternatural 69. *Encyclopedia Britannica*, XIV Edition, Encyclopedia Britannica, Inc., Chicago, London, Toronto.

70. Gordon Lindsay, "The Vision of Daniel," *The Prophecies of Daniel Series*, Vol. 11, Christ For The Nations, Dallas, Texas 75224, 1973.

71. Catholic Prophecy Update, Bi-Monthly Report from "Signs and Wonders For Our Times", Volume 1, Number 4, July/ August 1997, 109 Executive Drive, Sterling, Va. 20166

72. John Leary, *Prepare for the Great Tribulation and the Era of Peace*, Vol. 9, The Queenship Publishing Co., P.O. Box 42028, Santa Barbara, Ca. 93140

73. http://www.locutions.org/category/a-bridge-between-popes/ Joycelist2, Latest locutions to the world, Sunday March 3, 2013.

74. Laurinda Keys, "Consultant sees nothing but good in New ' Omen'," The Dallas Morning News, Thursday, March 12, 1981.

75. *St. Irenaeus of Lyons*, Book V, Ch. 30, 4; Ante-Nicene Fathers Vol. 1, The Apostolic Fathers Justin Martyr, Irenaeus, Hendrickson Publishers, P.O. Box 3473, Peabody, MA 01961-3473

76. Jerry Lucas and Del Washburn, <u>*Theomatics*</u> , Stein and Day Publishers, New York, 1977.

77. Del Washburn, <u>*Theomatics II - God's Best Kept Secret Revealed*</u>, Scarborough House, 4720 Boston Way, Lanham, Maryland 20706, 1994.

78. "Down the Ancient Appian Way," National Geographic, Vol. 159, No. 6, Page 714, National Geographic Society, 17th and M Streets N.W., Washington

79. "Digital Angel," Palm Beach, Fla. (BUSINESS WIRE) December 15, 1999 Applied Digital Solutions, Inc. (NASDAQ:ADSX- news).

80. Gordon Lindsay, "The Vial Judgments," *The Book of Revelation Made Easy Series*, Vol. 12, Christ For The Nations, Dallas, Texas 75224, 1973.

81. Oliver Greene, *The Revelation*, The Gospel Hour Inc., Greenville, South Carolina, 1963.

82. W.A. Criswell, "Bible <u>Land Travel Presents 16 Day Mediterranean Odyssey in</u> the Footstep of Jesus, John and Paul," Wholesale Tours International, Inc., New York 10003.

83. Charles R. Taylor, *World War III and Destiny of America*, Thomas Nelson Inc., Publisher, Nashville, Tennessee, 1979.

84. Robert Ritchie - America Needs Fatima robertritchie@america-needsfatima.org May 18, 2010

85. *The American College Dictionary*, Random House, New York.

86. Gordon Lindsay, "Two Babylons," *The Book of Revelation Made Easy Series*, Vol. 13, Christ For The Nations, Dallas, Texas 75224, 1973.

87. Ralph Woodrow, *Babylon Mystery Religion*, Woodrow Evangelistic Association, Riverside, California, 1966.

88. *Good News for Modern Man*, The New Testament in Today's English Version, Second Edition, American Bible Society, New York 1966.

89. "Places and Faces in Prophecy," The Gospel Truth, Vol. 20, No. 2, Southwest Radio Church

90. Harold Fuller, *Atlas of the World*, Westport Corp., New York.

91. Bill Salus, Israletine,The Ancient Blueprints of the Future Middle East, Highway, a division of Anomalous Publishing House, Crane 65633, 2008

92. Know that the 1000 years referred to in the Book of Revelation means just that. Monday, May 28th, 2012 http://www.thewarn-ingsecondcoming.com/know-that-the-1000-years-referred-to-in-the-book-of-revelation-means-just-that/

93. Louise Starr Tomkiel, Public communication – Joyce Lang e-mail, April 13, 2000.

94. Bob and Penny Lord, *This is My Body, This is My Blood – Miracles of the Eucharist* - Book 1, 25th printing 2003, ISBN 0-926143-02-6

95. Bob and Penny Lord, *This is My Body, This is My Blood - Miracles of the Eucharist* – Book II , 1994, ISBN 0-926143-33-6

96. Gordon Lindsay, "The New Heaven and the New Earth," *The Book of Revelation Made Easy Series*, Vol. 16, Christ For The Nations, Dallas, Texas 75224, 1973.

97. Bishop Robert J. Hermann, "Judgment is coming," St. Louis Review, Archdiocese of St Louis October 17, 2008

98. Gordon Lindsay, *The Story of Adam and Eve*, The Voice of Healing Publishing Co., Dallas, Texas 1963.

99. Downs Matthews, "The Monarchs of Mexico," The Dallas Morning News, Page 8, Section G, Sunday, March 19,1995, Dallas, Texas.

100. Message from the Lord to Maurice Sklar, a Messianic Jew – 7/29/10 (Internet) Maurice Sklar Prophecies & Ministries, 12127 Mall Boulevard, Suite A440, Victorville, CA 92392.

Michael D. Miesch Jr.
B.S. – Texas A&M 1955
M.S. – Purdue 1959
Ph.D. – Oklahoma State 1964

HOPE IS NOT ENOUGH !

We hear a lot about "hope" these days and that has caused me to reflect on my hopes and the efforts I made to achieve my life's objectives. I was born on a cotton farm in Northeast Texas two and one-half months premature. I possessed a severe hearing loss, which ultimately contributed to a severe speech impediment. There were no hospitals in our county and we lacked electricity and running water. My aunt told me that I weighed between two to three pounds at birth with fingers the size of matchsticks. They put me in a shoebox near the open oven door of a wood-burning cook stove, which served as an incubator to keep me warm. It took a year and a half before I was able to walk. Despite this beginning I did not lack intelligence and I started school at five years old in a two-room schoolhouse. My brother, Pete, who had just turned four on September 8th, went to school with me just to get my lesson assignments. He learned the lessons and was promoted along with me. Pete finished high school at the age of 15. Living on a farm, I hoed or chopped weeds out of cotton, corn, and vegetables, plowed the fields, and picked cotton, corn, vegetables and baled hay.

After finishing high school, we hoped to go to college. State employees who worked with the handicapped tried to discourage me from going to college. They said I would never be able to make it. I could hear vowels but not consonants. I did not move my lips or tongue but talked with the back of my throat. Only my immediate family and close friends could understand me. Since I depended on lip reading to understand people I could not read lips and write at the same time. My brother took notes for me through grade and high school. All through college, I depended on other students for notes. If a student did not take good notes, I was in trouble.

My brother and I went to Paris Junior College for two years where I received some speech therapy and then transferred to Texas A&M College. At mid-semester, I had one B, one C, two Ds, and two Fs. They put me on probation and tried to send me home. At the end of the semester, I finished with two Bs, two Cs, one D and one F. The F was due to a 25 on my first physics test. The second semester I made all Bs. A difficult first year but I survived and realized that hope would not carry the day. I had to work twice as hard as others who could hear and speak.

One of my English professors took an interest in me and on his own time, helped me with improving my speech. This is where I learned to relax while speaking.

After receiving my B.S. degree, I was accepted into graduate school. I received Cs in two graduate courses even though my test papers showed that I had an A and a B. My mother wrote the two professors asking what I made on my final exam. One professor did not answer. The other professor said I made 94 but he graded students more on their ability to carry on a discussion in the classroom than on grade points.

I spent the summer in 1955 working for Stroope Pest Control in Waxahachie, Texas checking cotton crops for insect infestation, doing house hold pest control and treating houses for termites. Anita, the wife of Clayton Wright (Purdue -1950), suggested that I go to Purdue University if I was interested in pest control. My mother called Dr. John Osmun in August 1956 and asked if I could get in Purdue. Dr. Osmun told me to come on up. I was told that Dr. Osmun was shocked when he saw that I was deaf with a severe speech impediment. Nevertheless, Dr. Osmun immediately introduced me to J.J. Davis, who had been the head of the entomology department and was famous for his work with pest control operators. Although at the time, I had no idea who J. J. Davis was, this experience stimulated me to pursue my career in the economic phases of entomology.

After finishing my M.S. thesis, everyone on my committee voted against me going for a Ph.D. except Dr. Daniel Shankland, my major professor. Whereas one respected professor told me that my thesis was not acceptable for an M.S. degree, Dr. Shankland reassured me that it was a good thesis. Dr. Leland Chandler agreed to be my major professor for my Ph.D. with the understanding that many on my committee had stated that they would vote against me for a doctorate. Obviously, Dr. Chandler thought I had a good thesis and respected my intelligence and drive or he would not have accepted me as a student for the Ph.D. Truthfully, I do not believe the highly respected professor thought my thesis was bad. More probably he was greatly concerned that a student with a severe hearing loss, speech impediment and one that had difficulty taking notes in the classroom would most likely be a bad reflection on the Entomology Department. He did not want to use my handicap as an excuse but criticized my thesis in an effort to discourage me from going for a Ph.D. Anyone can view my thesis in the Purdue University Library.

I spent the summer of 1959 at Purdue University doing research on my Ph.D. In September Dr. Chandler told me about a fellow from Ohio State with a speech impediment, who had described over 600 new species of leafhoppers. He put his "type insect specimens" up for sale. "Type insect specimens" are used as the museum standard to compare and identify other insect specimens. Dr. Chandler had written him about the type insect specimens and received a very bitter letter from him. Dr. Chandler said this person was upset that he did not get the job he wanted with a university or museum and that he probably wasted his time getting a Ph.D. as he was no longer working as an entomologist. As a consequence of this man's experience, Dr. Chandler recommended that I go out into the field and prove myself before continuing on for the Ph.D. Even Dr. Chandler admitted that my handicap was the reason he asked me to leave.

As an aside I must relate a few brief anecdotes of amusing events during my time at Purdue. In 1958 the Purdue Entomology Department was having a hard time with other departments on the campus taking over their classrooms in Ag Hall. After Christmas break, I brought about fifty scorpions from Texas that I found hibernating all clustered together. The scorpions were placed in a large open cylinder container, which rested on a glass plate. Someone may have picked up the cylinder unaware that there was no bottom. A few of the scorpions got out and scurried into one of the classrooms. The professor and students started screaming and hollering, and climbing on their chairs and desks. When the dust settled and the scorpions were returned to their container the professor asked Dr. Chandler how often these creatures got loose. Dr. Chandler said, "Quite often". The professor and students left giving the entomology department complete control of the classrooms and building.

I have often wondered if Dr. Chandler had purposely released a couple of scorpions under the door of the classroom to frighten the teacher and students. My classmate, Dr. Bill Bowers said this was something Dr. Chandler would do.

Since Dr. Chandler did his B.S. thesis on earthworms. I asked Dr. Chandler what he knew about the two and three-foot long earthworms from Texas. He had never heard of one that long and everyone gave me a hard time because the record for North America was twelve inches. Soon thereafter my mother and dad mailed a few two-foot earthworms from Texas. There was a professor on campus who was an expert on earthworms and Dr. Chandler asked him what he knew about two foot earthworms from Texas. He told Dr. Chandler that the "kid from Texas" must have glued two earthworms together. Dr. Chandler and I walked over to his office with the earthworm. He was stunned. He did not say anything. Soon thereafter a number of

526

live earthworms were mailed to Dr. Chandler including one, which measured 31 inches. Dr. Chandler said it was 29 inches when he received it. This earthworm was placed with the Purdue insect collection. Subsequently, I measured one earthworm at 36 inches. If my mother and dad had not mailed a few two-foot earthworms I believe I would have been kicked out of Purdue before I got my M.S. degree. One professor commented that Texas needed these earthworms to eat up all the bull we shoot in Texas.

The people at Texas Parks and Wildlife were shock to hear about these giant Texas earthworms. An article on these giant earthworms was published in their magazine in November 2008.

Although deeply disappointed in my career trajectory at this time I refused to give up my educational objectives and sought real world field experience. Clayton Wright helped me get a job in Dallas working for two brothers, Dr. Byron Williamson and Dr. Thurmond Williamson, both whom had Ph.D.'s in chemistry. They formulated and sold insecticides for livestock, poultry and pets. Clayton told me to go sweep the floors and do whatever they wanted me to do. The brothers did not have any one to work in the laboratory so they trained me to do laboratory formulation and product development. I spent four years doing research, formulating, developing and testing new products. I was responsible for raising houseflies, cockroaches, dog ticks, taking care of dogs, cats and cattle. We ran oral toxicity tests on white laboratory rats, chronic and dermal toxicity tests on dogs, cats and kittens to support new product registration.

While working in Dallas, I decided to take some more courses in organic chemistry at Southern Methodist University. Dr. Harold Jesky, who was the head of the chemistry department, taught the course. When I went in to register, we were in a small room. Dr. Jesky's booming voice echoed off the ceiling. I had to ask him to repeat three times before I understood what he said. He put his hands on the table and said, "Are you sure you want to take this course?"

527

I said, "Yes!" He would not have anything to do with me the first six week but he wrote everything on the blackboard so I had no problem taking notes. He gave everyone a copy of the questions he had asked on the previous two exams he had given his students in his last two courses. Each exam was an hour and a half. If you knew the answer and wrote as fast as you could write, you could finish the exam. After the first exam, 50% of the students dropped the course. A student next to me was majoring in Chemistry and was taking this course for the third time. He had three "A's, in three other courses in Chemistry. I made an 89 on the first test, which was the second highest grade in the class. The person who made 91 had taken the course before. From that day on Dr. Jesky took an interest in me and tried to get me to major in chemistry. He would stop in the middle of a lecture and say, "Miesch, do you understand?" I took two semesters of Organic Chemistry and felt like a walking textbook, when I finished.

Dr. John Osmun stopped at Love Field in Dallas in 1961. I told Dr. Osmun I would like to go back to Purdue to work on my Ph.D. Dr. Osmun would not give me any encouragement. Dr. Don Schuder told me later that the reason Dr. Osmun did not give me any encouragement was that the one professor who criticized my thesis, was the most influential economic entomologist in the department at Purdue.

I drove to Oklahoma State and talked with Dr. Mike Howell. He told me that they would not hold my handicap against me and for me to get started on my research before starting my residence at Oklahoma State. I had just spent two years working on a Face Fly syrup formulation that was applied to the face of beef cattle to control Face Flies. The company put DDVP into liquid fly syrup to kill the flies. They had to bring all the liquid bait back at the end of the season, as DDVP was not stable in the presence of moisture. I developed a powdered sugar DDVP formulation with a thixotropic ingredient and a stabilizer for the DDVP. It was stable until the farmer added water.

I was trying to come up with a project I could work on the year-round and not just when certain insects were available. I thought about coming up with a roach bait. I bought some dehydrated potatoes and mixed it with powdered sugar using DDVP and the same thixotrophic ingredient and stabilizer that were used for the Face Fly bait. The roaches loved it. I ran tests in roach infested apartments and picked up and counted the dead roaches every morning. At the end of two and/or four weeks I used a pyrethrum flush-out to determine the total number of roaches in each apartment. This enabled me to determine the percent control overnight, the first week and the second week, etc. In one apartment the bait gave 95% control overnight.

I took my bait and data to Oklahoma State and told Dr. Howell that I would like to work on roach bait. "Oh no", he said, "We already have a student working on roach bait." When I showed him my bait and data, he said I was so far ahead that he was going to stop this other person. He wanted me to work on food preferences of roaches. At Dr. Howell's direction, I spent two years working on food preferences for different species of roaches before attending Oklahoma State. I developed a statistical method to test four or nine baits per test. The tests were continued at Oklahoma State especially with liquid baits.

I won a fellowship from National Pest Control Association to attend Oklahoma State and Dr. Howell accepted all the graduate courses at Texas A&M and the three years at Purdue University. I went to Oklahoma State in September 1963 and earned my Ph.D. eleven months later in August 1964.

The U.S. Forest Service in Maryland wanted me to work for them because of my pesticide formulation experience, but had other candidates ahead of me. I came back to Dallas and visited with my friend, Dr. Ernest Laake who was formerly Director of USDA Man and Animal Research Laboratory in Dallas. Although Dr. Laake had moved the USDA Lab to Kerrville, Texas, he was now working for National Chemsearch at the time of my visit (Now NCH Corporation). Dr. Laake, was responsible for the original work with DDT and toxaphene on the control of insects and ticks on livestock and highly recommended me to National Chemsearch because of my formulation experience. The US Forest Service job offer came the day after I had accepted a position with National Chemsearch. Dr. Laake and I worked together for a year and a half when he retired at the age of 79. Dr. Laake was a graduate of Texas A&M in Entomology – Class of 1913 and lived to be 99. His close association with pesticides did not appear to endanger his longevity.

With more than thirty chemists working in their laboratories National Chemsearch grossed $15 million in 1964. On my retirement in 2000, 36 years later, they grossed over $800 million as a worldwide corporation.

At National Chemsearch I was the head of the pesticide and agronomy section responsible for the formulation and development of insecticides, herbicides, fungicides, rodenticides, fertilizers, growth regulators, wetting agents, etc. I was also in charge of the insectary. We had a colony of houseflies that were originally collected before World War II that had never been exposed to DDT. I kept this colony going by collecting eggs and raising them each week for thirty-six years. The company lost these houseflies within three months after I retired. They asked me to come back each week to maintain the insects which I did for six years after my retirement.

I reported the first case of Baygon resistant houseflies in the nation. They were discovered in a poultry house in Keller, Texas where I was performing some tests. Bayer Corporation did not believe that there were any houseflies resistant to Baygon. Resistant flies were collected and a colony was started in the lab. In a test, the non-resistant flies were dead in a few minutes, while the resistant flies were alive after one hour. Bayer representatives admitted that this was definitely a bona fide case of resistance.

My expertise was in making stable emulsifiable products. Some of my accomplishments include:

- Making the first Delnav formulation that passed the rigid USDA 90 days emulsion stability test that was approved for use in dipping vats in quarantine area to control ticks on cattle.
- Developing a stable emulsifiable Baygon formulation that did not separate or split when added to water.
- I did the original work in developing the Golden Marlin fly bait. DDVP was mixed with powdered sugar and pressed into flakes instead of coating sugar granulars to reduce the repellency of DDVP to houseflies.
- Running toxicity tests with rainbow trout and bluegill sunfish to support dibrom registration for use in trickling filters at sewage treatment plants to control filter flies. A room was constructed with refrigeration to get the temperature down to 45 degree F for the rainbow trout.
- The company sold the roach bait as Roach Strike.

Over the years, I have formulated hundreds of products. Some of the technical pesticides I formulated were DDT, toxaphene, chlordane, lindane, dieldrin, aldrin, heptachlor, DDVP, malathion, dursban, Baygon, Sevin, Lannate, pyrethrum, synthetic pyrethroids, boric acid, rotenone, plus many herbicides and fungicides, etc.

The struggle I went through has been a blessing. If it had been otherwise, I would not have had the opportunity to learn the whole field of formulation and product development, which turned out to be my life's work. I made a lot of friends and learned much everywhere I have been. I ended up with a career I really loved with very good bosses and spent forty years doing research, formulation and product development.

Despite the difficulties, I have kept in touch with all of my professors. Some of the best and happiest years of my life and some of my fondest memories were on the campus of Purdue University where I developed many close friends. The first year at Purdue I lived with a family in Lafayette with whom I have maintained contact through the years. I worked at the Zeta Tau Alpha sorority house next to the campus, washing pots and pans for my meals. Mabel Walker was the cook for the sorority house. My wife and I later spent the night at her house several times when we visited Purdue. Dr. Don and Mary Schuder spent a couple nights in our home during their visit in Irving, Texas. Dr. Leland Chlandler's family also spent a couple nights in our home. Dr. and Mrs. Schuder, and Dr. John Osmun have visited my laboratory and the plant manufacturing facilities where I worked. Dick Wright and I were lab partners in Dr. John Osmun's 515 pesticide formulation course where I did my first pesticide formulation. Clearly, this first experience with pesticide formulation was an important beginning of what became my life's work. Dr. Ralph Killough was a good friend who loaned me his class notes. Dr. Bill Bowers and I continue to keep in touch through e-mail.

One weekend, Mr. Arnold Mallis, the author of the "Handbook of Pest Control", honored us with a surprise visit. Mr. Mallis had an interest in the identification and study of ants. After a brief visit, we looked for ants in our yard and found some tiny black ants, which he put into a small vial and took with him.

I have a beautiful, lovely wife, a family of three married sons and now grandchildren. I retired in 2000, but still collect insects. I have 14 cases of insects on three walls in the house. My wife, Ann, taught science and was chosen as the Texas State Teacher of the Year in statewide competition in 1986.

Michael D. Miesch lll is a Senior Program Manager for Avaya. He is married to Jean Marie who is an accountant for St. Gabriel's Catholic Church. They have one son who was conceived after 16 years of trying to have a family. They reside in McKinney, Texas

Mark David Miesch is the Director of Project Management for a Design-Build-Developer in Houston. He is married to Tracy Lynn, who is self–employed in Sales and Marketing. They have three children, Margaret Ann, Meredith Estelle, and Donovan Andrew Miesch. They live in Magnolia, Texas which is northwest of Houston.

Paul Martin Miesch is a writer. He is married to Christy, who is a pharmacist. They have one son Nicholas Asher who was born on April 27, 2014. They live in Austin, Texas.

I am an Eagle Scout with 76 merit badges, a Vigil member of the Order of the Arrow, and have earned Scouting Wood Badge and Beads. I was awarded the Silver Eagle for the Explorer Scouts, which was supposedly equivalent to the Eagle Badge for the Boy Scouts. The Silver Eagle is no longer offered by the Boy Scouts of America. I have also studied Indian dancing and made numerous performances. The Greater Dallas Pest Control Association presented me a plaque as an honorary member of their association. In 2010 Paris Junior College inducted me into their Academic Hall of Honor for Science with a very beautiful plaque and my picture on the wall. This is a brief story of my life.

I am thankful and grateful for the education and experience I received at Paris Junior College, Texas A&M, Purdue, SMU and Oklahoma State Universities. Each of these fine academic institutions possessed great professors and teachers. I learned a great deal and made many friends that I cherish to this day. I am very thankful to my brother, Pete, for helping me through grade and high school, the students who willingly loaned me their notes and the professors who helped me reach my great desire in college education. My brother, Pete, was awarded a B.S. in petroleum engineering and later went on to receive his Ph.D. in petroleum engineering at Texas A&M. Two of my sons are graduates of Texas A&M University and the other son is a graduate of the University of Texas at Austin.

The professors at Texas A&M giving me C's in graduate school and Purdue sending me home was a blessing in disguise. Otherwise, I would have missed the opportunity to learn chemistry, research, formulation and product development which became my life work and to meet the beautiful and lovely lady who became my wife. It was also helpful that I was able to do two years research on my dissertation at the company before entering Oklahoma State which enabled me to get my Ph.D. in eleven months. I am truly thankful for my family, friends, and for all the blessings I have received. I had a very rewarding career and all of my dreams and desires have been fulfilled.

From this brief safari through my life's adventures I believe you will understand that my hopes were carried forward on a river of perspiration and that hope is not enough.

CPSIA information can be obtained
at www.ICGtesting.com
Printed in the USA
FSHW01n1754121018